Transnational Humans *and*
Transnationalisms in the Humanities

the americas in the world

THE AMERICAS IN THE WORLD

Jürgen Buchenau, Series Editor

The Americas in the World series publishes cutting-edge scholarship about the Americas in global and transnational history, politics, society, and culture as well as about the impact of global and transnational actors and processes on the hemisphere. The series includes both works on specialized topics as well as broad syntheses. All titles aim at a wide audience.

Also available in the Americas in the World:

Cocaine: Criminals, Routes, and Markets edited by Sebastián A. Cutrona
    and Jonathan D. Rosen
Embracing Autonomy: Latin American–US Relations in the Twenty-First Century
    by Gregory Weeks
The Dollar: How the US Dollar Became a Popular Currency in Argentina
    by Ariel Wilkis and Mariana Luzzi
North American Regionalism: Stagnation, Decline, or Renewal? edited by
    Eric Hershberg and Tom Long

Transnational Humans *and* Transnationalisms *in the* Humanities

Crossing Boundaries in the Americas

EDITED BY MAX PAUL FRIEDMAN, STEFAN RINKE, AND NÚRIA VILANOVA

UNIVERSITY OF NEW MEXICO PRESS | ALBUQUERQUE

Library of Congress Cataloging-in-Publication Data
Names: Friedman, Max Paul, editor. | Rinke, Stefan, 1965- editor. | Vilanova, Núria, editor. |
Castañeda, Ernesto, | Roniger, Luis, 1949– | Dhondt, Reindert, 1982– | Canessa, Andrew, 1965– |
Maio, Marcos Chor, 1956– | Lopes, Thiago da Costa, | Shukla, Sandhya. | Cabezas, Amalia L., |
Werth, Brenda G., | Friedman, Elisabeth J., 1966– | Feixa, Carles, 1962– | Hutchinson, Sydney,
1975– | Middents, Jeffrey, | Ledesma, Eduardo, 1972–
Title: Transnational humans and transnationalisms in the humanities: crossing boundaries in the
Americas / edited by Max Paul Friedman, Stefan Rinke, and Núria Vilanova.
Description: Albuquerque: University of New Mexico Press, 2025. | Series: The Americas in the
World | Includes bibliographical references and index.
Identifiers: LCCN 2025006803 (print) | LCCN 2025006804 (ebook) | ISBN 9780826368706 (cloth) |
ISBN 9780826368713 (paperback) | ISBN 9780826368720 (epub)
Subjects: LCSH: Transnationalism. | Transnationalism—Social aspects. | Transnationalism—
History. | Latin America. | America.
Classification: LCC JZ1320 .T728 2025 (print) | LCC JZ1320 (ebook) | DDC 305.8—dc23/
eng/20250219
LC record available at https://lccn.loc.gov/2025006803
LC ebook record available at https://lccn.loc.gov/2025006804

Cover illustration: Wifredo Lam, *Horizons Chauds*, ca. 1968. © Succession Wifredo Lam, Adagp,
Paris / ARS, NY 2025.
Designed by Felicia Cedillos
Composed in Adobe Jenson Pro

For Katharina and Martin
For Silke, Tilman, and Tobias
For Quim, Mariona, and Albert

Contents

List of Illustrations   ix

Acknowledgments   xi

Introduction. Transnational Humans and Transnationalisms in the
Humanities   1

    MAX PAUL FRIEDMAN, STEFAN RINKE, AND NÚRIA VILANOVA

Chapter 1. Overcoming the National: Typologies and Assumptions
in Studies of the Transnational   15

    ERNESTO CASTAÑEDA

Chapter 2. Political Exile and the Transnational Turn   39

    LUIS RONIGER

Chapter 3. The Transnational Turn in Hispanic Literary Studies   63

    REINDERT DHONDT

Chapter 4. Indigenous Transnationalism: An Enduring Paradox   85

    ANDREW CANESSA

Chapter 5. Transnationalism and the History of the Social Sciences in Brazil:
Race and Economic Development in the Sociology of Donald Pierson
and T. Lynn Smith   103

    THIAGO DA COSTA LOPES AND MARCOS CHOR MAIO

Chapter 6. Translations of the Transnational Americas:
Vito Marcantonio Through Harlem and Puerto Rico   125

    SANDHYA SHUKLA

Chapter 7. The Transnational Sphere and Sexual Labor   145

    AMALIA L. CABEZAS

Chapter 8. Transnational Genealogies of Performance Against Gender Violence in Argentina and Chile   163

BRENDA WERTH

Chapter 9. Transnational Intersections: Latin American Feminist Counterpublics and Digital Technology   181

ELISABETH JAY FRIEDMAN

Chapter 10. Multilateral Transnationalism: Gang Stories from the Latino Atlantic   201

CARLES FEIXA

Chapter 11. Transnationalism and the German Diaspora in Latin America: Content, Form, and the Revenge of the Nation-State   227

MAX PAUL FRIEDMAN

Chapter 12. Ghost Transnationalisms: Embodied Transborder Histories in Music and Dance in the Dominican Republic and the United States   245

SYDNEY HUTCHINSON

Chapter 13. "Without an Image, There Is No Story": The Indigenous and the Transnational Turn in Latin American Cinema and Video   269

JEFFREY ROMERO MIDDENTS AND NÚRIA VILANOVA

Chapter 14. Pocket Cinema and the Transnational Turn: Cell Phone Films as Global(ized) Counter-Cinema   289

EDUARDO LEDESMA

Bibliography   313

Contributors   339

Index   345

Illustrations

Figure 1.1 Types of colonialism and decolonialization   21

Figure 1.2 Immigrant integration pathways   21

Figure 1.3 Number of publications on transnationalism, 1978–2023   29

Figure 10.1 Gangs and transnationalism   221

Table 1.1 Types of transnationalism   24

Acknowledgments

The editors thank the contributors for their brilliant insights shared with one another during the workshop stage and for generating fascinating new ideas about a topic whose proliferation has been matched only by its flexibility. For financial, logistical, and intellectual support, we thank, at American University, Despina Kakoudaki, director of the Humanities Lab, and members of the lab's Transnationalism Group; the College of Arts and Sciences and former dean and provost Peter Starr; former director Eric Hershberg, Alexandra Flinn-Palcic, and Valery Valdez Pinto at the Center for Latin American and Latino Studies; and our colleagues in the Dean's Office and the Departments of History and World Languages and Cultures. At the Freie Universität Berlin, we thank Dr. Karina Kriegesmann and the Lateinamerika-Institut. Thanks also to the Alexander von Humboldt-Stiftung, the Ibero-Amerikanisches Institut, and the American Philosophical Society. At the University of New Mexico Press, thanks to Norman Ware for magnificent copyediting and to series editor Jürgen Buchenau and senior editor Michael Millman for believing in this project and bringing it to fruition.

For wise advice at every turn, Max Paul Friedman thanks Edith Mathilde Friedman and Elisabeth Jay Friedman, whose remarkable work he has been following since 1967. He thanks Katharina Vester for her boundless creativity across a quarter century of transnational partnership. And he thanks his favorite transnational human, Martin David Vester-Friedman, for delaying this book in the most delightful of ways. *Weiter so.*

Stefan Rinke thanks his students and colleagues in Germany and Latin America for their insightful criticism of his work.

Núria Vilanova wants to express her gratitude to her students, colleagues, and professors in her transatlantic world who throughout the years have taught her so much. She is also deeply thankful to Quim, Mariona, and Albert for their unfailing support and love.

Transnational Humans and Transnationalisms in the Humanities

MAX PAUL FRIEDMAN, STEFAN RINKE,
AND NÚRIA VILANOVA

ARE WE LIVING IN a transnational world? To judge by the 900 percent increase in the frequency of the word "transnationalism" in publications since 1995, it is an explosively significant phenomenon of our times.[1] The proportion of humanity who are international migrants—whose movement and transmission of culture and impact on politics are so decisive to the concept—has increased by 65 percent since 1980. The transnational circulation of capital, media, ideas, popular culture, and even plagues has accelerated at a dizzying pace. This in turn has prompted a ferocious backlash in the form of right-wing nationalist movements competing for power on six continents as well as reterritorializing projects from border walls to Brexit. A particular brand of transnationalism was the neoliberal claim that freeing capital, goods, and members of the elite from geographic constraints would help foster ideal societies everywhere. It reached its apogee shortly before the eruption of the COVID-19 pandemic shut down travel and trade around the world. The renationalizing lockdowns intersected with—and fueled—racial and ethnic supremacist forms of nationalism that challenged structures of transnational governance, from the United Nations and its World Health Organization to the European Union and its Schengen area free of border controls. In the twenty-first century, it has become clear that globalizing elites with their universalist claims and projects of regional integration failed to confront growing inequality and persuade anxious populations that increased migration was an unmitigated good. Transnationalism, it seems, may be in crisis, but it remains a defining feature of our world, if a highly contested one.

In scholarly research, the "transnational turn" has reshaped multiple disciplines in productive ways without generating a consensus on the meaning of the concept. Transnationalism thus can refer to migration, postcoloniality, cosmopolitanism, diasporism, Indigeneity, international relations, cultural production, and more. The dynamics of the transnational in the arts, in literature, and in cinema, for instance, are shaped by the many intertwined political, economic, and social layers of the national. In the late twentieth century, the concept of transnationalism was increasingly applied across disciplines and nation-states,[2] gradually evolving into a convenient notion that ran the risk of becoming an "empty vessel."[3] Many scholars have seconded the risk of using a category of analysis that can hinder its very purpose of being an effective tool and framework of cultural analysis, because it has often been used as either a "self-evident qualifier requiring only minimal conceptual clarification,"[4] "a hold-all term,"[5] or "a rather open term; at the same time [...] radically overdetermined."[6] However, there is also consensus that "trans" implies movement, "contests binary choices, and creates new images and new cultural landscapes to encompass novel ideas that are not in opposition to one another but instead evolve and are interconnected."[7] This breaking of predominant binary and dichotomic perspectives opens up productive ways to search for more specific categories of analysis.[8]

The movement of humans and their artifacts either physically, through travel, migration, and exile, or symbolically, through the circulation of texts, images, ideologies, music, film, dance styles, and the like, has long been a feature of the experience of the Americas. This anthology analyzes contemporary usage of the concept across disciplinary boundaries and fosters exchange among scholars working with transnationalism in order to enrich our understanding of people who live transnationally in the Americas, and to identify common and divergent approaches to the study of the concept that can contribute to the development of scholarly work informed by multidisciplinarity.

Transnationalism's widespread if diffuse usage seems likely to endure because it offers a useful analytical category distinct from other, similar concepts. It was initially welcomed by historians who found existing alternatives unsatisfying:

whereas world history aims for a comprehensive, coherent narrative allegedly if always insufficiently embracing the whole planet, and global history also takes the planet as a unit while often focusing on regions and their connections, historians have used transnationalism to study empires, diasporas, and the movement of people, goods, capital, ideas, and cultural practices across nation-state boundaries, without attempting to include the whole world.[9] The term has been embraced by scholars of the subaltern and the postcolonial for its potential to "do to the nation what gender did for sexed bodies: provide the conceptual acid that denaturalizes all their deployments, compelling us to acknowledge that the nation, like sex, is a thing contested, interrupted, and always shot through with contradiction."[10] Indeed, transnationalism suggests a rupture, a challenge to the nation. And yet nations have always been an invention requiring constant work of education, legislation, and narration to maintain.

Transnationalism transcends the very concept of the nation in which the term is grounded. In a preindependence Latin America not yet geographically or politically defined by borders between nation-states, symbolic and tangible artifacts, maps, stories, documents, and images exceeded their local circumscriptions and traveled to influence and be influenced by ongoing trends. Toward the second half of the twentieth century, this growing phenomenon, with its all-encompassing economic, political, social, and cultural consequences, became known as globalization.

Thanks to the transnational turn, we now know that nations neither evolved "naturally" from primordial roots nor did they spring up from a vacuum or in their own container. The relational character of the nation from its very beginnings in the late eighteenth century was covered up by the very elites—often historians—who knew very well that their construction depended on the myth of exclusivity. Since its emergence in the 1990s, the transnational perspective has become a traveling concept that not only moves across—and brings together—different disciplines of the humanities and social sciences in transdisciplinary settings but also transgresses historical periods. Indeed, many transnational phenomena that we now study in the era of modern nations can also be studied in earlier periods of history much like a transnational dimension *avant la lettre*. Breaking up the seemingly monolithic framework of the nation, the process has not stopped there. Today we also think of locality in terms of translocality, as the migration of people has forced us to do, or of the media as transmedia, as new forms of storytelling have gained in relevance. After the turning point of the multiple crises since 2020, has globalization come to its end? Must we rethink the relevance of the transnational perspective? Certainly, the world's present convulsions have taught a lesson that, beyond the transnational, the national dimension has continued to exist, sometimes in a defensive crouch, and that movement and connection cannot explain everything. The relevance of place has come back with a vengeance. However, transnational forces continue to thrive as they did at the high tide of nationalism, and it is now more important than ever to take them into account.

The concept of transnationalism has not been without its critics. Some scholars of the Global South have cautioned that transnational scholars must avoid replicating neoliberal narratives of globalization by jettisoning the nation-state, or even worse, reproducing global inequalities: the "fetishization" of transnational study is elitist, they warn, because such research demands substantial resources of time, funds, and language competence. Bearing those critiques in mind, transnational scholars are nonetheless interested not only in highlighting people and phenomena in motion beyond borders, but also in how "traffics traverse—while also at times reinforcing—the geographic boundaries of the nation-state."[11]

Other scholars have noted that transnational scholarship can inadvertently reinforce the national units and nationalist narratives that are reference points for boundary crossing. They emphasize instead the transimperial processes at work among Spanish, British, Portuguese, Dutch, French, Russian, and US empires reshaping the world since the nineteenth century.[12] Some Latin American scholars were initially skeptical of a term that might overlook hierarchies of power, erase the achievements of Marxist and postcolonial approaches focused on class or race, or flatten local specificities. It seemed to some to pose a counterpoint to the internationalism of the twentieth-century Left, although transnational solidarities appeared also in other channels not necessarily reflected in *internacionalismo*, including anticolonial and civil and human rights movements as well as peasant and Indigenous movements.[13] Some Latin American academics defended the centrality of the nation-state in a region where its sovereignty continues to be violated and were suspicious of a term that came from US-based American studies, in an intellectual version of the globalization paradigm.[14] As Reindert Dhondt writes in his contribution to this volume, the concept of transnationalism initially encountered resistance among scholars in Latin America, "who linked it to neocolonialism and homogenization through cultural imperialism," not least because in Spanish, the word *transnacional* was deeply associated with transnational corporations and their overweening power in inter-American affairs. (Their role is exemplified by the century-long trajectory of Chiquita Brands International, formerly the United Fruit Company, blamed for a massacre of striking workers in Colombia in 1928 and for contributing to the 1954 overthrow of Guatemala's President Jacobo Árbenz Guzmán, and found liable by a Florida court in 2024 for supporting paramilitary death squads in Colombia into the twenty-first century.) All this may help explain why *transnacionalismo* was slower to catch on in the intellectual field in Latin America. As Dhondt writes, "Because of this ideological freight, the term's connotation was perceived as pejorative in a decade characterized by the neoliberal policies of the Washington Consensus and the continent's subsequent disillusionment with these economics in the 2000s." In a process of South-North transmission familiar to recent scholars of Latin American culture and letters, some Latin American scholars reinterpreted and reappropriated the concept of transnationalism to address "a transcultural imaginary that blurs the binary between global and local" in a way that challenges both "postnational utopianism" and "national myths of cultural purity."[15]

Contested as it may be, the transnationalism concept seems to be here to stay.

Transnationalism, despite its charged connotation, opens an innovative and democratic way to explore a reality that comprises ongoing challenges. To combat the elusiveness that characterizes the term, scholars have made several attempts to produce categories of analysis that contribute to anchoring such a polysemantic concept. The collective contribution of the essays in this volume is not only to showcase the diversity implicated in the plural usage in the title: "Transnationalisms." It is to demonstrate that the state of the field has moved beyond a debate over whether transnationalism is a defining feature of our times, whether it is a conceptual stalking horse for the vested interests of corporate globalization, or whether it is a failed effort to overcome rhetorically the daunting real-world power of the nation-state. Instead, the latest work, well represented in this volume, shows how constructive conceptual creativity can be in helping us better understand the frameworks within which transnational humans make their own history. The concern that transnationalism serves only to further marginalize states and peoples of the Global South who already struggle to defend and implement their agency and sovereignty finds a qualified answer in the varieties of transnationalism such as Ernesto Castañeda's typology in this volume, dividing interpretations of the migrant experience into relational, reactive, elite, border, exile, and colonial transnationalisms, each with its own implications for the potential for integration and for the dignity and autonomy of the humans involved. The gloomy paradox that transnationalism may reify the nation-state by emphasizing its centrality even as a model under challenge can be weighed against Sydney Hutchinson's insights into the building of imagined communities through what she terms "ghost transnationalisms" detectable in music and dance. This describes transborder practices that are deliberately covered up ex post facto in the service of nationalist mythmaking, but that continue to draw present-day people and cultures together. Indeed, Sandhya Shukla's study of transethnic solidarity in Harlem suggests a kind of transnational cosmopolitanism that offers an appealing identity potential for progressive politics in the Americas.

The triumphalist strain of transnationalism's postnational utopianism is set against Max Paul Friedman's cautionary tale of one migrant diaspora—Germans in Latin America—who in the 1930s and early 1940s delicately navigated the efforts of the Nazi state to impose a virulent transnational solidarity upon them, only to see their communities destroyed by the backlash from defensive nationalist states. The fear that transnationalism will erase and smooth over local specificity and complexity meets the vivid demonstration of both in Carles Feixa's remarkable participant-observer depiction of the multilayered, Atlantic-spanning worlds of youth gangs, in which transnationalism from below (illicit solidarity expressed through a unique and symbolic language) confronts and adapts to transnationalism from above (neoliberal carceralism), producing a synthesis of multilateral transnationalism (through corruption, truce, or integration into licit social movements). Each essay in this volume shows that, rather than defend the term from its critics, we should recognize the ways in which varieties of transnationalism, like transnational humans themselves, can range from progressive, liberatory, and generative to ambivalent or destructive—or can even promise new forms of solidarity.

The chapters in this book, then, demonstrate how transnational forces have shaped ideas about racial difference, national belonging, immigrant exclusion and migrant agency, state power and layered sovereignties, cultural expression and appropriation, and the impact of gender, sexuality, and race on international advocacy movements. Several chapters investigate how cutting-edge digital technologies have complicated the whole notion of spatialization and given transnationalism new dimensions. All offer challenges to widely accepted tropes about the national and the transnational. Rather than attempting to impose a singular definition upon a diverse scholarly community, this collection provides the reader with tools to understand and then apply the meanings of the transnational condition in a variety of linked fields. While the humanities are at the center of the volume, we invited contributions from political scientists, anthropologists, and sociologists as well, because their often rigorously structural study of transnational communities and individuals in transnational spaces in the Americas has yielded important conceptual reference points for many aspects of the human experience that concern humanities scholars. These include migration and the development of transnational advocacy networks such as human rights organizations, ethnic affinity groups, feminist movements, and queer activism. They help us understand how transnational and international processes and actors have shaped local politics and experiences, and unpack the interweaving of the global, the local, and the glocal.

This anthology of fourteen chapters on transnationalisms from scholars across the humanities and allied fields presents concise overviews of the concept's meaning in each author's home discipline followed by their own illuminating case studies based on original research. In chapter 1, "Overcoming the National: Typologies and Assumptions in Studies of the Transnational," Ernesto Castañeda provides a typology of different understandings of transnationalism in migration studies, history, and social movements research. He cautions against overstating the reach, novelty, and implications of these transnationalisms and calls instead to continue to denaturalize the category of the "national." Chapter 2, "Political Exile and the Transnational Turn," traces the history of institutionalized exclusion in Latin America, where exile became part of the ground rules of political practice, targeting those who defied state power. Exiles played a key role in shaping the mental boundaries of nation-states, author Luis Roniger argues, while at the same time their presence challenged state claims of hegemonic control. While rulers still controlled citizens' lives and institutions and produced massive waves of territorial dislocation, exile also broadened the boundaries of identity and political debate beyond state horizons while helping to establish diasporic networks and legal regimes.

In chapter 3, "The Transnational Turn in Hispanic Literary Studies," Reindert Dhondt observes that although the field of Hispanic culture and literature may be understood as inherently transnational, the concept of transnationalism initially met some resistance among literary scholars in Latin America. Nonetheless, the concept was reappropriated by Latin American scholars studying texts that circulate across multiple geographies and authors and characters who travel; they especially sought to analyze the role of agency within a transcultural imaginary that blurs the binary between global and local. This transnationalism from below stresses a critical resistance to the homogenizing effects of globalization and challenges national myths of cultural purity. More recently, the transnational turn has spurred engagements with the transimperial and transcultural dimensions of Hispanophone cultures, contrasted with a number of conceptual trends including transatlantic studies, hemispheric studies, Iberian studies, and the global Hispanophone. Dhondt examines how these scholarly trends play out in the burgeoning genre of narcofiction.

Andrew Canessa, in chapter 4, explores how the condition of Indigeneity presents a paradox when considered through a transnational lens. On the one hand, Indigenous identities are rooted in space and time and cultural difference; they are often explicitly contrasted with transnational or globalized identities as local and "authentic." However, Indigenous identities are deeply transnational in the sense that they not only traverse national boundaries but also only make sense when considered transnationally. The chapter focuses on the Indigenous experience in the Americas, with special emphasis on Bolivia, to suggest that the transnationalism of Indigeneity is not merely a contemporary phenomenon but one that has had its roots in European expansion and modern state-building since the seventeenth century and fulfills the novel category of the glocal: rooted in local culture and specificity, they are part of a global network of people and ideas shaping Indigeneity.

In chapter 5, Thiago da Costa Lopes and Marcos Chor Maio examine the mutually constituting transnational intellectual currents circulating between Brazil and the United States that helped institutionalize social scientific thinking about race and development in both countries. They focus on the work of US sociologists Donald Pierson and T. Lynn Smith, who made distinct contributions to the institutionalization of sociology in Brazil in the mid-twentieth century. Subtle shifts in Pierson's and Smith's positions on race and economic development show how their own faith in US epistemic superiority veiled the substantial influence of Brazilian thinkers on their own work, problematizing the diffusionist model of North-South transfer.

Sandhya Shukla takes up the polyvalent life and work of the Italian American New York City congressman Vito Marcantonio (1902–1954), one of the most left-wing members of Congress of the twentieth century. Chapter 6, "Translations of the Transnational Americas: Vito Marcantonio Through Harlem and Puerto Rico," argues that his activism among the many diasporas in Italian Harlem and his polyglotism (Italian, Spanish, Yiddish, and English) represented a form of transnational cosmopolitanism. Shukla places special emphasis on language and its power effects in exploring how Marcantonio's border-crossing travels and transgressions, including championing Puerto Rican independence, promoted an expansive view of American identity akin to an "Americas" sensibility that brought the Caribbean into a conceptual geographical continuum with New York and Washington.

In chapter 7, "The Transnational Sphere and Sexual Labor," Amalia Cabezas examines two case studies that reveal how sex worker identity is articulated in processes of transnationalism. The first shows how sexual economic exchanges and the category of "prostitute" were racialized in the Panama Canal Zone in an early case of what would later be termed "sex tourism." "From the military language used, such as being on tour—to refer to time spent in a hostile environment—to the transient nature of the voyage, to the expectation of sexual adventure in meeting hypersexual natives, tourism and militarism are linked," writes Cabezas. The second case delves into the largest transnational sex worker network in the region, known as RedTraSex, headquartered in Argentina with locals in fourteen countries, generating a new social identity for sex workers as human rights activists. Both cases highlight how sex work has been constituted by the transnational sphere that has transformed the occupational identity of sex workers and enabled significant achievements in the political realm.

Chapter 8, "Transnational Genealogies of Performance Against Gender Violence in Chile and Argentina," takes up cases from theater and performative protest movements such as the scripted flash-mob dance *A Rapist in Your Path* in Chile in November 2019 and the *siluetazos* (a mass public depiction of human silhouettes as in a crime scene to represent the outline of a person who was disappeared or murdered) of the feminist movement NiUnaMenos in Argentina in March 2015. Brenda Werth argues that these movements linked gender violence to state violence orchestrated as part of the transnational network of terror Operation Condor (South American dictatorships' repression campaign backed by the United States, 1975–1983). Werth resituates foundational theatrical works of the transition to democracy such as Ariel Dorfman's *Death and the Maiden* (*La muerte y la doncella*, 1990) and Eduardo Pavlovsky's *Pas de deux* (*Paso de dos*, 1990) in a transnational framework, discussing the ways in which these works help explain the recent explosion of activist performances in the Southern Cone and how they draw on symbols, slogans, and practices from the dictatorship period. These links between past and present shed light on the role of the state and transnational networks in reinforcing and dismantling structural gender violence.

Elisabeth Jay Friedman in chapter 9 applies the concept of "counterpublics" to Latin American feminist movements that originated more than a century ago but irrupted massively across the region with the spread of digital technology. Bringing a transnational perspective to gender-focused and often women-led movements from Chile to Mexico helps reveal the distinct ways feminist counterpublics—the internal arenas of movements where they develop identities, build communities, and formulate strategies to affect larger publics—have encountered and interpreted the Internet. The chapter reveals the organizational and conceptual taproots of the contemporary cycle of anti–gender violence mass mobilization, including the historical twining of alternative media and counterpublic growth across the region and beyond.

In chapter 10, "Multilateral Transnationalism: Gang Stories from the Latino Atlantic," Carles Feixa does a deep dive into a street youth organization present on both sides of the Atlantic: the Latin Kings and Queens. Starting from the life stories of three gang leaders in the United States, Ecuador, and Spain, the chapter analyzes transnationalism at three levels. First, there are multiple transnationalisms "from above": visual imagery rooted in cinema, television series, and YouTube videos; "zero tolerance" policies toward street youth groups under the neoliberal penal state; and institutional racism that turns young migrants into precarious workers and scapegoats for "moral panic" campaigns. Second are transnationalisms "from below": the circulation of symbols, identities, and myths among the youth of a quasi-clandestine organization and a feeling of solidarity and mutual aid practices among the victims of globalization across vast expanses of space. The third level Feixa dubs "multilateral transnationalism": the circulation of intercultural experiences within and outside the group, which demonstrate the agency of its members in their capacity to lead a transnational life without dying in the attempt.

Continuing the theme of illicit transnationalisms, Max Paul Friedman observes in chapter 11 that transnationalism is often invoked, and sometimes cheered, by scholars to refer to the resistance by subaltern groups to the overwhelming power of the nation-state. But the fate of the German communities of Latin America during World War II illustrates the clash between transnational collective identities and national security imperatives that can arise during times of crisis, as German migrants in Latin America were placed under surveillance, blacklisted, arrested, deported, and interned by the thousands in camps in the United States—yet another case of the hazardous encounter between transnational people and states that prefer to treat them in neat national categories. German cultural transnationalism was exploited by the Nazis to try (with only limited success) to expand their influence abroad, calling into question whether the sustained links of expatriate communities to their homelands automatically equate to a form of resistance that scholars should celebrate. To cast transnationalism as the destroyer of nation-states, Friedman argues, is not likely to attenuate states' tendency to target migrants as a menace.

In Chapter 12, Sydney Hutchinson explores transnationalisms created and practiced by those without migration backgrounds who nevertheless engage, through music and dance, in practices that most freely travel across borders. Hutchinson's term "ghost transnationalisms" describes transborder practices that are deliberately covered up ex post facto in the service of nationalist myth-making, but that continue to haunt present-day people and culture in unexpected musical eruptions. Her chapter focuses on two cases, one from Dominican music history and one from US American country music, each revealing a forgotten era of past cooperation and cohabitation across borders, those of Haiti and the Dominican Republic and of the United States and Mexico, respectively. The ghost transnationalisms Hutchinson uncovers in merengue and country music are simultaneously carried in the body, intersecting with racial and gender identities while serving as archives of vanished transborder politics and relations.

Jeffrey Romero Middents and Núria Vilanova make a more deliberate and self-conscious effort to transform the understanding of Indigeneity during the transnational turn in Latin American cinema and video in chapter 13. The authors depict a challenge to traditional cinematic representations of Indigeneity, long adapted to an aesthetic common in international film festivals that are eager to highlight the "localness" and "authenticity" of Indigenous peoples in the collective imaginary. The emergence of digital media technologies in the 1990s that democratized filmmaking allowed Indigenous filmmakers to progressively expand their horizons and, in fluid transnational collaboration throughout the Americas, foster the production of films and audiovisuals in which self-representations of Indigeneity are linked to activism and advocacy for social justice. Indigeneity in Latin American film increasingly represents a decolonial challenge to the nation-state.

Where Middents and Vilanova note a democratization of filmmaking through the advent of digital media, Eduardo Ledesma sheds light on its current apex, "pocket cinema," produced by filming from cell phones. In chapter 14, Ledesma acknowledges the wide accessibility of the emerging "silicone screen" format but questions the technological utopianism that can overlook the darker side of ubiquitous filming, including the threat of widespread surveillance, cyber-stalking, and a simplification of social issues through a superficial engagement with images. Cell phone cinema constitutes an emergent transnational film format and a body of global movies that Ledesma sees as a counter-cinema to the commercial film industry: by literally placing filmmaking in the hands of ordinary people, this form serves as both affirmation of and resistance to transnational genre expectations.

Taken together, these essays demonstrate that "transnationalism" is far more than a word to describe movement across borders. The analytical categories these authors deploy and critique help to uncover power effects coursing through systems as diverse as diasporic communities, legal regimes, academic disciplines, computer networks, social movements, and popular culture. The transnationalisms they describe are constitutive of new realities, altering the sphere of sovereignty and individual and communal agency, enabling new identities and forms and genres of literary, artistic, and cinematographic expression, and spurring nation-states and supranational organizations to react with new norms and legislation or with ill-fated strategies of containment. Collectively, the volume presents a vivid picture of the state of scholarship on transnationalisms today.

Notes

1. Rarely in usage before 1990, the term began to appear more frequently in publications after 1995 and then boomed in the twenty-first century, continuing its rapid growth today. The Google Books Ngram Viewer, which charts the frequency of words in printed sources between 1500 and 2019 (some twenty-five million scanned texts), shows a 900 percent increase in the appearance of "transnationalism" between 1995 and 2019, the end of the scanning project. Google Scholar shows more than 23,000 appearances of "transnationalism" in academic publications since 2019, of which upward of 17,500 are since 2022.

2. Steven Vertovec, *Transnationalism* (Abingdon, Oxon., England: Routledge, 2009), 1.

3. Michael Peter Smith and Luis Eduardo Guarnizo, eds., *Transnationalism from Below: Comparative Urban and Community Research* (New Brunswick, NJ: Transaction Publishers, 1998), 4.

4. Mette Hjort, "On the Plurality of Cinematic Transnationalism," in *World Cinemas, Transnational Perspectives*, ed. Nataša Ďurovičová and Kathleen Newman (Routledge, 2010), 13.

5. Dolores Tierney, *New Transnationalisms in Contemporary Latin American Cinemas* (Edinburgh University Press, 2018), 6.

6. Kit Dobson and Áine McGlynn, *Transnationalism, Activism, Art* (University of Toronto Press, 2013), 5.

7. Lori Celaya and Sonja S. Watson, eds., *Transatlantic, Transcultural, and Transnational Dialogues on Identity, Culture, and Migration* (Lexington Books, 2021), 2.

8. Sophia A. McClennen, *Globalization and Latin American Cinema: Toward a New Critical Paradigm* (Cham, Switzerland: Palgrave Macmillan, 2018), 1–46.

9. See Christopher A. Bayly, Sven Beckert, Matthew Connelly, Isabel Hofmeyr, Wendy Kozol, and Patricia Seed, "*AHR* Conversation: On Transnational History," *American Historical Review* 111, no. 5 (December 2006): 1441–64; and Akira Iriye and Pierre-Yves Saunier, eds., *The Palgrave Dictionary of Transnational History* (Palgrave Macmillan, 2009).

10. Laura Briggs, Gladys McCormick, and J. T. Way, "Transnationalism: A Category of Analysis," *American Quarterly* 60, no. 3 (September 2008): 625–48, quoted at 627. Paul Giles sees transnationalism as a "Foucauldian exercise involving the renegotiation and redescription of power" in order to "hollow out pressing, peremptory [national] claims to legitimacy." *Transnationalism in Practice: Essays on American Studies, Literature and Religion* (Edinburgh University Press, 2010), 50, 44.

11. David Kazanjian and María Josefina Saldaña-Portillo, "Introduction: The Traffic in History," *Social Text* 25, no. 3 (92) (Fall 2007): 1–7, quoted at 4; and Andrew Zimmerman, "Africa in Imperial and Transnational History: Multi-Sited Historiography and the Necessity of Theory," *Journal of African History* 54, no. 3 (November 2013): 331–40.

12. See Kristin L. Hoganson and Jay Sexton, eds., *Crossing Empires: Taking U.S. History into Transimperial Terrain* (Duke University Press, 2020).

13. See Jessica Stites Mor, ed., *Human Rights and Transnational Solidarity in Cold War Latin America* (University of Wisconsin Press, 2013); Jessica Stites Mor, *South-South Solidarity*

and the Latin American Left (University of Wisconsin Press, 2022); Margarita del C. Zárate Vidal, "Resistencias y movimientos sociales transnacionales," *Alteridades* 25, no. 50 (2015): 65–77; and Andrew Canessa's contribution to this volume.

14. Kazanjian and Saldaña-Portillo, "Introduction: The Traffic in History," 1–3; and see the chapter by Reindert Dhondt in this volume.

15. All quotations are from Reindert Dhondt's chapter in this volume.

CHAPTER I

Overcoming the National

Typologies and Assumptions in Studies of the Transnational

ERNESTO CASTAÑEDA

THIS CHAPTER DISCUSSES THE origins of "transnationalism" as a term and phenomenon of study. It focuses on discussions, theories, empirical cases, and controversies around using a transnational focus within migration studies. It provides a typology of different understandings of transnationalism in migration studies and their theoretical and political implications. It then briefly discusses the use of the term in other areas, particularly history and social movements research. It concludes by warning against overstating the reach, novelty, and implications of transnationalism per se and calls instead to continue to denaturalize the category of the "national."

What Is Transnationalism?

The term "transnationalism" is used differently in various contexts and thus requires further specification. Early uses of the term referred to corporations such as HSBC, Citibank, and Sony, with branches in many countries and headquarters in global cities such as New York, London, or Tokyo.[1] Since the 1980s, scholars have used the term "transnationalism" to refer to a series of presences, identities, and movements that do not map easily within contemporary nation-states' geographical borders. Therefore, in its broadest sense, transnationalism is the movement of capital, people, and ideas back and forth across political borders. Not coincidentally, this characterization is similar to what people call "globalization."[2] Original proponents also linked an increase in transnational practices with a decrease in national policies' effect on economic outcomes. The rise of academic work on transnationalism took place during the same time as a rise of neoliberal policies, a decrease in economic development models such as import substitution industrialization in Latin America, and an increase in the conditioning of loans from the World Bank and the International Monetary Fund on structural adjustment programs that included reducing national deficits and funding for social programs while opening national markets to imports from the developed world.

In the 1970s, international relations scholars used the term "transnational" to describe international movements across state borders by nongovernmental actors.[3] Colloquially, the term was used in the 1980s to describe corporations with offices in multiple countries. Furthermore, starting in the 1980s, a business school professor defined globalization as transnational corporations selling the same products in multiple countries.[4] Later, many authors wrongly drew a causal connection whereby globalization increased migration and vice versa in a self-reinforcing loop.[5] Perhaps too quickly and eagerly, some scholars framed migration as globalization or transnationalism from below,[6] contrasting it with top-down policies opening borders to capital, goods, firms, and factories. Nevertheless, there was a theoretically and politically unwarranted conflation between migrant transnationalism and globalization. As historians have documented, this is misleading because we have had previous waves of globalization, and long-distance migrations preceded the most recent wave of globalization.[7] Furthermore, we should not equate "transnational" with "global" a priori. Most transnational processes are regional, within border areas, or from certain places into other particular places (e.g., migration between former colonies and the metropole).[8]

Nonetheless, there is still a theoretically and empirically sound manner of studying historical and contemporary migrant transnational practices. The so-called transnational turn made meaningful and lasting contributions. Migration scholars use the term "transnationalism" to describe migration from a perspective that takes into account the twin processes of emigration (leaving) and immigration (arriving),[9] and the social ties kept between emigrants and their communities of origin.[10] Therefore, I use the term *migration* in acknowledgment of emigration and transnational links as parts of the larger processes that are missed when we talk only about arrival or *immigration*. Nina Glick-Schiller and colleagues propose the term *transmigrant* for this "new type" of migrant,[11] but this term is misleading, since (1) to a degree, all migrants are transnational, (2) historically speaking, this is not a new phenomenon, (3) through time and immigrant generations, transnational behavior may decrease, (4) one can use a transnational frame without using the term "transmigrant," and (5) it did not catch on and is not widely used. This does not detract from Glick-Schiller and colleagues' theoretical contributions.

The consideration of the community of origin allows for the inclusion of internal migration, in which case the sending and receiving communities are part of the same national territory while at the same time having enough cultural, ethnic, or economic differences to be studied under this methodological framework. Mexican anthropologist Federico Besserer uses the term "translocalism" instead, which involves logic similar to a transnational framing even if no national borders are crossed.[12] An example would be women from Mayan communities in southern Mexico moving to Cancún to work, who send money to their nuclear families in their towns of origin.[13] This is a better theoretical term than "transnational," but it has not been taken up partly because of the division of labor between those who study international and internal migration.[14]

Transnationalism Within Migration Studies

Traditional migration theories emphasize long-term settlement and assume—or even prescribe—the end of all social, political, and economic ties with the community of origin. However, except for certain exiles and refugees, historically, migration has not entailed the complete severance of ties with the sending society.[15] Transnational studies show the strong connections that migrants have with their native country. Transnationalism gained scholarly attention in the 1990s, and it was proposed and described mainly by anthropologists, sociologists, and geographers.[16] Given the relative novelty of transnationalism as a theoretical perspective and its particular emphasis on multisited field research as a method,[17] there is still a lively debate about its theoretical implications and procedural definition. There has also been debate on whether transnationalism is a novel phenomenon or whether it existed before it was recognized and labeled as transnationalism.[18] The data show that long-distance connections and back-and-forth moves are not new, which makes keeping these ties in mind even more important as they will likely continue.

"Remittances" refers to money, gifts, and other resources that migrants send back to their place of origin—most commonly to their nuclear family or their parents and grandparents.[19] Many academic and policy papers have theorized about the economic and political implications of remittances, and some even present them as evidence of transnationalism. Some groundbreaking work expanding the field of transnational migration studies introduces the concept of social remittances to discuss cultural changes at the country of origin due to contact with people living abroad and adopting new cultural practices who stay in touch, visit, and return;[20] documents the role of religious institutions in transnationalism;[21] and studies the involvement of the sending state in fostering ties with the diaspora.[22] Over the past several decades, the academic subfield of migrant transnationalism has grown considerably, with a great deal of energy put in by many researchers to "prove" or even celebrate the existence of transnationalism by adding new case studies.

From being a novelty, transnationalism became quite central to migration studies in the 2000s. The term became fashionable, and many took for granted its relevance and eagerly provided new cases without questioning the theories and assumptions around it. Hyperbolically, perhaps, some talked about a "transnational turn." Despite its growing popularity, a consensus has not been reached on the extent to which immigrants who left their home countries at a very young age but grew up in their new country (the 1.5 generation), and second, third, and subsequent immigrant generations, engage in transnational activities.[23] This is because the level of transnationalism is impacted by the context of reception, the possibility of migrants' return to their country of birth, and levels of integration and racialization.[24]

As Algerian sociologist Abdelmalek Sayad explains, it is essential to see migrants both as emigrants (leaving a place) and immigrants (arriving in a new place) in order to understand their particular social and psychological conditions.[25] The traumas of migration and the nostalgia, sense of loss, and idealization of the land left behind by emigrants are also concerns in the psychoanalytical community.[26] An emphasis on transhumance (seasonal migration or, more generally, any circular migration) and an examination of migrants from the perspectives of both the sending and the receiving states have long been an interest of scholars of migration and international relations in Mexican academia.[27] The rise of transnational studies in the Anglo-American academic field also highlighted the importance of sending and receiving communities and the relation between the two in shaping the immigrant's social worlds.[28] The importance of studying both sending and receiving societies was also a significant part of Chicago School methodologies, as observed in the classic *The Polish Peasant in Europe and America* (1918–1920) by William Isaac Thomas and Florian Znaniecki.[29] Oscar Handlin's classic book *The Uprooted* (1951) focuses on displaced peasants moving into cities, losing their local culture and social ties. However, John Bodnar's *The Transplanted* (1985), while not fully transnational, shows that immigrants, through chain migration and the founding of ethnic halls and community institutions, try to re-create aspects of their culture to help them feel at home.[30]

Types of Transnationalism and Assumed Implications

Traditionally, migration studies has focused on the processes of immigrant integration into their host society.[31] Many studies show immigrant assimilation through time, while some alarmists frame immigration and ethnic enclaves as foreign communities or even "colonies" inside receiving countries.[32] The true colonial analogy mainly applies to the historical repopulation of the United States, Canada, Australia, and New Zealand by Europeans and later others.

Analytically, we could place immigrants along a continuum depending on the level of contact with their place of birth. The location on the scale is not meant to be normative. The length of the immigrant experience and the length of settlement (multigenerational) affect assimilation, integration, and mainstreaming, meaning becoming part of the majority society, being indistinguishable in terms of outcomes, and being protected from racialization's negative effects.[33]

Transnational practices are not incompatible with an upward path to integration and social mobility or exclusion.[34] I contrast *integration* (belonging despite cultural, religious, or racial differences) with *assimilation* (complete acculturation into the host society and loss of the culture of origin) and *ghettoization* (segregated access to political power and separate cultures and practices).

Ghettoization happens through the segregation of members of an ethnic or racial group and their stigmatization. Nonetheless, the growth of ghettos (either Jewish or Black) or colonias, barrios, Chinatowns, or ethnic enclaves can be perceived by some in the majority as an encroachment on national sovereignty and the formation of small foreign colonies within cities. But colonization is a different process. *Colonization* entails moving en masse in order to change and reshape society in the image of a new majority or elite in power or of a population backed up by an army using or threatening violence, largely for territorial and economic gain, which historically is predominantly associated with European settler colonialism. Historical cases in which this has become a reality include the arrival of Protestants to Texas when it was part of Mexico. Mexico allowed immigrants to settle as long as they promised to assimilate and not to secede. The numbers grew large, and they were led by people such as Sam Houston and Stephen Austin to declare independence from Mexico, which the United States recognized, leading to the Mexican-American War (1846–1848). The annexation of Texas led to the reinstatement of slavery in that large territory. And beyond Texas, the taking of half of Mexico's territory by the United States led to the overwhelmingly Native American and Spanish-descent populations in the West being dwarfed by Protestants, who took much of the land and enforced a second-class citizenship status for non-Anglos.[35] In another example, the French engaged in a failed attempt to make Algeria a permanent part of France by increasing the number of European people settling there.[36] Present-day migration to Europe and the United States does not have the goal of taking land for another country or declaring an independent one.

Circular migration through temporary work during a series of short-term stays can lead to transnationalism once people spend more time in the receiving place, often forming family relationships with locals and staying beyond seasonal work. Some research shows that the more integrated immigrants are, the more sporadic and intentional their transnationalism will be, while some migrants turn to transnationalism as a palliative for the racism and exclusion on the receiving side that often persists regardless of citizenship.[37]

Transnational behavior itself can vary depending on the conditions of exit, the context of reception, and the social position of a particular person or group. Most influential in the literature of the 2000s is a transnationalism that celebrates globalization and the declining significance of borders and the

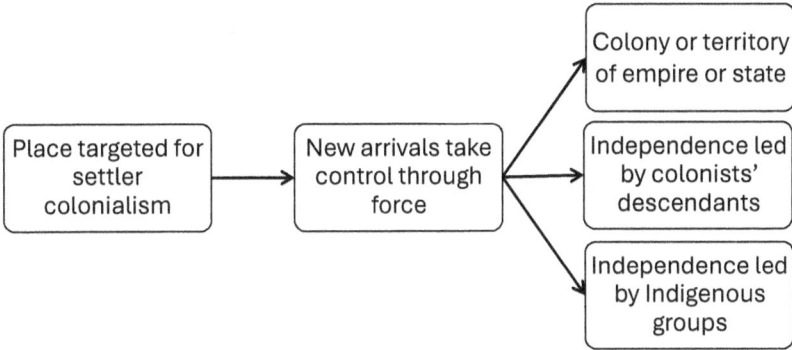

Figure 1.1. Types of colonialism and decolonialization.

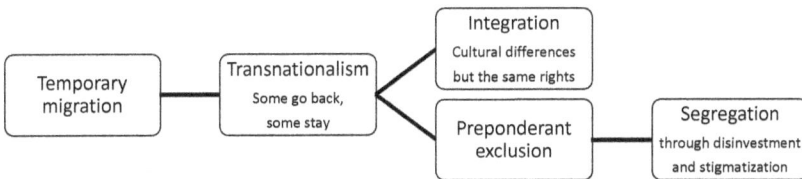

Figure 1.2. Immigrant integration pathways.

nation-state,[38] and that sees migration as evidence of this. In this framework, remittances are assumed to be an example of globalization and border effacement, and a way to produce economic development and reduce global inequality. In reality, the nexus between remittances and development is much more complicated.[39]

At the turn of the twenty-first century, some authors believed that people were experiencing a fast convergence of universal values and equal human worth. In this celebratory view, transnationalism empowers individuals across borders, opening new and limitless economic and political opportunities. Nonetheless, this cosmopolitan life is most often real for some elites, academics, and frequent flyers,[40] but not for working-class natives, immigrants, or those who are undocumented. Like those wrongly proposing the end of history after the fall of the Soviet Union, early proponents of globalization and transnationalism as a teleological destination ignored the deglobalization (the increase in the ratio of local transactions over global ones) brought about by pandemics, economic crises, economic sanctions, and war. Theorists also failed to account for the backlash from white blue-collar workers through Brexit and Donald Trump's presidential campaigns. These populist promises of Tories and Republicans did not solve any of the structural issues increasing inequality. They did not cause the end of transnational flows, nor did they stop everyone from engaging in some transnational practices or abandoning a cosmopolitan outlook. Not even tariffs can do this.

The theoretical framing of transnationalism as neoliberal globalization was a companion to an elite political project.[41] I call it "elite transnationalism" because it is mostly theoretical beyond the lives of a few. The framing of what I call "colonial transnationalism" is a political maneuver in which conservative restrictionists use the literature on transnationalism as evidence of a foreign invasion posing an existential threat to US and European populations and a great demographic replacement in which the white race becomes a minority.[42] These arguments are not only racist but also vastly overstate demographic change, the stability of ethnoracial labels, and the durability of transnationalism. Furthermore, it is important to recall that foreign-born labor plays a key role in creating wealth for established citizens; cheap labor from abroad has supplanted serfdom and the forced capture, transportation, and sale of slaves.

A more prevalent account of actually existing migrant transnationalism is what I call "relational transnationalism." In this process, migrants act on and react to the receiving society while simultaneously looking home. This constant comparison poses unique opportunities and problems in everyday life. For instance, parents who migrated with the explicit goal of sending remittances home will engage with relational transnationalism because the focus of what they are doing is rooted in the country of origin—sending money to their children or other relatives. This focus on earning as much money as possible through low-paid jobs means long hours and weekend work, making it harder for them to engage much beyond work in the communities where they live; they do not have the time to worry about new social mores, dispositions, or ideas.

Economically or socially, migrants may be in a disadvantaged position in their new communities, making achieving salience at the place of origin even more appealing. Politically, transnationalism allows interested actors to be active in two political communities without any deleterious effects on either.

Nonetheless, the type and extent of participation in the economy, the social landscape, and politics will depend on the immigrants' socioeconomic status and each community's characteristics. By shaping the context of reception, the receiving society and the state play a central role in regulating these people's social, economic, and political activity.

Remittances show migrants' strong social attachments to family members in their towns of origin. Remittances also constitute an "emotional investment" that goes beyond economic calculations. Their cost is often family separation that can last many years. Again, this cost partly depends on the remitter's economic success, legal status, and social networks, and the public policy sphere of the locality in which the immigrant lives. Things are better emotionally if family members have visas that allow them to visit each other periodically or if they can move as a family.[43]

One should not overlook that migrants also invest significant economic resources in the host society. In addition to working, immigrants pay income taxes, social security, rent, mortgages, and property taxes. They go to restaurants and shop in the areas where they live and work. They often start businesses that become community fixtures. Relational transnationalism is but one type of migrant transnationalism.

Table 1.1 shows the different understandings or types of transnationalism. While this typology is not meant to be strict or exhaustive, it is essential to discuss the many perspectives and manifestations of transnationalism. For the immigrants themselves, there are also multiple kinds of transnational experiences associated with their economic and legal capability to engage physically or intellectually with both their host and sending communities.

Colonial transnationalism reflects the exaggerated view of many residents—particularly in a city or country where many immigrants or refugees are perceived to be arriving for the first time or from new places—that immigrants represent an economic and cultural threat. It reflects a fear that immigrants will take over land, resources, and even government and change the place's culture. Beyond settler colonialism practiced historically by China as well as Great Britain and other European colonial powers, this is rarely the case in the West today. Colonial transnationalism frames remittances as resource extraction from the local economy. This framing pushes migrants to assimilate quickly or leave, as it presents them as a cultural threat and invasion.

TABLE I.I. Types of Transnationalism.

	Relational Transnationalism	Reactive Transnationalism	Elite Transnationalism	Border Transnationalism	Exile Transnationalism	Colonial Transnationalism
Definition	This is characterized by deep connections between immigrants, whether sanctioned or undocumented, and their place of origin. Internal and international migrants with visas will be able to visit home communities in some countries and historical periods, for instance those working in the US before the 2000s.	This is a type of restorative transnationalism. The children of immigrants look to the "country of origin" for affirmation and identity reasons.	We could also call this "cosmopolitan" or "resource-based" transnationalism.[1] It is the type of transnationalism engaged in by privileged individuals with access to papers and money who can choose to travel back and forth at will for profit and pleasure.	This occurs due to living in a border region where crossing often between countries is part of a survival strategy for the relatively privileged and for those for whom brokering between borders is the difficult but only way to make ends meet.[2]	This type of transnationalism is engaged by exiles, asylum seekers, and political refugees who cannot physically return to their home countries as long as the same regime is in power there. Nonetheless, they can be active in political opposition against the regime and keep in touch with family and friends.	In this alarmist framework, migrant enclaves show that immigrants are not adapting to their new society and thus pose a cultural threat to the host community.[3]

	Relational Transnationalism	Reactive Transnationalism	Elite Transnationalism	Border Transnationalism	Exile Transnationalism	Colonial Transnationalism
Arguments	Migrants act on and react to the receiving society while also looking home. This poses opportunities and problems. States and borders are not irrelevant. The state plays a central role in regulating migrants' social, economic, and political activity.[4]	This occurs when immigrants and their offspring are not happy with their standing in the host society. Transnationalism appears as nostalgia for a better past and the idealization of a better future outside of poverty and racialization within the host society.	Individuals in this category have the papers and resources to cross back and forth across political borders.	This occurs among individuals who constantly cross international borders for economic, social, and cultural reasons. It is real and unique but cannot be fully generalized to all the residents of a border area.	Political refugees and asylum seekers may form "governments in exile" to fight at a distance for political change in their country of birth. They may sometimes be labeled as terrorist groups (e.g., Sri Lankan immigrants in Paris who support the Tamil Tigers).	This gives credence to arguments about a "Reconquista" of the Southwest by Mexicans,[5] or the incompatible character of Muslims in Europe.
Assumptions	Migrants may be in a disadvantaged position in their host communities, making achieving salience in the sending side even more appealing.[6] However, a full return has to be postponed.[7]	In countries that have exclusivist cultures, minorities may have to look elsewhere for environments that are more tolerant of different religious and cultural practices.	This type of transnationalism was often implied in earlier discussions of the topic in terms of the weakening of the nation-state,[8] postnational membership,[9] and citizenship à la carte.[10]	People can go back and forth freely in a border city.	People cannot go back for fear of their lives.	Transnationalism distracts people from getting involved in local community service and politics. Transnational individuals show double loyalties and are thus a problem and/or opportunity for international politics.

	Relational Transnationalism	Reactive Transnationalism	Elite Transnationalism	Border Transnationalism	Exile Transnationalism	Colonial Transnationalism
The Implied Effects	Transnationalism allows interested actors to be active in two political communities without any deleterious effects to either.[11] Nonetheless, the type of participation will depend on each community's characteristics and the socioeconomic status of the immigrant in question.	Transnationalism is practiced to secure the dignity, identity, and cultural purity lost by the family's migration and downward assimilation. Transnationalism often remains aspirational, since return is not practical and many cultural differences remain.	Transnationalism erases borders and allows for new business and cultural connections but is limited to a small group.	It is embodied in bilingualism and biculturalism and is a form of everyday transnationalism (e.g., people living in Ciudad Juárez but working or studying in El Paso, Texas, who do not remit per se but carry cash with them and spend it in either country indistinctly).	Transnationalism is a way to stay involved in politics from a distance.	Remittances represent an extraction of resources from the host society.
Implications Regarding Remittances and the Development of the Sending Community	Remittances show strong social attachments to family members in the town of origin.[12] Remittances also constitute an "emotional investment" that goes beyond economic calculations. One should not overlook that important economic resources are also invested in the host society.	Remittances are not part of the return aspirations of second- and third-generation immigrants, since they have little money to remit and few family members to remit to. Transnationalism expresses itself more through nostalgic tourism, music, and cultural consumption.	Educated cadres, professionals, and business owners can make productive investments in the host and sending countries and help through charitable donations, yet the number of people in this position is relatively small.[13]	This form of brokerage is a back-and-forth movement as a strategy to overcome poverty and marginalization. It is contingent on citizenship, residency, or visas.	The goal is often to start a new life in exile or return to a country under a different political regime.	Remittances show that immigrants are only interested in the well-being of their place of origin.

1. José Itzigsohn and Silvia Giorguli Saucedo, "Immigrant Incorporation and Sociocultural Transnationalism," *International Migration Review* 36, no. 3 (2002): 766–98.
2. Howard Campbell and Josué G. Lachica. "Transnational Homelessness: Finding a Place on the US-Mexico Border, "*Journal of Borderlands Studies* 28, no. 3 (2013): 279–90; and Sergio R. Chávez, *Border Lives: Fronterizos, Transnational Migrants, and Commuters in Tijuana* (New York: Oxford University Press, 2016).
3. Samuel P. Huntington, *Who Are We? The Challenges to America's National Identity* (New York: Simon and Schuster, 2004).
4. Robert Courtney Smith, *Mexican New York: Transnational Lives of New Immigrants* (Berkeley: University of California Press, 2006).
5. Huntington, *Who Are We?*
6. Linda Basch, Nina Glick Schiller, and Cristina Szanton Blanc, *Nations Unbound: Transnational Projects, Postcolonial Predicaments, and Deterritorialized Nation-States* (London: Gordon and Breach, 1994).
7. Abdelmalek Sayad, *The Suffering of the Immigrant*, trans. David Macey (Cambridge: Polity Press, 2004).
8. Saskia Sassen, *Losing Control? Sovereignty in an Age of Globalization* (New York: Columbia University Press, 1996).
9. Yasemin Nuhoğlu Soysal, *Limits of Citizenship: Migrants and Postnational Membership in Europe* (Chicago: University of Chicago Press, 1994).
10. David Fitzgerald, *A Nation of Emigrants: How Mexico Manages Its Migration* (Berkeley: University of California Press, 2009).
11. Alejandro Portes and Rubén G. Rumbaut, *Immigrant America: A Portrait*, 4th ed. (Berkeley: University of California Press, 2014).
12. Viviana A. Zelizer and Charles Tilly, "Relations and Categories," in *The Psychology of Learning and Motivation*, vol. 47, *Categories in Use*, ed. Arthur B. Markman and Brian H. Ross (San Diego: Elsevier, 2006), 1–31.
13. Aihwa Ong, *Flexible Citizenship: The Culture Logics of Transnationality* (Durham, NC: Duke University Press, 1999); and AnnaLee Saxenian, *The New Argonauts: Regional Advantage in a Global Economy* (Cambridge, MA: Harvard University Press, 2006).

Exile transnationalism is the experience of exiles and asylum seekers—they engage transnationally but cannot visit their country of origin much less return permanently for fear of their lives. They may keep in touch with family or friends back home, but return is almost impossible. Border transnationalism is almost the opposite—the practice of people who live near a border and often cross for access to economic, social, or housing opportunities. Transnationalism is part of their everyday life through their physical engagement with the border, whereas the border in the mind of an exile is more of an idea; it is not physically in front of them.

In contrast, elite transnationalism refers to economic, artistic, or intellectual elites who migrate and, due to their secure legal status and abundance of economic resources, go back and forth as they please, even if their home country is not close by. This is increasingly the case for middle-class digital nomads from the Global North working in the Global South. Some of these diaspora members boast of their transnational activities by being active in hometown associations, sometimes running for office or sponsoring charities and cultural events through resources from their often transnational businesses; they are sometimes the heroes of some transnational ethnographies. However, they are far from representative of the larger immigrant community.

In contrast, relational transnationalism describes the experience of most economic migrants. Reactive transnationalism is experienced by the children of immigrants and 1.5 generation immigrants—embedded in their country of residence but looking to the other country to understand where they "come from," for identity and affirmation.

As previously noted, increasingly since the 1990s, scholars have used the term "transnationalism" to refer to a series of presences, identities, and movements that do not map easily within the geographical borders of contemporary nation-states. However, to paraphrase Bruno Latour, we have never been national. Therefore, examples of transnationalism can be uncovered throughout history and around the world, whether in Europe, Latin America, or the Middle East.[44] As figure 1.3 shows, the publication of papers on transnationalism has grown steadily since the 2000s. The Web of Science citation index shows that the most-cited papers about transnationalism concern migration. Nonetheless, transnational behavior is not limited to migration, as scholars have applied it to social movements, identity formation, and cultural diffusion, and to understanding historical events in a way that is not encumbered by national borders. Thus, the increasing call to move from the study and teaching of national histories toward a study of global history.[45]

Nonmigrant Transnational Studies

After transnationalism began to have influence in migration studies, and after the fruitful interrogation of methodological nationalism (which starts with the wrong assumption that political borders contain mutually exclusive units of analysis),[46] other academic fields, including sociology, anthropology, political science, and the humanities, have begun looking at practices, connections, and solidarities transcending national borders. Many chapters in this book take this approach. In doing so, they do not marginalize culture and practices; instead, they correct previous studies that artificially limited the scope of study of relations, contentious

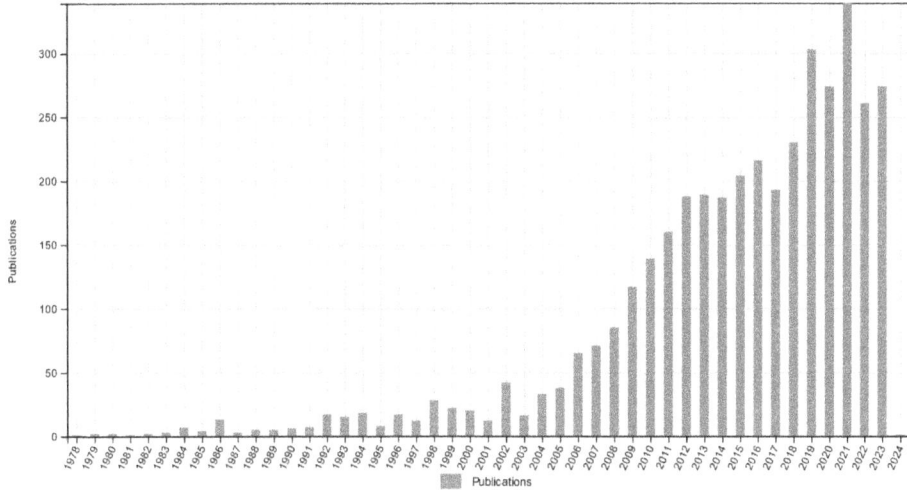

Figure 1.3. Number of publications on transnationalism, 1978–2023. Source: Web of Science citation reports, https://www.webofscience.com/wos/woscc/citation-report/
a5d1eaa5-c81f-41d8-b34b-2988628be647-fe5bf074.

performances, and social movements to the political limits of a nation-state. Flows of money, goods, people, and ideas across political demarcations are not new; nation-states are a more recent phenomenon.[47] Despite homogenizing national institutions and ideologies, most nation-states are ethnically diverse or plurinational. This is not pose a "problem" to solve. The ideal is not additional independentist movements to get to the lowest level of ethnic-cultural distinction, but further democratization to include all categorical groups and trust networks in local governing structures so that opportunities and results vary at the individual and not the group level, thus leading to true meritocracy.[48] It is not about having every tribe or possible ethnic subgroup with its own government but about having every individual represented and supported where they live.

In another example, social movements engage in what Charles Tilly calls "contentious performances," which are locally legible and legitimate ways to protest state policies or ask for more rights. Activists, performances, and agendas often diffuse across political jurisdictions. For example, in 2011, Occupy Wall Street was deeply influenced by the May 15 camps in Spain, which in turn were influenced by Icelandic protests against foreign debt as well as by the Arab Spring.[49]

To conclude, let us go back to migration as an example to discuss theoretical approaches—building partially on French sociologist Pierre Bourdieu's theories—that wrongly argue that transnational social fields transcend nation-state politics and make political borders less relevant.

Conclusion: Migration and Transnational Social Fields

Many authors have implicitly described remittances simultaneously as evidence, cause, and consequence of transnationalism. Remittances are attractive to transnational households because they connect two different labor fields. Whether or not they create a new social field, migrants become flexible labor power and cultural brokers between distinct social fields. Their uniqueness comes not from existing in closed ethnic enclaves with virtual halves in faraway lands, but instead from connecting different social fields such as Boston, Massachusetts, and Miraflores, Dominican Republic;[50] or towns in Puebla[51] or Guerrero,[52] Mexico, and New York City; or ranches in central Mexico and Albuquerque, New Mexico.[53] The separation of the place where one works from the place where one grows up and retires[54] creates transnational households divided across borders, resulting in teleparenting.[55] Nevertheless, during most of the waking day, immigrants live not in a transnational social field but in the receiving community. Immigrants must navigate the new places where they live and work but do so with the cultural frameworks they bring with them, all while thinking about their loved ones who had to stay in their place of origin and reproducing cultural and political activities with other people from their hometowns.

The growing interdisciplinary field of migrant transnational studies frequently uses the term "transnational social field" when describing the transnational activities of immigrant communities. This concept comes from transnational theory pioneers Nina Glick Schiller and Peggy Levitt, who conceptualize this "field" as the "place" where social interactions occur between people living physically apart in migrant-sending communities and migrant-receiving sites. These authors explicitly state that they draw on the work of Pierre Bourdieu when coining the term "transnational social field." The term has since been used to support the transnational perspective on immigration research[56] and to reify what anthropologist Arjun Appadurai would call an "ethnoscape" to refer to the global flows of people.[57] Other scholars reproduce the term "transnational social field" by using transnational methodological and theoretical frameworks. The concept of a "transnational social field" is a useful heuristic and abstraction, a theoretical construct to imagine, conceptualize, and discuss transnationalism. However, for readers who have not done fieldwork, the term may overstate the commonality and frequency of empirical transnational practices. The concept emphasizes a double presence rather than the double absence of emigrating and immigrating. It also excludes people in the receiving and sending communities who do not participate in transnational practices but who often interact with migrants or their families left behind. It is empirically limiting to study migration only through the lens of the long-term processes of immigrant integration into receiving societies, or only from the point of view of transnationalism, since the emphasis on the "transnational social field" alone could wrongly imply that immigrants have no real or meaningful interactions with locals beyond providing labor, or with those back in their previous place of residence besides sending money.[58] In more realistic theorizing, using a transnational lens does not then mean that all people involved in migration are equally exposed to transnational practices or that migration is the most meaningful experience of their lives. Indeed, Bourdieu's larger corpus describes the overlapping of multiple fields that shape people's social worlds.[59] Migration fueled by the goal of remitting is a process of brokering between economies in unequally developed geographies.

Bourdieu knew the challenges that migration created for embodied culture. It is not coincidental that one of his closest students and collaborators, Abdelmalek Sayad, used his theories to explain the experience of Algerian migrants in France.[60] Sayad was one of the earliest proponents of the conceptualization of migration as including both sending and receiving communities. In this sense, Sayad anticipated the theoretical need for a multisited transnational methodology—meaning conducting fieldwork in multiple geographic locations of origin and destination. Sayad's approach is still useful because it does not depend on abstract "transnational social fields" or a monolithic "immigrant culture" but rather on a theory in which cultures of origin are carried by migrants in their own particular manner through their individual habitus—dispositions and social history embodied in individuals, structure becoming flesh. What Sayad calls "the suffering of the migrant" is due to the fact that communities of origin and destination have different (field-specific) types and valuations of cultural capital—know-how about the practices, unspoken rules, and hidden curricula of prestigious and powerful social circles and institutions.[61] But contrary to a "clash of cultures" perspective, I argue that this embodied culture is flexible and changes through time and continued interactions with others. Contrary to how states often frame this, the challenge is not rooted in theology, economic competition, racial character, or national security but is a matter of interpersonal relations—as messy and complicated as they are. Clearly, the state can moderate and incorporate, or further alienate, vilify, and escalate, ethnic and racial tensions and social boundaries.[62]

A relational understanding of migration and transnationalism provides a better approach to understanding human mobility.[63] Migration scholars would do well to reassess transnationalism and integration through these powerful theoretical lenses, because the premigration experience sets up expectations and the reference through which immigrants evaluate their integration and success postmigration. The term "transnationalism" was probably first used to denote the supposed novelty of the described phenomenon. Nevertheless, the field of transnational history shows that sending money and keeping in touch with the place of origin is not new, but has often accompanied human mobility.[64] Long-distance migration predates the nation-state.[65]

Some migration scholars used the transnational social field as the theoretical scaffolding for descriptive studies of cultural maintenance and long-distance communication among immigrants and their families, which in itself has produced useful findings and empirical descriptions. Using Bourdieu's concepts of field, capital, and habitus together opens a new door to understanding contemporary migration. This does not take away from the important empirical research and fieldwork findings by all the many scholars contributing to studies of immigrant transnationalism. Future research bringing the concepts of cultural capital and habitus into discussions of migration can offer a more holistic description of the complex empirical reality behind the human migration experience. In the meantime, relational transnationalism—a procedural and mechanism-based approach to immigration based on transactions, social relations, actual networks, and contentious politics—provides a useful way to design social research and case studies to theorize about the political and cultural implications of transnationalism, whether in real-life spaces or cyberspace, or through movies and other cultural products.

Notes

I thank the editors of this book, as well as Eric Hershberg, Carlos Coleman, Isabella Goris, and fellow authors in this volume for useful feedback.

1. Saskia Sassen, *The Global City: New York, London, Tokyo*, 2nd ed. (Princeton University Press, 2001).

2. Ernesto Castañeda and Amber Shemesh, "Overselling Globalization: The Misleading Conflation of Economic Globalization and Immigration, and the Subsequent Backlash," *Social Sciences* 9, no. 5, article 61 (2020), https://www.mdpi.com/2076-0760/9/5/61.

3. Emanuel Deutschmann, *Mapping the Transnational World: How We Move and Communicate Across Borders, and Why It Matters* (Princeton University Press, 2021), 3.

4. Theodore Levitt, "The Globalization of Markets," *Harvard Business Review* 61, no. 3 (May 1983): 92–102.

5. Castañeda and Shemesh, "Overselling Globalization."

6. Alejandro Portes, "Globalization from Below: the Rise of Transnational Communities," Working Paper 98:8, 1997, University of Oxford; and Michael Peter Smith and Luis Eduardo Guarnizo, eds., *Transnationalism from Below: Comparative Urban and Community Research* (New Brunswick, NJ: Transaction Publishers, 1998).

7. Ewa Morawska, "Immigrants, Transnationalism, and Ethnicization: A Comparison of This Great Wave and the Last," in *E Pluribus Unum? Contemporary and Historical Perspectives on Immigrant Political Incorporation*, ed. Gary Gerstle and John Mollenkopf (Russell Sage Foundation, 2001), 175–212; Charles Tilly, Ernesto Castañeda, and Lesley J. Wood, *Social Movements, 1768–2018*, 4th ed. (Routledge, 2020); and Nancy L. Green, *The Limits of Transnationalism* (University of Chicago Press, 2019).

8. Deutschmann, *Mapping the Transnational World*, 35–38.

9. Abdelmalek Sayad, *The Suffering of the Immigrant*, trans. David Macey (Polity Press, 2004); and Abdelmalek Sayad, *L'immigration ou les paradoxes de l'altérité*, vol. 1, *L'illusion du provisoire* (Éditions Liber, 2006).

10. Robert Courtney Smith, *Mexican New York: Transnational Lives of New Immigrants* (University of California Press, 2006); and Charles Tilly, "Trust Networks in Transnational Migration," *Sociological Forum* 22, no. 1 (March 2007): 3–24.

11. Nina Glick Schiller, Linda Basch, and Cristina Blanc-Szanton, "Transnationalism: A New Analytic Framework for Understanding Migration," *Annals of the New York Academy of Sciences* 645, no. 1 (July 1992): 1–24.

12. Federico Besserer, *Topografías transnacionales: Hacia una geografía de la vida transnacional* (Universidad Autónoma Metropolitana, Iztapalapa; Plaza y Valdés Editores, 2004); and Rocío Gil Martínez de Escobar, *Fronteras de pertenencia: Hacia la construcción del bienestar y el desarrollo comunitario transnacional de Santa María Tindú, Oaxaca* (Universidad Autónoma Metropolitana, Iztapalapa; Ediciones Casa Juan Pablos, 2006).

13. M. Bianet Castellanos, "Adolescent Migration to Cancún: Reconfiguring Maya Households and Gender Relations in Mexico's Yucatán Peninsula," *Frontiers* 28, no. 3 (2007): 1–27.

14. Joshua Dietz, Bulin Li, and Ernesto Castañeda, "Keeping in Motion or Staying Put: Internal Migration in the United States and China," *Societies* 13, no. 7, article 162 (July 2023), https://www.mdpi.com/2075-4698/13/7/162.

15. William Isaac Thomas and Florian Znaniecki, *The Polish Peasant in Europe and America: Monograph of an Immigrant Group*, 5 vols. (Gorham Press, 1918–1920); Nancy Foner, *From Ellis Island to JFK: New York's Two Great Waves of Immigration* (New Haven, CT: Yale University Press; New York: Russell Sage Foundation, 2000); and John Bodnar, *The Transplanted: A History of Immigrants in Urban America* (Indiana University Press, 1985).

16. Smith and Guarnizo, *Transnationalism from Below*; Linda Basch, Nina Glick Schiller, and Cristina Szanton Blanc, *Nations Unbound: Transnational Projects, Postcolonial Predicaments, and Deterritorialized Nation-States* (Gordon and Breach, 1994); and Michael Kearney, "The Local and the Global: The Anthropology of Globalization and Transnationalism," *Annual Review of Anthropology* 24 (1995): 547–65.

17. George E. Marcus, "Ethnography in/of the World System: The Emergence of Multi-Sited Ethnography," *Annual Review of Anthropology* 24 (1995): 95–117.

18. Morawska, "Immigrants, Transnationalism, and Ethnicization"; Foner, *From Ellis Island to JFK*; and Roger Waldinger and David Fitzgerald, "Transnationalism in Question," *American Journal of Sociology* 109, no. 5 (March 2004): 1177–95.

19. Ernesto Castañeda, "Remittances," in *The Palgrave Dictionary of Transnational History*, ed. Akira Iriye and Pierre-Yves Saunier (Basingstoke, Hants., England: Palgrave Macmillan, 2009), 904–7.

20. Peggy Levitt, "Social Remittances: Migration Driven Local-Level Forms of Cultural Diffusion," *International Migration Review* 32, no. 4 (Winter 1998): 926–48; and Peggy Levitt, *The Transnational Villagers* (University of California Press, 2001).

21. Peggy Levitt, *God Needs No Passport: Immigrants and the Changing American Religious Landscape* (New Press, 2007).

22. David Fitzgerald, *A Nation of Emigrants: How Mexico Manages Its Migration* (University of California Press, 2009); Robert C. Smith, "Diasporic Memberships in Historical Perspective: Comparative Insights from the Mexican, Italian and Polish Cases," *International Migration Review* 37, no. 3 (Fall 2003): 724–59; Gustavo Cano and Alexandra Délano, "The Mexican Government and Organised Mexican Immigrants in the United States: A Historical Analysis of Political Transnationalism (1848–2005)," *Journal of Ethnic and Migration Studies* 33, no. 5 (2007): 695–725; Natasha N. Iskander, "Innovating Government: Migration, Development, and the State in Morocco and Mexico, 1963–2005" (PhD diss., Massachusetts Institute of Technology, 2006); and Alexandra Délano, *Mexico and Its Diaspora in the United States: Policies of Emigration Since 1848* (Cambridge University Press, 2011).

23. Peggy Levitt and Mary C. Waters, eds., *The Changing Face of Home: The Transnational Lives of the Second Generation* (Russell Sage Foundation, 2002).

24. Ernesto Castañeda, Maria Cristina Morales, and Olga Ochoa, "Transnational Behavior in Comparative Perspective: The Relationship Between Immigrant Integration and Transnationalism in New York, El Paso, and Paris," *Comparative Migration Studies* 2, no. 3 (2014): 305–34; Tineke Fokkema, "'Return' Migration Intentions Among Second-Generation Turks in Europe: The Effect of Integration and Transnationalism in a Cross-National

Perspective," *Journal of Mediterranean Studies* 20, no. 2 (2011): 365–88; and Justice Richard Kwabena Owusu Kyei, Elizabeth Nana Mbrah Koomson-Yalley, and Peter Dwumah, "Transnational Political Practices and Integration of Second Generation Migrants," *Journal of Ethnic and Migration Studies* 48, no. 5 (2020): 1–16.

25. Pierre Bourdieu and Abdelmalek Sayad, *Le déracinement: La crise de l'agriculture traditionnelle en Algérie* (Éditions de Minuit, 1964); Sayad, *The Suffering of the Immigrant*; and Sayad, *L'immigration ou les paradoxes de l'altérité*.

26. Salman Akhtar, *Immigration and Identity: Turmoil, Treatment, and Transformation* (Jason Aronson, 1999); Salman Akhtar, "A Third Individuation: Immigration, Identity, and the Psychoanalytic Process," *Journal of the American Psychoanalytic Association* 43, no. 4 (August 1995): 1051–84; León Grinberg and Rebeca Grinberg, *Psychoanalytic Perspectives on Migration and Exile*, trans. Nancy Festinger (New Haven, CT: Yale University Press, 1989); and Joseba Achotegui, "La atención a la salud mental de los inmigrantes y demandantes de asilo / Attention to Mental Health of Immigrants and Asylum Seekers," *Avances en Salud Mental Relacional / Advances in Relational Mental Health* 15, no. 1 (2016), https://psiquiatria.com/trabajos/1494.pdf.

27. Francisco Alba, "Comercio, migración y esquemas de integración económica: Los casos de la CEE y el TLCAN," *Foro Internacional* 41, no. 2 (April–June 2001): 299–308; and Jorge A. Bustamante, "Mexico–United States Labor Migration Flows," *International Migration Review* 31, no. 4 (Winter 1997): 1112–21.

28. R. Smith, *Mexican New York*; Levitt and Waters, *The Changing Face of Home*; and Peggy Levitt and B. Nadya Jaworsky, "Transnational Migration Studies: Past Developments and Future Trends," *Annual Review of Sociology* 33, no. 1 (December 2007): 129–56.

29. Ernesto Castañeda, "Transnationalism in the Lives of Migrants: The Relevance of Thomas and Znaniecki's Work to Understand Migration," in *Contemporary Migrations in the Humanistic Coefficient Perspective: Florian Znaniecki's Thought in Today's Social Science Research*, ed. Jacek Kubera and Łukasz Skoczylas (Frankfurt am Main: Peter Lang, 2017), 171–86.

30. Charles Tilly, "Transplanted Networks," in *Immigration Reconsidered: History, Sociology, and Politics*, ed. Virginia Yans-McLaughlin (Oxford University Press, 1990), 79–95.

31. Milton Myron Gordon, *Assimilation in American Life: The Role of Race, Religion, and National Origins* (Oxford University Press, 1964); Richard D. Alba and Victor Nee, *Remaking the American Mainstream: Assimilation and Contemporary Immigration* (Harvard University Press, 2003); José Itzigsohn, *Encountering American Faultlines: Race, Class, and the Dominican Experience in Providence* (Russell Sage Foundation, 2009); and Rogers Brubaker, *Ethnicity Without Groups* (Harvard University Press, 2004).

32. Samuel P. Huntington, *Who Are We? The Challenges to America's National Identity* (Simon and Schuster, 2004); and Christopher Caldwell, *Reflections on the Revolution in Europe: Immigration, Islam, and the West* (Doubleday, 2009).

33. Alba and Nee, *Remaking the American Mainstream*.

34. Castañeda, Morales, and Ochoa, "Transnational Behavior in Comparative Perspective"; and Alejandro Portes, Cristina Escobar, and Renelinda Arana, "Divided or Convergent Loyalties? The Political Incorporation Process of Latin American Immigrants in the United States," *International Journal of Comparative Sociology* 50, no. 2 (2009): 103–36.

35. Laura E. Gómez, *Manifest Destinies: The Making of the Mexican American Race* (New York University Press, 2007).

36. Andrea L. Smith, *Colonial Memory and Postcolonial Europe: Maltese Settlers in Algeria and France* (Indiana University Press, 2006).

37. Castañeda, Morales, and Ochoa, "Transnational Behavior in Comparative Perspective."

38. Saskia Sassen, *Losing Control? Sovereignty in an Age of Globalization* (Columbia University Press, 1996); and Thomas L. Friedman, *The World Is Flat: A Brief History of the Twenty-First Century* (Farrar, Straus and Giroux, 2005).

39. Ernesto Castañeda, "Living in Limbo: Transnational Households, Remittances and Development," *International Migration* 51, no. 1 (2013): 13–35; Matt Bakker, *Migrating into Financial Markets: How Remittances Became a Development Tool* (University of California Press, 2015); and Alejandro Portes and Patricia Fernández-Kelly, eds., *The State and the Grassroots: Immigrant Transnational Organizations in Four Continents* (Berghahn Books, 2015).

40. Craig J. Calhoun, "The Class Consciousness of Frequent Travelers: Toward a Critique of Actually Existing Cosmopolitanism," *South Atlantic Quarterly* 101, no. 4 (Fall 2002): 869–97.

41. Quinn Slobodian, *Globalists: The End of Empire and the Birth of Neoliberalism* (Harvard University Press, 2018).

42. Huntington, *Who Are We?*; and Ernesto Castañeda, *Building Walls: Excluding Latin People in the United States* (Lexington Books, 2019).

43. Ernesto Castañeda and Daniel Jenks, *Reunited: Family Separation and Central American Youth Migration* (Russell Sage Foundation, 2024); and Jason DeParle, *A Good Provider Is One Who Leaves: One Family and Migration in the 21st Century* (Viking, 2019).

44. Akram Fouad Khater, "Becoming 'Syrian' in America: A Global Geography of Ethnicity and Nation," *Diaspora: A Journal of Transnational Studies* 14, nos. 2–3 (Fall–Winter 2005): 299–331.

45. John Coatsworth, Juan Cole, Michael P. Hanagan, Peter C. Perdue, Charles Tilly, and Louise Tilly, *Global Connections: Politics, Exchange, and Social Life in World History*, 2 vols. (Cambridge University Press, 2015).

46. Andreas Wimmer and Nina Glick Schiller, "Methodological Nationalism and Beyond: Nation-State Building, Migration and the Social Sciences," *Global Networks: A Journal of Transnational Affairs* 2, no. 4 (October 2002): 301–34; Ernesto Castañeda, "Introduction to 'Reshaping the World: Rethinking Borders,'" *Social Sciences* 9, no. 11, article 214 (2020), https://www.mdpi.com/2076-0760/9/11/214; and Charles Tilly, *Big Structures, Large Processes, Huge Comparisons* (Russell Sage Foundation, 1984).

47. Tilly, *Big Structures*.

48. Ernesto Castañeda and Cathy Lisa Schneider, eds., *Collective Violence, Contentious Politics, and Social Change: A Charles Tilly Reader* (Routledge, 2017).

49. Ernesto Castañeda, "The Indignados of Spain: A Precedent to Occupy Wall Street," *Social Movement Studies* 11, nos. 3–4 (2012): 309–19; Eduardo Romanos, "Immigrants as Brokers: Dialogical Diffusion from Spanish Indignados to Occupy Wall Street," *Social Movement Studies* 15, no. 3 (2016): 247–62; Manuel Castells, *Networks of Outrage and Hope: Social Movements in the Internet Age* (Polity Press, 2015); and Tilly, Castañeda, and Wood, *Social Movements*.

50. Levitt, *The Transnational Villagers.*

51. R. Smith, *Mexican New York*; Marcela Ibarra Mateos and Liliana Rivera-Sánchez, *Entre contextos locales y ciudades globales: La configuración de circuitos migratorios Puebla–Nueva York* (Puebla, Mexico: Universidad Iberoamericana Puebla, 2011); and Liliana Rivera-Sánchez, "Expressions of Identity and Belonging: Mexican Immigrants in New York," in *Indigenous Mexican Migrants in the United States*, ed. Jonathan Fox and Gaspar Rivera-Salgado (La Jolla, CA: Center for US-Mexican Studies; Center for Comparative Immigration Studies, University of California, San Diego, 2004).

52. Castañeda, "Living in Limbo."

53. Deborah A. Boehm, *Intimate Migrations: Gender, Family, and Illegality Among Transnational Mexicans* (New York University Press, 2012).

54. Michael Burawoy, "The Functions and Reproduction of Migrant Labor: Comparative Material from Southern Africa and the United States," *American Journal of Sociology* 81, no. 5 (March 1976): 1050–87.

55. Ernesto Castañeda and Lesley Buck, "A Family of Strangers: Transnational Parenting and the Consequences of Family Separation Due to Undocumented Migration," in *Hidden Lives and Human Rights in the United States: Understanding the Controversies and Tragedies of Undocumented Immigration*, vol. 2, ed. Lois Ann Lorentzen (Santa Barbara, CA: Praeger, 2014), 175–202; Ernesto Castañeda and Lesley Buck, "Remittances, Transnational Parenting, and the Children Left Behind: Economic and Psychological Implications," *The Latin Americanist* 55, no. 4 (December 2011): 85–110; and Castañeda and Jenks, *Reunited.*

56. Basch, Glick Schiller, and Szanton Blanc, *Nations Unbound.*

57. Arjun Appadurai, *Modernity at Large: Cultural Dimensions of Globalization* (University of Minnesota Press, 1996).

58. Castañeda, *Building Walls*, 165–83.

59. Pierre Bourdieu, *The Rules of Art: Genesis and Structure of the Literary Field*, trans. Susan Emanuel (Stanford University Press, 1996); Pierre Bourdieu, *The State Nobility: Elite Schools in the Field of Power*, trans. Lauretta C. Clough (Polity Press, 1996); Craig J. Calhoun, "Habitus, Field, and Capital: The Question of Historical Specificity," in *Bourdieu: Critical Perspectives*, ed. Craig J. Calhoun, Edward LiPuma, and Moishe Postone (University of Chicago Press, 1993), 61–88; Craig J. Calhoun, "For the Social History of the Present: Bourdieu as Historical Sociologist," in *Bourdieu and Historical Analysis*, ed. Philip S. Gorski (Duke University Press, 2013), 36–66; and Gil Eyal, "Spaces Between Fields," in *Bourdieu and Historical Analysis*, ed. Philip S. Gorski (Duke University Press, 2013), 158–82.

60. Pierre Bourdieu and Loïc Wacquant, "The Organic Ethnologist of Algerian Migration," *Ethnography* 1, no. 2 (December 2000): 173–82; Emmanuelle Saada, "Abdelmalek Sayad and the Double Absence: Toward a Total Sociology of Immigration," *French Politics, Culture and Society* 18, no. 1 (Spring 2000): 28–47; and Craig J. Calhoun, "Pierre Bourdieu and Social Transformation: Lessons from Algeria," *Development and Change* 37, no. 6 (2006): 1403–15.

61. Bourdieu and Sayad, *Le déracinement*; Sayad, *The Suffering of the Immigrant*; Sayad, *L'immigration ou les paradoxes de l'altérité*; Abdelmalek Sayad and Éliane Dupuy, *Un Nanterre algérien, terre de bidonvilles* (Éditions Autrement, 1995); and Saada, "Abdelmalek Sayad and the Double Absence."

62. Ernesto Castañeda, *A Place to Call Home: Immigrant Exclusion and Urban Belonging in New York, Paris, and Barcelona* (Stanford University Press, 2018); and Castañeda, *Building Walls*.

63. Ernesto Castañeda, "Understanding Inequality, Migration, Race, and Ethnicity from a Relational Perspective," in *Immigration and Categorical Inequality: Migration to the City and the Birth of Race and Ethnicity*, ed. Ernesto Castañeda (Routledge, 2018), 1–25.

64. Castañeda and Buck, "Remittances"; Morawska, "Immigrants, Transnationalism, and Ethnicization"; and Waldinger and Fitzgerald, "Transnationalism in Question."

65. Eric R. Wolf, *Europe and the People Without History* (University of California Press, 1982); and Peter Sahlins, *Boundaries: The Making of France and Spain in the Pyrenees* (University of California Press, 1989).

CHAPTER 2

Political Exile and the Transnational Turn

LUIS RONIGER

FOLLOWING WESTPHALIAN PRINCIPLES, NATION-STATES since the seventeenth century have increasingly claimed exclusive control over sovereign territories and socialized residents to see themselves as belonging to distinct nations, defining the modern parameters of membership in a political community. As countries consolidated their rule, state and nation became coterminous, with states promoting and expecting commitment and devotion from those enjoying citizenship rights. Through various institutions, practices, and ceremonies, states purposely instilled a sense of identity and obligation among citizens.

In Latin America, the process of nation-state building was protracted and incomplete. Given their close cultural and linguistic connections, low population density and porous borders, conflicting administrative boundaries, and abrupt shifts in legitimacy (or breakdown, as in the Spanish realm), the nascent states were more a project in the making than a consummated reality. As such, they hardly could obliterate cross-border interactions or erase the persistent visions of transnational realignment.[1] Early struggles for political independence installed exile—a colonial practice for maintaining social order and populating border outposts—as a major mechanism for dealing with political conflict. At that stage, exiles played a key role in shaping the conceived boundaries of nation-states, while at the same time their presence challenged state claims of overcoming transnational undercurrents and linkages.[2] Since those early days, territorial displacement has become ubiquitous throughout Latin America. Standing out among displacement's various forms is exile, used and abused to deal with political opponents.[3]

Despite the recurrent use of exile, most historians and social scientists long ignored its systemic significance, addressing it just as a note or chapter in the biographies of major political and intellectual figures. Few tried to explain its crystallization and systemic development. Rather, exile was taken for granted, being the expected lot of those defying power. Moreover, studies tended to look at exile as a dependent variable, paying little attention to its formative role and transformations. For instance, it was customary to downplay the impact of exile communities, whose transnational experiences shaped the ideational boundaries of nations and the ground rules of political practice while affecting both host and home countries. This approach changed in the late twentieth century with increased awareness of massive territorial displacement and accelerated globalization, and as observers called into question the ideological and symbolic centrality of the nation-state. While state rulers still controlled citizens' lives and institutions and produced massive waves of territorial dislocation, both displaced persons and individuals staying at home increasingly witnessed the weight of transnational networks that were not fully confined to state borders. Correlated with these changes, the study of political exile has burgeoned in recent decades.[4]

Studying exile led necessarily to the recognition that, beyond the logic of states claiming control over "national" territories and citizens, any country or region that expelled or received exiles was likely to experience an insistent transnational dynamic. The concept of transnationalism, as considered in this work, addresses the interconnectivity between individuals, groups, and nations that is often triggered by, and in turn conditions, social processes, political movements, and cultural ideas and networks extending beyond national boundaries and state borders.[5] Such interconnectivity may develop—although not necessarily—along organizational lines. Often, it becomes equally visible in cultural bonds, historical memories, cross-border networks, and unstructured migration flows, including forced migration and displacement.[6] Diaspora networks are, by definition, a major instance of such dynamics.[7]

Studies of exile have also indicated that transnational linkages were in existence much earlier and that nation-states never superseded completely the transnational connections and entanglement of Latin America as a multistate region. On the contrary, the policies of state closure and authoritarian exclusion necessarily re-created cycles of banishment and partial return, which projected partisan political and historical debate beyond state borders and shaped transnational dynamics, subverting the claims of exclusive control by the expelling states. In this sense, beyond their empirical findings, studies of political exile have compelled a transnational turn.

Hereafter, I address the interplay between states' claims of controlling territories and citizens and the transnational impact of forced displacement on political systems and institutions. I suggest that political exile can account for several transnational impacts. First is its character as a generalized mechanism of institutionalized exclusion in Latin America, where it has become part of the ground rules of political practice, targeting anybody defying those in power or not paying them homage. Second is the transformative impact of forced displacement in broadening the boundaries of identity and political debate beyond state horizons.

Third, politically active exiles have energized the development of diaspora communities interacting with one another, with social and political forces in the host countries, and increasingly with transnational networks of solidarity. Fourth, exile has prompted the crystallization of regional diplomatic and legal mechanisms of territorial displacement and asylum. Last but not least is the transference of new ideas, practices, and organizational principles. This particularly follows amnesties and pardons allowing return to a home territory, yet it is also prompted by those who, while remaining abroad, maintain an interest in and contacts with their home societies.

The chapter starts with a characterization of political exile among forms of territorial displacement, followed by a succinct review of the paradigmatic shifts of exilic studies in recent decades. Next, analysis moves to the impacts of exile. Approaching the transformative experience of living transnational lives, I then address the re-creation of transnational visions and horizons. The following sections cover the development of a regional normative of asylum, the transnational political and cultural projects prompted by exiles, and the variable impact of Latin American diasporas grounded in their resonance through the multiplier factor of transnational advocacy networks and international organizations. The final section discusses the transference of ideas, practices, and emergent forms of transnational networking prompted by exiles and returnees.

Political Exile and Other Forms of Territorial Displacement and Relocation

Since immemorial times, journeys across geographical spaces, time lines, and cultures have been a major means of understanding the world and expanding frameworks of reference. For millennia, migrants, exiles, internally displaced people, and refugees have fled repression, religious clashes, ethnic conflicts, and natural disasters with huge implications for their societies of origin and places of relocation, just as much as cosmopolitan wanderers, nomads, tourists, diplomats, and diasporic sojourners have been part of global displacements and crossings. What has changed has been the variable willingness to recognize these relocations as constitutive forces of society, culture, and political order.

We should start this inquiry by identifying the analytical characteristics that, when converging, define political exile. The first characteristic is the forceful institutional exclusion and displacement of exiles linked to their strong will to retain control of life decisions, all under constraining conditions and persecution. A second trait is that exiles cross onto new ("host") environments, where they re-create life strategies and images of homeland. The third is the exiles' impaired yet persistent will to return to their country of origin (the "home" country). Each of these elements separately is insufficient to define exile, yet as they converge, they provide a phenomenological characterization of the exilic experience, particularly of political exile as distinct from related phenomena of territorial displacement and relocation.

Taken separately, these elements characterize other forms of territorial decoupling as well. One example is massive coercion in the formation of classical diasporas, such as that of African slaves taken to the New World, of Jewish people expelled from their sites of residence, or of Irish people forced by a policy of enclosures and famine to migrate across the Atlantic Ocean. Likewise, internally displaced persons leave their homes due to violent conflict, natural or human disasters, or even under the impact of developmental projects disrupting their habitat. The element of relocation prevails as well in cases of transmigration, namely of individuals who live in border regions and move back and forth periodically across state borders, even if—unlike in exile—the concepts of home and host countries are blurred. In addition, the elaboration of a life vision of return and reconstruction is not particular to exiles, as many other migrants and internally displaced individuals engage such ideas as they live and interact in their sites of relocation.[8] Finally, the longing for a home society left behind and the temporary impossibility of returning also characterize long-term migrant groups, as well as *Gastarbeiter* and diplomats. When coming together, however, the above three elements form a cluster that singles out political exiles within the wider set of individuals and groups who experience their lives in motion.

Studying Political Exile: From Narrating Biographical Episodes to Tracing Systemic Impacts

Since the turn of the twenty-first century, the systemic significance of political exile has adumbrated as researchers, intellectuals, and in some cases also policy makers have shifted attention to the profound impact of exile and advocacy networks during the last phases of the Cold War. Connected to such awareness, researchers attributed the widespread use of banishment to the biased format of citizenship, focusing on the far-reaching personal and institutional implications of exile, many of them bearing a transnational impact. The new approaches created awareness that exile can be an independent variable with constitutive effects of transnational order on sociopolitical systems and the collective imagination of societies or sectors thereof.

Key to the new approaches is the role of exile as a mechanism of institutional exclusion regulating political struggle in elitist polities. In the transition to political independence, all Latin American states incorporated exile as a major political practice, along with other mechanisms of punishment. Territorial displacement and expulsion, instrumental in colonial times for dealing with social offenders and reinforcing defenses on the margins of empire, became commonly used and abused in the realm of politics. In the collective imaginary and in the public spheres of Latin American countries, exile became a central mode of "doing politics." Those who defied power could expect the fate of *encierro, destierro o entierro*, that is, prison, exile, or death, as put colorfully by historian Félix Luna for those opposing Argentine dictator Juan Manuel de Rosas.[9] With the transition to state independence, exile developed a special political profile and role, which, although transformed, persisted into the twentieth and early twenty-first centuries. Forced displacement became a mechanism to lessen the impact of interelite conflict. While factionalism was widespread, elites perceived it as extremely dangerous, as it could develop into a zero-sum struggle that could decimate the ruling class and upper strata. By sending away those who led a defeated faction, rulers could claim to be working to restore the organic unity of society, which they asserted they embodied legitimately. Without forcing territorial displacement, Latin American hierarchical societies would face the possible annihilation of an entire political class resulting from a zero-sum game for power that often involved the mobilization of wider strata.

Political exile has implied the institutional exclusion of individuals and groups from a home territory and its body politic, or the projection of politics onto transnational arenas. Reclaiming their agency in those arenas, exiles could contest the official partisan histories that authoritarian regimes tried to impose on those residing within the national territory.[10]

Exile ensued from the reluctance of power holders to open public spheres and the political realm to full participation. In the nineteenth century, territorial banishment was reserved for narrow elite circles who dared to challenge those in positions of power, while lower-class people defying power structures were usually put to death. With the passing of time, exile increasingly affected a wider range of individuals connected to the public domain such as intellectuals, professionals, publicists, academics, and trade union and student activists. Whether banishment was the lot of a few prominent individuals or wide social groups depended on the shifting definition of political boundaries in various settings and historical circumstances. Paradoxically, the opening of Latin American public arenas to new publics by the twentieth century was accompanied by exponential growth in the number of citizens and residents expelled from the national territories or fleeing for their lives and physical integrity. In turn, by midcentury, the additional growth of exile resulting from Cold War confrontations in the Americas increased exiles' contact with transnational advocacy networks as well as interest in and research about political exile and a growing awareness of its transnational functions.[11]

The Transformative Experience of Living a Transnational Life

Regulating the political domain, exile has generated complex processes at different levels of articulation, spanning from local domains to the transnational realm. For people socialized in nation-state horizons, displacement from the national territory and its body politic triggers a series of issues of crucial personal and collective transcendence. The exilic experience demolishes well-established beliefs. As they find themselves detached from the environment in which routines were meaningful, many displaced individuals lose their "markers of certainty"[12] and may question issues once taken for granted, including the assumption of a nation's convergence with its territorial boundaries.[13] This dynamic deepens as territorial displacement follows the defeat of political projects. Unsurprisingly, exile has prompted the reconstitution of those life projects and paradigms.

Rooted in displacement and translocation, political exile has a clear territorial dimension. However, the time dimension is no less crucial, as exile forces leaps from past to present and backward, with eruptions of remembrance and imagination. As soon as they arrive in a host society, exiles begin to live in several time frames and often dive into "a state of memory," as in Tununa Mercado's autobiographical text, which brings alive the disjointed sense of time she experienced once exiled.[14] This dynamic prompts a constant redefinition of political and cultural premises that, until recently, those individuals took for granted. In this sense, exile is a harbinger of reflexivity and change, both at the personal and the collective level.

While the surrounding society reinforces in them an acute sense of their collective identity and historical particularity, at the same time exiles may dialectically stress human solidarity and universal values. Furthermore, the reconstitution of political movements and cultural networks beyond nation-state borders brings about transnational awareness. As exile triggers questions of identity, it leads to rethinking the tension between the political and the primordial components embedded in the idea of the nation-state conflating citizenship and national identity. Individuals and networks crossing physical borders undergo shifts in their worldview that transcend the nation-state optic. While abroad, many exiles start reflecting on the embeddedness between their sense of nationality and their broader Latin American experiences.

To be an exile is constraining in the short term. For some, banishment is a trigger of depression; for others, it prompts activism. In all cases, existential plight forces a process of individual and collective change, rooted in confrontation and exposure to new environments, institutions, and ideas. For those who try to remain relevant to developments in their home society, a mere acculturation and adaptation to their place of relocation, as is typical of migrants, is not enough. Being abroad forces many of them to learn to perform in terms of the wider transnational, international, and global arena. Activist or "proactive" exiles wish to contribute to a change in the conditions that forced them to move abroad. For years, many of them have tended to defy settled power in their home country, creating the conditions for political change, pressing for a return, replacing the expelling power holders, and perhaps attaining power themselves. Often, the proactive types become agents of transformation and serve as a bridge between societies, ideas, and institutional paradigms, many of these shifting in a transnational "key."[15]

Displacement and Diasporas: The "National Soul" and Transnational Horizons

The existential state of living through a destierro—especially for those who were actively engaged in politics in their home country—necessarily shifts the terms of reference from internal public spheres to the transnational arena and the international realm. One of the central issues distinguishing exiles from other people who suffer forced displacement, such as refugees, is their will to retain control of their constrained decisions, choices, and self-image.[16]

When nation-states were first emerging, exiles could relocate as a tactical move, find a source of living, and rebuild their lives in a new host country. Yet, the very fact of staying in another territory often deepened a dual sense of finding a shared ground of identity while bearing a distinct identity. Standing out before independence were the Jesuits, who, once exiled, wrote chronicles and panoramic descriptions of their home "kingdoms" left behind, embedding their texts with a sense of local patriotism. Once independent, the new states garnered those texts to create a sense of national identity.[17]

Once states consolidated, territorial displacement brought to the fore tensions between the principle of national membership and the principle of citizenship. People pressed to go into exile lost the entitlements attached to citizenship. Yet, concurrently, many felt a strong attachment to the covert yet potent dimension of identity rooted in the sense of homeland. This dimension often emerged in exile, if for no other reason as a reaction to accusations of being foreigners who expressed ideas "out of place." The following example from Costa Rica in the 1890s is illustrative. At that time, President Rafael

Yglesias embarked on a wide program of public works and institution building. Francisco Pereira Castro, the editor of *Prensa Libre*, dared to criticize the "electoral fraud" resulting from the constitutional reform that President Yglesias promoted with an eye to being reelected. A liberal, Pío Víquez, then demanded the expulsion of Pereira Castro—a Colombian national—from the country, because "it is not convenient, nor should it be tolerated, that other parties should come to tell us that we are weak, cowardly, and stupid." He was expelled.[18]

Many Latin American exiles discovered, rediscovered, or invented that sense of nationhood in primordial or spiritual terms. At the same time, their situation led them to identify with exiles proceeding from other latitudes and working as they were to establish transnational networks of advocacy. Exile contributed to reshaping collective identities from afar, yet not just in the sense that exile has been the "mother of nationality," as often claimed by those following Benedict Anderson.[19] Exile equally re-created transnational bonds, to be refracted back later onto the countries of origin. Moreover, exile reinforced the transnational concerns of elites and their global outlook. This was especially evident as the structure of exile, originally triadic—built upon the interaction between the state of origin, the country of relocation, and the exile communities—added increasingly a fourth dimension by the twentieth century, that of the transnational networks of solidarity and the international community.[20]

It was often abroad that exiles rekindled the sense of attachment to "sister nations" in the Americas. Such re-creation of a national imagery along with transnational reconnections took place in the midst of communities of exiles. While engaging in power struggles, displaced individuals contributed to the tension-ridden dual process of defining both national and transnational identities, a process closely tied to shaping the boundaries of the emerging states in this part of the Americas. Since early independent times, many exiles reinforced the recognition that the citizens of various states shared not just cultural, linguistic, and historical links but also common political challenges and interests.

Exiles and expatriates elaborated and re-created pan–Latin American ideas after relocating beyond the borders of their home countries. Already in the nineteenth century, displaced individuals claimed to represent the "true spirit" of the home countries on transnational terms. One example is Colombian José María Torres Caicedo (1830–1889), who, after forced to become an expatriate in 1850, remained abroad until his death. Torres Caicedo represented Colombia in London and Paris, was Venezuelan consul general and chargé d'affaires in France and the Netherlands, and later chargé d'affaires of El Salvador in France and Belgium. Significantly, he developed from afar a continental approach, being among the first to coin, no later than 1856, the term "Latin America" as a common denominator for the Hispanic, Portuguese, and French Americas. "We love our native country with passion," he said in 1864, "and yet, we consider the beautiful Latin American land as a common fatherland."[21] As a prolific writer and literary critic in Paris, he projected the voice of an entire continent in the Association Littéraire et Artistique Internationale (International Literary and Artistic Association) led by Victor Hugo and supported the idea of a Latin American union, founding an association with that purpose in mind.[22]

Political exiles have been major agents re-creating not just a sense of discrete nationality but also transnational horizons in the Americas. Many exiles recovered their voice abroad, claiming that they and not the powers at home were true representatives of their nation and of the imagined Patria Grande, in the spirit of Bolivarianism. As politically active Brazilians left their country after the military coup of 1964 and relocated to other South American countries, Mexico, or European sites, they discovered common challenges and struggles with exiles from other South American nations and recognized a pan–Latin American identity:

> José Maria Rabêlo, a Brazilian who lived as an exile in Bolivia, Chile, and France with his wife and seven children, remembers that it was soon after his arrival in Bolivia that he first "discovered" Hispanic America. [. . .] Later, during his exile in Chile, this Latin Americanism was reinforced by the presence of exiles from the entire continent. [. . .] [Rabêlo:] "These discoveries produced a special feeling in us with regards to the cultural, political, economic and social complexity of the other side of Latin America. When we left Brazil we thought that we were going to teach; soon we realized that we had much to learn." [. . .] The similarity between the political processes experienced by Brazil and the countries of the Southern Cone amazed the Brazilian exiles and led them to recognize that they were part of Latin America as well.[23]

The constant flow, serial exile, and back-and-forth movement across borders contributed to making Latinx diasporas not just a long-standing presence in the region but at times also a global phenomenon deserving international attention.

Transnational Systemic Mechanisms: Regulating Exile Through Asylum

Before the nineteenth century, rulers often welcomed migrants and refugees into their realms, anticipating that the newcomers would introduce new skills and resources, contribute taxes, enlarge the number of those serving in their armies, and provide other benefits. With the consolidation of nation-states, refugees and migrants were increasingly seen as threats to countries' security and cohesion, portrayed sometimes as introducing subversive ideas or even diseases. Nation-states adopted restrictive policies toward outsiders, aiming to turn borders into walls.[24] Still, host governments had to deal with the presence of exiles on their territory, granting them residence, controlling their politics, or co-opting them as allies in their own geopolitical adventures beyond state boundaries. The recurrent use of exile expanded political horizons beyond borders while prompting rulers to define and consolidate those borders. Some states, like Chile, even routinized the cycles of banishment by recurrently promulgating pardons for those interested in returning home, while banishing others or encouraging their flight as they faced persecution, prison, or perhaps a death penalty.[25]

Used widely throughout the Americas, political exile prompted Latin American states to discuss asylum starting in the late 1860s, which was a precocious development from a comparative perspective. Those in power could use exiles to harass political enemies in neighboring countries, and when they were reluctant to concede asylum to "troublemakers" from other states, they could not ignore that eventually they themselves might need a refuge if ousted from power. Unsurprisingly, asylum turned into a subject of common concern, with representatives meeting already in 1867 in Lima to discuss it, even if they did not reach an agreement at the time. The initial document on asylum was drafted at the First South American Congress of International Private Law, meeting in Montevideo in 1889. In December 1907, representatives of Costa Rica, Guatemala, Honduras, Nicaragua, and El Salvador met in Washington, DC, and signed a Treaty of Peace and Friendship, by which the parties undertook a commitment not to allow political émigrés "to reside in the border regions of the countries, the peace of which they could disrupt." In 1911, the Andean countries reached agreement on extradition in a congress in Caracas. The Central American countries reached a parallel agreement in Guatemala in 1934. In other words, entwined in a multistate system, Latin American countries debated asylum even before the issue reached global attention after World War I and more confidently after World War II.[26]

Inter-American treaties on asylum and political refuge were signed in Havana (1928), Montevideo (1933), and Caracas (1954). The 1928 treaty denied the right of asylum to common felons, while the 1933 agreement clearly defined the legal framework of political asylum. Most countries adhered to the treaty and ratified it, with the exception of Venezuela, Bolivia, and the United States. The Tenth Inter-American Conference in 1954 produced an agreement on political asylum. In Article 2, the agreement recognized that "every state has a right to concede asylum but cannot be forced to concede it, nor to explain the reasons why it denies it."[27] This reflected the consensus shaped during the interwar period concerning the perception of asylum as a state prerogative.[28]

While the 1928 and 1933 treaties dealt with asylum mainly in terms of crossing borders, the 1954 treaty devoted concurrent attention to the topic of diplomatic asylum and obtaining safe conduct to exit one's home country. The Caracas meeting dealt with this topic explicitly as it confronted the case of Víctor Raúl Haya de La Torre, founder of the Alianza Popular Revolucionaria Americana (APRA) movement in Peru. With his party outlawed in 1948, Haya de La Torre spent five years at the Colombian embassy in Lima, given the reluctance of Peruvian authorities to grant him the right to leave the national territory.[29]

After the United Nations created the Office of the High Commissioner for Refugees (UNHCR, or in its Spanish abbreviation, ACNUR) in 1950 and adopted the Convention Relating to the Status of Refugees in 1951, followed by a protocol in 1967, the regulatory norms became increasingly binding globally. The Declaration on Territorial Asylum adopted by the UN General Assembly in December 1967 recognized that granting asylum "is a peaceful and humanitarian act and that, as such, it cannot be regarded as unfriendly by any other state."[30] Still, the massive entry of Cuban political refugees to the United States and the exodus of Haitians, Paraguayans, Bolivians, Dominicans, Nicaraguans, and Hondurans from their respective home countries prompted the Inter-American Commission on Human Rights to recognize that the system could fail under the great pressure put on countries of asylum.[31]

The process of formalization of these provisions went even further in the 1980s and 1990s. Then, following the displacement of hundreds of thousands of refugees in Central America, a series of Latin American meetings organized by the UNHCR brought together government officials, UN agents, professional experts, and NGOs to discuss the humanitarian and legal problems of asylum and refugees. Starting with a program of cooperation between the Organization of American States (OAS) and the UNHCR signed in 1982 and the 1984 Cartagena Declaration on Refugees, which resulted from a colloquium on the international protection of refugees in Central America and Mexico, numerous inter-American meetings and summits have further endorsed the normative framework for the protection of refugees in the Americas. This framework, sanctioned once again in the San José Declaration on Refugees and Displaced Persons of 1994 and in later meetings, has stressed the humanitarian and apolitical character of their treatment, the rejection of forced repatriation, and the need to reinforce legality.[32] The principle of *non-refoulement*, by which no contracting state should "expel or return ('refouler') a refugee in any manner whatsoever to the frontiers of territories where his life or freedom would be threatened," is now fully established in principle.[33] Nonetheless, the normative framework is not lacking in contradictions and tensions, as Niklaus Steiner points out in his discussion of western European cases around the turn of the twenty-first century.[34] And US border enforcement in the twenty-first century also attenuates the principle of non-refoulement, using public health as a rationale during the COVID epidemic.

Due to the massive and complex character of the refugee problem, especially in Central America since the 1980s, legal and normative frameworks of exile have increasingly incorporated international norms for refugees, broadening the scope of the normative framework shaped originally in the context of elite politics. Accordingly, the legal frameworks endorsed in the region have increasingly conflated the categories of refugees, persons devoid of citizenship (*apátridas*), and asylees. Since 1998, the international community has also addressed the growing problem of internally displaced persons, affecting many countries in recent history, among them Guatemala and Colombia.[35]

Transnational Political and Cultural Projects

Under certain historical circumstances, exile led to the emergence of transnational political and cultural projects. Illustrations abound. José Martí (1853–1895) and fellow Cubans, while in exile, befriended Ramón Emeterio Betances (1827–1898), a founding father of Puerto Rican nationalism, and organized patriotic clubs aimed at attaining the independence of both Cuba and Puerto Rico from Spain. At one point, these patriots collaborated on a project of a future Confederation of the Antilles, partially thought of as a preemptive move aimed at precluding US political hegemony after the envisioned independence. Another prominent example is that of Eugenio María de Hostos y Bonilla (1839–1903). A native of Puerto Rico educated in law in Spain, he left Spain in 1869 and became a wandering expatriate. He moved to New York City and became a member of the Cuban revolutionary junta. Shortly thereafter, he left for a four-year trip through Colombia, Peru, Chile, Argentina, and Brazil, campaigning for the independence of Cuba and Puerto Rico, for a Confederación Antillana that would include Cuba, Puerto Rico, and the Dominican Republic, and for the abolition of slavery. His championing of maltreated Chinese laborers in Peru changed public opinion, as did his advocacy for female admission to professional schools in Chile and his educational work in the Dominican Republic.[36]

Likewise, in the 1910s–1920s, thousands of unionists tried to re-create the lost unity of Central America, wandering and preaching their vision in the isthmus.[37] A generation later, Augusto César Sandino (1895–1934), Farabundo Martí (1893–1932), and many others led an armed struggle against international intervention and domestic dictatorships in Central America, inspired and led by transnational experiences and forces. Starting in 1920, Sandino experienced life in the economic enclaves of the Caribbean coast of Central America, where he was able to witness the diversity of the circum-Caribbean area populated by Garifunas ("British West Indian Blacks"), US plantation and farm managers, and a multinational labor force that included foreign radicals and adventurers. Wandering through the Americas, Sandino developed a vision of resistance to international intervention and of Bolivarian, transnational commitments. Although his revolutionary activities took place in Nicaragua, his key officers and part of the rank-and-file soldiers came from other Central American countries, and some even from Mexico and the Dominican Republic. Imbued by such a vision, he and his transnational cadre resisted the US military presence in Nicaragua from 1927 to his assassination in 1934.

In the late twentieth century, the reverberations of the Cold War re-created transnational connections and horizons. In the Southern Cone, for example, expulsions and exile, migrations, and relocations had a strong impact on redefining political agendas. That impact took on different forms. Provided there were no major constraints in their choice of destination, a large percentage of individuals forced to flee their home states chose to settle in neighboring countries, hoping to return within a short time. Yet democracies collapsed one after another, and there was justifiable urgency to escape repression, particularly where it was harsh and as the circle woven by Operation Condor (a campaign of transnational repression led by several right-wing dictatorships) closed on activists defying the established social and political order within an increasingly authoritarian South America.

Under such circumstances, new relocations took place in a kind of "serial exile." In the cases of Uruguayans, Chileans, and Argentines, this led to the emergence of diaspora communities in sites far removed from their home countries. Paraguayans were more concentrated in Argentina and less dispersed globally. Dispersion made communication more difficult yet granted resonance to the plight of exiles. Crucial, however, was the extent to which different communities of conationals posed a proactive challenge to their home dictatorships, and how they did so effectively by cooperating transnationally. The authoritarian governments of Chile and Argentina, followed by that of Uruguay, would soon discover that while in the short run they could succeed in secluding and indoctrinating sectors of domestic public opinion, in the long run the massive use of political exile backfired. Given the connections that displaced individuals maintained with transnational advocacy networks in the global arena, their plight was highly resonant.

The Variable Transnational Impact of Latin American Diasporas

Focusing on the Latin American diasporas formed or enlarged in the 1960s–1980s, all faced similar challenges derived from the policies of persecution and disinformation carried out by their home dictatorships, from their disconnection from their home society, from their will to continue organizing, and from the need to survive under the varied circumstances of the sites of exile. Those diasporas differed in their numerical weight and dispersion patterns, and furthermore in terms of the centrality of exile activism in their midst—that is, the extent to which exiles managed to claim the representation of entire diaspora communities or major parts thereof.[38]

The image that a diaspora assumes in the framework of the foreign policy considerations of a host country, especially if the latter has a pivotal place in the international system, is another important variable. To various degrees, exiles have participated in the emerging global human rights movement, establishing links with committees of solidarity and transnational networks of advocacy. There have been variations in their ability and their impact on international public opinion, due to the distinct circumstances of their geopolitical environment. Paradigmatic perhaps is the case of Cubans who have played such a role since the late nineteenth century, at that time primarily from Paris and New York and in the twentieth century from both Mexico in the 1950s and the United States before and after the 1959 revolution. As Cuba adopted communism, Cuban Americans were portrayed as an exile community escaping authoritarian rule. This was in sharp contrast to the fate of thousands of Haitians who tried unsuccessfully to achieve similar recognition while attempting to enter the United States illegally since the mid-twentieth century. Instead, the media portrayed them as economic migrants, and their entrance was strictly controlled and curtailed.

Probably the paradigmatic case of an actively engaged exile diaspora is that of Chileans, who stood out for their international clout, which beyond sheer numbers (estimated at four hundred to six hundred thousand) reflected their emblematic standing, the high profile of their leadership, and the activism of rank-and-file members. The images of the airstrikes on the Chilean presidential palace on September 11, 1973, left a profound mark on the global consciousness, similar to those of the 9/11 attack on the Twin Towers in Manhattan a generation later. The brutality and magnitude of repression following the military takeover made Chile into the cause célèbre of both the Left and liberal democratic forces. The military takeover did constitute a breakdown of Chilean constitutional tradition, and it ended the country's first experiment of a leftist administration reaching power through the ballots and professing to endorse socialism through constitutional means. The Chilean military rulers closed the political sphere and alienated many Christian Democrats and members of other nonrevolutionary and centrist parties, creating a constellation of forces that transcended the East-West divide of the Cold War and mobilized transnationally.

The citizens who fled abroad, or were expelled, became the core of a vibrant diaspora that projected the plight of a society undergoing massive repression and human rights violations into global awareness. Chilean exiles came from a country with an articulated political system and with political parties that found almost immediate resonance with sister parties and intellectual circles in western Europe, communist states, Latin America, and many other distant lands. They proactively projected themselves through transnational networks of solidarity and international organizations.

Like any other group of exiles, the Chileans were a diverse group in terms of age and gender, occupational and class background, and regional and ethnic composition. In terms of class background, workers were a minority versus middle- and upper-class individuals. A relatively large group of Mapuches (a group particularly targeted by the military), five hundred strong, found their way into western Europe, where they founded their own organization, the Comité Exterior Mapuche, which coordinated actions with other organizations and networks of Chilean exiles. The Chilean diaspora involved a critical mass of politically proactive exiles who endowed their banner with a strong moral claim, in addition to the heroic, Byronic image many of them proudly projected. Their common denominator was the banning of their respective political organizations back home, in which they had been active or at least in sympathy with, and the brutal state repression that had driven them into exile. This commonality led to the reestablishment of their political parties abroad: the Socialist Party, the Communist Party, the Movimiento de Acción Popular Unitaria (MAPU) and MAPU Obrero-Campesino, the Radical Party, the Christian Left, and the Movimiento de Izquierda Revolucionaria (MIR), all associated with the former coalition of Salvador Allende and reconstituted in exile, mainly in Europe. The Christian Democrats were also reestablished overseas.

The extension of the Chilean Dirección de Inteligencia Nacional (DINA) counterintelligence service's activities into Latin America, the United States, and Europe, and coordinated transnational repression in the framework of Operation Condor, led to the assassination of several prominent exiles, among them former foreign affairs minister Orlando Letelier, murdered in Washington, DC, in 1976. However, repression was ineffective in silencing an opposition whose voice gained resonance through the multiplier factor of transnational advocacy networks and international organizations. Augusto Pinochet, Chile's new military head of state and dictator, would soon have to face the political implications of losing international public opinion, despite his claim of being at the forefront of the struggle against communism. By becoming a voice for the entire diaspora, while being transformed by their global exposure, exiles had a crucial impact on the internationalization of human rights and the struggle for the return of democracy in Chile.

The potent and clear-cut message put forward by Chilean exiles and their transnational allies contrasted with the initial conditions of Argentine political and social activists fleeing abroad. The Argentine diaspora resembled the Chilean in terms of the dispersal of exile communities and their drive to create their own organizations, geared on the one hand to the political domain and on the other to supporting exiles socially. Equally important, Argentine exiles seemed to be able to establish links with networks of solidarity. Yet the lack of a clear-cut party system similar to that of the host countries became a hindrance. It was hard for outsiders to position themselves toward Argentina, a country where democracy had broken down and massive repression begun already in the early 1970s under a democratic Peronist administration. Indeed, within the Peronist multiclass coalition, left-wing and right-wing forces decimated one another several years before the 1976 military coup. The propaganda of the Argentine military junta characterizing exiles as violent individuals who remained committed to armed struggle struck a chord among transnational audiences as well. It would take time, and the emblematic example of the Madres de Plaza de Mayo and other NGOs demanding truth and justice, for the international community to become sensitive to their plight.

The Paraguayan diaspora, with a majority living in Argentina, faced similar difficulties. Its political fragmentation and personal rivalries, and the presence of thousands of spies and collaborators in its midst, diminished effectiveness. Adding to the equation was the strategy of General Alfredo Stroessner's dictatorship of retaining the formalities of electoral democracy and relying on the backing of the Colorado Party, a major political force that had strong popular backing and enjoyed ancestral loyalties. Neighboring countries' descent into dictatorship also limited the transnational reach and effectiveness of the Paraguayan diaspora, despite the great sacrifices that many exiles suffered while trying to bring down Stroessner's rule.

A major factor differentiating the transnational impact of those diasporas stemmed from the ability of exiles to become the voice and image of entire communities of conationals, which was partly dependent on the relative mix of political and economic motivations projected. In the case of Central Americans fleeing generalized violence and repression spreading in their countries of origin, their image abroad was ambiguous: some were considered refugees and others economic migrants, the latter unable to attain the protections granted to refugees.

The Uruguayan diaspora was comparatively substantial and included several prominent political figures such as Senator Zelmar Michelini and Speaker of the House Héctor Gutiérrez Ruiz (both abducted and murdered in Argentina in 1976), and others who escaped that fate, such as Senators Wilson Ferreira Aldunate and Enrique Erro. Nonetheless, its impact on global public opinion was limited, mostly geared to high-level contacts and not derived from massive transnational mobilizations. Only toward the end of the dictatorship, Uruguayan exiles managed to regain centrality in the process of democratization.[39]

Return: The Transference of Ideas and Transnational Networking

The last aspect of exile worth mentioning, although due to reasons of space it cannot be fully developed here, is the impact of the exilic phenomenon on the transference of ideas and transnational networking. In a study focusing on four South American countries, we have fully analyzed this impact, particularly in the academic and professional realms, in which societies have opened themselves to transnational cooperation, the promotion of new scientific disciplines, the launching or consolidation of subfields, and the transference of ideas and innovative practices.[40] As examples, I shall mention the development of social history by Gabriel Salazar in Chile and the introduction of bioethics related to genome research in Argentina by Dr. Víctor Penchaszadeh. The latter did a great service to the Abuelas de Plaza de Mayo, who were trying to locate the grandchildren abducted with their parents whose whereabouts were unknown. No less crucial was the exposure of exiles to European feminism and the transference of ideas of gender equality by those rebelling against the *machista* attitudes that had once prevailed even among the most radical leftist circles. Augusto Roa Bastos, the renowned author of *Yo el supremo* (I the Supreme), tried upon his return to Paraguay to advance such ideas politically, though he was unsuccessful. Others managed somehow to change paradigmatic approaches in various disciplines, such as Noé Jitrik, who explicitly incorporated the work of authors from the diaspora in a multivolume collection of Argentine literature, disengaging national literature from confinement to those writing within the national territory. In Uruguay, the reincorporation of returnees into leading roles in the public higher education system—for instance, Samuel Lichtensztejn, Rafael Guarga, Rodrigo Arocena, and Ricardo Ehrlich—revolutionized academic institutions and scientific research, producing major innovations. In all four countries, returning exiles also renewed the editorial industry, while others in cinematography, theater, and the arts challenged younger generations into recognizing and confronting legacies of human rights violations. Exiles also encouraged policy makers to adopt strategies for reconnecting with conationals living abroad, shifting conceptions of brain drain into paradigms of "brain gain," leading to transnational openings and international cooperation in science and technology. In Chile, the experience of territorial banishment also strongly influenced ideological and political change; this led a large number of former exiles to play an important role in the transition to democracy and then occupy key ministerial positions in the administrations of the Concertación de Partidos por la Democracia and in nongovernmental organizations promoting human rights.

Summing up, while the recurrent use of forced territorial banishment reflected the exclusionary nature of Latin American nation-states, the other side of the coin has been the reception of political exiles by sister nations in the Americas and encounters with other exiles in diaspora communities worldwide. Exiles became a major bridge re-creating transnational connections and political visions, with implications for the introduction of new ideas, practices, and institutional changes in the region. Studying political exile enables one to follow the Janus-like character of the Latin American multistate system, embedding nations in a regional matrix of transnational connections and global networks. Following developments in history and other social sciences that highlight the centrality of transnationalism, mobility, and diasporas, this chapter suggests that exile is a topic of central concern, whose systematic study leads to new readings of history and society in Latin America, away from the scripts of nation-states and toward regional and transnational dimensions.

Notes

1. Luis Roniger, *Transnational Politics in Central America* (University Press of Florida, 2011).
2. During the transition to independence, the terms denoting exile were *destierro*, *expatriación*, and *proscripción* (and the counteraccusation of being a *prófug@*—i.e., a runaway

from justice—rather than a banned individual or *proscript@*). See María Gabriela Mizraje, "Argentina, siglo XIX y exilios: La dislocación de los lenguajes," in *Políticas del exilio: Orígenes y vigencia de un concepto*, ed. Marcelo G. Burello, Fabián Javier Ludueña Romandini, and Emmanuel Taub (Caseros, Argentina: Editorial de la Universidad Nacional de Tres de Febrero, 2011), 147–59.

3. Edward Blumenthal, *Exile and Nation-State Formation in Argentina and Chile, 1810–1862* (Cham, Switzerland: Palgrave Macmillan, 2019), 171–218; and Mario Sznajder and Luis Roniger, *The Politics of Exile in Latin America* (Cambridge University Press, 2009), 40–90.

4. On this development, see Luis Roniger, *Destierro y exilio en América Latina: Nuevos estudios y avances teóricos* (Editorial Universitaria de Buenos Aires, 2014); and Luis Roniger, "Forced Migration and Exile: Analytical and Historical Perspectives," in *The Routledge History of Modern Latin American Migration*, ed. Andreas E. Feldmann, Xóchitl Bada, Jorge Durand, and Stephanie Schütze (Routledge, 2023), 172–85. Among representative works, see José del Pozo Artigas, ed., *Exiliados, emigrados y retornados: Chilenos en América y Europa, 1973–2004* (RIL Editores, 2006); Silvia Dutrénit Bielous, ed., *El Uruguay del exilio: Gente, circunstancias, escenarios* (Ediciones Trilce, 2006); Pablo Yankelevich and Silvina Jensen, eds., *Exilios: Destinos y experiencias bajo la dictadura militar* (Libros del Zorzal, 2007); Luis Roniger, James N. Green, and Pablo Yankelevich, eds., *Exile and the Politics of Exclusion in the Americas* (Eastbourne, E. Susx., England: Sussex Academic Press, 2012); Silvina Jensen and Soledad Lastra, eds., *Exilios: Militancia y represión; Nuevas fuentes y nuevos abordajes de los destierros de la Argentina de los años setenta* (La Plata, Argentina: Editorial de la Universidad Nacional de La Plata, 2014); and Ludger Pries and Pablo Yankelevich, eds., *European and Latin American Social Scientists as Refugees, Émigrés and Return-Migrants* (Cham, Switzerland: Palgrave Macmillan, 2019). See also the burgeoning research agenda at the *Jornadas de Trabajo sobre Exilios Políticos del Cono Sur en el siglo XX*, for example http://jornadasexilios.fahce.unlp.edu.ar/vi-jornadas-2023/otrasEdiciones.

5. Claus Leggewie, "Transnational Citizenship: Cultural Concerns," in *International Encyclopedia of the Social and Behavioral Sciences*, ed. Neil J. Smelser and Paul B. Baltes, (Pergamon, 2001), 15857–62; Nina Glick Schiller, Linda Basch, and Cristina Szanton Blanc, "From Immigrant to Transmigrant: Theorizing Transnational Migration," *Anthropological Quarterly* 68, no. 1 (January 1995): 48–63; Ulf Hannerz, *Transnational Connections: Culture, People, Places* (Routledge, 1996); Ann Curthoys and Marilyn Lake, eds., *Connected Worlds: History in Transnational Perspective* (Australian National University Press, 2005); and Eliezer Ben-Rafael, Yitzhak Sternberg, Judit Bokser Liwerant, and Yosef Gorny, eds., *Transnationalism: Diasporas and the Advent of a New (Dis)order* (Brill, 2009).

6. Luis Roniger, *Transnational Perspectives on Latin America: The Entwined Histories of a Multi-State Region* (Oxford University Press, 2022).

7. Gabriel Sheffer, *Diaspora Politics: At Home Abroad* (Cambridge University Press, 2003); Judit Bokser Liwerant, Eliezer Ben-Rafael, Yosef Gorny, and Ranaan Rein, eds., *Identities in an Era of Globalization and Multiculturalism: Latin America in the Jewish World* (Brill, 2008); and William Safran, "The Diaspora and the Homeland: Reciprocities, Transformations, and Role Reversals," in *Transnationalism: Diasporas and the Advent of a New (Dis)order*, ed. Eliezer

Ben-Rafael, Yitzhak Sternberg, Judit Bokser Liwerant, and Yosef Gorny (Brill, 2009), 75–100.

8. On the complexity of forced displacements and their semantic and legal implications, see Martín Lienhard, ed., *Expulsos, desterrados, deslocados: Migrações forzadas na América Latina e na África* (Iberoamericana Vervuert, 2011); and Flor Edilma Osorio Pérez, "Más allá de las migraciones internas: Destierro y despojo en la guerra," *Iztapalapa: Revista de Ciencias Sociales y Humanidades* 76, no. 35 (June 2014): 19–51.

9. Félix Luna, *Historia integral de la Argentina* (Planeta, 1995), 202.

10. This differs from circumstances in democratic regimes, where debates over history can take place within state boundaries. See the claim by Max Paul Friedman and Padraic Kenney, "History in Politics," in their edited book *Partisan Histories: The Past in Contemporary Global Politics* (Palgrave Macmillan, 2005.)

11. Luis Roniger, "Exílio massivo, inclusão e exclusão política no século XX," *Dados: Revista de Ciências Sociais* 53, no. 1 (2010): 91–123; Silvina Jensen, "Agendas para una historia comparada de los exilios masivos del siglo XX: Los casos de España y Argentina," *Pacarina del Sur* 1, no. 8 (2011): 1–32; and Maria Cláudia Badan Ribeiro and Mario Ayala, "Exílios latino-americanos e solidaridade transnacional durante a Guerra Fria," *Cuadernos de Historia: Serie Economía y Sociedad*, no. 29 (2022): 135–43.

12. The concept follows Claude Lefort, *Democracy and Political Theory*, trans. David Macey (University of Minnesota Press, 1988); and Shmuel N. Eisenstadt, "Modernity and the Reconstitution of the Realm of the Political," in *The Modern Prince and the Modern Sage: Transforming Power and Freedom*, ed. Ananta Kumar Giri (SAGE Publications, 2009), 3–24. Similar is Jürgen Habermas's concept of "lifeworld."

13. Hannah Arendt, *The Origins of Totalitarianism* (Meridian Books, 1968), 296.

14. Tununa Mercado, *En estado de memoria* (Ada Korn Editora, 1990).

15. Soledad Lastra, *Volver del exilio: Historia comparada de las políticas de recepción en las posdictaduras de la Argentina y Uruguay (1983–1989)* (La Plata, Posadas, and Los Polvorines, Argentina: Universidades Nacionales de La Plata, Misiones, y General Sarmiento, 2016); Luis Roniger, Leonardo Senkman, Saúl Sosnowski, and Mario Sznajder, *Exile, Diaspora, and Return: Changing Cultural Landscapes in Argentina, Chile, Paraguay, and Uruguay* (Oxford University Press, 2018); and Enrique Coraza de los Santos and Soledad Lastra, eds., *Miradas a las migraciones, las fronteras y los exilios* (Consejo Latinoamericano de Ciencias Sociales, 2020).

16. See Martha Nussbaum's analysis of Diogenes (404–323 BC) in *Cultivating Humanity: A Classical Defense of Reform in Liberal Education* (Harvard University Press, 1997), 56; and Ariel Dorfman, *Heading South, Looking North: A Bilingual Journey* (Farrar, Straus and Giroux, 1998), 236–39.

17. See Sznajder and Roniger, *The Politics of Exile*, 46–49.

18. Tatiana Lodo, "Costa Rica imaginaria," in *Costa Rica imaginaria*, ed. Alexander Jiménez and Jesús Oyamburu (Heredia, Costa Rica: Editorial Fundación, Universidad Nacional Costa Rica, 1998), 29–39, quoted at 36.

19. Benedict Anderson, *Long-Distance Nationalism: World Capitalism and the Rise of Identity Politics* (Centre for Asian Studies, 1992). See also Nina Glick Schiller, "Long-Distance Nationalism," in *Encyclopedia of Diasporas: Immigrant and Refugee Cultures Around the*

World, ed. Melvin Ember, Carol R. Ember, and Ian Skoggard (Springer, 2005), 1:570–80; and Daniele Conversi, "Irresponsible Radicalisation: Diasporas, Globalisation and Long-Distance Nationalism in the Digital Age," *Journal of Ethnic and Migration Studies* 38, no. 9 (2012): 1357–79.

20. Sznajder and Roniger, *The Politics of Exile*, 136–92.

21. José María Torres Caicedo, *Ensayos biográficos y de crítica literaria* (Guillaumin y Cia, 1868), 274.

22. Arturo Ardao, *Génesis de la idea y el nombre de América Latina* (Centro de Estudios Latinoamericanos Rómulo Gallegos, 1980).

23. Cristián Doña-Reveco, "The Unintended Consequences of Exile: The Brazilian and Chilean Cases in Comparative Perspective, 1964–1990," Latino/Latin American Studies Faculty Publications no. 11, Fall 2012, University of Nebraska Omaha, https://digitalcom-mons.unomaha.edu/cgi/viewcontent.cgi?article=1010&context=latinamstudfacpub. The interior quotation is from José Maria Rabêlo and Thereza Rabêlo, *Diáspora: Os longos caminhos do exílio* (Geração Editorial, 2001), 26–27.

24. For a twentieth-century case, see Pablo Yankelevich, *Los otros: Raza, normas y corrupción en la gestión de la extranjería en México, 1900–1950* (El Colegio de México; Iberoamericana Vervuert, 2019).

25. Brian Loveman and Elizabeth Lira, *Las suaves cenizas del olvido: Vía chilena de reconciliación política (1814–1932)* (LOM Ediciones, 1999).

26. Jaime Esponda Fernández, *La tradición latinoamericana de asilo y la protección internacional de los refugiados* (Siglo XXI Editores, 2003); and Edward Blumenthal, "Droit d'asile, droit d'expulsion et représentations de l'exilé en Amérique du Sud au XIXe siècle," *Diasporas: Circulations, Migrations, Histoire*, no. 33 (2019): 91–103.

27. *Convención sobre asilo diplomático suscrita en la X Conferencia Interamericana*, Caracas, March 1–28, 1954 (Unión Panamericana, 1961); and Luis Miguel Díaz and Guadalupe Rodríguez de Ita, "Bases histórico-jurídicas de la política mexicana de asilo diplomático," in *Asilo diplomático mexicano en el Cono Sur*, ed. Silvia Dutrénit Bielous and Guadalupe Rodríguez de Ita (Instituto Mora; Secretaría de Relaciones Exteriores, 1999), 63–82.

28. See, e.g., "Asile," in *Larousse du XXe siècle* (Éditions Larousse, 1928), 1:384.

29. David Alejandro Luna, *El asilo político* (Editorial Universitaria, 1962), 39–40; and International Court of Justice, "Haya de la Torre (Colombia v. Peru)," https://www.icj-cij.org/case/14.

30. UN General Assembly, Declaration on Territorial Asylum, A/RES/2312 (XXII), December 14, 1967, https://www.refworld.org/legal/resolution/unga/1967/en/10415.

31. María Claudia Pulido and Marisol Blanchard, "La Comisión Interamericana de Derechos Humanos y sus mecanismos de protección aplicados a la situación de los refugiados, apátridas y solicitantes de asilo," UN High Commissioner for Refugees, https://www.acnur.org/fileadmin/Documentos/BDL/2014/2578.pdf.

32. Leonardo Franco et al., "Investigación: 'El asilo y la protección de los refugiados en América Latina'; Acerca de la confusión terminológica 'asilo-refugio'; Informe de progreso," in *Derechos humanos y refugiados en las Américas: Lecturas seleccionadas* (Inter-American Institute for Human Rights; Office of the UN High Commissioner for Refugees, 2001),

176–77; and Alberto D'Alotto, "El sistema interamericano de protección de los derechos humanos y su contribución a la protección de los refugiados en América Latina," https://www.corteidh.or.cr/tablas/r12443.pdf.

33. Office of the UN High Commissioner for Refugees, Convention Relating to the Status of Refugees, adopted by the United Nations on July 28, 1951, entry into force on April 22, 1954.

34. Niklaus Steiner, *Arguing About Asylum: The Complexity of Refugee Debates in Europe* (St. Martin's Press, 2000), 15–16. For Latin America, see Juan Ignacio Mondelli, "Reshaping Asylum in Latin America as a Response to Large-Scale Mixed Movements: A Decade of Progress and Challenges (2009–2019)," UNHCR, Americas Bureau, December 1, 2020, https://www.unhcr.org/people-forced-to-flee-book/wp-content/uploads/sites/137/2021/10/Juan-Mondelli_Reshaping-Asylum-in-Latin-America-as-a-Response-to-Large-Scale-Mixed-Movements.pdf.

35. Pulido and Blanchard, "La Comisión Interamericana de Derechos Humanos y sus mecanismos de protección"; César Walter San Juan with Mark Manly, "El asilo y la protección de los refugiados en América Latina: Análisis crítico del dualismo 'asilo-refugio' a la luz del Derecho Internacional de los Derechos Humanos," https://www.acnur.org/fileadmin/Documentos/Publicaciones/2012/8945.pdf; and Osorio Pérez, "Más allá de las migraciones internas."

36. Roberto Cassá, "Historiography of the Dominican Republic," in *General History of the Caribbean*, vol. 6, *Methodology and Historiography of the Caribbean*, ed. B. W. Higman (UNESCO Publishing; London: Macmillan, 2003), 395.

37. Marta Elena Casaús Arzú and Teresa García Giráldez, *Las redes intelectuales centroamericanas: Un siglo de imaginarios nacionales (1820–1920)* (F&G Editores, 2005); and Roniger, *Transnational Politics in Central America*, 94–101.

38. This section follows Luis Roniger, "'Latinos' in Exile: Latin American Political Diasporas and Their National and Transnational Struggle," in *Global Latin(o) Americanos: Transoceanic Diasporas and Regional Migrations*, ed. Mark Overmyer-Velázquez and Enrique Sepúlveda (Oxford University Press, 2017), 231–54.

39. Luis Roniger, "Transitional Justice and Protracted Accountability in Re-Democratised Uruguay, 1985–2011," *Journal of Latin American Studies* 43, no. 4 (November 2011): 693–724.

40. Roniger et al., *Exile, Diaspora, and Return*, 187–266.

CHAPTER 3

The Transnational Turn
in Hispanic Literary Studies

REINDERT DHONDT

The Transnational as a Traveling Concept

This chapter scrutinizes how the "transnational turn" has affected Hispanic studies and, more precisely, Hispanic literary studies. Hispanic studies has traditionally been understood as a domain of humanistic enquiry broadly concerned with the Spanish language and the cultures of Spanish-speaking countries (or areas of Hispanic origin), from Roman Hispania to the present, from Tenerife to Los Angeles. In what follows, I will specifically focus on the analytic potential and adaptability of transnationalism as a conceptual construct. In this sense, I will study the modulations of the concept of the transnational in literary studies as a consequence of its own transnationalization. As cultural theorist Mieke Bal has pointed out, concepts are not given, fixed, nor innocent but are constantly changing, often normative and ideologically tinted. According to Bal, concepts provide a common language that facilitates discussion beyond disciplinary boundaries and national cultures of research. Yet these conceptual transfers always assume a recontextualization that defies the theoretical consistency and precision of the concepts, as well as the very idea of translatability of cultures. Thanks to this equivocality, the importation of concepts into other research domains can lead to new insights: "[Concepts] travel—between disciplines, between individual scholars, between historical periods and between geographically dispersed academic communities.

Between disciplines, their meaning, reach and operational value differ."[1] In this sense, Bal's idea of traveling concepts fosters but also probes the limits of the development of transnational approaches to literature or culture.[2]

Although its origins can be traced back to the nineteenth century,[3] the concept of the transnational was for the first time systematically used in the late 1960s in the field of political science as a way to differentiate international relations, with their focus on nation-states and institutional actors, from transnational relations, with their focus on networks of noninstitutional and nonstate actors that transcend borders such as NGOs, social movement organizations, and migrant communities.[4] The concept was applied with greater frequency during the 1990s, in order to designate a new condition of the postindustrial, globalized society. The transnational developed an association with transnational corporations, global financial institutions, and neoliberalism—what Michael Peter Smith and Luis Eduardo Guarnizo have called "transnationalism from above."[5] In the public discourse of a large part of the Hispanic world, the qualifier "transnational" is frequently used in a substantivized form (*una transnacional*) in order to refer to both historical, mostly colonial corporations such as the Dutch East India Company, and current-day multinationals, thus sidestepping the difference between a centralized and decentralized management structure of companies with divisions in several countries.[6]

It is therefore not surprising that, whereas "transnational" became an increasingly fashionable buzzword for the study of literature in Euro-US academia from the late 1990s onward, the concept initially met some resistance among literary scholars in Latin America, who linked it to neocolonialism and homogenization through cultural imperialism. Because of this ideological freight, the term's connotation was perceived as pejorative in a decade characterized by the neoliberal policies of the Washington Consensus and the continent's subsequent disillusionment with these economics in the 2000s. This explains, at least partly, why some scholars had to overcome an initial rejection before accepting its operationality when studying texts that circulate across multiple geographies and authors and characters who travel, and especially the role of agency within a transcultural imaginary that blurs the binary between global and local. This latter use of "transnational," which stresses a critical resistance to the homogenizing effects of globalization and challenges national myths of cultural purity, corresponds to what Smith and Guarnizo have termed "transnationalism from below."[7]

Transnationalizing Hispanic Studies

In the past decades, the transnational has set new agendas for scholarship and has fundamentally reshaped the edifice of Hispanic studies. As Steven Vertovec has observed, "transnationalism (as long-distance networks) certainly preceded 'the nation.'"[8] Despite the relatively recent emergence of the term "transnational," transnational interactions and mobility are not new; what is different today is their greater intensity and speed as a consequence of intensified globalization. To a certain extent, the field of Hispanic culture and literature is inherently transnational, since the very idea of the Hispanic or Hispanophone world goes beyond the framework of the nation-state. More recently, the transnational turn has spurred engagements with the "transimperial" and transcultural dimensions of Hispanophone cultures, from the Sephardic and Morisco diasporas in medieval and early modern times to current-day intercultural performances in the Caribbean. The view of the Spanish Empire as the site of the "first globalization,"[9] in which the Spanish language crossed numerous territories and contact zones and literary works were produced at the intersection of a myriad of cultures, helped to overcome the view of transnationalism as anachronistic when applied to objects of inquiry before the rise of nationalism and before the term "nationhood" came into being. Because of this, the impact of the transnational turn in Hispanic studies is lower than in American studies in the sense that Hispanic studies has already transcended a nation-bound approach and has been practically comparative since its conception, through the convergence of Latin American studies and peninsular studies. Nonetheless, since the turn of the millennium, transnational approaches have been reshaping the field of Hispanic studies and its curricula, which are often accompanied by an intensive meta-disciplinary reflection and a methodological eclecticism. These reconfigurations of the research and curricular agendas problematize place-defined identities and the nation-state as the central point of reference, presenting the national and the transnational as interpenetrating and mutually constitutive instead of antithetical.[10] Broadly speaking, one can distinguish four major disciplinary realignments of Hispanic studies with a clear transnational dimension that influence the current academic landscape.

Transatlantic studies emerged at the turn of the twenty-first century when some university programs and departments adopted an approach that breaks

away from an Ibero-centric understanding of Hispanic culture. The main pro-
ponent of transatlantic studies is Julio Ortega, who founded the Transatlantic
Project in 1999. Ortega's geo-textualist approach to cultural transatlanticism
focuses on the exchange of narrative strategies, patterns of discourse circulation,
and interpretative configurations between the two sides of the Hispanic Atlantic
and foregrounds the possibility of translation or transcodification, which often
leads to hybridization and *mestizaje*: "Translation implies the possibility of constructing an intermediate setting, which would frame interpretations as dialogical."[11] This view also has implications for the study of peninsular culture: for
instance, the Spanish baroque cannot be studied solely from a European vantage
point, since it is deeply intertwined with the "discourse of abundance" of the
New World, according to Ortega.[12] Although the paradigm has been criticized
for sidestepping asymmetrical power relations when studying creative counter-
responses to the European colonist gaze and has been dismissed as "renovated
Pan-Hispanism,"[13] it has led to a critical reassessment of Atlantic archives,
including South-South relationships through intersections with African cultures, but also to revisit contemporary phenomena such as the imaginary of
political transitions and the aesthetics of postdictatorship cultures on both sides
of the Atlantic. Transatlantic studies provides a cross-regional and transnational
model of comparison that has been gathering increased scholarly attention
through yearly conferences and book series such as Líneas y Estudios Transatlánticos de Literatura (LETRAL) of the scholarly publishing house Iberoamericana Vervuert.

    Hemispheric studies focuses on North-South or inter-American relations. It
broadens the scope of classical American studies by presenting the United States
as a part of the Americas, thus superseding the nation as the basic frame for
analysis and criticizing the co-optation of the continental designation for a
national, unifying identification. This is not merely a question of geographical
semantics: essentially, hemispheric studies not only pays attention to a considerable body of American literature written in languages other than English but
also foregrounds transnational imaginaries through a broad range of topics, such
as the similarities between the regional imagination of the US South and Latin
American fiction,[14] foundational texts such as José Martí's *Nuestra América*
(1891), the afterlife of the character Caliban from Shakespeare's *The Tempest*
(1611), and the cultural representation of hyphenated Americans. Through its

transnational frame and its effort to decenter and provincialize the United States, hemispheric studies questions center-periphery models and revisits earlier continental frameworks such as pan-Americanism, even though it has also been perceived as an expansionist attempt of American studies.[15]

More recently, *Iberian studies* has been proposed as a reframing of peninsular Spanish studies that opens up to the multilingualism and cultural diversity of Spain and rejects a neo-imperial nostalgia closely connected to the ideology of *hispanidad* (hispanicity). By focusing on two nation-states and by incorporating the Galician, Basque, and Catalan languages and literatures, Iberian studies unsettles previously held ideas about the centrality of the Castilian language and unravels monolithic conceptions of literary history. It opens up new avenues for translation studies and complicates models of comparison of comparative studies (with their traditional focus on national literary productions) through a focus on diaspora communities and interliterary relations within a pluri-national state, as part of the Spanish literary polysystem.[16] The signifier "Iberia" is historically associated with extensive multiregional exchanges and with being a crossroad of Mediterranean cultures since pre-Roman times. Iberian studies revisions historical ideas of the *convivencia*, the multiethnic coexistence in al-Andalus, but also addresses Spain's multicultural identity in twenty-first-century narratives written by Afro-Iberian writers like Najat El Hachmi. The focus on a transnational cultural field and a relational, nonhierarchical "federalist approach"[17] revisits Spain's historical eccentric position vis-à-vis European culture and the "peripheral" cultures within the peninsula itself. By doing so, it also draws attention to the continued significance of the national, which is paradoxically reconfigured as the central object of critique. Iberian studies implies a transnational turn away from an increasingly suspect methodological nationalism of traditional peninsular studies, which was historically informed by the nationalizing agenda of the Francisco Franco government and the post-Franco Spanish state with its political centralization and cultural homogenization.

Finally, the emergent *global Hispanophone* is influenced by other disciplinary and epistemic categories such as *littératures francophones* and global Anglophone literature, which examine texts produced at both the center and the peripheries of the former French and British empires, respectively. Heavily indebted to postcolonial studies and the field of world literature, the global Hispanophone incorporates the historical experiences of territories that once belonged to the Spanish Empire, such as Equatorial Guinea and the Maghreb (Hispano-African literature) and Southeast Asia (Hispano-Philippine literature).[18] As such, it decenters national narratives and the Hispanic world (often reductively equated with Spain and Spanish America) and revisits and reframes the cultural diversity of the Iberian Peninsula itself. Even though the global Hispanophone primarily draws on a linguistic criterion instead of spatially defined categories, it recognizes transnational linguistic areas and the multilingual nature of cultural production within its geographic scope, in close contact with languages over which Castilian has exerted a hegemonic influence beyond the Iberian Peninsula (often interpreted in terms of "linguistic imperialism") such as Moroccan Arabic, Tagalog, and Guaraní; or inversely, in contact with dominant languages such as English in the United States, which places Castilian—or, more precisely, US Spanish—in a minoritized or even "racialized" position as a language of poor immigrants.[19]

These four areas of study and learning are not merely a strategic rebranding of Hispanic studies, but forms of transnationalization that reinvigorate and expand the field with new critical questions. By displacing the centrality of Spanishness and hispanicity, by deterritorializing Spanish-language culture and questioning the cultural construction of national or continental identities, these transnational perspectives have strengthened the discipline and broadened its scope.

Transnational Approaches to Hispanic Literature

Hispanic literary studies have also been profoundly influenced by the transnational turn. The interest in transnationalism in literary studies was anticipated by the spatial turn in the humanities at the end of the 1980s, when space replaced time as a central analytical axis. This paradigm shift led to a more politicized approach to space as a social and symbolic construction, especially in relation to mobility, as opposed to a more static, topographical approach to the literary representation of space and place.[20] Indebted to evolutions in the social sciences, especially in human geography and social anthropology, the methodological tools and concepts put forward by scholars who subscribed to the spatial turn or to the broader mobile turn (e.g., Edward Soja's *Thirdspace* and Arjun Appadurai's "scapes")[21] are particularly apt to render accounts of phenomena such as (trans)migrancy and disjunctive global flows that lead to new hybrid cultural forms.

The 1990s saw technological, political, and economic transformations that seemed to herald a borderless world: the emergence of the Internet with its promise of a cosmopolitan and boundaryless civil society, the fall of the Berlin Wall and the collapse of the Soviet Union (which launched Francis Fukuyama's optimism about the "end of history," understood as the ascendency of liberal democracy, the triumph of free-market capitalism, and the arrival of a postideological world), and an increased economic integration that would erode the nation-state, as exemplified by the North American Free Trade Agreement (NAFTA, 1994). After an initial phase in which celebratory discourses on globalization and the "postnational constellation" were dominant,[22] the focus shifted toward more complex interrelations between the national level and other levels of cultural production, be they local, regional, or global.[23] The transnational turn reshaped debates not only in literary studies but across the humanities by foregrounding the impact at a local level of cultural exchanges beyond the nation-state, similar to what Roland Robertson has termed "glocalization."[24]

In this sense, transnational literary scholarship is understood not only as a corrective to a methodological nationalism by decentering the nation-state as an analytical category and by denaturalizing it as an ideological invention, but also as a critical reaction against a postnational utopianism and a triumphalist discourse of globalization that dismisses the nation-state as moribund and analytically irrelevant. Far from being a uniform and coherent method of inquiry, transnationalism in literary scholarship promotes rethinking borders both within and outside the nation, emphasizing the interrelation of cultures on a global, national, and local scale.

In Hispanic studies, transnational literary studies has been thriving in recent years. Film scholar Mette Hjort makes a useful distinction between marked and unmarked transnationality, and applying this distinction to literature can be insightful.[25] Marked transnationality is situated on the level of the story or the narrative discourse, whereas unmarked transnationality pertains to the production, distribution, and reception of literary texts across national borders. The first form of transnationality invites the reader to think about transnationalism by thematizing it, often as a social phenomenon or a historical condition that characterizes our current era of instant interconnectedness, which reduces the constraints of space by means of a "time-space compression"[26] or through the use of specific narrative techniques; whereas unmarked transnationality cannot be rendered visible through an immanent or text-internal approach but only by means of a contextualizing, literary-sociological, or materialist approach, examining the ways in which both texts and authors circulate and are received.

Although the transnational is a lens that enables us to complement and complicate the study of literature in a national context without supplanting it, rather than an ontological category that allows us to classify or label specific text types or genres, literature with marked transnational features presents a set of identifiable subjects such as transnational subjectivities and the tourist gaze, which generally trigger a transnational approach. Studies on cultural representations of transnational phenomena, such as new forms of mobility and migration, started to burgeon in the 1990s and 2000s, paralleling scholarly developments in the social sciences. One example of this is Latino literature. Since "transnational studies at its origins were, to a significant degree, a Latin America-related phenomenon"[27] because of the large diasporic Latino communities living in the United States, it comes as no surprise that scholars working in the field of Latino studies and its institutional predecessors, Chicano studies and Puerto Rican studies, were among the first to adopt the term.[28] This explains why the scholarship initially privileged transnational relationships between the United States, Mexico, and the Caribbean over other areas. Contemporary narratives on the Latino diaspora and the US-Mexican border that do not entail a radical break with the place of origin for first- and second-generation migrants but highlight the bilingual and bicultural life of the protagonists, unsettle ideas of ethnocultural purity and the common view of literature as the expression of a national essence, thus providing a new cartography for understanding contemporary Latinidad in terms of the back-and-forth movement of ideas and individuals across imaginary and geographical borders. Consequently, there is a growing scholarly interest in cultural remittances of transmigrants and their inscription in a dual nation-state context, what Bill Ashcroft has called the "Chicano Transnation," which "captures the fluidity of national subjects moving within and between the borders of the state."[29] Literary studies on migrant literature increasingly thematizes phenomena such as cultural hybridity, linguistic code-switching, and the dual lives transmigrants lead thanks to new communication technologies and affordable flights. Think, in this respect, of the metaphor of the *guagua aérea* (air bus) used to describe the circular mobility between the mainland United States and

Puerto Rico as a "commuter island" or a "nation on the move."[30] Unlike the more politically engaged literature of exile of previous decades, contemporary migrant literature does not highlight cultural assimilation to the host culture and nostalgia for the lost homeland but rather calls attention to the constant movement between the country of settlement and the country of origin, going beyond a territorialized conception of identity.

These works enabled departments of English literature and American studies to overcome the restraints of the nation-state framework and question the rigidity of a binary center-periphery model, as illustrated by Paul Jay's definition of a transnational context, which "moved beyond and explicitly questioned older Eurocentric models of 'comparative' analysis."[31] In his analysis of Junot Díaz's Pulitzer prize–winning novel *The Brief Wondrous Life of Oscar Wao* (2007), for instance, Jay focuses on the cultural bifocality of the Dominican American characters who are not fully anchored in one of the nation-states. A decade later, Jay redefined a transnational approach to literature not only in terms of transit but first and foremost in terms of intersubjectivity. The transnational reorients the reader toward the (sexual, ethnic, etc.) other and to experiences that foster a sense of national identity, but at the same time connect people "across, over, and through geographic and human-made borders"; while individual subjectivity "may be shaped by forces within the nation, those forces often have their origins outside it."[32]

An interesting case in point is literature written by Latin American migrants who settled abroad for professional reasons, often in Spain as a consequence of the transnationalization of the editorial market[33] or of reverse migration (i.e., Latin American migrants returning to the country from which their ancestors came). The often autofictional nature of the *crónicas* and novels of major contemporary authors such as Valeria Luiselli, Eduardo Halfon, Roberto Bolaño, Rodrigo Rey Rosa, and Andrés Neuman, and their discursive self-fashioning, hint at a kind of "rooted cosmopolitanism."[34] The reterritorialization of these *escritores radicantes*[35] within a Hispanophone transnational territory contrasts with the self-proclaimed deterritorialized, postnational posture of previous generations of writers, such as the McOndo or Crack movements,[36] which were seen as advocates of globalization. In a context of cultural globalization and the emergence of cyberspace, writers have become increasingly disconnected from their locality and no longer write national or continental allegories. Case studies on contemporary writers such as Luiselli and Halfon often deal with wandering and related concepts (e.g., nomadism, *errabundia*, and *flâneur*).[37] These studies also approach mobility from a more formal and aesthetic perspective,[38] often as part of a transnational "poetics of movement."[39]

Hispanists have paid special attention to the marked transnational dimension of the contemporary essay as a genre with a strong tradition in the construction of national (and continental) identities, both in Spain and in Latin America. These new discourses of cultural self-affirmation have led to a deconstruction of national identity discourses, but also to a revision of the previous discourses of *panlatinoamericanismo* and *panhispanismo*.[40]

The recent surge of memory studies has given way to an engagement with national and (marked) transnational memory formations in literary works and the discourse of activism. Novels like Antonio Muñoz Molina's *Sefarad* (2001) or Pablo Montoya's *Tríptico de la infamia* (2015) engage with "traveling" or "multidirectional" memories that circulate across nations and intersect with one another,[41] while cultural narratives on crises and populism, and their digitization, show the potential of local memories to form countermemories in a progressively nationalizing and globalizing world. Of particular interest are narratives that draw on the dialogic nature of Spanish Civil War legacies with Latin American experiences of violence, for instance through the desaparecido as a transnational figure.[42]

Unmarked transnationalism, on the other hand, primarily deals with networks of literary exchange and the infrastructure of the literary system, but also with reinterpretations of canonical literature through a transnational lens, for instance William Childers's rereading of Cervantes from the present moment, whose afterlife invites us to interrogate received ideas of Spanish nationhood: "Appropriated by the Spanish state as a symbol of national pride, at the same time he [Cervantes] has often appealed to those in exile who consider him a symbol of everything the Spanish nation excludes and rejects."[43] These reinterpretations, close to reception studies, have also led to a critical assessment of the circulation of literature and the empirical study of literature. The digitization of communication media has given an impetus to transnationalism, as can be deduced from the emergence of criticism through blogs and other ways by which writers nowadays communicate with vast transnational virtual communities. The literary blog El Boomeran(g) and cultural magazines such as *Letras Libres*, with separate Mexican and Spanish editions, are important tools to foster discursive (cyber)communities beyond nation-state borders, preserving a sense of belonging in times of deterritorialization. Inspired by the literary-sociological approach of Pierre Bourdieu and his disciples Anna Boschetti, Gisèle Sapiro, and Pascale Casanova, numerous scholars have approached the literary and cultural field in the Spanish-speaking world from a transnational angle.

Of particular interest are the studies on what Víctor Barrera Enderle has called the *alfaguarización*, or the impact of transnational publishing conglomerates on Latin American literature, the prize circuit, and the book market.[44] The transnational acts here as a corrective to classical conceptions of world literature, which were still informed by a center-periphery model and assumptions about the hegemony of the Global North. Scholars such as Ana Gallego Cuiñas, Gustavo Guerrero, Gesine Müller, and Liliana Weinberg have proposed an institutional analysis of the book publishing industry, cultural markets, and translational circulation.[45] Their vision of world literature does not celebrate a planetary connectedness or borderless cosmopolitanism that obviates the nation, but starts from a polycentric geography that asserts the interdependence of national and supranational frameworks.

Transnationalizing Narcofiction

In order to make this overview of transnational literary scholarship more tangible, we will now illustrate the benefits of a transnational approach by examining narcofiction—the artistic representation of drug trafficking and the violence it generates. Narcofiction addresses transnational crime, but as a genre it is also characterized by exchanges between the local and the global. Nowadays, it has become almost a commonplace to state that narconovels or novels about cartel-related violence have replaced magical-realist and dictator novels as the dominant Latin American literary genre. Indeed, drug violence has gone mainstream in Latin American culture and is no longer constrained to the formerly marginal genre of drug ballads (*narcocorridos*). Best-selling writers like Élmer Mendoza in Mexico and Jorge Franco in Colombia have incorporated drug smuggling into their literary universe, not merely as a background setting but as the center of the action, which has led the Mexican writer Jorge Volpi to posit that narcoliterature has become the new paradigm of Latin American literature.[46]

According to Volpi, the rise of narcofiction is a facile way to satisfy a foreign readership in search of exoticism and clichés after the turn-of-the-century postnational literature of the McOndo and Crack movements.[47] These two movements portrayed the globalized condition and defended a deterritorialized view of literature, dismissing national or supranational categories such as Latin American literature. By doing so, many writers from Volpi's generation reacted against stereotypical representations of Latin American reality, which they mainly associated with post-Boom, supposedly lowbrow writers such as Isabel Allende and Antonio Skármeta.[48] Instead, they deliberately distanced themselves from the outworn, commercialized magical-realist formula and challenged fixed, essentialist notions of a cultural discourse that opposed Anglo and Latino. Calling themselves "La Compañía Antirruralista," the Crack movement did not delve into an indigenous or rural reality from a civilizing or supernatural perspective, but set their novels in non–Latin American, mostly urban settings such as Nazi Germany. Their fiction integrates numerous elements from US pop culture and global youth culture, which enabled them to inscribe their work strategically in world literature and a tradition of cosmopolitanism within Latin American literature. In the global market, this postnational tendency has been replaced to a large extent by narcofiction, which presents violence as the new trademark of Latin American literature.

The current proliferation of narconovels is often explained as a resurgence of regionalist and rural literature, the kind of literature that flourished before the emergence of the Boom. According to this regionalist view, many narconovels are deeply anchored in the reality of the Mexican state of Sinaloa and its capital Culiacán, or the Colombian department of Antioquia and its capital Medellín, home to Pablo Escobar. The regionalist view of Mexican narcofiction is best represented by Rafael Lemus, a literary critic who framed the commercial success of narcofiction in a discussion of northern Mexican literature (*literatura norteña*). His essay reads as an attack on the crude realism and *costumbrismo* of authors who engaged with provincial "narco folk" at the margins of the mainstream literary system. Lemus argues that these highly readable and marketable novels are imbued with *couleur locale* and glorify premodern, violent narcoscenes that never challenge the horizon of expectations of readers in Mexico City or in metropolitan areas around the world. As a literary critic advocating an autonomist stance, Lemus rejects the conformism of what he considers a second-rank,

leisure-time literature. In his polemical article, Lemus critiques the aestheticiza-
tion of the violence, the hyperbolic masculinity, and the semirural imaginary of
regional *narcocorridos* and Élmer Mendoza's hard-boiled novels. These works
make the reader aware of the ubiquity of narcoculture in daily life through
details like slang and dress code—*norteño*-style hats, expensive alligator boots,
embroidered belts, golden relics of *Santa Muerte* or the narcosaint Jesús Malverde—in sum, the flamboyant and exaggerated *chero* (cowboy) style of the narcos, which is often equated with a vulgar, nouveau-riche taste. Lemus's reading
is reductive because he only approaches narcofiction from a center-periphery
opposition: "Mientras más se insista en la particularidad de la región, más se
escribe para el centro."[49] He leaves aside the *transnational* nature of the narcocorridos themselves, which are extremely popular among California's Chicano
youth and are often produced in the United States.[50] Moreover, even though his
novels are invariably set in Culiacán, Mendoza—who expressed his discomfort
with classifying northern literature as paraliterary narcoliterature—is far from
being an author whose significance is limited to his own region: he largely fore-
went the local literary field by publishing his novels with the transnational publishing house Tusquets and by acquiring significant symbolic capital upon being
consecrated as a member of the *Academia Mexicana de la Lengua*.

Colombian narcofiction is also studied through this regionalist lens. The
Colombian writer Héctor Abad Faciolince coined the term *novela sicaresca* to
refer to an aesthetic trend that originated in Antioquia in the early 1990s.[51] The
protagonists of these testimony-like novels are usually young hit men (*sicarios*)
who are employed by the drug lords and eventually diversify into political assassination. The authors resort to *parlache*, a vernacular language spoken in Medellín's shantytowns, in order to enhance the verisimilitude and localism. Abad
Faciolince describes the Medellín-centered *sicaresca* as the artistic expression and
sociological portrait of these new characters coming from local *comunas*: drug
trafficking supposedly spurred the creation of a more realist mode of writing that
suits the reality of inequality and everyday violence. The features of the sicaresca
are remarkably similar to the characteristics Lemus puts forward: "lenguaje colo-
quial, violencia plástica, orgullo regionalista, populismo, picaresca."[52] The term
"sicaresca" is indeed a derivative of the Spanish designation for the picaresque
novel, with its sociological orientation and focus on local customs, realistic language and detail, and cynical attitude of the outsider protagonist.

A good illustration of this localist or regionalist approach is *Narrating Narcos* (2013), in which Gabriela Polit Dueñas undertakes ethnographic fieldwork in both Culiacán and Medellín by interviewing authors, journalists, and cultural agents, documenting their responses to the portrayal of narcoculture. According to the author, the narconarratives can only be understood in relation to the local context. Even if Polit Dueñas manages to demonstrate that speaking of the "Colombianization of Mexico" is incorrect because of the different genealogies of violence in the two countries, she does not really adopt a comparative perspective, nor does she attempt to define a transnational poetics. Interestingly, she aims to offer insights about the origins and development of illegal drug trafficking within a network of local memories, stories, and human dramas: "[L]iterature provides an alternative perspective on our ordinary perception of narcocultures and brings us closer to *paisa* and *culichi* realities, both as locations of violence and as imaginary places created in fiction."[53] By incorporating these local memories and affiliations, Polit Dueñas offers a meticulous, close reading of the milieu of popular, locally based cultural texts, without however comparing generic or formal features of Colombian *sicaresca* or the Mexican *narconovela*.

Other critics adopt a globalist approach when studying Latin American narcoliterature, whereby narcofiction is seen as a site-specific way of thematizing the excrescences of globalization. In *Beyond Bolaño: The Global Latin American Novel* (2015), Héctor Hoyos examines a series of post-1989 Latin American novels that offer valuable insights into processes of globalization by starting from the observation that these narratives "*matter* beyond their immediate national contexts." Hoyos proposes to use the narconovela, which he terms an "emerging world literary genre," as a "springboard to critique the hegemonic global order that underwrites narcotrafficking,"[54] but by doing so, he tends to lose sight of how deeply these narratives are embedded in both a regional and a national context. Indeed, one of the novels analyzed by Hoyos, *La virgen de los sicarios* (1994) by Fernando Vallejo, can be read as a cynical commentary on the difficult process of nation building in Colombia and the role intellectuals played in it. Other, more political readings also tend to delocalize the violence in Latin American narcoliterature. Rebecca E. Biron, for instance, sees in these *hit men* the ultimate expression of late hypercapitalism. According to Biron, these novels are first and foremost narratives about unequal power relations and the instrumentalization of human life, which supports global capitalism.[55] Likewise, works such as *Capitalismo gore* (2010) by philosopher-activist Sayak Valencia marginalize the local and the particular of the violence by presenting the drugs, the dead bodies, and the representation of the violence as Third World commodities in a global neoliberal system of hyperconsumerism.[56] These readings reject the view of violence as something innate or intrinsically bound up with the region, and are critical of the romanticization and glorification of violence, but frequently overlook the local and the particular and tend to downplay the potential of literature and popular culture to create counternarratives against global capitalism and the symbolic violence exercised by Hollywood. In other words, they privilege transnationalism from above over transnationalism from below.

These visions of narconovels as a regionalist or global genre are both equally reductive. Only a transnational perspective can do justice to the complex negotiations between the local, the national, and the supranational. Several scholars have adopted an approach that perceives narconovels simultaneously as a local and a global genre, without abandoning the intermediate level of the national. For example, such a perspective has been adopted by Miguel Cabañas in his work on narcocorridos. Cabañas compares Mexican narcocorridos with Colombian *corridos prohibidos* and examines to what extent they articulate a transnational identity.[57] His approach focuses on the tensions between the local and the global, without ignoring the importance of the national level, which is rearticulated in many narconarratives. In Mexico, the massive increase in drug-related killings is often seen as an ironic consequence of the democratization process: the transition from a one-party authoritarian and clientelistic state, dominated by a hegemonic Institutional Revolutionary Party (Partido Revolucionario Institucional, PRI), to a three-party system and more competitive democracy coincided with a rise in lawless violence among the drug gangs and weak rule of law. Sinaloa is not only the paradigmatic place to understand the genealogy of drug trafficking, but it is also a place traumatized by actions committed by the Mexican state. Mendoza's novels mythologize kingpins but also provide a counterdiscourse to the "consistently negative representation of lower-class and rural narcos"[58] and insist on state corruption and impunity as an endemic problem of Mexico. Colombian novels such as *La virgen de los sicarios* can also be read as a commentary on *colombianidad* and *narcodemocracia*, while others portray capos as present-day *caudillos* in regions that have never been under the control of the central government. Contract killers and the drug wars in Colombia are often represented as a continuation of the period of intense civil strife and bloodshed called La Violencia (1948–1958). Little critical attention has been paid to transnational artistic collectives such as Narcochingadazo (US-Colombia-Mexico), who produced event-actions tied to national independence celebrations amid the drug wars. Another example of the interconnectedness of the local, national, and international levels is the Mexican movie *El infierno* (2010) by Luis Estrada, which is set against the same background of Mexico's bicentennial and underscores the failed project of the nation by depicting a deported Mexican migrant emulating local kingpins.

Narcofiction is created and consumed transnationally, and is not only tailored by local authors for a niche domestic audience. Drug narratives are written across the hemisphere, and in Spain, Colombian sicarescas, Mexican narconovelas, and Chilean and Galician narcofiction can be seen as articulations of an overarching transnational crime fiction focusing on today's drug business, without subsuming it to "world literature," which erases the singularity of a regional space of cultural production. Moreover, cultural representations on narcoviolence have become increasingly transnationalized and re-mediatized. From a transnational and transmedial perspective, Arturo Pérez-Reverte's *La reina del sur* (2002) constitutes an interesting example of how a foreign writer dialogues with the oral tradition of narcocorridos and the narrative schemata, stereotypes, and patterns of framing that are characteristic of the Mexican narconovel. Pérez-Reverte's plot, which is based on the lyrics of a popular corrido by the norteño band *Los Tigres del Norte* and moves the center of action to the Iberian Peninsula, led to a popular Spanish-language telenovela produced by the US television network Telemundo (2011–2023) as well as an English-language remake (*Queen of the South*, 2016–2021). It also sparked the Galician narcoliterature boom.

Another intriguing example of this dynamic is the plurimedial constellation around Escobar, from the Colombian narcotelenovela *Escobar: El patrón del mal* (Caracol TV, 2012), which is based on Medellín's former mayor Alonso Salazar Jaramillo's biography *La parábola de Pablo* (2001), to the English-language Colombian-Spanish drama film *Loving Pablo* (2017) or Netflix's *Narcos* (2015–2017) and its multiple spin-offs such as comic books and games. Many of these narcoseries are transnational coproductions or have inspired intermedial adaptations or intramedial remakes abroad. Consequently, they require transmedia and transcultural approaches to map their circulation and unravel the complex entanglement of regional, national, and supranational imagined memoryscapes. These cultural depictions recycle and adjust memory figurations to cater to different audiences, or revision Colombia's historical memory, as seen in *Narcos* episodes on the theft of Simón Bolívar's sword and the Palace of Justice siege.

The transnationalism of present-day Latin American filmic and literary narcofiction invites us to go beyond both the local level and the national level, without providing a merely deterritorialized interpretation that reduces these fictions to an illustration of neoliberalism's role in making human beings disposable. Several recent studies demonstrate the validity of a dialectical transnational approach that considers the local roots and translocal scope of the cultural artifacts. Alejandro Herrero-Olaizola examines how local marginalities and ethnic differences are niche-marketed and commercialized globally, by pointing out the role played by transnational publishers like Alfaguara, which, in their search for an international best seller, universalize what is essentially a local phenomenon of the slums of Medellín.[59] Likewise, Hermann Herlinghaus, in his study on "transnational Latin American narcoepics," combines an interest in place-specific writing and localism with attention to different regional and national forces and their transnational points of intersection.[60] This also involves calling attention to the transnational genealogies of local drug cultures. Narconovels are not just *Heimat* literature or expressions of a generalized globalism, but also a market-driven commodification of cultural otherness that caters to local, national, and foreign audiences. This requires reading across and beyond borders while acknowledging the singularity of the national space of cultural production and regional networks of circulation.

Epilogue

A heightened sensitivity to transnational flows and the obstacles encountered by these flows (e.g., language barriers and cultural stereotypes) has prompted many fields of study to rethink their underpinning assumptions. This chapter has presented various ways in which Hispanic (literary) studies have been transformed since the turn of the twenty-first century as a consequence of the transnational turn. The transnational has fundamentally changed the way in which Hispanic scholarship and teaching are organized. This overview is not in any way exhaustive, as it has touched only briefly on digital culture and translation and left out a discussion of the transnational turn in Hispanic literary studies in relation to key interlocutors such as borderlands studies, island studies, and postcolonial and decolonial studies, which have given rise to a "minor transnationalism" that decenters a Eurocentric perspective.[61] Nor have I engaged with the ongoing debates on cosmopolitanism and on resurgent forms of isolationist and anti-immigrant nationalism in Europe and the Americas, which have sparked a growing interest in transnational fascism and populist movements and their genealogies.[62] Studies on the literary representation of undocumented migrants and on colonial literature also clearly benefit from a transnational approach. The rich diversity of the contributions to this volume shows how multifaceted and promising the field of transnational studies is.

Notes

1. Mieke Bal, *Travelling Concepts in the Humanities: A Rough Guide* (University of Toronto Press, 2002), 13.

2. Ansgar Nünning, "Transnational Approaches to the Study of Culture," in *English and American Studies: Theory and Practice*, ed. Martin Middeke, Timo Müller, Christina Wald, and Hubert Zapf (Verlag J. B. Metzler, 2012), 267.

3. Pierre-Yves Saunier, *Transnational History* (Basingstoke, Hants., England: Palgrave Macmillan, 2013), 17.

4. Pierre-Yves Saunier, "Transnational," in *The Palgrave Dictionary of Transnational History*, ed. Akira Iriye and Pierre-Yves Saunier (Basingstoke, Hants., England: Palgrave Macmillan, 2009), 1047–55, quoted at 1051.

5. Luis Eduardo Guarnizo and Michael Peter Smith, "The Locations of Transnationalism," in *Transnationalism from Below: Comparative Urban and Community Research*, ed. Michael Peter Smith and Luis Eduardo Guarnizo (New Brunswick, NJ: Transaction Publishers, 1998), 3–34, quoted at 3.

6. The term was first recorded in the twenty-second edition of the *Diccionario de la lengua española* (2001) of the Real Academia Española. According to the academy, the frequency of "transnacional" has tripled since the year 2000.

7. Guarnizo and Smith, "The Locations of Transnationalism," 3–5.

8. Steven Vertovec, *Transnationalism* (Abingdon, Oxon., England: Routledge, 2009), 3.

9. Serge Gruzinski, *Les quatre parties du monde: Histoire d'une mondialisation* (La Martinière, 2004); and Ivonne del Valle, Anna More, and Rachel Sarah O'Toole, eds., *Iberian Empires and the Roots of Globalization* (Vanderbilt University Press, 2019).

10. Nadia Lie, "Lo transnacional en el cine hispánico: Deslindes de un concepto," in *Nuevas perspectivas sobre la transnacionalidad del cine hispánico*, ed. Robin Lefere and Nadia Lie (Brill/Rodopi, 2016), 17–35, quoted at 20.

11. Julio Ortega, *Transatlantic Translations: Dialogues in Latin American Literature*, trans. Philip Derbyshire (Reaktion Books, 2006), 83.

12. Julio Ortega, "Post-teoría y estudios transatlánticos," *Iberoamericana* 3, no. 9 (March 2003): 109–17, quoted at 114.

13. Abril Trigo, "De lo transcultural a/en lo transnacional," in *Ángel Rama y los estudios latinoamericanos*, ed. Mabel Moraña (Instituto Internacional de Literatura Iberoamericana, 1997), 147–51.

14. Deborah Cohn, *History and Memory in the Two Souths: Recent Southern and Spanish American Fiction* (Vanderbilt University Press, 1999).

15. Shelley Fisher Fishkin acknowledges the importance of Latino/Latina scholarship and borderlands scholars like Gloria Anzaldúa and José David Saldívar for the transnational turn of American studies. See Shelley Fisher Fishkin, "Crossroads of Cultures: The Transnational Turn in American Studies; Presidential Address to the American Studies Association, November 12, 2004," *American Quarterly* 57, no. 1 (March 2005): 17–57.

16. Joan Ramon Resina, "Iberian Modalities: The Logic of an Intercultural Field," in *Iberian Modalities: A Relational Approach to the Study of Culture in the Iberian Peninsula*, ed. Joan Ramon Resina (Liverpool University Press, 2013), 1–19, quoted at 12–13.

17. Joan Ramon Resina, *Del hispanismo a los estudios ibéricos: Una propuesta federativa para el ámbito cultural* (Biblioteca Nueva, 2009).

18. Adolfo Campoy-Cubillo and Benita Sampedro Vizcaya, "Entering the Global Hispanophone: An Introduction," *Journal of Spanish Cultural Studies* 20, nos. 1–2 (2019): 1–16.

19. Eric Calderwood, "Spanish in a Global Key," *Journal of Spanish Cultural Studies* 20, nos. 1–2 (2019): 53–65.

20. Sigrid Weigel, "On the 'Topographical Turn': Concepts of Space in Cultural Studies and *Kulturwissenschaften*; A Cartographic Feud," *European Review* 17, no. 1 (February 2009): 187–201.

21. Tim Cresswell, *On the Move: Mobility in the Modern Western World* (Routledge, 2006); and John Urry, *Mobilities* (Polity Press, 2007).

22. Jürgen Habermas, *Die postnationale Konstellation: Politische Essays* (Frankfurt am Main: Suhrkamp Verlag, 1998).

23. Vertovec, *Transnationalism*.

24. Roland Robertson, "Glocalization: Time-Space and Homogeneity-Heterogeneity," in *Global Modernities*, ed. Mike Featherstone, Scott Lash, and Roland Robertson (SAGE Publications, 1995), 25–44.

25. Mette Hjort, "On the Plurality of Cinematic Transnationalism," in *World Cinemas, Transnational Perspectives*, ed. Nataša Ďurovičová and Kathleen Newman (Routledge, 2010), 12–33, quoted at 13–14.

26. David Harvey, *The Condition of Postmodernity: An Enquiry into the Origins of Cultural Change* (Blackwell, 1990).

27. Juan Poblete, "The Transnational Turn," in *New Approaches to Latin American Studies: Culture and Power*, ed. Juan Poblete (Routledge, 2018), 32–49, quoted at 33.

28. See Frances R. Aparicio, "Reading the 'Latino' in Latino Studies: Toward Re-Imagining Our Academic Location," *Discourse* 21, no. 3 (Fall 1999): 3–18.

29. Bill Ashcroft, "Chicano Transnation," in *Imagined Transnationalism: U.S. Latino/a Literature, Culture, and Identity*, ed. Kevin Concannon, Francisco A. Lomelí, and Marc Priewe (Palgrave Macmillan, 2009), 13–28, quoted at 14.

30. Marc Priewe, "The Commuting Island: Cultural (Im)mobility in *The Flying Bus*," in *Kulturelle Mobilitätsforschung: Themen—Theorien—Tendenzen*, ed. Norbert Franz and Rüdiger Kunow (Potsdam, Germany: Universitätsverlag Potsdam, 2011), 135–47.

31. Paul Jay, *Global Matters: The Transnational Turn in Literary Studies* (Cornell University Press, 2010), 2.

32. Paul Jay, *Transnational Literature: The Basics* (Abingdon, Oxon., England: Routledge, 2021), 10.

33. Burkhard Pohl, "Estrategias transnacionales en el mercado del libro (1990–2010)," *Aleph*, no. 25 (2012): 13–34.

34. Kwame Anthony Appiah, "Cosmopolitan Patriots," in *Cosmopolitics: Thinking and Feeling Beyond the Nation*, ed. Pheng Cheah and Bruce Robbins (University of Minnesota Press, 1998), 91–114, quoted at 91.

35. Dagmar Vandebosch borrows the term "radicant" from Nicolas Bourriaud's aesthetic theories. Dagmar Vandebosch, "Introducción," in "Escritores hispanoamericanos en España," ed. Dagmar Vandebosch, special issue, *Aleph*, no. 25 (2012): 10–11.

36. In the satirical manifesto to their short-fiction anthology *McOndo* (1996), Alberto Fuguet and Sergio Gómez reject magical-realist literature's tropes and techniques (supposedly exhausted by the "literatura *light*" of some of the post-Boom novelists) in favor of a so-called virtual realism that captures the societal and cultural transformations wrought by neoliberalism. The setting of their novels is no longer a mythical, archetypal town (epitomized by Macondo in Gabriel García Márquez's literary universe) that symbolizes Latin America's age-old isolation disrupted by the forces of Anglo-European modernity, but the non-place of the shopping mall and a McDonald's restaurant as symbol of a globalization that erases national distinctions. In the same year, the *generación del Crack*, led by Jorge Volpi and Ignacio Padilla, published their manifesto in Mexico. Volpi and his peers also undertook a rupture (hence the onomatopoeia of an explosive noise) by breaking away from nationalism/regionalism and magical realism, adopting a distinctly cosmopolitan attitude in an attempt to portray a global imagined community.

37. Alexis Grohmann, *Literatura y errabundia: Javier Marías, Antonio Muñoz Molina y Rosa Montero* (Rodopi, 2011); and María Paz Oliver, "A pie: *Wandering* y cotidianidad en *Simone* de Eduardo Lalo," *Neophilologus* 99, no. 4 (October 2015): 569–79.

38. Graciela Speranza, *Atlas portátil de América Latina: Arte y ficciones errantes* (Editorial Anagrama, 2012); and Fernando Aínsa, *Palabras nómadas: Nueva cartografía de la pertenencia* (Iberoamericana Vervuert, 2012).

39. Ottmar Ette, *Literature on the Move*, trans. Katharina Vester (Rodopi, 2003).

40. Reindert Dhondt and Dagmar Vandebosch, eds., *Transnacionalidad e hibridez en el ensayo hispánico: Un género sin orillas* (Brill, 2017).

41. Dagmar Vandebosch, "Transnational Memories in Antonio Muñoz Molina's *Sepharad*," *European Review* 22, no. 4 (October 2014): 613–22; and Reindert Dhondt, "Tríptico de la

infamia de Pablo Montoya como cuadro barroco," *Mitologías Hoy: Revista de Pensamiento, Crítica y Estudios Literarios Latinoamericanos* 16 (2017): 307–19.

42. Silvana Mandolessi and Mariana Eva Perez, "The Disappeared as a Transnational Figure or How to Deal with the *Vain Yesterday*," *European Review* 22, no. 4 (October 2014): 603–12; and Gabriel Gatti, ed., *Desapariciones: Usos locales, circulaciones globales* (Siglo del Hombre Editores; Universidad de los Andes, 2017).

43. William Childers, *Transnational Cervantes* (University of Toronto Press, 2006), xiii. See also Theo D'haen and Reindert Dhondt, eds., *International Don Quixote* (Rodopi, 2009).

44. Víctor Barrera Enderle, "Entradas y salidas del fenómeno literario actual o la 'alfaguar-ización' de la literatura hispanoamericana," in *Ensayos sobre literatura y culturas latinoameri-canas* (LOM Ediciones, 2002), 91–111.

45. Ana Gallego Cuiñas, *Las novelas argentinas del siglo 21: Nuevos modos de producción, cir-culación y recepción* (Peter Lang, 2020); Gustavo Guerrero, *Paisajes en movimiento: Literatura y cambio cultural entre dos siglos* (Eterna Cadencia, 2018); Gesine Müller, "Transnational Challenges for World Literatures: Publishing Caribbean Writers," in *The Transnational in Literary Studies: Potential and Limitations of a Concept*, ed. Kai Weigandt (De Gruyter, 2020), 44–55; Gesine Müller, *Wie wird Weltliteratur gemacht? Globale Zirkulationen lateina-merikanischer Literaturen* (De Gruyter, 2020); and Liliana Weinberg, "The Oblivion We Will Be: The Latin American Literary Field After Autonomy," in *Institutions of World Lit-erature: Writing, Translation, Markets*, ed. Stefan Helgesson and Pieter Vermeulen, 67–78 (Routledge, 2016).

46. Jorge Volpi, "Cruzar la frontera," *Milenio* (Monterrey), October 24, 2009.

47. See Timothy R. Robbins and José Eduardo González, "Posnacionalistas: Tradition and New Writing in Latin America," in *New Trends in Contemporary Latin American Narra-tive: Post-National Literatures and the Canon*, ed. Timothy R. Robbins and José Eduardo González (Palgrave Macmillan, 2014), 1–19.

48. The Boom refers less to a movement or style than to an explosion of creativity and mar-keting in Latin American narrative fiction, detonated by Carlos Fuentes's *La muerte de Arte-mio Cruz* (1962), which gained international acclaim and best-seller status for novelists such as Julio Cortázar, Mario Vargas Llosa, Gabriel García Márquez, and Fuentes. Although the label "post-Boom" is often regarded as too reductive to encapsulate the heterogeneity of Latin American novelistic production after the disintegration of the unified aesthetic (mod-ernist, experimental) and political (leftist, pro-Cuba) project of the Boom, it is commonly used to refer to the more readable novels that emerged from the mid-1970s onward.

49. "The more one insists on the particularity of the region, the more one writes for the center." Rafael Lemus, "Balas de salva: Notas sobre el narco y la narrativa mexicana," *Letras Libres* 7, no. 81 (September 2005): 39–42, quoted at 42.

50. The music is inspired by North American gangsta rap and is often produced by Califor-nia-based and Grammy Award–winning musicians who seek inspiration on the Internet. See Elijah Wald, *Narcocorrido: A Journey into the Music of Drugs, Guns, and Guerrillas* (HarperCollins, 2001).

51. Héctor Abad Faciolince, "Estética y narcotráfico," *Revista de Estudios Hispánicos* 42, no. 3 (2008): 513–18.

52. "[C]olloquial language, tangible violence, regional pride, populism, the picaresque." Lemus, "Balas de salva," 40.

53. Gabriela Polit Dueñas, *Narrating Narcos: Culiacán and Medellín* (University of Pittsburgh Press, 2013), 5.

54. Héctor Hoyos, *Beyond Bolaño: The Global Latin American Novel* (Columbia University Press, 2015), 1, 128, 28.

55. Rebecca E. Biron, "It's a Living: Hit Men in the Mexican Narco War," *PMLA* 127, no. 4 (October 2012): 820–34.

56. Sayak Valencia, *Capitalismo gore* (Santa Cruz de Tenerife, Spain: Editorial Melusina, 2010).

57. Miguel Ángel Cabañas, "El narcocorrido global y las identidades transnacionales," *Revista de Estudios Hispánicos* 42, no. 3 (2008): 519–42, quoted at 525.

58. Diana Palaversich, "The Politics of Drug Trafficking in Mexican and Mexico-Related Narconovelas," *Aztlán: A Journal of Chicano Studies* 31, no. 2 (Fall 2006): 85–110, quoted at 88.

59. Alejandro Herrero-Olaizola, "'Se vende Colombia, un país de delirio': El mercado literario global y la narrativa colombiana reciente," *Symposium: A Quarterly Journal in Modern Literatures* 61, no. 1 (2007): 43–56.

60. Hermann Herlinghaus, *Narcoepics: A Global Aesthetics of Sobriety* (Bloomsbury, 2013), 31.

61. Françoise Lionnet and Shu-mei Shih, eds., *Minor Transnationalism* (Duke University Press, 2005).

62. Reindert Dhondt, Monica Jansen, and Maria Bonaria Urban, eds., *Transatlantic Practices of Fascism(s) and Populism(s) from the Margins: The Cultural Politics of "Us" Versus "Them"* (Abingdon, Oxon., England: Routledge, 2025).

CHAPTER 4

Indigenous Transnationalism

An Enduring Paradox

ANDREW CANESSA

IN THIS CHAPTER, I explore what I see as a central paradox inherent in the condition of Indigeneity. On the one hand, Indigeneity seems closely bounded by the nation-state, and Indigenous identities travel with difficulty, if at all, across national boundaries. In addition, if we consider Indigenous identities against contemporary globalized identities and culture, the former would appear to be diametrically opposed to the latter: Indigenous identities are quintessentially rooted in space and time and cultural difference. Even further: transnational and globalized identities are often explicitly contrasted with Indigenous ones, which appear to many to be more "authentic." The paradox is that Indigenous identities are deeply transnational in the very simple sense that they not only traverse national boundaries but also only really make sense when considered transnationally. A people may have a very specific culture rooted in a particular place, but what makes their identity Indigenous is how this people and culture relate to the broader nation-state and their shared identity with other Indigenous peoples. With no appreciation of the transnational context in which they exist, they are simply a marginalized local group. Another way of thinking about this is seeing Indigenous identities as quintessentially "glocal"; they are rooted in a very local culture and specificity, but they are inevitably part of a global network of people, organizations, and, perhaps most importantly, ideas that identify Indigenous people.

I will explore these themes below, drawing on more than thirty years of working with Indigenous people in Bolivia,[1] a country that has a special place in transnational Indigeneities because it elected an Indigenous president in 2005, Evo Morales, who has sometimes been described as the "world's (first) Indigenous president" and who powerfully articulated Indigeneity in his political rhetoric and operationalized it as a tool of governance.[2] I will also draw more broadly on the Indigenous experience in the Americas and across the world to explore the paradox outlined above and suggest that the transnationalism of Indigeneity is not merely a contemporary phenomenon but one that has roots in European expansion and modern state-building since the seventeenth century.

When considering the position of Indigenous peoples in the Americas, the most readily available lens through which to see five hundred years of history offers the image of myriad peoples conquered by Europeans and then enduring centuries of struggle to maintain their identities and their very existence. By the end of the nineteenth century, the Mapuches had succumbed in Chile, the Conquest of the Desert had sounded the death knell of Indigenous independence in Patagonia, and the nomadic peoples of the North American Plains had finally been defeated. In countries such as Mexico and Peru, the much larger farming populations were absorbed into the colonial and then republican states as subordinated, ethnically differentiated peasantries. Some Indigenous groups maintained their autonomies longer than others by fleeing ever farther upriver or by occupying sparsely populated areas that Europeans did not want, but by the twenty-first century there are very few Indigenous peoples who live an autonomous lifestyle beyond the nation-state.

One way of understanding Indigenous peoples, then, is as survivors of history who have demonstrated endurance because they have managed to eke out an existence on the margins of the nation-state. In this reading, Indigenous peoples have little if any role in the development of the nation-state, much less in relations between states. As such, they can only be understood as existing outside modernity if not actually antithetical to it. Being resolutely outside the nation-state, they can neither traverse nor transcend its borders and are resolutely constituted as being on the *boundaries* of the nation, in opposition to the nation and consequently beyond any transnational experience.

Another approach takes seriously the possibility of Indigenous transnational-ism in the form of migration, especially from Latin America to the United States. In the case of the Guatemalan Mayas, many of these were fleeing war. Here, Shelton Davis and Patricia Foxen have chronicled in great detail the flows of people to the United States and the importance of remittances back to Gua-temala in a series of quite complex and enduring transnational currents.[3] Foxen, in particular, has noted that even though the Mayan language and other cultural elements travel to the United States, the former is rarely transmitted across gen-erations and the latter, inevitably, go through profound changes in a new cultural context. More significantly, Guatemalan migrants' sense of being specifically Indigenous is transformed as they are considered Guatemalans or even simply as American migrants by the host population.[4] Indeed, Indigenous Mexicans are perceived as simply "Mexicans" when they cross the border to the United States, their Indigeneity erased in the eyes of the nationals of their new home, even as they continue to speak, for example, Mixtec and maintain a distinct identity.[5] In a similar vein, Aymara and Quechua migrants from Bolivia to São Paulo are merely regarded as "Bolivians" by their hosts. What is striking about this exam-ple is the speed with which they slough off a specifically Indigenous identity; in fact, they resist any such identification.[6]

This experience is reproduced even further afield with Aymara migrants in Madrid and Jerez de la Frontera in Spain. When I have met Aymara migrants in these and other places such as Buenos Aires, they are usually delighted and always surprised to meet a European who speaks Aymara. Their joy in finding someone outside their (usually small) group of family and friends who speak Aymara does not, however, extend to articulating a specifically Aymara identity, let alone an Indigenous one. This is in part because their Indigeneity has little meaning within their lived experiences in Spain (or Argentina), but also because migration can be an opportunity to slough off what is still a stigmatized identity. Bolivian migrants are further stigmatized for their association with Indigeneity in Buenos Aires, so there is an additional reason here to downplay any identifica-tion with an Indigenous identity or culture.

On a different plane, because Indigeneity is seen as being rooted in a very geographically circumscribed culture, moving out of that space can open migrants to accusations of lacking authenticity and thus undermining their political impact, as Virginia Tilley demonstrates for El Salvador.[7] Under the

Morales regime in Bolivia (2006–2019), the president and vice president regularly denounced Indigenous, especially lowland, groups as being manipulated by foreign agents and Indigenous NGOs, asserting that they could not organize themselves internationally, so any international organization must be false and because Indigenous mobilization *by definition* could only be conceived as being located within the nation-state.

At root here is the very conception of Indigeneity and how it relates to the nation-state. Modern political theorists who are concerned with Indigenous people often explicitly define Indigeneity as a condition outside that of the modern sovereign state,[8] and the progressive political project is inclusion within the sovereign state. They thus share a position with Locke and Hobbes in seeing Indigenous people as *fundamentally* outside the development of a political form that arose out of the double collapse of ecclesiastical and feudal authority in the early modern period in Europe.

I heed James Scott's caution against being blind to the complex relationship between the state and those that it somehow has not quite managed to control.[9] In many cases, he argues, ethnicity is a product of a conscious effort by people to escape state control. Egalitarian political structures that are often features of people considered to be Indigenous or tribal are not simply cultural forms *sui generis* but active strategies in avoiding the state. Scott quotes Ernest Gellner, who argues that the political autonomy and tribalism of the Berber population of Morocco "is not a tribalism 'prior to government' but a political and partial rejection of a particular government."[10] In Scott's own words: "[E]thnicity and tribe began, by definition, where sovereignty and taxes ended,"[11] and this is not far from Pierre Clastres's formulation that sees Indigenous peoples as societies "against the state."[12] One is also reminded of Fredrik Barth's seminal work on ethnicity in which he notes that the substantive difference between Pathans and Baluchis in Pakistan and Afghanistan is not linguistic (since many people speak both) or cultural but essentially political: Pathans are independent, and to become politically subordinate is, inevitably, to change one's ethnic affiliation.[13]

The work of Scott and others is instructive because it shifts attention away from Indigenous groups as "survivors" to a more dynamic model of relations with a state and opens up the space for seeing Indigenous people not simply as being contained by nation-states but as existing in a very transnational space where ideas circulate rapidly and powerfully. However, not only are Indigenous people not constituted by the rejection of the state, but the state itself is constituted by the rejection of and by the Indigenous, or indeed by the rhetorical devices it adopts for the absorption of Indigeneities. I follow Scott, who states the need to imagine marginalized Indigenous people as a dramatic counterpoint to legitimate state rule.[14] Anna Tsing states this rather more strongly when she writes that the "Meratus [of southern Borneo] construct the state locally by fleeing it."[15] This is true of the Meratus and Indonesia today; it was also true in the sixteenth century when Europeans were developing their own modern states. Indigenous peoples were *necessary* to how Europeans imagined the nation-state, and, especially in the Americas, they have played a major role in its development right up to the present day, which is why Karena Shaw describes Indigenous people as Hobbes's "border guards"; she argues:

> "[S]avages" and the other "others" without sovereignty are produced as "different," as marking the outside, the margins, of "our" new political imaginary. It tells those of us "inside" how to think about the world (and those "outside"); it provides for us the limit that enables us to evade the problem of "infinity" or "difference." Most remarkably it does so openly, explicitly, self-consciously.[16]

Up to this point it is clear that, in so many ways, Indigeneity is defined in terms of the nation-state. We could argue that Indigeneity is a core part of our modern understanding of the nation-state, since Indigeneity was a condition against which European philosophers founded or imagined their modern Westphalian nation-states.[17]

Herein lies an enduring paradox, however: Indigenous people are widely defined as living *within* the boundaries of nation-states, and yet the very concept of Indigeneity is resolutely and ambiguously transnational. In fact, Indigeneity only arose out of a moment of European expansion, when the hitherto ethnically diverse peoples inhabiting the Americas were suddenly all imagined as sharing a particular identity and that identity is being *Indigenous*. Seeing Indigenous Americans as foundational in the development of Western modernity[18] not only inserts Indigenous Americans into modern history but also points to their role in international relations. To put it another way: Indigeneity was only ever transnational; it made no sense at all until Europeans expanded across the globe and took with them this transnational concept, which was Indigeneity.

Indigeneity in International Law and Practice

Indigeneity continues to be a transnational concept today. When one considers the attendees at the UN's annual Indigenous Peoples' Forum in New York, one can see Maasai from Tanzania, Aborigines from Australia, Lakotas from the United States, Mohawks from Canada, and so on. They come from every continent and are urban and rural, agriculturalists and pastoralists, hunter gatherers and construction workers. They speak myriad languages and have as many histories. What unites them is not any kind of culture or even shared values, but a particularly transnational idea of the nation-state and the ways certain peoples fit into that idea or not.

An important element here is that of scale: Indigenous people live in countries and are defined by those borders. Native Papuans may be considered Indigenous if they live in the Indonesian province of Irian Jaya but not if they live in the state of Papua New Guinea across the border, since Papua New Guinea is an independent state with a majority Papuan population. One could consequently argue, although to my knowledge no one has yet, that there are no Indigenous people in Bolivia, since the majority population and the one most clearly represented in Morales's government, and indeed the current administration of Luis Arce, is composed of those descendants of the pre-Conquest population. Morales brought Indigeneity into his statecraft and came close to articulating a vision of Bolivia as an Indigenous state,[19] but even if he had succeeding in doing so, there is no precedent in international law for recognizing Indigenous states. The Indigenous state of Bolivia would be no more recognized as Indigenous as any other country previously dominated by Europeans such as Fiji or Botswana. What did happen, however, in Bolivia was that when the state identified as Indigenous, there was a clear conflict between those Indigenous groups that felt marginalized by the new state and others who saw Indigeneity as part of the national identity.[20] To put it another way, the "Indigenous state" produced its own relationships with other(ed) Indigenous groups. The key point here is that Indigeneity as a concept can only be imagined in terms of states and, specifically, as being marginal and, in some way, in opposition to those states. This leads to a further paradox that even, or rather *because*, Indigeneity is defined in terms of states, Indigeneity is a concern of states and international organizations. It is thus worth looking at how international organizations have attempted to define

Indigeneity and consider further the very transnational way such definitions are operationalized.

In advance of announcing an International Decade of the World's Indigenous People (1995–2004), the United Nations appointed José Martínez Cobo to report to the UN Sub-Commission on Prevention of Discrimination and Protection of Minorities, in which he defined Indigenous people as such: "Indigenous communities, peoples and nations are those which, having a historical continuity with pre-invasion and pre-colonial societies that developed on their territories, consider themselves distinct from other sectors of the societies now prevailing in those territories, or parts of them."[21] Martínez Cobo's report has become a key reference document for other international agencies and nations in defining Indigeneity,[22] and even for anthropologists.[23]

Over the same period, the International Labour Organization was drafting its Resolution 169, which for the first time recognized Indigenous people in international law when it came into force in 1991. As with the UN, the ILO saw Indigeneity as primarily a relationship between colonized and colonizers. Article 1(b) of the resolution defines Indigenous people as "[p]eoples in independent countries who are regarded as Indigenous on account of their descent from the populations which inhabited the country, or a geographical region to which the country belongs, at the time of conquest or colonization."[24]

Finally, the World Bank's Operational Directive 4.20 of September 1991 inaugurated the bank's policy toward Indigenous people, having identified them as being particularly marginal and the sectors of a given population who were most likely to be poor.[25] It is through these policy documents and treaties that the concept of Indigenous people and rights has been established in international law and discourse, drawing on Enlightenment principles of rights and Western concepts of descent and territorial legitimacy.[26]

These discourses have circulated back to communities who have begun, in turn, to express who they are in the language of Indigeneity. It is important to underline that, even as international organizations consulted with Indigenous groups about definitions, the starting point is located not within Indigenous communities but in the very transnational framework of international relations. To draw from my own experience studying Indigenous peoples in Latin America, in particular in Bolivia, there is no term in any language that I am aware of that is a comfortable gloss for the word "Indigenous" that can apply to a wide range of groups. To take a particular example, the Aymara people I have worked with do not have a word that can be translated as "Indigenous." They do have a word that allows them to distinguish themselves from people with racialized identities other than their own (e.g., white and mixed-race people), and this word is *jaqi*, a word that, like with so many Indigenous titles of self-ascription, simply means "people."[27] Jaqi, however, would not usually include other people usually identified as Indigenous by outsiders, such those people who live in the Bolivian Amazon. Until very recently—that is, this century—and then only in a very limited fashion, Aymara speakers did not see any kinship with lowland Indigenous peoples at all. It was only with the election of President Morales (who was born in an Aymara community), who used Indigeneity as a tool of governance, that people really developed a broad and shared sense of Indigenous identity across the country and across ethnic boundaries.

Michael Hathaway's work on the development of Indigenous consciousness and identity in rural China is quite illustrative.[28] Hathaway notes that the term *tu zhu ren*, which literally means "people of the mountains," has been adopted as a translation of that globalized concept, "Indigenous." Although increasingly used in a very positive sense to identify Indigenous people, the phrase was much more generally used pejoratively in the past. As he points out:

> First, finding equivalents to "Indigenous people" in China is not simply a matter of translation. Second, and more importantly, [. . .] even if a Chinese term for Indigenous people became acceptable to some, the very concept of Indigenous would have to contend with ongoing legacies of ethnic and social hierarchies. My fieldwork showed that it was not people like Old Wang who rallied under the identity of Indigenous, but mainly Chinese public intellectuals who used this transnational concept in a diverse effort to reshape notions of ethnicity, citizenship, and rights.[29]

The role of transnational Indigenous networks cannot be underestimated in creating a globalized sense of Indigeneity, and it is very often these transnational networks that introduce the very concept of Indigeneity where none hitherto existed. Maria Sapignoli provides a very good example of this for the San Bushmen of the Kalahari, where it was international NGOs that worked with the San to articulate an Indigenous identity in order to defend their land rights within the Kalahari reserve.[30]

Redefining oneself as an *Indigenous* group, or simply rediscovering one's Indigenous identity,[31] can be an important strategy for marginalized groups to gain recognition and resources from the nation-state, where lobbying through international NGOs can be much more effective than organizing nationally.[32] Indeed, many Indigenous activists have much better access to international organizations than they do to local bureaucracies and national power structures in their own countries, and accessing transnational Indigenous networks can be an effective way of circumventing antagonistic local bureaucracies.

These and other agencies do vary in how they define Indigeneity and usually add elements such as attachment to a territory, a particular relationship to the environment, language, religion, and so on. There are, however, two concepts that are common to all: the first is understanding Indigenous people primarily in terms of their being descended from pre-Conquest or precolonial peoples; and the second is self-definition as a key component in Indigenous identity. These criteria are also included in Sidsel Saugestad's attempt to arrive at a synthetic definition of Indigeneity; they are the first and the last of her four criteria: they were the first to come (i.e., they were there before the dominant group); nondominance; cultural difference; and self-ascription.[33] Even the first term is, however, problematic, as many countries refuse to accept Indigenous peoples within their (postcolonial) borders. The Chinese state, although advocating for Indigenous groups in Taiwan, insists that all Chinese in China are Indigenous.[34] The state of Botswana similarly argues that all Botswanans are Indigenous as it resists the recognition of San Bushmen as Indigenous in order to curtail their rights.[35]

There is no question that Indigenous groups are connected to a very globalized network of activists, organizations, and institutions with very developed and rapid communication between the various nodes. Where there is paradoxically much less communication is in academic scholarship across different regions. Scholars note, and with some regularity, that Indigeneity in Africa and Asia is rather different from that in settler states such as Australia and Argentina.[36] In the latter countries, who is and is not Indigenous appears to outside observers to be relatively unproblematic. In Africa and Asia, however, many national governments often declare the entire population to be Indigenous; Indigeneity is presented as being controversial, a threat to divide people, and a very recent import. The issue of Indigeneity in Latin America, in contrast, is understood to be intimately associated with colonization by Europeans in the fifteenth and sixteenth centuries; in Africa, fewer Europeans settled (and many left), and most countries have overwhelming majorities of people who are of non-European descent. Nevertheless, as I have demonstrated above, Indigeneity as an identity is thoroughly modern: when colonized peoples in the Americas and Africa resisted the state (colonial or otherwise), they did not do so as Indigenous people per se but rather as local, subordinated people opposing whatever state oppressed them. It was only in the late twentieth century that Indigenous peoples began to develop shared political identities across borders.

It is in this globalized context that scholars noted an "Indigenous awakening" or "resurgence" in Latin America.[37] It is no coincidence that a new, globalized Indigeneity is emerging at the very moment that the Western nation-state is facing its greatest challenge, quite possibly since the Treaty of Westphalia established the modern rules of relations between states in 1648.[38]

The rising international profile of Indigenous people and especially the development of a parallel environmental and ethical discourse have contributed greatly to the two most celebrated success stories of Indigenous mobilization in Latin America: the Zapatistas, who declared war against the Mexican state in 1994, and the presidency of Evo Morales in Bolivia. Both cases were explicit critiques of the state and economic globalization.

Morales, not unlike the Zapatistas, used inclusive language and took Indigeneity to articulate a wide range of social causes as well as the defense of natural resources for the nation. In fact, especially in the first years of his presidency, he was rather fond of quoting Zapatista slogans.[39] Manifestly influenced by the Zapatistas, he declared Indigenous people to be the "moral reserve of humanity."[40] The association of Indigenous people with social ethics, morality generally, politically progressive ideologies, and environmental consciousness is not only modern but explicitly constructed as a counterpoint to the globalized world, where the local is sacrificed for the global. In a context in which many people feel that the state is subordinated to a globalized economy and multinationals, Indigeneity offers a powerful and explicit critique.

These Mexican and Bolivian examples underline the ways in which modern Indigenous movements arise out of critiques of globalization and in themselves form critiques of the nation-state.

Contemporary Indigeneity and the International Order

Although contemporary Indigenous identities usually draw on historical local struggles for justice, in practice, it is very often the case that people come to identify as Indigenous through a dynamic and dialectical engagement with international actors, reflecting their interaction with the discourses of global networks of international institutions and NGOs.

The 1990 Bolivian *March for Territory and Dignity*, which many see as an important turning point in Indigenous mobilization,[41] actually drew enormously on NGOs not only for the organization of the march but also for its very conception. This is not to say that activists such as Marcial Fabricano did not also have a key role, but it is important to recognize the role of the Confederation of Indigenous Peoples of Bolivia (Confederación de Pueblos Indígenas de Bolivia, or CIDOB), which organized the march. CIDOB and Support for Peasant-Indigenous Peoples of Eastern Bolivia (Apoyo para el Campesino Indígena del Oriente de Bolivia, or APCOB) were founded, respectively, in 1980 and 1983 by German anthropologists Jürgen Riester and Berndt Fischermann in collaboration with Guaraní leader Bonifacio Barrientos Iyambaei. Riester continued to play a major role in CIDOB well into this century, and he was able to draw on international political and financial support for the organization. In Bolivia, as elsewhere in Latin America, international NGOs have a huge role to play in shaping the expression of local struggles as explicitly Indigenous ones.[42]

The 1990 march, an eight-hundred-kilometer trek from the tropical lowlands to the capital city, was a turning point for Indigenous mobilization for a number of reasons. The residents of La Paz were stunned to see thousands of lowland Indigenous people descend on their city, appearing to contradict the idea that lowland Indigenous people were inexorably disappearing from history.[43] Another significant point about the march is that there was an alliance between highland and lowland Indigenous people for the first time. For much of the 1990s, however, highlanders did not, by and large, see themselves as Indigenous but rather still held onto the 1950s euphemism for Indian, "*campesino*" (peasant). Urban people also generally avoided an identity label, even if they had rural Aymara or Quechua roots. When I first went to Bolivia in the late 1980s, I was surprised that people who were "obviously" Indigenous in my eyes were rather taken aback at the suggestion that they would be considered as such. As I was forcefully told, "Indigenous people live in the jungle." Within a decade, however, this had begun to change—and not only in Bolivia—as there was a veritable explosion of groups in the world identifying as Indigenous. The 1990 march was also significant because it resulted in huge international pressure on the Bolivian government to recognize Isiboro Sécure National Park as the first Indigenous territory in the country.[44] And this is critical: it was the transnational connections made by Indigenous people that made that march effective.

This combination of mobilization around local issues, NGO involvement, and international media recognition proved to be a potent recipe for success, and it was by no means only in Bolivia that such an alliance of interests produced results. Aside from the Zapatista rebellion mentioned above, in Brazil some Afro-Brazilian groups developed new Indigenous identities;[45] in Africa, marginal and threatened groups such as San in Botswana,[46] Maasai in East Africa,[47] and Ogoni in Nigeria[48] positioned themselves as Indigenous people with concomitant discourses in their struggle for land and other rights;[49] and in Asia, a number of subaltern people successfully argued for their rights as Indigenous peoples[50] and, in some cases, even set up their own individual autonomous regions.[51]

Conclusions

The condition of Indigeneity points to an enduring paradox: the very concept as well as its practice is inherently transnational even as it is rooted in very local custom and culture. As we have seen, very local Indigenous identities do not travel well across nations, and Indigenous people who migrate across international borders find that their Indigenous identities may have little meaning in their new homes, where they are often ascribed a national identity that is very often denied them in their country of birth. This is not to say that there are not transnational flows of people and ideas—of course there are—but, rather, that it is challenging to maintain an Indigenous identity when removed from its source of origin. In fact, even within nation-states, Indigenous people have difficulty maintaining and asserting their identities when they move to cities, as they are then deemed "inauthentic" and "unrooted."[52] These issues are intensified when Indigenous people leave their country of birth and engage in transnational migration.

Indigenous identities are, however, profoundly transnational in another way. The very concept of Indigeneity is rooted in European history, which imagined a new, post-Westphalian state in the context of colonial discovery and expansion. The European idea of the "wild man"[53] was developed and exported to the New World and projected onto a complex and diverse group of populations who hitherto had nothing in common. It is that transnational moment of conquest that creates Indigenous identities for people who were hitherto known to themselves and others as Inca and Maya, Lakota and Uru, with absolutely no sense of sharing any common identity. Although Indigenous peoples were first imagined and invented in the Americas, the concept was also applied to other parts of the world such as Australia.

In the late twentieth century there was a renewed interest in Indigenous peoples as the United Nations, the International Labour Organization, and multilateral agencies such as the World Bank took an interest in populations around the world that seemed to be particularly marginalized. Indigeneity was transformed in these international forums, going substantially beyond the understanding rooted in European colonization that had hitherto been prevalent, and expanded to include a range of marginalized populations. In this way, the numbers of recognized Indigenous people grew significantly: whereas the majority of Indigenous peoples up to the twentieth century were considered to reside in the Americas, by the twenty-first century, a clear majority of recognized Indigenous people were seen by agencies such as the World Bank to live in Asia.

The United Nations, a transnational organization par excellence, has initiated a number of efforts, declarations, conventions, and forums directly concerned with Indigenous peoples: the UN Declaration on the Rights of Indigenous Peoples (UNDRIP) in 2007, the Indigenous and Tribal Peoples Convention in 1991, the UN Permanent Forum on Indigenous Issues (UNPFII), the Expert Mechanism on the Rights of Indigenous Peoples (EMRIP), and the UN Special Rapporteur on the Rights of Indigenous Peoples (UNSR).

The UNPFII has had a particular role in fostering Indigenous identities by inviting Indigenous groups from around the world and creating a global sense of Indigeneity that had hitherto never existed.[54] Empowered and emboldened, Indigenous activists are returning to their countries of birth and their communities and using these connections with international forums to argue for improved conditions and to defend their territories and rights. This circulation of ideas is what Margaret Keck and Kathryn Sikkink have described as the "boomerang effect," which, when applied to Indigenous people, describes a powerful tool whereby local groups can access international agencies to bring pressure to bear on their nation-state's government.[55] This is as true when Indigenous people mobilize on a march in Bolivia as when they oppose a pipeline in Standing Rock, North Dakota. It is not simply that Indigenous issues play out on a world stage because of modern forms of communication and media; Indigenous issues play out on a world stage because they always did, from the very moment Europeans invented the concept when they developed their modern states and began colonial expansion. Indigeneity is thus profoundly transnational.

Notes

1. See, for example, Andrew Canessa, *Intimate Indigeneities: Race, Sex, and History in the Small Spaces of Andean Life* (Duke University Press, 2012).

2. Robert Albro, "The Indigenous in the Plural in Bolivian Oppositional Politics," *Bulletin of Latin American Research* 24, no. 4 (October 2005): 433–53; Andrew Canessa, "Conflict, Claim and Contradiction in the New 'Indigenous' State of Bolivia," *Critique of Anthropology* 34, no. 2 (2014): 151–71; and Nancy Postero, *The Indigenous State: Race, Politics, and Performance in Plurinational Bolivia* (University of California Press, 2017).

3. Shelton H. Davis, "Migration, Remittances, and Ethnic Identity: The Experience of Guatemalan Maya in the United States," in *Moving Out of Poverty*, vol. 1, *Cross-Disciplinary Perspectives on Mobility*, ed. Deepa Narayan and Patti Petesch (World Bank; Basingstoke, Hants., England: Palgrave Macmillan, 2007), 333–54; and Patricia Foxen, *In Search of Providence: Transnational Mayan Identities* (Vanderbilt University Press, 2008).

4. Foxen, *In Search of Providence*.

5. Adriana Cruz-Manjarrez, *Zapotecs on the Move: Cultural, Social, and Political Processes in Transnational Perspective* (New Brunswick, NJ: Rutgers University Press, 2013).

6. Aiko Ikemura Amaral, "Making Money and Ends Meet: Racialization, Work, and Gender Among Bolivian Market Vendors," in *Urban Indigeneities: Being Indigenous in the 21st Century*, ed. Dana Brablec and Andrew Canessa (University of Arizona Press, 2023), 93–118.

7. Virginia Q. Tilley, *Seeing Indians: A Study of Race, Nation, and Power in El Salvador* (University of New Mexico Press, 2005).

8. Quentin Skinner, *Reason and Rhetoric in the Philosophy of Hobbes* (Cambridge University Press, 1996); James Tully, *An Approach to Political Philosophy: Locke in Contexts* (Cambridge University Press, 1993); and James Tully, *Strange Multiplicity: Constitutionalism in an Age of Diversity* (Cambridge University Press, 1995).

9. James C. Scott, *The Art of Not Being Governed: An Anarchist History of Upland Southeast Asia* (New Haven, CT: Yale University Press, 2009).

10. Quoted in Scott, *The Art of Not Being Governed*, 29.

11. Scott, *The Art of Not Being Governed*, 30.

12. Pierre Clastres, *Society Against the State: Essays in Political Anthropology*, trans. Robert Hurley and Abe Stein (Zone Books, 1987).

13. Fredrik Barth, ed., *Ethnic Groups and Boundaries: The Social Organization of Culture Difference* (Universitetsforlaget, 1969).

14. Scott, *The Art of Not Being Governed*.

15. Anna Lowenhaupt Tsing, *In the Realm of the Diamond Queen: Marginality in an Out-of-the-Way Place* (Princeton University Press, 1993), 26.

16. Karena Shaw, *Indigeneity and Political Theory: Sovereignty and the Limits of the Political* (Abingdon, Oxon., England: Routledge, 2008), 38.

17. For a fuller treatment of these themes, see Andrew Canessa and Manuela Lavinas Picq, *Savages and Citizens: How Indigeneity Shapes the State* (University of Arizona Press, 2024).

18. Walter D. Mignolo, *The Idea of Latin America* (Blackwell, 2005); and Aníbal Quijano, *Modernidad, identidad y utopía en América latina* (Editorial El Conejo, 1990).

19. Postero, *The Indigenous State*.

20. Andrew Canessa, "Indigenous Conflict in Bolivia Explored Through an African Lens: Towards a Comparative Analysis of Indigeneity," *Comparative Studies in Society and History* 60, no. 2 (April 2018): 308–37.

21. The full text reads: "Indigenous communities, peoples and nations are those which, having a historical continuity with pre-invasion and pre-colonial societies that developed on their territories, consider themselves distinct from other sectors of the societies now prevailing in those territories, or parts of them. They form at present non-dominant sectors of society and are determined to preserve, develop and transmit to future generations their ancestral territories, and their ethnic identity, as the basis of their continued existence as peoples, in accordance with their own cultural patterns, social institutions and legal systems." José Martínez Cobo, *The Study of the Problem of Discrimination Against Indigenous Populations*, vols. 1–5, United Nations publication E/CN.4/Sub.2/1986/7 (United Nations, 1986), para. 379.

22. Simone Cecchini, Raúl Holz, and Humberto Soto de la Rosa, eds., *A Toolkit for Promoting Equality: The Contribution of Social Policies in Latin America and the Caribbean*, United Nations publication LC/TS.2021/55 (UN Economic Commission for Latin America and the Caribbean, 2021), 3; and Sidsel Saugestad, *The Inconvenient Indigenous: Remote Area Development in Botswana, Donor Assistance, and the First People of the Kalahari* (Uppsala, Sweden: Nordic Africa Institute, 2001).

23. Justin Kenrick and Jerome Lewis, "Indigenous Peoples' Rights and the Politics of the Term 'Indigenous,'" *Anthropology Today* 20, no. 2 (April 2004): 4–9.

24. International Labour Organization, Indigenous and Tribal Peoples Convention, no. 169 (1989), Article 1.

25. "Implementation of Operational Directive 4.20 on Indigenous Peoples: An Independent Desk Review," World Bank, Washington, DC, January 10, 2003, http://documents.worldbank.org/curated/en/570331468761746572/Implementation-of-Operational-Directive-4-20-on-Indigenous-Peoples-an-independent-desk-review.

26. Cecchini, Holz, and Soto de la Rosa, *A Toolkit for Promoting Equality*; Kenrick and Lewis, "Indigenous Peoples' Rights"; and Ronald Niezen, *The Origins of Indigenism: Human Rights and the Politics of Identity* (University of California Press, 2003).

27. Indeed, it is striking how many Indigenous peoples in the Americas refer to themselves as "people."

28. Michael Hathaway, "The Emergence of Indigeneity: Public Intellectuals and an Indigenous Space in Southwest China," *Cultural Anthropology* 25, no. 2 (May 2010): 301–33.

29. Hathaway, "The Emergence of Indigeneity," 302.

30. Maria Sapignoli, "'Bushmen' in the Law: Evidence and Identity in Botswana's High Court," *Political and Legal Anthropology Review* 40, no. 2 (November 2017): 210–25.

31. Alcida Ramos gives the example of the Portuguese-speaking Pataxó of northeastern Brazil, who have been learning the language of their distant relatives, the Maxakali of Minas Gerais in central Brazil. No longer speaking a Native language, they have concluded that when their Indigenous identity is better secured, they will be able to argue and negotiate more effectively with the Brazilian government and other agencies. Alcida Rita Ramos, "The Hyperreal Indian," *Critique of Anthropology* 14, no. 2 (1994): 153–71.

32. Kay B. Warren and Jean E. Jackson, eds., *Indigenous Movements, Self-Representation, and the State in Latin America* (University of Texas Press, 2002).

33. Saugestad, *The Inconvenient Indigenous*, 43. These criteria would seem to have a broad appeal, but they throw up important anomalies. I will be dealing with the one of self-ascription below, but if we consider that the majority of Bolivia's population is Indigenous and the government is led by a party a majority of whose deputies (if no longer the leader) identify as Indigenous, then the question of who, if anyone, is Indigenous in Bolivia gets thrown into even greater confusion.

34. Hathaway, "The Emergence of Indigeneity."

35. Sapignoli, "'Bushmen' in the Law."

36. See, for example, Peter Geschiere, *The Perils of Belonging: Autochthony, Citizenship, and Exclusion in Africa and Europe* (University of Chicago Press, 2009); Dorothy L. Hodgson, *Being Maasai, Becoming Indigenous: Postcolonial Politics in a Neoliberal World* (Indiana University Press, 2011); Kenrick and Lewis, "Indigenous Peoples' Rights"; and Michaela Pelican, "Complexities of Indigeneity and Autochthony: An African Example," *American Ethnologist* 36, no. 1 (February 2009): 52–65.

37. Xavier Albó, "El retorno del indio," *Revista Andina* 9, no. 2 (1991): 299–345; Alison Brysk, *From Tribal Village to Global Village: Indian Rights and International Relations in Latin America* (Stanford University Press, 2000); Rodolfo Stavenhagen, "Indigenous Peoples and the State in Latin America: An Ongoing Debate," in *Multiculturalism in Latin America: Indigenous Rights, Diversity and Democracy*, ed. Rachel Sieder (Basingstoke, Hants., England: Palgrave Macmillan, 2002), 24–44; and Donna Lee Van Cott, ed., *Indigenous Peoples and Democracy in Latin America* (Basingstoke, Hants., England: Palgrave Macmillan, 1994).

38. Canessa and Picq, *Savages and Citizens*.

39. Albro, "The Indigenous in the Plural."

40. Amy Goodman, "Evo Morales: 'Los pueblos indígenas son la reserva moral de la human-idad,'" Rebelión, October 4, 2007, https://rebelion.org/evo-morales-los-pueblos-indigenas-son-la-reserva-moral-de-la-humanidad/.

41. For example, see Xavier Albó, "Making the Leap from Local Mobilization to National Politics," NACLA Report on the Americas 29, no. 5 (March–April 1996): 15–20.

42. Erick Langer and Elena Muñoz, eds., Contemporary Indigenous Movements in Latin America (Scholarly Resources, 2003).

43. Xavier Albó, "And from Kataristas to MNRistas? The Surprising and Bold Alliance Between Aymaras and Neoliberals in Bolivia," in Indigenous Peoples and Democracy in Latin America, ed. Donna Lee Van Cott (Basingstoke, Hants., England: Palgrave Macmillan, 1994), 55–81.

44. The march gained rapid international attention and was reported even in European regional newspapers.

45. Jan Hoffman French, Legalizing Identities: Becoming Black or Indian in Brazil's Northeast (University of North Carolina Press, 2009).

46. Francis B. Nyamnjoh, "'Ever-Diminishing Circles': The Paradoxes of Belonging in Botswana," in Indigenous Experience Today, ed. Marisol de la Cadena and Orin Starn (Berg, 2007), 305–32.

47. Hodgson, Being Maasai, Becoming Indigenous.

48. Michael J. Watts, "Antinomies of Community: Some Thoughts on Geography, Resources and Empire," Transactions of the Institute of British Geographers, n.s. 29, no. 2 (June 2004): 195–216.

49. See also Stephanie Rupp, Forests of Belonging: Identities, Ethnicities, and Stereotypes in the Congo River Basin (University of Washington Press, 2011).

50. B. G. Karlsson, Contested Belonging: An Indigenous People's Struggle for Forest and Identity in Sub-Himalayan Bengal (Abingdon, Oxon., England: Routledge, 2000).

51. Alpa Shah, In the Shadows of the State: Indigenous Politics, Environmentalism, and Insurgency in Jharkhand, India (Duke University Press, 2010).

52. Dana Brablec and Andrew Canessa, eds., Urban Indigeneities: Being Indigenous in the 21st Century (University of Arizona Press, 2023).

53. Anthony Pagden, The Fall of Natural Man: The American Indian and the Origins of Comparative Ethnology (Cambridge University Press, 1982).

54. Sylvia Escárcega, "Authenticating Strategic Essentialisms: The Politics of Indigenousness at the United Nations," Cultural Dynamics 22, no. 1 (March 2010): 3–28; and Marjo Lindroth, "Indigenous-State Relations in the UN: Establishing the Indigenous Forum," Polar Record 42, no. 3 (July 2006): 239–48.

55. Margaret E. Keck and Kathryn Sikkink, Activists Beyond Borders: Advocacy Networks in International Politics (Cornell University Press, 1998).

CHAPTER 5

Transnationalism and the History of the Social Sciences in Brazil

Race and Economic Development in the Sociology of
Donald Pierson and T. Lynn Smith

THIAGO DA COSTA LOPES AND MARCOS CHOR MAIO

AS THE SOCIAL SCIENCES became institutionalized in Brazilian universities in the 1930s and 1940s, they were heavily influenced by so-called foreign missions and the arrival of academics from Europe and the United States to teach the new courses.[1] The articulation between local actors, institutions, and agendas on the one hand and multilateral agencies and international forums on the other was also an important ingredient during this initial phase. The aim was to consolidate a professional and scientific status for the new disciplines through the routinization of empirical research.[2] In studying these transnational flows of people and ideas across borders, the literature has examined the logic through which Brazilian social scientists absorbed foreign patterns of intellectual work, highlighting the specificities of local traditions of thought and, simultaneously, problematizing the earlier diffusionist view—the idea that the standard of the work produced by European and US academics spread naturally due to their intrinsic epistemic value and represented a cognitive leap forward for the social sciences in the country.[3]

Early Brazilian sociological production has also been explored through broader cartographies, no longer centered exclusively on national frameworks, in studies that underline the similarities and connections with ideas and actors located in Latin America and, more generally, in peripheral regions of the world.[4] Reflecting the global and transnational turns in intellectual history and the history of science, the interest in thinking about transborder circulation as a constitutive dimension of the social sciences in Brazil has led researchers to reexamine the meanings usually attributed to the flows between the Global North and South.[5] In this case, it becomes relevant to understand not only how foreign academics influenced the development of these disciplines in Brazil but also the marks that the latter context left on them, without losing sight of the frequently asymmetrical nature of these intellectual exchanges and the specific historical circumstances in which they transpired.

Looking to contribute to this debate, the present chapter analyses the ways in which the trajectories and academic production of the American sociologists Donald Pierson and T. Lynn Smith were associated with the Brazilian intellectual world during the Good Neighbor era of the 1930s–1940s. In particular, we reflect on the dialogues that these two scholars had with local authors working in the area of social thought concerning problems linked to race relations, community development, and the transformations undergone by Brazilian society in a context of growing urbanization and industrialization. As we argue, the works of Pierson and Smith, influential in the Brazilian context during a period when the social sciences were first taking shape in a developing academic environment, emerged from the intersection of diverse intellectual traditions. Examining the forms of sociological knowledge they produced about Brazil in the specific historical contexts in which their ideas emerged allows us to highlight the traces left by their circulation between North and South America.

Among the foreigners who were involved in the construction of an academic and scientific space for the social sciences in Brazil, the name of the US scholar Donald Pierson has a special prominence. His first contact with the country dates back to the mid-1930s when, as part of an ample comparative studies project coordinated by sociologist Robert Park on interethnic relations in various parts of the planet, Pierson carried out research in Salvador, Bahia, collecting the empirical material that would serve as the basis for his doctoral thesis. This work was completed at the University of Chicago in 1939 and published a few years later under the title *Negroes in Brazil: A Study of Race Contact at Bahia.*[6] In 1939, amid the first timid initiatives of the Franklin Roosevelt administration in the area of scientific, intellectual, and artistic exchanges and cooperation with Latin America (what were called "cultural relations" in the diplomatic circles of the time), Pierson would return to Brazil, this time settling in São Paulo as a professor of sociology and social anthropology at the Free School of Sociology and Politics (Escola Livre de Sociologia e Política, ELSP).[7]

During his stay in the country, which lasted until the beginning of the 1950s, Pierson developed a series of activities the general direction of which he himself would encapsulate in a motto he used in his correspondence with students and colleagues: "For the establishment of the social disciplines as sciences."[8] Supported by the belief in the unequaled epistemic development of the social sciences in the United States, Pierson, in a process not without its setbacks and tensions, sought to take advantage of the favorable setting for exchanges with Latin America, fostered by the Good Neighbor policy, to advance his project for consolidating "scientific sociology" in Brazil through systematic empirical investigation and the professional training of higher-education researchers.[9] As well as helping set up the Department of Sociology and Social Anthropology at ELSP, which he headed in its early years, organizing a Research Methods and Techniques seminar, in 1941 the sociologist founded, along with the anthropologists Herbert Baldus and Emílio Willems, the first postgraduate course in social sciences in the country. Pierson was a member of the editorial board of the journal Sociologia, one of the first scientific periodicals in the area, while also being involved in organizing collections and translating books into Portuguese. Liaising with US agencies like the Rockefeller Foundation, he negotiated scholarships for Brazilians to study at universities in the United States. His interest in training students was also visible in the collective research projects he coordinated after settling in Brazil. In the early 1940s, he conducted surveys on eating habits and housing in São Paulo city and, in the second half of the decade, surveys in cities in the interior of the state, selecting the municipality of Araçariguama for a community study. A decisive factor for the funding of Pierson's work in Brazil was his affiliation, from 1945, with the Brazilian section of the Institute of Social Anthropology (ISA) at the Smithsonian Institution. Amid Washington's diplomatic efforts to boost ties with Latin America, the institute launched an academic cooperation program with countries in the region, aiming to promote teaching and research in the social sciences, inspired by the initiatives developed by Pierson in São Paulo. Also under the auspices of the ISA, in the 1950s Pierson directed an ambitious series of studies in rural locations in the São Francisco River Valley with the aim of examining the sociocultural transformations under way in the region in the wake of urbanization, industrialization, and economic development programs.[10] The gradual deterioration of Pierson's health after he contracted a viral disease during fieldwork precipitated his return to the United States in the middle of the decade.

Although he never took up residence in Brazil like Pierson, T. Lynn Smith not only conducted studies in the country but also sought to build a network of interlocutors and potential practitioners of rural sociology, an area to which his name was linked in the United States. A graduate of the University of Minnesota, where he had been a student of Pitirim Sorokin and Carle Zimmerman, Smith, who became a professor at Louisiana State University, belonged to the generation committed to imbuing rural sociology with its own cognitive identity. This seemed to be an urgent task in the face of the Mertonian expectations of the mainstream groups of professional sociologists in the United States, who were eager to establish the discipline as a purely scientific endeavor, setting it apart from any practical or reformist undertaking.[11] In the 1930s, like rural sociologists in general, Smith became involved in experiments in planning and social reform for rural populations under Roosevelt's New Deal, which gave impetus to research in the area despite the severe economic depression.[12] Although Smith sought to delimit the scope of rural sociology in accordance with the scientific aspirations then dominant in the US academic world—defining it as an eminently theoretical discipline, an effort visible in his The Sociology of Rural Life (1940), in which he adheres closely to canonical methodological conceptions and approaches, such as those of the Chicago sociological tradition—the substantive contents of his sociological analysis were marked by an undeniably applied and normative flavor congruent with the tendencies exhibited by the discipline in the United States.[13] In this case, unlike Pierson, concerned at the same time with affirming the strictly academic nature of his research in Brazil and the scientific status of the sociology he represented, striving to insulate it from political values and immediate utilitarian interests, Smith displayed no reservations about associating his Brazilian studies with technical advisory activities, especially in the context of intergovernment cooperation.[14]

Smith's first visit to Brazil, made in late 1939 a few months after Pierson's arrival in São Paulo, was part of a reconnaissance trip to South American countries, reflecting Louisiana State University's interest in implementing inter-American agreements in the area of academic exchange. Carried out with resources from the Julius Rosenwald Fund, well known for financing research and educational programs targeted at the Black population of the US South, the trip convinced Smith that the stratifying logic imposed by the plantation system, responsible for producing rigid hierarchies and extending to various regions of the Americas, helped explain the low levels and standards of life, as well as the lack of cohesion and civic participation of their rural communities.[15] Although his work was not centered on the study of interethnic dynamics, focusing particularly on what he called "man's relation to the land," the racial dimension of social processes was not absent from his studies, as we will see. In the mid-1930s, Smith's interest in examining the social effects of the plantation system on the Black population of the Deep South, who constituted a significant portion of the region's farm tenants and landless farmworkers, led him to develop close ties with Robert Park, who subsequently took up a post at Fisk University in Nashville to continue his research on race relations, making frequent visits to the rural sociologist in Louisiana. During this period, the contact with Park stimulated Smith's academic interest in comparative studies involving Brazil.[16]

However, Smith's investment in the Brazilian rural world as an object of study was only cemented with the development of the Good Neighbor policy, especially from 1942 with the US war effort, when the sociologist worked as an agricultural analyst linked to the US embassy in Rio de Janeiro. After staying for about a year in Brazil, making trips to various states, Smith published his monumental *Brazil: People and Institutions* (1946), a work that he would seek to complement and update on various shorter visits to the country over the following decades. The Brazilian experience, combined with official missions in Colombia, consolidated the sociologist's reputation as an expert on Latin America. At the end of the Second World War, Smith participated in structuring area studies of the region, initially at Vanderbilt University, where he was one of the founders of the Institute for Brazilian Studies, and subsequently at the University of Florida, where he would remain until the end of his career. In the 1950s, amid the US international aid policy embodied in President Harry Truman's Point Four Program, his trips to Brazil were marked by the defense of agrarian reform based on the family farm model, the sociologist having participated in 1952, at the request of the Getúlio Vargas government, in the work of the National Agrarian Policy Commission.

Juxtaposing these two sociologists, who, despite coming from the same US academic context, ended up establishing distinct professional ties with Brazil, allows us to consider the US presence in the country's social sciences in a more nuanced form, showing that it did not constitute a homogeneous block in terms of intellectual and scientific interests and projects. With this approach, we can shed light on part of the specific and complex circuits through which the United States, at the end of the war, gradually emerged as the hegemonic force in the social sciences practiced in the Americas, in a process not without its tensions, difficulties, failures, and, no less importantly, adaptations and exchanges with other actors on the continent. For the purposes of this analysis, we are primarily interested in showing how the work of Pierson and Smith in the Brazilian intellectual context, especially in the world of the social sciences then under construction, did not represent a one-way flow of ideas from the Global North to the South but was also shaped by debates on the country among the local intelligentsia. As much as the US sociologists' evaluation of the development of sociology in Brazil assumed the notion of backwardness relative to what was believed to be the progress shown in their own country in terms of research techniques and methods—a salient view in the work of Pierson, who classified a considerable portion of the sociological work produced in the country as prescientific—the substantive visions that they developed about Brazilian society were to a large degree based on interpretations by local authors.

These inter-American dialogues become particularly visible when we consider the early research conducted by the two US sociologists about race relations (Pierson) and the structuring and functioning of rural communities (Smith) in the context of the Good Neighbor policy. Even if their immediate objects of inquiry were different, both analyses were marked by underlying views regarding the modernizing changes that were taking place in Brazil. In other words, both worked with a dynamic framework, seeking not only to uncover the historical roots of the social processes being observed in the present but also to anticipate how these would unfold over time. By turning to Brazilian history to make its society intelligible, Pierson and Smith eventually engaged in decisive dialogues with prestigious writers known for their efforts to identify and decode Brazil's cultural specificities vis-à-vis other nations.

Until at least the first half of the 1940s, both Pierson and Smith embraced an optimistic diagnosis of Brazil's entry into modernity, relying largely on authors such as Francisco José de Oliveira Vianna and Gilberto Freyre, who had a strong influence on the Brazilian context of the 1930s. Each in his own way, Pierson and Smith believed that the country would find its own path during this process of change, its particular sociocultural traditions allowing it to avoid the negative effects of capitalist development in the United States, like the exacerbated racial conflicts and individualism that dissolved community ties—phenomena that had emerged as the other side of the technical progress and material abundance of the North American nation. Even if they did not altogether abandon an evolutionist conception of the historical process and tended to see different aspects of Brazilian society as symptoms of its backwardness—a previous stage of development in the history of the Western, industrialized world represented by the United States—Pierson and Smith sought to emphasize Brazil's specificities while examining the country's development toward modernity. As we argue in the following pages, while the intellectual atmosphere of the New Deal and the Good Neighbor policy helped foster positive perspectives on Latin American social and historical experiences among US intellectuals, reformers, and social scientists, equally important for Pierson's and Smith's assessments of social change was their involvement with debates around nation-building promoted by Brazilian intellectuals.

Donald Pierson's study of Black and white relations in Salvador, Bahia, was part of the efforts of the group gathered around Robert Park, his supervisor, and the seminar on race and cultural contacts at the University of Chicago to develop a comparative sociology of the various patterns of interethnic interaction that had crystallized in the world following European colonization.[17] Chicago sociologists' keen interest in Brazil as an object of study was fueled by the long-held shared imagination between the two countries regarding the striking differences between their respective racial situations.[18] As registered in a note published in the University of Chicago's *Bulletin of the Society for Social Research* announcing Pierson's trip to South America, "the fact that the former slave class [in Brazil] has achieved relatively complete economic, social and political equality with the former master class is a notable point of contrast."[19]

The favorable view of the Brazilian racial experience by Americans was fueled by the intellectual atmosphere of the New Deal and the Good Neighbor policy, marked by attitudes of benevolence and growing interest in Latin America. At a time when reformers and progressive intellectuals, in the wake of the 1929 economic crisis, were reflecting critically on the direction of capitalist development in their own country, Latin America tended to be valued as a source of original societal experiences and a locus of traditional forms of sociability not yet completely disturbed by the forces of modernity. In its historical evolution, the region could offer alternative routes to progress, eventually counterbalancing the harmful effects of urban-industrial civilization to social life, the epitome of which were the US metropolises.[20]

The idea that Salvador, Bahia, was part of a traditional society constitutes an important premise of Pierson's analysis. In his assessment, the preponderance of personal and family relationships and face-to-face interaction had contributed to the construction of a social order less prone to racialized forms of conflict when compared to the United States. In an environment relatively untouched by the fierce economic struggles and anonymity typical of the modern city, the Brazilian patriarchal tradition had paved the way for a form of social stratification favorable to the rise of Blacks and mixed-race people and their incorporation into the broader community. Following the typology suggested by Park, who was primarily interested in the problem of social mobility of the Black population in the United States, Pierson identified Bahia with a multiracial class society, distinct both from the Indian caste structure, with rigidly closed strata, and from the US South, where a Black minority, although rising economically, was not accepted equally by the white community, forming a separate middle class.[21] By stating that the social classes in Bahia were porous, and that it was only a matter of time before a larger contingent of Blacks would climb to the upper echelons, Pierson had in mind the trajectory of mulattos who assumed positions of prestige among whites, compensating for the stigma of their color with socially valued attributes and skills. As they gained social recognition, these individuals contributed to gradually undermining the negative attitudes toward their phenotypic traits, a kind of prejudice that Pierson saw as residues of the old caste-based, slave-owning society, destined to disappear.[22]

Critics of Pierson's work have particularly questioned his hypothesis that prejudice directed at the Black population was more class based than race based, since it was associated with the subordinate social status in which most of these individuals still found themselves. Throughout his fieldwork, Pierson came across an intricate and ambiguous ethnographic context that led him to hesitate as to the nature of the discrimination suffered by these groups, as indicated in his research reports.[23] Instead of a racial paradise, the sociologist recorded the framework of inequalities that persisted in the post-abolition period in Brazil, as well as various situations of conflict in everyday life in which an individual's race or color came to the fore as a salient element of dispute.[24]

Faced with an empirical universe that was admittedly contradictory and lacking in information, Pierson had to rely on interpretations of the formation of Brazilian society produced by writers who at the time enjoyed recognized intellectual authority in the country, among whom Gilberto Freyre stood out. Although not deserving, in the eyes of Pierson, the credentials of a professional sociologist, Freyre, alongside Park, offered the US sociologist guidance in his effort to decode Bahia's interethnic arrangement. Pierson's optimistic thesis about the gradual dismantling of racial barriers and the emergence of a system of free competition in Brazil was shaped by intellectual perspectives with strong affinities, despite being rooted in different national contexts. On one hand, it drew from Park's analytical framework for studying interracial dynamics in the United States, which aligned with Booker T. Washington's gradualist political vision and critique of the Reconstruction era. On the other, it resonated with Freyre's idea that the patriarchal family played a positive role in fostering a relatively cohesive society in Brazil from the colonial period onward, despite the acute forms of stratification produced by the plantation and the ethnic heterogeneity of its constituent elements.

Not only Freyre but other well-known authors of Brazilian intellectual traditions, notably Oliveira Vianna, had highlighted the preponderant role of the patriarchal family in the country's history as compared to other institutions, such as the state and the Church, pointing to its influence on the particularistic forms of conduct that were crystallized in Brazilian mores.[25] Pierson drew on this interpretative tradition by stating that the personalized nature of social relations, still largely observed in Salvador, prevented individuals from being evaluated exclusively based on external markers such as skin color. Because of intimate knowledge derived from kinship and *compadrio* relations, Blacks and whites were considered more than merely members of abstract categories such as "race."[26]

It is Freyre's work, nevertheless, that was central to Pierson's interpretation.[27] Appropriating Freyre, who points to the miscegenation that occurred within the patriarchal family as a factor of "social democratization," Pierson argued that face-to-face contacts within the Brazilian mansion house had fostered the creation of moral and blood bonds that crossed color lines, paving the way for the slow integration of Blacks and mulattos into the upper strata through kinship relations that united masters and their illegitimate enslaved descendants.[28] Particularly relevant to Pierson's argument are Freyre's observations, developed in *Sobrados e mucambos* (1936) (The Mansions and the Shanties), about the insertion of mulattos into the liberal professions in the second half of the nineteenth century, amid the growth of cities and the disintegration of the slave regime, a process of vertical mobility favored by the patriarchal logic of the social protection of the mansion house.[29] This model of ascension, which relied on seeking the approval of white people rather than producing adverse attitudes, led Pierson to assert that abolition, in the Brazilian context, represented the culmination of a slow and gradual process of social integration of the Black population. This experience contrasted, in turn, with the US experience, marked by the racialization of conflict and the institution of segregationist laws in the South after Reconstruction.

Far from reflecting only Freyre's perspective on the socially constructive role of patriarchalism—the author's family origin was linked to the old aristocratic classes of the sugar plantation area of Pernambuco, in the northeastern part of Brazil—Pierson's praise of tradition and gradualism as a path to racial integration was reinforced by Park's sociological diagnosis of the US context. This view dates to the political work that Park carried out at the beginning of his career, while still a journalist, with the Black leader Booker T. Washington. Washington's well-known criticism of the abruptness of the change in the legal status of the Black population after the Civil War and his commitment to the gradual incorporation of this population into the world of citizenship through technical and professional education found support in the sociological work of Park and his students in Chicago.[30] According to the sociologist, the armed conflict and the sudden change in the social position of Blacks during the Reconstruction era had implied a rupture with the "moral order" that masters and slaves had been building on the plantation through close and regular contacts. Like Freyre, Park evaluated these close relations positively, seeing them as capable of producing social unity and avoiding racialized forms of conflict. In the old South, however, this "traditional etiquette of race relations" had been swept away by abolition, paving the way for the racialization of conflict, which tended to be exacerbated as the forces of urbanization and industrialization brought with them the anonymity of large cities and the intensification of economic competition.[31]

Precisely because it managed to preserve the integrationist legacy of patriarchalism, gradually modifying its caste structure without abrupt ruptures with the past, Bahian society was in a better position, in Pierson's assessment, to achieve the modern liberal ideal of equal opportunities. It was progressively moving toward a meritocratic social order whose forms of stratification, instead of reflecting the racial origins of its members, would be the result of the effort and skill of individuals in free competition.

The willingness to see Brazilian traditions as the basis for a path toward modernity was also evident in T. Lynn Smith's early works on the country, written during the Second World War and the intensification of US efforts to build a broad range of inter-American alliances against Axis influences on the continent. During 1942 and 1943, while serving at the US embassy in Rio de Janeiro as an agricultural analyst, Smith traveled through different states and municipalities in the vast Brazilian hinterland, collecting demographic and economic data from government agencies and recording his field observations in a travel diary. Similarly significant, he began reading authors of Brazilian social thought whose ideas helped the sociologist organize and comprehend the mass of information that he had gathered in a short space of time. In reports to the US government and in academic articles, Smith drew on the history of the country's settlement to give meaning to the social landscape he observed in the present, especially drawing attention to Oliveira Vianna's theses on the shaping power of the large rural domains over the structure of Brazilian society, paradigmatically expressed in *Populações meridionais do Brasil* (1918). He also relied on authors such as Freyre to present an optimistic perspective on the process of formation of Brazilian rural communities, highlighting the country's tradition of interethnic integration as an element that, unlike what was observed in the United States, favored the formation of bonds of solidarity among local groups.

Given the explanatory value that Oliveira Vianna attributed to the "rural origins" of Brazilian society to elucidate its main features, it is not surprising that the author played a central role in Smith's analyses, linked to the tradition of US rural sociology. Revealing an affinity with Oliveira Vianna's focus on the links between land structure and societal dynamics, rural sociologists in the United States prioritized the study of "man's relations to the land" to understand the forms of human grouping, asking themselves about the effects of the types of land tenure, division, and settlement on the patterns of social interaction and the associative capacity, or communitarian potential, of individuals and families in rural areas.

From Oliveira Vianna's work, Smith retained the idea that the colonization of Brazilian territory through large landed estates (latifundio) represented a break with the Portuguese tradition of small properties, which ended up being decisive in the way Brazilian culture and society were structured.[32] Large-scale farming was at the origin of the routine and primitive way in which agriculture was practiced, with excessive use of labor to the detriment of investment in technology.[33] The agricultural practices of the Portuguese peasant influenced the habit of burning to prepare land for planting. Combined with the strong stigma regarding manual labor, a legacy of slavery, large estates were at the root of a rudimentary social structure, composed on the one hand of a mass of rural workers, landless and itinerant, and on the other of agricultural elites averse to manual tasks, leaving no room for a middle class of small, progressive farmers.[34] Considering its social effects, especially on the type of rural worker who could be counted on for the war effort, the country's land structure constituted an obstacle to a medium-term increase in agricultural productivity, an issue that became central to the US government's hemispheric defense plans.[35]

Smith's writings in Brazil during this period were not only marked by the immediate concerns of Americans with the war. They also reflect the reformist impetus to think, on a broader, inter-American scale, of alternative societal models to the old laissez-faire liberalism, a search for a less individualistic and atomized society whose political expression, in the United States, was Roosevelt's New Deal. The strengthening of community life was the goal of US rural sociologists to counterbalance what they saw as the deleterious effects of the modernization process, which led on the one hand to the dissolution of traditional social ties and, on the other, to the expansion of the political and administrative structures of the state. Halfway between the individual and the impersonal forces of the market and the state, the community was imagined as an informal network of social protection and mutual aid, as well as a locus for political participation and self-rule within the reach of rural populations.[36] Although they started from the classic definition of Ferdinand Tönnies, who conceived of community in the manner of ideal types, as a pattern of relationships marked by proximity, cooperation, and consensus, rural sociologists tended to reify the concept. Following the example of Charles Galpin, considered one of the founding fathers of the discipline in the United States, they strove to identify the precise limits of the geographic areas in which these forms of interaction were observable, mapping, in the apparently isolated corners of the countryside, the networks of sociability that linked families scattered throughout the land.[37]

According to Smith, the proximity of dwellings, combined with the convergence of interests, beliefs, and values of their residents, gives life to a community. Its embryonic form would be the neighborhood, a group of families living side by side and willing to cooperate with one another. The community itself, however, should cover a larger territorial extension, exhibiting features of relative socioeconomic self-sufficiency.[38] In the United States, its precise boundaries were sometimes difficult to pin down on the map. Artificial administrative divisions, the localist tendency of small towns to seek emancipation at the expense of their connections with the surrounding rural districts (incorporation), the construction of schools in areas that did not coincide with the associative forms existing in any locality, and racial and religious divides among the population were among the factors that made more difficult the emergence of communities with clear contours.[39]

Smith's interest in studying the community would accompany him on his travels to Brazil. In this case, Oliveira Vianna would also be an important interlocutor. According to Smith, the form of settlement centered on the large landed estate had resulted in a dispersed and isolationist distribution of the population throughout the territory, affecting the way in which local groups were formed, marked by weak ties of interfamily solidarity. Oliveira Vianna's thesis on Brazil's lack of social solidarity ties (*insolidarismo*) is what seems to inform Smith's diagnosis of the "amorphous state" of its rural communities.[40] According to his argument, such had been the weight of the great landowner, with his family, servants, and slaves, in the historical process of land occupation, and such was the socioeconomic independence demonstrated by the large landed estate that the emergence of associative ties aimed at common interests remained restricted to these private groups, or "clans," constituting the "only form of social solidarity that [we Brazilians] really *feel*, [. . .] the only one that we really practice."[41]

Smith saw Oliveira Vianna's "clan" as a "neighborhood group," defined as the social unit prior to the community in the scale of development of associative ties. He noted that, in Brazil, these groups were generally formed by families that orbited the domains of a landowner. In accordance with Oliveira Vianna's observations, Smith concluded that such ties absorbed almost all the concerns of individuals. Considering the physical isolation, the narrow social horizon, and the small number of relationships they maintained, limited to the area of their residences, the locality groups did not form communities in the US sociological sense, that is, a *locus* of coordinated action aimed at common ends in which individuals from different neighborhoods participated. In addition to geographic isolation, the self-sufficiency of large estates and a polarized class structure, the predominance of subsistence agriculture among the poor, and the low level of education of the population made it difficult for families and neighborhoods to integrate into broader areas of social interaction.[42]

Making optimistic projections, Smith believed, however, that the lack of social solidarity identified by Oliveira Vianna, far from being chronic, would tend, over time, to give way to forms of association beyond the sphere of family and clan. The development of means of communication and transportation would contribute to connecting farming populations more closely to the small rural centers represented by the seats of each *município*, Brazil's basic political and administrative unit.[43] Likewise, colonization and land redistribution programs centered on the small family farm would help change the rigid class structure derived from the plantation system, a hindering factor in building social ties of a communitarian nature.[44]

According to Smith, these modernizing forces were to be joined by tendencies inscribed in the Brazilian tradition propitious to the formation of integrated communities. In fact, Smith even considered that the country could come to realize, in the future, Galpin's utopia of "rurban communities," that is, areas of strong social cohesion and of well-defined territorial physiognomy, formed by the integration of the dispersed populations of the farms into a single village center toward which the political, religious, social, and commercial functions of the locality would converge. Smith noted that, in contrast to US local political units, Brazilian municípios reflected a more centralized pattern. By force of law, they necessarily encompassed both the towns that served as their seats and the districts and rural areas under their influence. They were thus the ideal unit around which a community could set its boundaries. Families from the surrounding areas also flocked to the municipal seats due to their ties to the dominant Catholicism; there was at least one church in each village. Unlike in the US countryside, where various denominations had established houses of worship, the Brazilian community gained even more cohesion due to the homogeneity of its members' religious beliefs.[45]

Smith also pointed out that the absence of rigid racial divisions reinforced the community potential of rural Brazilian locations: "Within the limits of the same community there are not many places where overlapping neighborhoods of whites and Negroes may be distinguished, as is so generally the case in the southern parts of the United States." Like Pierson, he observed that "class differences [are] closely correlated with color shades," but, since there was no segmentation of neighborhoods along color lines, the racial element did not act, as in the United States, as a complicating factor in the structure of the emerging communities.[46] The sociologist also drew on Freyre's work when tracing the Brazilian pattern of racial relations to the miscegenationist role of the patriarchal family.[47] Despite occasionally noticing that Blacks and whites did not seem to mingle in public gatherings such as the traditional evening strolls in the villages' central plazas, as was the case during his visit to Barretos, a rural locality in São Paulo State, Smith followed the prevailing view among Brazilian intellectuals of the period regarding the integrative traits of its culture.[48] Tradition would help Brazil build strong and cohesive rural communities in the face of the modernizing changes.

In the years of the Good Neighbor policy, Pierson and Smith imagined Brazilian traditions stemming from the country's rural, patriarchal past not simply as archaisms hindering progress but as a source of alternative patterns of social development potentially capable of bypassing some of the shortcomings of US urban-industrial civilization. Grounding a significant part of their work in authors who were widely read in Brazilian intellectual circles of the 1930s, they believed that the country could move away from either racism and racial barriers (Pierson), or communitarian fragmentation and social atomization (Smith), in the process of becoming modern.

Establishing a dialogue mainly with the work of Gilberto Freyre, Pierson saw in the integrating forces set in motion by the patriarchal family a path toward the disintegration—gradual and without acute conflicts—of the old slave-owning caste society. Although he did not deny the existence of forms of prejudice and discrimination directed at the Black population, he saw them as residues destined to disappear with the gradual emergence of a multiracial class society, organized in open layers. More than in the contradictory ethnographic context with which he was confronted, Pierson relied on readings of the Brazilian past consecrated by authors such as Freyre to cast a positive perspective on the changes in progress in Bahia's race relations. This view is reinforced by the way in which the sociologist and his mentors in Chicago positively contrast the abolition process that occurred in Brazil with that observed in the United States, which had created a drastic rupture, in Park's understanding, with the forms of interracial coexistence and the common moral order that were being developed on Southern plantations before Reconstruction. Thus, instead of merely juxtaposing ideas drawn from different national contexts, Pierson's work was constructed based on the affinities that existed between them, of a transnational nature.

This is also how we can understand Smith's early research in Brazil. His dialogue with Brazilian authors, especially Oliveira Vianna, benefited from the convergences that they presented with the tradition of US rural sociology by focusing, at the level of sociological explanation, on the relationships between land structure, patterns of settlement, and societal dynamics. Smith based his diagnosis of the incipient nature of community development in rural Brazil on Oliveira Vianna's well-known theses on the historical role of the large landed estate in the structuring of Brazilian society and the country's insolidarismo. Following in Oliveira Vianna's footsteps, he concluded that the existing forms of social solidarity, of mobilizing groups for activities of common interest, were still largely restricted to the particularist sphere of extended families structured around the farmer, his relatives, and his employees. In the early 1940s, however, Smith was optimistic about the community potential inscribed in Brazilian culture. The development of means of transportation and communication, combined with a land settlement policy centered on small family properties and capable of alleviating the class divisions produced by large estates, could converge with trends that the sociologist identified in the country's traditions, such as the absence of racial divides in the locality groups' structure.

The consideration of inter-American dialogues that preceded Pierson's and Smith's diagnoses on social change in Brazil, and the role that the country's traditions, stemming from its rural and patriarchal past, played in their optimistic projections about the transformations in progress in the country, invite us to reassess the usual narratives about the production of US sociology regarding the themes of modernization and development in the world's peripheries. In the context of the Good Neighbor policy, Latin America was read not only as a region of backwardness and archaisms to be transformed by the modernizing process, as in the dualistic interpretations that became common in the postwar period with modernization theory, but also as a source of original societal experiences that could contribute to a reexamination of the paths followed by capitalist development in the West. Examining the dialogues between Americans like Pierson and Smith and Brazilian authors highlights how intellectual production on social change processes was a transnational undertaking. Although teleological assumptions inform their understanding of history, which is perceived to be moving inexorably toward the development of urban-industrial civilization, the destiny of Brazilian society does not converge, in their analysis, with what was imagined to be the present of the United States. Comparisons, sometimes explicit and sometimes implicit, with the US context, instead of reaffirming the latter as the societal model or paradigm, suggest that the Latin American country would follow a sui generis path in its own modernization process.

Notes

1. Fernanda A. Peixoto, "Franceses e norte-americanos nas ciências sociais brasileiras: 1930–1960," in *História das ciências sociais no Brasil*, vol. 1, ed. Sérgio Miceli (Editora Sumaré; Instituto de Estudos Econômicos, Sociais e Políticos, 1989), 410–60; and Heloisa Pontes, "Brasil com Z: A produção estrangeira sobre o país, editada aqui, sob forma de livro, entre 1930 e 1988," in *História das ciências sociais no Brasil*, vol. 2, ed. Sérgio Miceli (Editora Sumaré; Instituto de Estudos Econômicos, Sociais e Políticos, 1995), 443–77.

2. Marcos Chor Maio, "UNESCO and the Study of Race Relations in Brazil: Regional or National Issue?," *Latin American Research Review* 36, no. 2 (2001): 118–36.

3. Glaucia Villas Bôas, *A recepção da sociologia alemã no Brasil* (Rio de Janeiro: Topbooks, 2006); Marcos Chor Maio and Thiago da Costa Lopes, "'For the Establishment of the Social Disciplines as Sciences': Donald Pierson e as ciências sociais no Rio de Janeiro (1942–1949)," *Sociologia e Antropologia* 5, no. 2 (August 2015): 343–80; and Marcia Consolim, "Circulação de intelectuais e recepção das novas ciências do homem francesas no Brasil: 1908–1932," *Tempo Social* 33, no. 1 (January–April 2021): 17–51.

4. Antonio Brasil Jr., *Passagens para a teoria sociológica: Florestan Fernandes e Gino Germani* (Hucitec Editora, 2013); and João Marcelo Maia, "History of Sociology and the Quest for Intellectual Autonomy in the Global South: The Cases of Alberto Guerreiro Ramos and Syed Hussein Alatas," *Current Sociology* 62, no. 7 (October 2014): 1097–115.

5. Thiago da Costa Lopes, *Em busca da comunidade: Ciências sociais, desenvolvimento rural e diplomacia cultural nas relações Brasil-EUA (1930–1950)* (Rio de Janeiro: Fundação Oswaldo Cruz, 2020); Marcos Chor Maio and Thiago da Costa Lopes, "Modernization, Race, and the Rural Past in Brazil: A Transnational Analysis of Donald Pierson's Sociology (1930–1950)," *Latin American Research Review* 57, no. 2 (2022): 298–315; and Ian Merkel, *Terms of Exchange: Brazilian Intellectuals and the French Social Sciences* (University of Chicago Press, 2022). For an illuminating account of the inter-American histories of social scientific knowledge centered on US-Mexico relations, see Karin Alejandra Rosemblatt, *The Science and Politics of Race in Mexico and the United States, 1910–1950* (University of North Carolina Press, 2018).

6. Donald Pierson, *Negroes in Brazil: A Study of Race Contact at Bahia* (University of Chicago Press, 1942).

7. On Pierson's activities in Brazil and his early impact on the social sciences, see Donald Pierson, "Algumas atividades no Brasil em prol da antropologia e outras ciências sociais," in *História da antropologia no Brasil (1930–1960): Testemunhos; Emílio Willems e Donald Pierson,* ed. Mariza Corrêa (Campinas, Brazil: Editora da Unicamp, 1987), 30–116; Sebastião Vila Nova, *Donald Pierson e a escola de Chicago na sociologia brasileira: Entre humanistas e messiânicos* (Coleção veja Universidade, 1998); Fernando Limongi, "A escola livre de sociologia e política," in *História das ciências sociais no Brasil*, vol. 1, ed. Sérgio Miceli (Editora Sumaré; Instituto de Estudos Econômicos, Sociais e Políticos, 1989), 217–33; and Lúcia Lippi Oliveira, *A sociologia do Guerreiro* (Rio de Janeiro: Editora Universidade Federal do Rio de Janeiro, 1995), chap. 3.

8. Donald Pierson to Luiz de Aguiar Costa Pinto, April 19, 1944, Universidade Estadual de Campinas, Donald Pierson Collection, folder 39; and Darcy Ribeiro to Oracy Nogueira, November 8, 1943, Universidade Estadual de Campinas, Donald Pierson Collection, folder 37.

9. Marcos Chor Maio and Thiago da Costa Lopes, "Between Science and Politics: Donald Pierson and the Quest for a Scientific Sociology in Brazil," *Sociologias* 24, no. 60 (May–August 2022): 228–66.

10. Marcos Chor Maio, Nemuel da Silva Oliveira, and Thiago da Costa Lopes, "Donald Pierson e o Projeto do Vale do Rio São Francisco: Cientistas sociais em ação na era do desenvolvimento," *Dados: Revista de Ciências Sociais* 56, no. 2 (June 2013): 245–84.

11. Robert C. Bannister, *Sociology and Scientism: The American Quest for Objectivity, 1880–1940* (University of North Carolina Press, 1987).

12. Charles Camic, "On the Edge: Sociology During the Great Depression and the New Deal," in *Sociology in America: A History*, ed. Craig Calhoun (University of Chicago Press, 2007): 225–80.

13. On the history of rural sociology in the United States, see Olaf Larson and Julie Zimmerman, *Sociology in Government: The Galpin-Taylor Years in the U.S. Department of*

Agriculture, 1919–1953 (Pennsylvania State University Press, 2003); and Lowry Nelson, *Rural Sociology: Its Origin and Growth in the United States* (University of Minnesota Press, 1969).

14. On Smith's career and his connections with Brazil, see T. Lynn Smith, *How I Became a Rural Sociologist*, 1973, T. Lynn Smith Papers, Center for Southwest Research, University of New Mexico, box 2, folder 61; T. Lynn Smith, "Sociology and Sociologists in Brazil and the United States: Some Aspects of Their Interrelationships," in *Brazilian Society* (University of New Mexico Press, 1974), 8–24; and Lopes, *Em busca da comunidade*.

15. T. Lynn Smith to M. R. Benedict, September 11, 1939, T. Lynn Smith Papers, box 3, folder 58.

16. Smith, "Sociology and Sociologists in Brazil."

17. The research conducted by Chicago social scientists outside the United States, as well as the cross-border dialogues they established, constitute a little-known chapter in the history of this sociological tradition, generally analyzed from a strictly national framework, referring to the domestic context of large US cities. See, for example, Jean-Michel Chapoulie, *La tradition sociologique de Chicago (1982–1961)* (Éditions du Seuil, 2001).

18. On the intrinsically relational nature of defining racial dynamics in both countries, see Micol Seigel, "Beyond Compare: Comparative Method After the Transnational Turn," *Radical History Review*, no. 91 (Winter 2005): 62–90.

19. University of Chicago, "News About Members," *Bulletin of the Society for Social Research* 3 (March 1935), Fisk University Special Collections and Archives, Robert E. Park Collection (Supplement 1), 1923–1943, box 15, folder 1, quoted at 3.

20. Fredrick B. Pike, *FDR's Good Neighbor Policy: Sixty Years of Generally Gentle Chaos* (University of Texas Press, 1995). It is well known how Chicago sociology tended to see the US metropolis as the space par excellence of processes such as harsh economic competition, interethnic conflict, and social disorganization. Chicago's first ethnographic projects in small, rural villages in Latin America, such as those developed by Robert Redfield in Tepoztlán (Mexico) in the 1920s, stressed, on the other hand, the cooperative, cohesive, and communitarian mode of life engendered by local tradition. See Clifford Wilcox, *Robert Redfield and the Development of American Anthropology* (Lexington Books, 2004).

21. Robert Park to Pierson, February 11, 1936, Donald Pierson Collection, folder 62; Pierson to Robert Park, September 9, 1936, Donald Pierson Collection, folder 62.

22. Donald Pierson, *Negroes in Brazil: A Study of Race Contact at Bahia*, 2nd ed. (Southern Illinois University Press, 1967).

23. Pierson to Robert Park, Robert Redfield, and Louis Wirth (Report no. 3), June 19, 1936, Donald Pierson Collection, folder 62; and Pierson to Robert Park, Robert Redfield, and Louis Wirth (Report no. 6), December 19, 1936, Donald Pierson Collection, folder 62. On Pierson's research experience, see Christophe Brochier, "De Chicago à São Paulo: Donald Pierson et la sociologie des relations raciales au Brésil," *Revue d'Histoire des Sciences Humaines* 25, no. 2 (2011): 293–324; and Anadelia A. Romo, *Brazil's Living Museum: Race, Reform, and Tradition in Bahia* (University of North Carolina Press, 2010).

24. For a detailed analysis of conflict in Pierson's ethnography, see Marcos Chor Maio and Thiago da Costa Lopes, "Entre Chicago e Salvador: Donald Pierson e o estudo das relações raciais," *Estudos Históricos* 30, no. 60 (January–April 2017): 115–40.

25. Unlike Freyre, Oliveira Vianna's works were not translated into English. Oliveira Vianna stood out as an ingenious interpreter of Brazilian social formation and a critic of the liberal political institutions of the First Republic in Brazil, denouncing their incongruity with the deeper, heterogeneous social reality of the country. However, his racialist bias and authoritarian inclinations did not age well in Brazilian intellectual circles. For an appraisal of his controversial work, see Élide Rugai Bastos and João Quartim de Moraes, *O pensamento de Oliveira Vianna* (Campinas, Brazil: Editora da Unicamp, 1993).

26. Pierson, *Negroes in Brazil*, 2nd ed. 123.

27. Not as central as Freyre in shaping Pierson's vision of the Brazilian racial situation, Oliveira Vianna nevertheless offered important reading keys for diagnosing Brazil developed by Smith, as we will see below.

28. Gilberto Freyre, *Casa-grande e senzala: Formação da família brasileira sob o regime da economia patriarcal* (Global Editora, [1933] 2003), 33.

29. Gilberto Freyre, *Sobrados e mucambos: Decadencia do patriarchado rural no Brasil* (Companhia Editora Nacional, 1936), chap. 7; and Pierson to Robert Park, Robert Redfield, and Louis Wirth, October 17, 1936 (Report no. 5), Donald Pierson Collection, folder 62.

30. On the relationship between the two and the importance of the political debate between the leaders of American Black activism at the beginning of the twentieth century for the sociology of Chicago, see Aldon D. Morris, *The Scholar Denied: W. E. B. Du Bois and the Birth of Modern Sociology* (University of California Press, 2015).

31. Robert E. Park, "Racial Assimilation in Secondary Groups with Particular Reference to the Negro," *American Journal of Sociology* 19, no. 5 (March 1914): 606–23; and Robert E. Park, "The Conflict and Fusion of Cultures with Special Reference to the Negro," *Journal of Negro History* 4, no. 2 (April 1919): 111–33.

32. T. Lynn Smith, *Brazil: The Population and the Relations of the People to the Land* (report), August 20, 1943, US Department of Agriculture, Office of Foreign Agricultural Relations, T. Lynn Smith Papers, box 3, folder 58.

33. T. Lynn Smith, *Brazil: The Brazilian Labor Force in Relation to Agriculture* (confidential report), January 20, 1943, National Archives and Records Administration, Record Group 166, box 80, folder "Restricted 1942–1945 labor."

34. Both Oliveira Vianna and Smith stressed the consequences of the relative absence of a class of small landowners, organized around the family farm model, for Brazilian history and society.

35. Assessing the potential of the labor force and the living conditions of the populations involved in agriculture was one of Smith's tasks on this trip to Brazil, on a joint mission by the US Department of State and the US Department of Agriculture. At stake in this case was both the guarantee of the production of strategic materials such as rubber and quinine, typical of tropical areas, and the supply of agricultural food products in the north of Brazil, a region directly involved in the war effort. Smith, *Brazil: The Brazilian Labor Force*.

36. Lopes, *Em busca da comunidade*.

37. On the role of sociological definition of the contours of rural communities for social planning during the Roosevelt era, see Jess Gilbert, *Planning Democracy: Agrarian Intellectuals and the Intended New Deal* (New Haven, CT: Yale University Press, 2015).

38. T. Lynn Smith, *The Sociology of Rural Life* (Harper and Brothers, 1940).

39. Smith, *The Sociology of Rural Life.*

40. Smith, *Brazil: The Population,* 100.

41. Francisco José de Oliveira Vianna, *Populações meridionais do Brasil,* 4th ed. (Companhia Editora Nacional, 1938), 219.

42. Smith, *Brazil: The Population,* 99–103.

43. T. Lynn Smith, "The Locality Group Structure of Brazil," *American Sociological Review* 49, no. 1 (February 1944): 41–49.

44. T. Lynn Smith, *Brazil: People and Institutions* (Louisiana State University Press, 1946), chap. 16.

45. Smith, "The Locality Group Structure."

46. Smith, "The Locality Group Structure," quoted at 43–44.

47. Smith, *Brazil: People and Institutions,* 634–35.

48. T. Lynn Smith, *Brazil: Field Notes,* 1942, T. Lynn Smith Papers, box 10, folder 18.

CHAPTER 6

Translations of the Transnational Americas

Vito Marcantonio Through Harlem and Puerto Rico

SANDHYA SHUKLA

WHEN PUBLIC INTELLECTUAL RANDOLPH Bourne in 1916 touted the "transnational" as a political and cultural ideal, his primary concern was the United States. In the middle of a war and witnessing continuous waves of migration, Bourne contemplated how diversity and globality might be conjoined under the rubric of a new kind of Americanism, writing: "Only America [. . .] can lead in this cosmopolitan enterprise. Only the American, and in this category I include the migratory alien who has lived with us and caught the pioneer spirit and a sense of new social vistas—has the chance to become that citizen of the world."[1] While the foregrounding of the United States, in a somewhat chauvinistic tone, suggests serious limitations for the expansiveness of Bourne's ideas, the proposal that cosmopolitanism could live inside the nation remains quite generative. In fact, this casting of the transnational, from over a hundred years ago, broke down critical oppositions between home and abroad that continue to structure even the most sophisticated studies of culture and history.

It is with this insight (and critique) in mind that I consider Vito Marcantonio, one of the most left-wing members of Congress in US history, as a figure who conjures up many pasts and possibilities for thinking about locality, nation, and globe, all at once.[2] Marcantonio brings into clearer focus interventions of this volume about reimagining transnationalism through an Americas lens. Marcantonio's border-crossing practices emerged from East Harlem, the very diverse place that he was from and represented in Congress, and actively engaged spheres outside of that district as he worked to challenge narrow forms of nationalism predicated on unbridgeable divides. His working-class cosmopolitanism built an anti-imperialist, nonexclusivist approach to "transnational America." This included support for independence movements and deep sympathy for the rights and conditions of poor people in the United States and all over the world.

Marcantonio's sustained and committed support of Puerto Rico opens up important questions about the bounds of nations and movement across their boundaries with which any formation of the Americas must be concerned. To invoke Puerto Rico with reference to a US congressman is to ask what the relationship between the two formations of the United States and Puerto Rico really is. Colonialism and imperialism, in general and especially in this case, have brought together areas of the world with the influence and power dynamics of deep political, cultural, and economic connection. Through this spatial field, Harlem and Puerto Rico might be seen as in a geographic continuum of an extended Caribbean[3] or "Americas" framework, in both cases contested ideas. Further complicating the matter is the existence of diasporas, uneven communities that result and persist. Puerto Rican Harlem was indexed to the place of origin of many of its peoples; migrants maintained bonds with those back home and established changing points of reference for islanders. There was an exceptionality in Marcantonio's ability to effectively and enduringly effect connection, but it is important to remember that his cosmopolitanism also emerged from conditions of possibility, namely the left-wing (anti-imperial and antiracist) currents of the late 1930s to the early 1950s. Marcantonio could simultaneously embody the nation and articulate internationalist and regional sensibilities because an ideology brought those projects together. One effect was to collapse distances between the diverse worlds of East Harlem and Puerto Rico. The work of that historical moment continues to raise important political and conceptual questions, including those that haunt our fields of US-American and Latin American studies today, about what kinds of dialogue are possible when such vast differences exist.[4]

Born and raised in Italian Harlem, Marcantonio was an embodiment of place and a figure of an ethnicity that was, like others, itself densely constituted. By the time of Marcantonio's rise, the area of Manhattan between 96th and 125th Streets from Lexington Avenue to the East River had become populated by people from Italy beginning in the 1890s and reaching a climax of population concentration in about 1930.[5] The "Italianness" of this part of Harlem comprised people from Bari, Sicily, Calabria, Sarno, and elsewhere, some of whom were immigrants; others were children of immigrants.[6] Still, America's discourse of immigrant integration was predicated on national origins, and being Italian American enabled belonging. These categorical complexities faced many migrants, like those from Latin America, whose primary identity could only be processed through reference to states that they may or may not have felt fully defined by, not to mention racial frameworks different from those by which they had been shaped.[7]

If the area where Italians settled in Harlem was geographically delineated, its boundaries, like those of any neighborhood, were porous. Italian Harlem was in and of a space that had been occupied by Irish Americans and Jewish Americans, many of whom stayed on when Italians arrived, just as Italians may have left en masse by the 1950s (but some of course continued to live there); and it was a historical destination for Puerto Ricans beginning well before the 1940s, which saw migration on a larger scale. To further complicate the picture, Black populations could be found all over Harlem, East Harlem included.[8] Such heterogeneity was part of the fabric of the place, even if not always apparent in the day-to-day community activities based in shared backgrounds and language, or reflected by broader public associations of one area of Harlem with a particular ethnic and/or racial group. And dramatic separations were another result of this heterogeneity, as in all urban areas. Many actively sought to distinguish Black (West) Harlem and immigrant (East) Harlem not only to indicate region but also because of anti-Blackness. And within East Harlem, rifts developed between prominent groups like Italians and Puerto Ricans, the former increasingly associated with a developing "white" ethnicity and the latter excluded from that group because they spoke Spanish (even when the "race" of at least some Puerto Ricans was ambiguous before they immigrated). Marcantonio represented this district in the US House of Representatives from 1936 to 1950 as a member of the Republican,

Democratic, and then American Labor Parties and explicitly addressed civil rights, economic and social class, and imperialism.

One key to Marcantonio's expansiveness was a working-class cosmopolitanism that grew from shared interests and extended across cultural differences. It started with the political world of Italians and radiated outward from there. By the early twentieth century, trade unions in areas across the country had many Italian members and leaders. Left-wing formations shaped those labor organizations and constituted the ideological ambience in which Marcantonio became politicized. In high school from 1917 to 1921, he was awash in conversations about and activism around unions as well as housing rights (Marcantonio organized the East Harlem Tenants League). Crucially, for that developing imagination, Marcantonio's socialist teacher also inspired arguments against colonialism (especially the British occupation of Ireland).[9] It was in high school, too, that Marcantonio first became associated with reformer and activist Leonard Covello, whose social justice initiatives in East Harlem assumed the same cross-cultural shape that Marcantonio's politics would come to take. All these inclinations combined intense interest in the locality of East Harlem and in the world outside of it.

In the 1930s and 1940s, Marcantonio's district, and East, Central, and West Harlems in general, were undergoing demographic shifts. By 1930, East Harlem was already the destination for Irish, Jewish, African American, Cuban, and Puerto Rican people, and there were many exchanges and conflicts. But the central tension of the area became that between Italians and Puerto Ricans. When a famous Italian American priest, Peter Rofrano, in 2005 noted about this period that "they had to get Italians out, so they brought in the Puerto Ricans from Puerto Rico; now Mexicans are coming in, pushing Puerto Ricans out,"[10] he drew on an ethnic succession narrative of urban society characterized by both racialized anxiety and ambivalence about neighborhoods changing, as much about the time in which he spoke as about a represented past.

Competition between Italians and Puerto Ricans was iconic, represented in media and literature and widely discussed by residents in the area. A 1967 memoir about East Harlem during the 1930s to 1950s by Puerto Rican writer Piri Thomas, *Down These Mean Streets*, describes in vivid detail the turf conflicts between Puerto Ricans and Italians, resulting in both physical violence and delicate negotiations.[11] Yet Thomas also noted in an interview about

Marcantonio: "The Puerto Ricans and Italians were always fighting and he was helping everybody out." In that recollection, Thomas brought ethnic misrecognition to the fore—"I thought he was Puerto Rican because he helped everybody, all nationalities"—but also, however unintentionally, he illuminated the difficulty of balkanizing "Spanish Harlem" and "Italian Harlem."[12] Moreover, the invocation of "helping" highlighted the aspect of service in how Marcantonio acted and was received, more generally, alongside an obvious but still remarkable ability to connect, or translate, across differences.

Economic realities created vexed relationships to the state among different groups of people, and even as a US legislator, Marcantonio could ally himself to activist goals to address those difficulties. One community group, the East Harlem Organizers, opined that Marcantonio was a friend, a "fearless fighter for the Latin-American and specially for the Porto Ricans."[13] In 1947, Marcantonio joined with local politicians in the important Harlem Legislative Conference to demand that the New York City administration address basic economic and political issues of the "Negro and Puerto Rican citizens of Harlem" regarding public welfare and the "full citizenship rights and equality for the Negro and Puerto Rican people and other minorities."[14] His support for social security explicitly addressed resources for multiple groups, including older Italians as well as Jewish people who lived just across the borders of East Harlem.

That expansiveness was evident in how Marcantonio spoke to civil rights struggles locally and nationally. He worked with educational activist Leonard Covello, the principal of the integrated Benjamin Franklin High School in East Harlem,[15] to help defuse racial tensions in 1945 between African American and Italian students. Marcantonio established camaraderie with Black intellectuals, particularly on the Left.[16] That solidarity underlay a project that included efforts to desegregate public facilities, to provide sufficient funding for the Fair Employment Practices Commission, and to inquire into exclusions of African American players from national baseball organizations years before Jackie Robinson integrated the Major Leagues.

What is clear in all these cases is that for Marcantonio, the rights of working people and immigrants, the issues of discrimination against Puerto Ricans, Italians, and African Americans, and questions of racial justice in the United States and the world are connected. That could not be more evident than when he intoned in 1943: "The effects of anti-poll-tax legislation extend beyond our own borders. Not only will the abolition of the poll tax lift the morale of the 13,000,000 loyal Negro Americans in this country, and thereby forge that national unity which is so essential to victory, but it will be living evidence and reaffirmation to our United Nations Allies and to the colonial peoples in India, Africa, Latin America, and the Caribbean, of our earnest and high resolve to win the battle for a free and democratic world."[17] Here, Marcantonio was indexing domestic concerns to a well-known, almost clichéd, Americanist global project, the "battle for a free world," but he was subtly undoing that with a reference to quite another kind of transnationalism, one that saw anticolonial struggle as a matter of justice.

And Marcantonio's working-class cosmopolitanism was especially vivid in his advocacy on behalf of Puerto Rico and Puerto Rican people. Unlike a more elite worldliness, Marcantonio's version was left-wing and patterned by the negotiations he had engaged in "at home." In arguing for the social welfare of Puerto Rican residents or the political independence of Puerto Rico, Marcantonio could still somehow manage to be the congressman from Italian Harlem, to inhabit a subjectivity shaped by those neighborhood blocks. Territorial tensions of the time in Harlem might have generated a question of whether it was possible to be Italian and pro–Puerto Rican at the same time—the notion that Italians were "pushed out" by the newer Puerto Rican populations is predicated on a vision of hardened spatial compartments. When Marcantonio held both populations close, he revamped local concerns but also lit up a geography that could push beyond the limits of nationality. He argued against US occupation or annexation of Puerto Rico, all the while emphasizing both connectedness and autonomy. No less importantly, how Marcantonio saw this world beyond Harlem manifested a leftist internationalism, as he made explicit in a speech before the House of Representatives in 1939: "My interest in Puerto Rico is due not only to the fact that I represent the largest Puerto Rican constituency [. . .] but also to my desire as a progressive to defend the most exploited victims of a most devastating imperialism."[18]

Astonishingly, Marcantonio served Puerto Ricans in Puerto Rico just as he served his formal constituents. They asked him for help in making claims to the US government regarding back pay for military service, or obtaining Works Progress Administration (WPA) jobs, or even addressing more personal issues regarding impoverishment and displacement.[19] The intensity of effort bears further comment. In one case, Marcantonio intervened with Harold Ickes, the secretary of the interior, on behalf of an eighty-year-old man who was unable to pay the taxes on his land in Puerto Rico.[20] In another, a poor painter from Puerto Rico, Guadalupe Ruiz, wrote first to the mayor of New York and then, after receiving no response, to Marcantonio to explain that his son had been imprisoned in New York City and that he could not visit him from such a distance; Marcantonio wrote to the New York Department of Corrections and then had personal correspondence with the Parole Commission, with positive consequences. The mother of the prisoner wrote about contacting Marcantonio: "*Un rayo de luz illuminó mi cerebro, y el nombre del valeroso y ferviente defensor de los puertorriqueños el Hon. Vito Marcantonio resplandeció en mi mente como un astro*" (A ray of light illuminated my mind, and the name of the brave and fervent defender of the Puerto Ricans, the honorable Vito Marcantonio, gleamed in my mind like a heavenly body). Marcantonio's translator put it more economically, but certainly less poetically, as "I know that you are very good to all the Puerto Ricans and that is the reason why I appeal to you." In both versions, the grandeur of relating to and defending all Puerto Ricans resounds.[21]

While the expressed needs of Puerto Ricans on the island made reference to specific experiences, their quality of bald economic and political disadvantage resonated with the lives of Harlem's inhabitants, who were constituents in a more formal sense. This helps us to understand how connections could be made across different places and spatial registers, one an island territory and the other an urban area in the United States. A transnational *political* relationality superseded the anxiety in the United States at the time about that which lay outside the country's borders, as well as the carefully managed, and contradictory, ideologies of colonial annexation and effective inclusion.[22] If Puerto Rico was apart from and a part of the United States, in varied ways, so was Marcantonio both outsider and insider, a left-wing activist from a poor city and a national congressman. And this framing of solidarities across boundaries of the nation-state that enabled local investments and attentions in Puerto Rico bore a structural similarity to the cross-cultural sensibility of Harlem, always processing racial and ethnic exchanges while maintaining roots in Italian communities.

For the case of Puerto Rico, like that of Italians in Harlem, an attention to the disempowerment of working people provided a foundation for Marcantonio's political vision: Puerto Rican unions formally supported Marcantonio, and he supported them. In representative cases, he appeared before the Wage and Hour Division of the US Department of Labor on behalf of the United Railroad Workers Union to argue for increasing the wages of WPA workers.[23] The worker-centric orientation was inextricable from a critique of colonial power; thus, Marcantonio moved from supporting statehood to independence for Puerto Rico. When he went to Puerto Rico in 1936 to defend independence leader Pedro Albizu Campos, he was met by huge, supportive crowds; he returned to Harlem, where there were also large rallies advocating independence.[24] Through the 1930s and 1940s, Marcantonio maintained intense relationships with a number of Puerto Rican independence leaders and intellectuals. There is no question that his frank socialism could find a congenial home in a space that experienced, and protested, the continuing exploitation of capital— big sugar companies, for example—and that many, though not all, migrants who came to settle in Harlem shared that political sensibility, just as many in Italian Harlem had been shaped by leftist currents back home.

Citizenship cases were predicated on narrow conceptions of nationality yet inevitably raised the complications of more global belonging. The status of those in and from a place that was continually colonized and only semiautonomous in the best of times could not be anything but problematic.[25] So many people in Puerto Rico (like those at home in East Harlem) wrote to Marcantonio about difficulties in obtaining citizenship rights, not least because of the ambiguities of the rules surrounding the distinct situation of Puerto Rico, neither state nor country. Not surprisingly, there were mixtures that reflected other historical encounters, and those did not fit neatly into the limited boxes of identity that the US nation-state imagined. Many described being denied citizenship in the United States despite having been born in Puerto Rico, because of having Italian rather than Spanish fathers. Some of those cases involved Corsicans who had migrated to Puerto Rico in the late 1800s to work in the coffee industry and intermixed with populations already living there. This fact makes plain that cultural and racial diversity was not just a feature of the United States but could be found in most, if not all, societies, and it would be a mistake to think of "Spanish" or Latin America, or the Caribbean, as homogeneous; we might imagine that Marcantonio would have been especially able to process this insight, however unconventional at the time, precisely because his working grammar was transnational and comparative.

Such social complexities rippled through migrant communities in East Harlem and elsewhere. As Jesús Cariel, whose father was Italian, explained it to Marcantonio: "If I am not a citizen, there must be about a half million of Porto Ricans who are voting and using the rights of an American Citizen although they are still aliens without knowing it. In the Spanish colony in Harlem in New York, half of the population are the same way, as I know quite a few people from my home town and others."[26] Marcantonio argued for and helped pass a bill in 1940 that granted citizenship to all those who had been born in Puerto Rico, thus extending birthright citizenship across the borders of the continental United States and its annexations, to provide another continuous zone of identification for those in Harlem and Puerto Rico while also incorporating all sorts of mixtures of diasporic subjectivity. The two sites of Puerto Rican diaspora were naturally linked in cultural and familial terms, but Marcantonio provided some political glue, mapping a transnational space and in that way remaking the territories of both *el barrio* and Puerto Rico.

One of Marcantonio's central causes, with which he was identified both positively and negatively, was Puerto Rican independence. Not every Puerto Rican in New York, or for that matter in Puerto Rico, supported independence,[27] which only reinforces the argument that Marcantonio's relational approach to the island was deeper and more personally transformative than electoral interests would compel. This can be seen in feeling as much as advocacy: Marcantonio took on Puerto Rico and its citizens from outside his zone of operation and brought them inside a political body (of constituents, of the working class, of racialized minorities), and into his own subjective experience of those formations, all while respecting the constitutive integrity and difference of Puerto Rico. Marcantonio maintained relationships with Puerto Rican activists and political figures throughout his career. It is also clear that he read Puerto Rican newspapers and other materials regularly. Interestingly, Marcantonio was also recognized in the United States as an authority on Puerto Rico; in one case, a Princeton University professor even sought Marcantonio's expertise on the issue of Puerto Rican independence.[28] There is much material that testifies to reciprocal affect: Puerto Ricans wrote letters evoking the need for services and also the sensibility that Marcantonio *cared* about people who were unlike him.

When Pedro Biaggi contacted Marcantonio in 1936, after his one congressional election defeat, to request an interview for an article on Puerto Rico for

Latin American newspapers, he appealed to felt connections across the usual parameters of time and space, offering to treat Marcantonio to "some Spanish or Italian lunch."[29] Biaggi wrote: "Puerto Rico fully realizes that you have made a supreme sacrifice for *our* sacred cause of independence" (my emphasis) and acknowledged the adversity that Marcantonio faced in "our homeland," referring to his own relationship to Puerto Rico. But the represented affective bond gets deeper and more complicated as Biaggi goes on to remark that when he had first learned of Marcantonio "in connection with the Harlem political and social struggles," he had misrecognized Marcantonio as Puerto Rican, because he had known in Puerto Rico a Corsican family named Marcantonio who had relatives living in Harlem, "rather blond or blue blood." Less important than the accuracy of this perception is Biaggi's inclination to read Marcantonio through a more personal experience—his own family had come to Puerto Rico from Corsica—and he writes to Marcantonio that recalling struggles in Corsica "makes me think if there is not some spiritual bond tying you to our beloved and so ignominiously treated homeland." In this discourse, "homeland" serves as a double signifier to a Corsican writer raised in Puerto Rico (and who seems recently to have spent time in Buenos Aires), who is ever conscious of diasporic space reaching across to Harlem and identified with Marcantonio. Different, dynamic, and comparative accounts of disempowerment come to settle on this moment of the late 1930s in and through three spaces—Corsica, Puerto Rico, and Harlem—that might be variously understood as colonial. In this way, too, "the Americas" of exile and migration might even exceed a continental formation.

Just as it did for Biaggi, Puerto Rico would become an important space for Marcantonio to work through important questions of nationality and globality. Marcantonio's leftist inclinations certainly seamlessly assimilated Puerto Rican nationalism, but one cannot rule out the possibility that the experience of relation also wrought something less predictable. In the 1930s and 1940s, as through all periods of history, the United States was under construction, and its relationship to other places and regions was changing, too. If Marcantonio was articulating a different vision of what "place" could look like at home, he was also ever conscious of the world, and about the allegiances (always shifting, too) of its constituting regions—when he spoke Spanish in public broadcasts, he suggested that his audience was not only Puerto Rican, that people of other Latin American countries were listening, too. Puerto Rico could in this way be seen as articulated to the Spanish-speaking Americas, not only to the United States, and thus centers and peripheries were redrawn, just as the limits of the frame of the nation-state for thinking about place and difference were laid bare.

Solidarity is always a complicated endeavor, requiring boundary crossing and also, to work fully, a profound sense of connection, relation, and understanding. Language, as a means of expression, as a sign of cultural knowledge, and as an essential practice of the everyday, provides a space in which to convey and receive understanding—one can think of language as a preferred vehicle for cross-culturality—and it was a vehicle that Marcantonio worked on and through with great commitment. No doubt there was an electoral aspect to his legendary ability to speak Italian, Yiddish, and Spanish (as well as English) in a district that had significant populations of constituents who primarily spoke those languages. Like his predecessor Fiorello La Guardia, Marcantonio made political speeches in multiple languages to appeal to a diverse East Harlem, and, one might presume, also to adequately represent the area's people locally and nationally. The idea that language is a sign of difference and can potentially mark exclusion for migrants from other countries helps establish that Marcantonio's multilingual practice serviced the aspiration of inclusion, national and otherwise. And considering how this instance of multilingualism emerged from East Harlem also links it to the working-class cosmopolitanism that Marcantonio staged in other realms.

Marcantonio's relationship to Spanish bears closer exploration because it was unusual and multifaceted, expressed in a range of political and even personal spheres. In 1941, Angelita Santaella, who shared a godchild with Marcantonio, wrote from Puerto Rico: "*Yo le escribo en español, porque he sabido por Ada y Gilberto que usted sabe nuestro idioma, y aún que sé un poco de inglés, suficiente para expresarme, lógicamente, lo hago mejor en mi idioma*" (I write to you in Spanish, because I know from Ada and Gilberto that you know our language, and although I do know a little English, enough to clearly express myself, I do better in my own language).[30] But when the letter was translated at the time for Marcantonio's review, it read slightly differently: "I have been informed [. . .] that you master our language pretty well." We may for a moment consider what the deeper sentiment around knowledge is, what it might mean for Santaella to think that Marcantonio knows *her* language. She intimates that she feels more comfortable communicating with him in Spanish, with the expectation that she will be understood. Santaella ends another letter with a more direct statement about Marcantonio's role in Puerto Rico: "*. . . con los deseos de que sea usted siempre nuestro querido REPRESENTANTE, y que tiene los votos de los puertorriqueños, que le han elegido y reelegido, por sus grandes méritos. Los de aquí y de allá tenemos los mismos gustos.* (. . . with the hope that you will always be our beloved REPRESENTATIVE, who has the votes of the Puerto Ricans, who have elected and reelected you for your substantial merits. Those of us from here and there have the same desires).[31] It is in Spanish that Santaella can close a number of gaps between herself and a US congressman—she emphasizes identification by using uppercase letters to announce that Marcantonio is *her* representative— as well between East Harlem Puerto Ricans who have formally voted for him and those, like herself, on the island, who have not.

Marcantonio frequently utilized Spanish to connect to a broad audience of constituents and others. In a radio program during his 1949 mayoral campaign, Marcantonio began by saying that he was pleased to be speaking to listeners in the "language of Cervantes," gesturing toward high literary Spanish, possibly European, traditions, but he quickly undid any potential elitism when he followed up with: "*Yo no estudié español en Salamanca, España. [. . .] Mi español es del hombre común que trabaja y sufre.*" (I did not study Spanish in Salamanca, Spain. [. . .] My Spanish is that of the common man who works and suffers).[32] Identifying his kind of Spanish, imperfect because not formally studied and not that of the colonizer, could only be in service of working-class Puerto Ricans (and some other Spanish-speaking inhabitants) of New York City. In other nods to the daily lived experience of Puerto Ricans feeling like second-class citizens, Marcantonio mentioned that he was aware that they had been targeted by the police: "*víctimas de los más horrendos ataques de la polizia [sic]*" (victims of the most horrendous attacks by the police) and had been subject to prejudice from the Relief Office. When Piri Thomas referred in his 1967 memoir to the similar position that Puerto Ricans, Italians, and others found themselves in with regard to the Relief Office, writing: "It seemed that every mother had brought a kid to interpret for her,"[33] he raised questions about legibility that were about both language and class, which here we can see Marcantonio tapping into for his own solidarity with Puerto Ricans.[34]

Mikhail Bakhtin's discussion of discourse as built through the diversity of social phenomena (dialects, voices, worldviews) and not bound by the expectations of a singular literary language provides an important way to understand Marcantonio's verbal utterances. His very self-aware complexity of address has to do with his establishment of one kind of cultural authority, in knowing Spanish and its origins, but also in understanding the lived and shared experience of speaking in a language of workers and residents. Both rhetorics, and more than just those, can be seen to be present and even in tension in what he said. As Bakhtin puts it: "The centripetal forces of the life of language, embodied in a 'unitary language,' operate in the midst of heteroglossia. At any given moment [. . .] language is stratified not only into linguistic dialects [. . .] but also [. . .] into languages that are socio-ideological: languages of social groups, 'professional' and 'generic' languages, languages of generations and so forth."[35] And the very use of one language or another, at any point in time, is significant.

The sense of language as open interestingly engages questions related to translation, like cultural trace, comparison, and legibility. Marcantonio's style of Spanish was Italian-inflected in terms of both vocabulary and accent. Throughout his time in Congress, he clearly employed someone who translated constituent letters and other materials, but Marcantonio also himself read and communicated in Spanish.[36] In audio recordings, one can hear the difference between Spanish speeches that were written for him, grammatically correct and with precise word choice, and recordings such as interviews in which he spoke Spanish on the fly, using many Italian words, like "polizia." Yet what also resonates from one radio program in particular is an awkwardly worded yet compelling expression "*Ustedes me conocen, yo lo conozco*" (You know me, I know it). Here, Marcantonio appeals to reciprocal understanding, *knowing*—it may take shape in Spanish but cannot but supersede narrow expectations, articulated as it is in a heavy Italian accent. The sonic and more formally textual aspects are components of what Bakhtin has referred to as "dialogized heteroglossia."[37]

To read Marcantonio's language use as an instance of translation is to consider cross-culturality in another way. Here, as in other elements of his politics, he does not effect a completed move across borders but self-presents in a dynamic exchange in which his identity is both familiar and porous enough to accommodate otherness. Just as Bakhtin directs us to pay attention to the "authentic environment of an utterance," how could we not understand Marcantonio's choices for communication vis-à-vis his campaign in the early 1940s to reverse policies in Puerto Rico that mandated English as the main language of instruction? The argument that Marcantonio pragmatically used Spanish to connect to voters can be complicated by the possibility of an authentic recognition of difference and respect for the experience of place. If recent work in translation studies has reminded us to be attentive to the limits of moving from one language or culture into another, we might see Marcantonio's crossings as deeply aware of boundaries, too.[38] His linguistic translations, imperfect and registering multiplicity, were nonetheless legible, and thus the intimacy of communicating in the same language need not always entail mastery. Marcantonio here is translating, and he is also being actively translated. Language itself, and its use, can build a space for identification that incorporates all kinds of differences, rather than simply be used as a tool of authority.

These translations raise, then, the question of comparison—moving from one language to another (or one culture to another) is to interrogate what is shared and what is different therein. Marcantonio's ability to communicate in Spanish may indeed have been aided by his fluency in Italian, precisely because of certain exchanges among southern European–derived linguistic practices. To put it more simply, Italian is sort of like Spanish. And if spoken Italian in the United States is already a mix of dialects (from the melting pot of Italy itself), competence in it may include a kind of built-in linguistic flexibility. In this way, it is not structurally dissimilar to Spanish in former colonies, which is necessarily not spoken as it was in the land of Cervantes, undergoing change and hybridization and, in the world of Marcantonio's time, also shaped by diasporic movements. More difficult to determine is whether the language parallels and exchanges were matched by other kinds of cultural compatibility, controversial as "culture" itself is. Nonetheless, the cultures of place, in which peoples who were ethnically different were in continuous contact and exchange, and their politics of solidarity, in which there was a practiced communication, were the stuff of Marcantonio's cross-culturality.

Marcantonio's translational practices were deeply transnational, stretching across the boundaries of the nation and the constitution of belonging for a range of peoples, and ultra-conscious of differences. Even in a period of anxiety about the "foreign," Marcantonio held out the "noncitizen" as entitled to US rights, capturing those migrants not yet eligible for citizenship but also extending, one might imagine, to Puerto Ricans on the island, ambivalently, and liminally, part of the United States. Here was a more flexible understanding of nation and its

limits, indeed a project that Marcantonio was working on in many ways throughout his lifetime.

In fact, Marcantonio's experience in Harlem helped him conceive of a different kind of imagined community, of solidarity and sympathy across nations,
with one of those endpoints in an Americas sensibility. Central to the discursive
toolkit of Marcantonio's politics were the ideals of human rights and national
openness, which could be put to use for many purposes. In 1939, Marcantonio
supported the Wagner-Rogers Bill, which would have allowed the entry of
twenty thousand German Jewish children and which failed to pass Congress,
ignominiously. In that same year he protested practices by the Immigration and
Naturalization Service to remove Puerto Ricans from boats arriving at mainland
US ports and require them to prove the citizenship of their parents.[39] These
interventions occurred at borders, but one could also argue that they sought to
transform the limits of the nation-state at the same time. Like many on the Left,
Marcantonio supported US efforts during World War II, and his own angle was
from cross-cultural and working-class formations within the broader space of
Harlem, a localized take on the popular front. He worked with Adam Clayton
Powell and Black, Puerto Rican, Jewish, and Italian political activists in groups
like the Harlem Victory Council, the Harlem Defense Committee, the Jewish
Peoples Committee, the National Negro Congress, and the Italian Club, not to
mention the American Labor Party, Communist Party, and Youth Communist
League, to argue in favor of the rights of the "foreign born," for their full participation in the armed forces and industries, and for economic and social justice,
while also supporting the war.[40] All of these engagements had some Harlem
content while also being articulated to other political-national projects like the
Popular Front, espousing not only a wartime vision but also a future-looking,
antiracist, and economically equitable United States in and of the world.

If, when we think about the Americas, particularly Puerto Rico, and necessarily understand the United States as an imperial actor, we might also look
toward the uneven and layered nature of the constituting formations. Flashes of
anti-imperialism coming from a US space certainly complicate the direction of
movements and the possibilities of resistance through the transnational. Marcantonio's life and work, exceptional but maybe not altogether unusual, help us
open up a field for reconceptualizing nation and region, and for engaging with
deeper questions about global citizenship: how we connect, and how we are

fundamentally different, across borders. Those are the complexities and possibilities that transnationalism puts onto the critical table.

Notes

1. Randolph S. Bourne, "Trans-National America," *Atlantic Monthly* 118, no. 1 (July 1916): 86–97, quoted at 96.

2. Some of the material in this chapter is from my book *Cross-Cultural Harlem: Reimagining Race and Place* (Columbia University Press, 2024) and reprinted with permission from Columbia University Press.

3. Immanuel Wallerstein has made an economic argument for a category of the "extended Caribbean" to refer to a region from Brazil to Maryland in *The Modern World-System II: Mercantilism and the Consolidation of the European World-Economy, 1600–1750* (University of California Press, 2011). Lara Putnam has taken that concept to develop an understanding of Harlem as one point in a broader geography through the Americas of influence and habitation for Caribbean migrants in "Provincializing Harlem: The 'Negro Metropolis' as Northern Frontier of a Connected Caribbean," *Modernism/Modernity* 20, no. 3 (September 2013): 469–84.

4. Sandhya Shukla and Heidi Tinsman, eds., *Imagining Our Americas: Toward a Transnational Frame* (Duke University Press, 2007).

5. A few works have discussed Italian Harlem. The classic work, with a focus on religious history, is Robert Anthony Orsi's *The Madonna of 115th Street: Faith and Community in Italian Harlem, 1880–1930* (New Haven, CT: Yale University Press, 1985). Jonathan Gill's synthetic history, *Harlem: The Four Hundred Year History from Dutch Village to Capital of Black America* (Grove Press, 2011) contains descriptions of Italian migrant formations in East Harlem, particularly in relation to Jewish ones. Material on Italian Harlem can also be found in Workers of the Federal Writers Project, Works Progress Administration of the City of New York, *The Italians of New York: A Survey* (Random House, 1938).

6. Gerald Meyer accesses data compiled by Irving Sollins in the latter's "A Socio-Statistical Analysis of Boys' Club Membership" (PhD diss., New York University, 1936) for his own discussion of diversity in Italian Harlem. Gerald Meyer, *Vito Marcantonio: Radical Politician 1902–1954* (State University of New York Press, 1989).

7. Wendy D. Roth, *Race Migrations: Latinos and the Cultural Transformation of Race* (Stanford University Press, 2012).

8. See Christopher Bell, *East Harlem Remembered: Oral Histories of Community and Diversity* (McFarland, 2013), for a discussion of the African American presence in East Harlem.

9. Bell writes about the influence of a leftist history teacher named Abraham Lefkowitz on Marcantonio in *East Harlem Remembered*, 59.

10. Peter Rofrano, interview with the author, April 5, 2005.

11. Piri Thomas, *Down These Mean Streets* (Alfred A. Knopf, 1967), chap. 6.

12. Cited in Bell, *East Harlem Remembered*, 65.

13. "Manifesto," reel 2, microfilm 54, Vito Marcantonio Papers, 1902–1954, Manuscripts, Archives, and Rare Books, New York Public Library, New York (hereafter Marcantonio Papers).

14. Folio titled "Call for an Emergency Conference to the People of Harlem," box 3, Marcantonio Papers.

15. Gerald Meyer notes that, in 1945, the school's population was 37 percent Italian, 13 percent African American, 9 percent Puerto Rican, and 41 percent "other" (presumed to include a significant portion of Jewish students). See Gerald Meyer, "When Frank Sinatra Came to Italian Harlem: The 1945 'Race Riot' at Benjamin Franklin High School," in *Are Italians White? How Race Is Made in America*, ed. Jennifer Guglielmo and Salvatore Salterno (Routledge, 2003), 161–76.

16. Marcantonio's personal papers are filled with correspondence with Adam Clayton Powell, and many African American luminaries spoke at his memorial service.

17. Annette T. Rubinstein et al., eds., *I Vote My Conscience: Debates, Speeches, and Writings of Vito Marcantonio, 1935–1950* (Vito Marcantonio Memorial Association, 1956), 175.

18. Vito Marcantonio, speech before the House of Representatives, March 11, 1939, in Rubinstein et al., *I Vote My Conscience*, 374.

19. Marcantonio's personal papers are filled with correspondence from people in Puerto Rico regarding these issues. See especially boxes 54–55 and reel 2, microfilm 54, Marcantonio Papers. Gerald Meyer, *Vito Marcantonio: Radical Politician*, contains a wealth of detail on Marcantonio's efforts on behalf of Puerto Rican workers. There is also important material in Félix Ojeda Reyes, *Vito Marcantonio y Puerto Rico: Por los trabajadores y por la nación* (Ediciones Huracán, 1978).

20. Olivor L. Chapman to Vito Marcantonio, March 26, 1940, reel 1, microfilm 54, Marcantonio Papers; Vito Marcantonio to Harold L. Ickes, March 18, 1940, reel 1, microfilm 54, Marcantonio Papers; Vito Marcantonio to José Kailan Melicio, March 18, 1940, reel 1, microfilm 54, Marcantonio Papers; and José Kailan Melicio to Vito Marcantonio, March 26, 1940, reel 1, microfilm 54, Marcantonio Papers.

21. Guadalupe Ruiz to Vito Marcantonio, undated, reel 2, microfilm 54, Marcantonio Papers (the first translation is my own).

22. Laura Briggs, *Reproducing Empire: Race, Sex, Science, and U.S. Imperialism in Puerto Rico* (University of California Press, 2002); and César J. Ayala and Rafael Bernabe, *Puerto Rico in the American Century: A History Since 1898* (University of North Carolina Press, 2007).

23. See the materials in boxes 54 and 55, Marcantonio Papers.

24. "Spurred by the comment of Representative Vito Marcantonio, who recently returned from a two-weeks' visit to the island and denounced conditions there, the paraders shouted 'Free Puerto Rico!' and 'Down with Yankee Imperialism!' so loudly that thousands of other residents in the area, populated mostly by Negroes and Spaniards, leaned out of windows and over the edges of roof-tops and added their protests to those of the demonstrators." "10,000 Parade Here for Puerto Ricans," *New York Times*, August 30, 1936, 24.

25. See Daniel Acosta Elkan's fine PhD dissertation, "The Colonia Next Door: Puerto Ricans in the Harlem Community, 1917–1948" (Bowling Green State University, 2017), chap. 2, for a discussion of citizenship for Puerto Ricans.

26. Jesús Cariel to Vito Marcantonio, June 23, 1939, box 55, "Puerto Rico—Citizenship" folder, Marcantonio Papers.

27. José Ramón Sánchez, *Boricua Power: A Political History of Puerto Ricans in the United States* (New York University Press, 2007), 115–18.

28. William P. Maddox to Vito Marcantonio, September 18, 1936, reel 2, microfilm 54, Marcantonio Papers; William P. Maddox to Vito Marcantonio, September 28, 1936, reel 2, microfilm 54, Marcantonio Papers; and Vito Marcantonio to William P. Maddox, September 30, 1936, reel 2, microfilm 54, Marcantonio Papers.

29. Pedro J. Biaggi to Vito Marcantonio, December 1, 1936, reel 2, microfilm 54, Marcantonio Papers.

30. Angelita Santaella to Vito Marcantonio, December 18, 1941, reel 3, microfilm 55, Marcantonio Papers (here and below, my translation).

31. Angelita Santaella to Vito Marcantonio, November 5, 1941, reel 3, microfilm 55, Marcantonio Papers.

32. Radio Address bajo dirección de Salvador Mercedo, with interviewer Alfred Barrea, Audiotape 01644, Marcantonio Papers.

33. Thomas, *Down These Mean Streets*, 42. Thomas here is referring to a program developed by the Federal Emergency Relief Administration (1933) and/or the Works Progress Administration (1935) that provided federal assistance to states for projects that addressed the effects of the Great Depression.

34. Marcantonio understood the importance to his constituents of language and familiarity with Puerto Rico. In a radio endorsement, the announcer begins by describing Marcantonio as a person "que habla hispana, que ha vistado este país" (who speaks Spanish, who has visited this country), which draws on both potential sources of connection. Political announcement, undated (probably 1949, during Marcantonio's mayoral campaign), audiotape 01649, Marcantonio Papers.

35. Mikhail Bakhtin, "Discourse in the Novel," in *The Dialogic Imagination: Four Essays*, ed. Michael Holquist, trans. Caryl Emerson and Michael Holquist (University of Texas Press, 1981), 271–72.

36. Marcantonio refers to some newspaper articles and other materials in Spanish-language papers in Puerto Rico, and there is no evidence in the correspondence of translations, suggesting that he had at least a working fluency with Spanish. In a February 7, 1939, letter, Marcantonio writes to J. Enamorado Cuesta about having enjoyed a poem he wrote in *Prensa Libre*; box 54, Marcantonio Papers.

37. Bakhtin, "Discourse in the Novel," 272. The full quotation reads: "The authentic environment of an utterance, the environment in which it lives and takes shape, is dialogized heteroglossia anonymous and social as language, but simultaneously concrete, filled with specific content and accented as an individual utterance."

38. See, for example, Susan Bassnett and Harish Trivedi, eds., *Postcolonial Translation: Theory and Practice* (Abingdon, Oxon., England: Routledge, 1999).

39. Vito Marcantonio to Immigration and Naturalization Service, July 13, 1939, Box 54, Marcantonio Papers.

40. "Letter from Harlem Victory Council," March 28, 1942; "Minutes from Saturday afternoon meeting of Harlem Defense Conference," January 17, 1942; and "Letter from Bernard Harkavy, National Secretary of Jewish Peoples Committee," May 26, 1942, box 2, Marcantonio Papers.

CHAPTER 7

The Transnational Sphere and Sexual Labor

AMALIA L. CABEZAS

WHETHER ENSLAVED, INDENTURED, OR waged laborers—whether employed in brothels, cabarets, or taverns, or simply working in public spaces—sex workers have long been entwined with social history and empire building across the globe.[1] In Latin America and the Caribbean (LAC), protagonists range from women who worked in Havana's service economy during the sixteenth century to Brazilian *travestis* who currently walk the streets in Spain.[2] Historians have documented the experiences of nineteenth- and twentieth-century migrant sex workers from Mexico to Costa Rica and Panama to Argentina, but generally, investigations into the sex trade have been limited to accounts of victims lacking agency who need rescuing and rehabilitation—or else as simply vectors of disease.[3] There has been a lack of research specifically regarding the intersection of gender, race, and sexual labor; indeed, sex workers and sex worker communities have been historically left out of—or even rejected from—labor and women's social movements. And yet they have persevered, organizing to demand rights, decriminalization, and legitimacy from societies that have relied on the image of the whore to discipline all women. While others have long seen sex work as moral depravity, sex workers themselves have tended to see their work simply as labor, and hard-earned labor at that. Their activism and sheer perseverance force us to rethink our understanding of what constitutes "work."

In this chapter, I explore two case studies that examine how sex worker identity is articulated in processes of transnationalism. First, I analyze migrant circuits to Central America, investigating how sexual economic exchanges and the category of "prostitute" were racialized in the Panama Canal Zone after US intervention. I propose that this is an early case of what was later termed sex tourism. Second, I delve into the transnational sex worker network, which has generated a new social identity for sex workers as human rights activists by focusing on the largest network in the region, known as RedTraSex. In both these cases, I highlight how the social construction of the prostitute/sex worker identity is fluid as well as political, particularly in the transnational sphere.[4]

US Military Occupation

Over the course of the nineteenth and twentieth centuries, multiple US military occupations enabled, promoted, and protected expanding US financial interests. At the beginning of the twentieth century, the United States solidified its power as a world empire through global military interventions—particularly in the LAC region, including Cuba, the Dominican Republic, Haiti, Nicaragua, Panama, and Puerto Rico. These interventions greatly expanded the demand for sex work. US military troops' sexual access to women of color was undeniably a part of the process during which the United States expanded its power. At the least, some believed that military bases required women's sexual labor to occupy the soldiers. But in addition, as Andrew Byers explains in *The Sexual Economy of War*, the military "tended to believe that soldiers had irrepressible sexual needs that, when inevitably indulged, could cause harm to the army."[5] Thus, military-based sex work buttressed heterosexual military masculinity—in other words, it prevented same-sex relations between soldiers.

The US rhetoric of imperial conquest called for spreading civilization to supposedly backward, childlike peoples who needed moral, scientific, and political tutelage. The US military envisioned itself as being simultaneously chivalrous civilizers of savage, primitive races and as "benevolent father figures" who needed to control the loose sexual customs of backward peoples.[6] Thus, the gender, racial, and sexual discourses of US empire were instrumental in rationalizing the project of military occupation. Ultimately, financial markets, foreign direct investments, and militarism were all interlinked.

In the mid-nineteenth century, US investment in Central America also led to large-scale migratory patterns. Afro-descendant workers from the British colonies were recruited to toil in the banana, coffee, and sugar plantations as well as in extensive infrastructure projects like the construction of railroads and the Panama Canal on the Central American isthmus.[7] Many more men and women immigrated on their own initiative. Contract labor from India, China, and Java added to the mixing of cultures in the region. Altogether, the Caribbean and Central American region became a transnational field of action and exchange.

The United States imposed a system of apartheid in both social segregation and payroll; West Indian workers building the Panama Canal earned less than their white counterparts and other laborers, though they worked in the most dangerous and wretched conditions.[8] Social segregation extended to all aspects of social life. For instance, Panamanians and West Indian migrants crossing into the Zone found themselves suddenly subject to the discipline and sometimes punishment enforced by a vastly superior military power.[9]

During and after the construction of the Panama Canal, thousands of sailors, marines, and soldiers, some as young as nineteen, flooded occupied Panamanian cities in search of alcohol, erotic entertainment, and the exoticism of the tropical destination. The disembarking of US forces—when the sailors in white uniforms went ashore and inundated the streets—was known as the *sabana blanca*, or the white wave. Some had been at sea for over six months and accumulated substantial funds to spend in the nearby towns and cities.[10] "Leaving the [US military] Zone and crossing into Panama, Americans delighted in finding 'everything "wide open" and raging,'" explains historian Julie Greene. "The journey to Cocoa Grove, where the streets were filled with saloons, brothels, Chinese shops, and lottery ticket sellers, provided American [military personnel] with an easy escape from the regimented Zone."[11]

When ships docked in the Canal Zone, businesses were crowded with men looking for exotic rest and recreation. Local merchants, many of whom were transnational migrants, duly strove to make Panama live up to the expectation of endless fiesta and tropical hospitality. They manufactured this fantasy by selling parakeets, monkeys, parrots, and snakes, which sailors used to adorn their heads and shoulders as they walked the streets of the Zone. When an orientalist trend swept the United States, merchant emigrants from China and South Asia sold jade, silk, clothing, games, and souvenirs. Cabarets staged orientalist shows, and even the Kelley Ritz, an upscale nightclub, had a room for private parties—a "beautiful Mandarin room . . . in Japanese style"—to cater to orientalist allure.[12] The military experience resembled a touristic diversion, with all the temptations of colonial, exotic fantasies. Central to the experience was the perception that local women were sexually available.

US canal workers, tourists, military troops, and administrative personnel attached to the canal had sexual access to both white and Afro-descended women. But when West Indian construction workers purchased sex, they mostly did so from women of color. Ultimately, the racism of the US imperial project deemed women, particularly Afro-descended women, as prostitutes, whether they sold sex or not. Thus, for most of the US troops, "anything local in a skirt was a whore."[13] Widespread tolerance for male debauchery, as well as the "boys will be boys" attitude that ascribed irrepressible sexuality to men, was common, often at the expense of West Indian women.[14] Numerous military men, many of whom circulated among various bases in the South Pacific and the Caribbean, already suffered from venereal disease—and yet they were not criminalized for either purchasing sex or spreading that disease.

Women from other LAC countries also tried their luck in Panama, which became a magnet for entrepreneurs, laborers, and performers. Argentine dancer María Estela Martínez Cartas met exiled Argentine president Juan Perón at a cabaret in Panama. Known more widely as Isabel, she became Perón's third wife and, when he was elected president of Argentina for the third time in 1973, his vice president. When he died the following year, she became president herself. Whether from Argentina, Barbados (and other Caribbean islands), Chile, Colombia, Costa Rica (and other Central American countries), Ecuador, Mexico, Peru, or Venezuela; or from the United States, Canada, or western European countries (especially Belgium, France, Italy, and Spain), migrant sex workers journeyed to Panama to seek their fortune with the sailors who enjoyed their furlough in the bustling sexual entertainment districts filled with saloons, dance halls, bars, hotels, and brothels.[15] All were lively cosmopolitan meeting places offering sexualized entertainment for US male personnel.[16]

The traffic of steamships from the United States brought women mostly of southern and eastern European ancestry to Panama to work in the entertainment district. Some were recruited, and others traveled of their own volition from Chicago, New Orleans, New York, and San Francisco. Some of these women contracted to perform in the taverns and bars, which often operated as thinly veiled sex businesses, and they eventually made their way into commercial sex. Due to the pervasiveness of US migrant women in the sex trade during the construction era, one canal official observed that "the term 'American women' had become the 'isthmian name for whores.'" Likewise, in local parlance, "American houses" was a slang term for brothels, connecting sexual commerce to the ubiquity of women from the United States making a living in the sex trade.[17] In contrast to West Indian women, Euro-American women became proprietors of brothels, saloons, and cabarets, connecting Panama to entertainment districts in the United States.

West Indian migrant women were the most disadvantaged of sojourners gravitating to the isthmus, subject to enforced registration with the state as sex workers, forced to undergo vaginal examinations, and criminalized if they left the red-light district. While Euro-American labor migrants were able to forge a new path that moved them from alterity to respectability,[18] no such path was available for women of color, who carried the stigma of being sex workers whether they participated in the sex trade or not.

The Panamanian sexual entertainment district was hierarchical and stratified. The high-end cabaret scene became an enclave of white privilege as nightclub owners contracted all-white theatrical groups from Chicago, New Orleans, or New York. White women benefited from racial and class privilege in relation to Afro-descended female sex workers. Historian Jeffrey Parker elucidates this when he writes: "Although women from many nationalities prospered in the entertainment districts selling alcoholic beverages and sex, white women from the States tended to dominate the 'respectable' or high-end brothel business."[19] US ideas and practices about race and gender, exemplified in Jim Crow social policies, permeated every aspect of commercial sex businesses.

Euro-American migrant women in the brothel districts achieved a high degree of notoriety and financial independence. Sadie Kohn and Violet Nelson managed a saloon called the Tuxedo, where, as independent businesswomen, they could reject undesirable clients and control the terms of sale. Likewise, Mary Lee Kelley found fame and fortune in owning and managing a cabaret, the Kelley Ritz—the cabaret with the fancy Mandarin-Japanese room mentioned earlier—with a transnational reputation and clientele, featuring Panama's best nightlife. Kelley's prestigious cabaret aimed for bourgeois respectability. One of its advertisements proclaimed: "A café and cabaret that has set the standard in Panama offering high-class and refined American entertainment nightly." Other racially segregated nightclubs, such as the Casino Vista Alegre, also declared in advertisements that their venues were exclusive places. One such announcement professed "a place where only respectable people are admitted."[20] White-owned establishments maintained white supremacy and concealed sexual commerce. "Respectability" became a marker for race.

As the owner of the Kelley Ritz, Mary Lee Kelley was careful to cultivate an image of whiteness. By positioning herself as a successful entrepreneur with clubs and connections in the United States, she created the image of an upscale club far removed from the seedy associations of the red-light district. But the quest for nightclub owners like Kelley was a difficult one: to spearhead a route to whiteness, wealth, and respectability in the sex industry. Unhelpful rumors circulated that Kelley was a brothel madam during the construction of the canal and that her performers were working-class ethnic whites who at the time were considered to have racially inferior backgrounds, or that she was suspected of being a "white slave" trafficker. It did not help that her club was also geographically adjacent to the red-light district, where Black sex workers lived. Nevertheless, Kelley sought to renegotiate the boundaries of race and gender in the tropics to make sexual labor discreet and respectable. Since high-end clubs were not licensed for sex work, the women working there could maintain a fictitious identity as entertainers, dancers, and singers. Another way was to rework racial identities. Racial realignment served this purpose because, in Panama, North American migrants of Jewish, Irish, Italian, and Polish background—considered racially inferior in the United States during the early twentieth century—were able to reformulate their identities. Further, the exclusion of women of color from the clubs facilitated a regime of respectability produced by anti-Blackness that was otherwise unavailable in the sex trade.

The reputational tension of white cabarets—and the many ways in which white women's reputations could be imperiled—were never fully resolved. The Kelley Ritz became known as both a respectable business establishment *and* a whorehouse, emphasizing the contested process of sexuality and racialization where white, working-class, undesirable ethnics could gain access to the benefits of whiteness by working in the sex trade.

Attempts to create respectability through whiteness paid off personally for the notorious Mary Lee Kelley in both financial success and fame. While traveling to the United States, she gave interviews to major newspapers, and various columns praised her for exemplifying that "high-class respectable entertainment could exist in the tropic environment."[21] Kelley's financial success facilitated her investment in cabarets in US cities and allowed her to remodel the famous bar the Old Absinthe House in New Orleans.[22] Her reputation was eventually sanitized enough for depiction in US cultural productions. She inspired Cole Porter's character Miss Hattie in the 1940 Broadway musical hit show *Panama Hattie*, which the Hollywood studio Metro-Goldwyn-Mayer turned into a film in 1942 and a television production in 1954.

Panama became a backdrop for white women's respectability in Hollywood film productions.[23] *Panama Lady* (1939) and *Panama Sal* (1957), in which "dancehall girls, nightclub singers, or hoteliers" were a cover for prostitution, reflect the longevity of the narrative in US popular culture about the white working-class gal in danger in the tropics.[24] In *Panama Hattie*, Cole Porter's catchy tune "(Did I Get Stinkin') at the Club Savoy" references getting drunk at a famous bordello in Colón, a city adjacent to the Panama Canal. Another tune, "I've Still Got My Health," speaks to one of the major concerns for soldiers, venereal disease. Stage and film productions like *My Sin* (1931), *Sailor Beware!* (1932), *Panama Flo* (1932), *Sensation Hunters* (1933), *Marie Galante* (1934), and *Swing High, Swing Low* (1937) portray white women as naïve and susceptible to corruption, racial mixing, and sexual violation but who are ultimately saved by a white man and returned to the United States.

For Euro-American women, prostitution and the prostitute identity could be concealed or elided within the context of US intervention in Panama. Women with, for instance, southern European heritage could sell sex with impunity while forging a path to "full whiteness." Unlike West Indian women, who were automatically marked as prostitutes, Euro-American migrant sex workers who labored in fancy entertainment venues could potentially bypass the stigma associated with their ethnic identity and their sexual labor by claiming the "white" category in a colonial setting. The sexual-economic exchange can have different meanings, as Panama's case shows. But the figure of the prostitute, a stigmatized and criminalized woman, can be used to discipline all women into conforming; otherwise, they are considered sluts or bitches—who can be killed or raped with impunity.

US military bases in Panama and the Caribbean islands were contested spaces that paved the way for the entrance of multinational tourism conglomerates. As scholars have begun to unlock the connections of engagement between militarism and tourism in the twentieth century, we can see how sex and sexuality underscored transnational spaces. As Vernadette Vicuña Gonzalez explains, the roots and routes of the US military "are foundational to tourist itineraries and imaginations."[25] From the military language used, such as being on tour—to refer to time spent in a hostile environment—to the transient nature of the voyage, to the expectation of sexual adventure in meeting hypersexual natives, tourism and militarism are linked in their contours. The notion of the sabana blanca is replicated when cruise ships disembark hordes of tourists in Panama City, San Juan, or Santo Domingo. As Vicuña Gonzalez attests: "Indeed, the world of the soldier and that of the tourist were often one and the same, illuminating how the routes of travel were mapped out and shared by military and civilian alike."[26] American military dominance in the Pacific and the Caribbean region shaped economies and desires for modern tourism. As with military settings, the sexual economies, both formal and informal, maintain the dominant structures of tourism. For the Caribbean region, Greg Thomas argues: "The power politics of sex are writ so large in the practice of tourism that the phrase 'sex tourism' seems redundant."[27] These earlier histories are important to excavate because they acknowledge the interconnectedness of US empire and sex work.

In the next section, I explore the possibilities for collective action by and for sex workers' rights. As with the case of Panama discussed above, the transnational sphere constitutes sexual labor in LAC.

Sex Workers' Mobilization

Sex workers in LAC have a long history of organizing, publicly challenging and resisting unjust regulations and policies. Notwithstanding that most accounts of the origins of the sex worker movement reference Global North precursors, in the Americas sex workers have been organizing collectively since the end of the nineteenth century. The conception of prostitution as a form of labor—and not sin, vice, or the depravity of "fallen women"—was first articulated by a Caribbean collective of prostitutes. An often ignored forerunner to the global movement for sex worker rights began in Cuba. In the late nineteenth century, during a period of increased trans-Caribbean migration, women traveled from the Canary Islands, European countries, Mexico, Panama, Puerto Rico, Spain, the United States, and Venezuela to cosmopolitan Havana to eke out a living. Many ended up in the red-light district. Some of the brothel owners, or madams, were prosperous: having earned large sums of money in their youth, they invested in venues that offered prostitution, gambling, and dancing.[28] As brothel owners, they used their economic power to influence public opinion and challenge the Spanish colonial administration over their role in society. As historian María del Carmen Barcia Zequeira points out, sex workers self-defined as a marginal and exploited class because they were victims of the continuous extortion of the authorities who controlled their activities.[29]

In Havana at the end of the nineteenth century, women who made a living in the regulated brothel system envisioned a political party that would demand their labor rights. A group of Havana sex workers created a newspaper to voice their views against the colonial government, opposing corruption in the regulation of prostitution and calling for a political party led by sex workers. It was financed by wealthy sex workers and edited by a Spanish immigrant anarchist, Victorino Reineri Jimeno. The short-lived newspaper was intended as a publication for and by prostitutes and a medium for protest against discriminatory laws and unethical officials in the colonial government.[30] *La Cebolla: Periódico ilustrado, órgano oficial del partido de su nombre* (The Onion: Illustrated newspaper, official organ of the party with the same name) was widely distributed throughout Havana and other Cuban provinces to advocate openly for the rights of prostitutes in Havana.

In four issues during the month of September 1888, articles in *La Cebolla* ridiculed and protested the high regulatory fees and the medical checkups imposed on brothel-based prostitutes by government regulations. The "horizontals"—the name used in the newspaper for prostitutes—did not shy away from protesting the control over their lives by challenging an exploitative administrative system paid for with all the regulations enacted over their bodies. Another *La Cebolla* article advocated the formation of a prostitutes' professional guild to back their demands. These women challenged the social order of late nineteenth-century Havana by calling for a collective that demanded the recognition of sexual services as a form of labor. Using humor and candor, sex workers publicly exposed their exploitation in print media, inspiring the creation of a new identity for prostitutes as laboring women.

The rebellious and demanding spectacle of so-called public women who had no shame in posing for pictorials and calling for recognition in *La Cebolla* was an act of defiance against a Spanish colonial administration already under attack by the independence movement. Government officials retaliated by quickly banning the newspaper and incarcerating the editor. Nevertheless, the harm to the colonial regime was done, public visibility was established, and sex workers' demands were voiced. The short campaign highlighted the fact that prostitutes did not have to be politically powerless, invisible, and easily vilified.

There does not appear to be a continuous movement of organizing sex worker collectives, but there are many legal cases in which women united to demand more control over their working conditions. For instance, sex workers continued to exercise whatever agency was available to them, as Jeffrey Parker argues of the many legal cases women launched in Panama to challenge the regulations governing the sex trade. Sex workers were also active in regional political movements. For instance, in Nicaragua, sex workers were instrumental in the resistance movement against US imperialism during the early twentieth century.[31] The close contact between US soldiers and sex workers during the military occupation facilitated information sharing between sex workers and US military personnel. Sex workers would pass on information—effectively working as spies—to Nicaraguan rebel leader Augusto Sandino and his guerrilla fighters. They led the Sandinista fighters to precise military targets and helped extract and even transport weapons (it is said that they partially hid some weapons in their clothing). Whether working in bars or other public spaces, sex workers played a vital role by assisting Sandino and his crew, earning his respect and recognition. Thereafter, Sandino often acknowledged that the women had risked their safety to contribute to the struggle strategically.

In the early twentieth century, sex workers were pivotal to a tenants' rights social protest effort in Veracruz, Mexico, where they initiated a citywide tenant strike. "¡Estoy en huelga y no pago renta!" (I am on strike and not paying rent!), declared posters throughout Veracruz. Sex workers were the first tenants to burn their mattresses and throw them into the street while suspending payment to their landlords. After that, the women working in the city's red-light district also mobilized to complain publicly to the mayor at a public meeting about the extremely high rates they paid for their rooms and the extortion they experienced from the administrators who collected the rent. Theirs was the first step in inspiring a statewide tenant movement (*el movimiento inquilinario*) to appear on the political scene. Many other impoverished women took inspiration from their leadership and joined the movement. Their fruitful actions of popular resistance resonated not only with tenants throughout the port city, who were also paying excessive fines, but with anarchists, communists, and syndicalists, who joined the strike. The renters' movement would eventually spread to other Mexican cities.[32]

Lizabeth Paravisini-Gebert points out that several migrant Cuban sex workers in Haitian brothels in the 1940s and 1950s, "prized for their light skins [. . .] returned home to join the anti-Batista movement, leading the effort to combat the exploitation of women, particularly young girls, in the infamous Cuban brothels of that dictator's reign."[33] Once again, women working in the sex industry participated in mobilization against oppression. The historical accounts discussed above reveal how sex workers were part of social movements and at the forefront of struggles for social justice in the region. However, whether anarchist, communist, or feminist, no social or political movement took up sex workers' rights in the region.

Transnational Sex Worker Organizing

By the end of the twentieth century, the identity of the prostitute had begun to shift into new terrain, in part due to their transnational collective action and advocacy. Starting in the 1980s, social movement mobilization took place across national borders, with RedTraSex an example of the processes of transnationalism. The flow of information and ideas and the social production of a new subjectivity have allowed for building cross-border solidarities and politics in the transnational realm. This is a movement by and for sex workers.[34]

RedTraSex—Red de Mujeres Trabajadoras Sexuales de Latinoamérica y el Caribe (Network of Women Sex Workers of Latin America and the Caribbean)—headquartered in Argentina, is the largest transnational sex worker network in LAC. Currently, RedTraSex includes fourteen member countries across the region whose representatives meet regularly and coordinate action plans, research, and advocacy efforts.[35] As sociologist Jorgelina Loza explains, RedTraSex is a "contemporary transnational experience directly influenced by the national contexts of its members, while receiving the impact of regional and international events."[36] Loza establishes that "the central claim of the women that make up RedTraSex is their demand to be recognized by the nation states to which they belong as subjects of rights, that is, as workers who have the right to access decent working conditions and social benefits: housing, health, retirement, and pensions."[37] Through a feminist, rights-based approach, RedTraSex coordinates programs to unite sex workers around issues that impact their lives, including conducting investigations and advocating for improved access to medical care free of discrimination, antiviolence initiatives, safe working environments, sexual health, and mobilization in opposition to human trafficking. The connections produced by transnational ties within the region and internationally have fortified activists' image and legitimacy and created a platform to denounce the normalized violence that sex workers routinely face.

Since the 1980s, sex workers have been organizing and networking across national borders. RedTraSex emerged from these regional struggles to transform policies into a transnational formation. The sex worker movement in LAC first arose in the early 1980s, when collective action was taken up in Ecuador. In 1982, a group of sex workers challenged police violence against them and the system of exploitation by brothel owners by starting an organization called the Asociación de Trabajadoras Autonomas "22 de Junio" de El Oro (Association of Autonomous Workers "22 June" of El Oro [a province of Ecuador]).[38] This was followed by other prostitute collectives that emerged later that decade: the Asociación de Meretrices Profesionales del Uruguay (Association of Professional Female Prostitutes of Uruguay), created in 1986, and the Brazilian Network of Sex Workers in 1987. The proliferation of groups has been steady for the past forty years. There are now separate organizations for cisgender and trans sex workers in most countries in LAC; some countries, such as Ecuador, have an organization in each province.

Sex workers' second entry point into the transnational realm emerged through their responses to governments' and supranational health associations' increased attention to the role that sex workers played in preventing and eradicating HIV. Global programs to eradicate the HIV virus, from supranational health associations such as the World Health Organization to aid programs from individual European countries, mobilized sex workers and spurred conferences and research projects that sought to integrate sex workers into prevention efforts. While the HIV/AIDS pandemic created an entry point for renewed attempts to survey and treat sex workers as vectors of sexually trans-mitted infections, sex workers took an active role in raising political conscious-ness and articulating demands for recognition as laborers, for policy change, and for fair treatment from local governments.

The NGO boom in the LAC region has also facilitated research and advo-cacy efforts.[39] A 1996 meeting in Costa Rica, funded by the government of the Netherlands and carried out by the Instituto Latinoamericano de Prevención y Educación en Salud (ILPES; the Latin American Institute of Prevention and Education on Health), brought together sixty sex workers. Elena Reynaga, the current executive secretary of RedTraSex, recalled: "We were pure enthusiasm, discovery, strength. A tingle ran through our bodies with increasing intensity when another colleague took the microphone and shared her reality. Her reality was the reality of all."[40] According to Reynaga, it was at the ILPES conference that sex workers decided to organize transnationally in the region to demand the recognition of their labor and demand rights from their respective govern-ments.[41] The ILPES meeting led to the founding of RedTraSex.

By the twenty-first century, the groundwork had been laid for transnational sex worker solidarity from international bodies. Transnational advocacy calling for the decriminalization of sex work has generated support for sex workers' rights from global health bodies such as the Joint United Nations Programme on HIV/AIDS (UNAIDS) and the World Health Organization. Human rights organizations Amnesty International and Human Rights Watch (HRW) have raised attention to the violence inflicted with impunity on both cisgender and trans sex workers. In 2016, Amnesty International joined a group of organiza-tions, including the Global Alliance Against Traffic in Women, the Global Commission on HIV and the Law, and the UN Special Rapporteur on the Right to Health, to advocate for the decriminalization of consensual sex work.

In 2017, the Inter-American Commission on Human Rights (IACHR) of the Organization of American States (OAS) hosted leaders from RedTraSex in Washington, DC, for the first time. At the meeting, sex workers presented infor-mation about the high rate of killings and institutional violence carried out by security forces and other state agents.[42] OAS commissioner Margarette Macaulay stated: "The information the Commission received is extremely troubling, and we are going to ensure that whenever we are dealing with the rights of women [. . .] we bring up the issue of the rights of sex workers in the entire hemisphere."[43]

It is in the transnational sphere that RedTraSex has articulated demands and garnered support for their claims against institutional violence, including abuse and exploitation by national police and military forces, and discrimination and stigma in access to social services. State policies of necropolitics are being laid bare.[44] However, the struggle is only getting started, and there are many vulnerabilities in cross-border collective actions. Even within RedTraSex, issues of linguistic, racial, ethnic, cultural, political, ideological, and historical difference are vast and generate cross-cultural conflict. State approaches to the regulation of commercial sex are also not uniform in LAC. Dependence on funding from Global North philanthropic and intergovernmental organizations poses another vulnerability. These are only some of the issues, along with many others, that will continue to challenge RedTraSex.

Conclusion

These two disparate case studies propose that sex work has a multivalent meaning and is constituted by the transnational sphere—a field of action that reveals the plasticity of the sex worker category. In the case of Panama, the Eurocentric concept of prostitution was socially constructed to convey notions of gender, sexuality, race, and class. In the discursive domain, what counted as prostitution and whose labor was discounted was also embedded in the category. US women whose status as whites was contested, migrating to Panama, were able to enter a transnational realm that enhanced their racial categorization by distancing them from a stigmatized ethnic identity and occupation. Their occupational identity became more malleable as a product of class and racial formations in an imperial setting. In contrast, anti-Black politics rendered all women of African descent as prostitutes.

The case of RedTraSex suggests that the transnational realm offers a level of richness at the global institutional level that builds on advocacy, networking, and alliance building. Beyond the nation-state, RedTraSex has been able to form networks and coalition campaigns that have transformed the meaning of the category. In the 1980s, a reformulation of sex work by and for sex workers within the transnational sphere proved key to transforming the discursive domain. Incomparable momentum has been gained in the transnational realm, where the long process and tense path toward public and private recognition of sex worker rights has begun.

Notes

1. Magaly Rodríguez García, Lex Heerma van Voss, and Elise van Nederveen Meerkerk, *Selling Sex in the City: A Global History of Prostitution, 1600s–2000s* (Brill, 2017).

2. Alejandro de la Fuente, *Havana and the Atlantic in the Sixteenth Century* (University of North Carolina Press, 2008); Adriana Piscitelli, "Amor, apego, e interesse: Trocas sexuais, econômicas e afetivas em cenários transnacionais," in *Gênero, sexo, amor e dinheiro: Mobilidades transnacionais envolvendo o Brasil*, ed. Adriana Piscitelli, Gláucia de Oliveira Assis, and José Miguel Nieto Olivar (Campinas, Brazil: Núcleo de Estudos de Gênero Pagu; Editora da Unicamp, 2011), 537–82; and Joseli Maria Silva and Marcio Jose Ornat, "Intersectionality and Transnational Mobility Between Brazil and Spain in *Travesti* Prostitution Networks," *Gender, Place and Culture* 22, no. 8 (2015): 1073–88.

3. Lara Putnam, *The Company They Kept: Migrants and the Politics of Gender in Caribbean Costa Rica, 1870–1960* (University of North Carolina Press, 2002); Donna J. Guy, *Sex and Danger in Buenos Aires: Prostitution, Family, and Nation in Argentina* (University of Nebraska Press, 1991); and Jeffrey Wayne Parker, "Sex Work on the Isthmus of Panama," in *Trafficking in Women, 1924–1926: The Paul Kinsie Reports for the League of Nations*, vol. 2, ed. Jean-Michel Chaumont, Magaly Rodríguez García, and Paul Servais (United Nations, 2017), 166–71.

4. Adriana Piscitelli, "Tránsitos: Circulación de brasileñas en el ámbito de la transnacionalización de los mercados sexual y matrimonial," *Horizontes Antropológicos* 15, no. 31 (June 2009): 101–36.

5. Andrew Byers, *The Sexual Economy of War: Discipline and Desire in the US Army* (Cornell University Press, 2019), 3.

6. Micah Wright, "'Protection Against the Lust of Men': Progressivism, Prostitution and Rape in the Dominican Republic under US Occupation, 1916–24," *Gender and History* 28, no. 3 (November 2016): 623–40.

7. Ronald N. Harpelle, "Racism and Nationalism in the Creation of Costa Rica's Pacific Coast Banana Enclave," *The Americas* 56, no. 3 (January 2000): 29–51.

8. Koufi Boukman Barima, "Caribbean Migrants in Panama and Cuba, 1851–1927: The Struggles, Opposition and Resistance of Jamaicans of African Ancestry," *Journal of Pan-African Studies* 5, no. 9 (March 2013): 43–62; and Bonham C. Richardson, *Panama Money in Barbados, 1900–1920* (University of Tennessee Press, 2004).

9. Julie Greene, *The Canal Builders: Making America's Empire at the Panama Canal* (Penguin Press, 2009), 73–74.

10. A 1923 *New York Times* article reported that when 146 naval ships anchored in the US port in the Canal Zone, sailors spent three million dollars within two months, an amount equal to half the money circulating in the entire country. "Panama Profits by Fleet's Visit," *New York Times*, April 18, 1923, quoted in Jeffrey Wayne Parker, "Empire's Angst: The Politics of Race, Migration, and Sex Work in Panama, 1903–1945" (PhD diss., University of Texas at Austin, 2013), 203.

11. Greene, *The Canal Builders*, 73–74.

12. "New Cabaret Opens Today," *Panama Star and Herald*, June 1, 1918, quoted in Parker, "Empire's Angst," 200.

13. Michael E. Donoghue, *Borderland on the Isthmus: Race, Culture, and the Struggle for the Canal Zone* (Duke University Press, 2014), 141.

14. Joan Flores-Villalobos, "'Freak Letters': Tracing Gender, Race, and Diaspora in the Panama Canal Archive," *Small Axe: A Caribbean Journal of Criticism* 23, no. 2 (July 2019): 34–56.

15. Parker, "Empire's Angst," 109.

16. Greene, *The Canal Builders*.

17. Parker, "Empire's Angst," 23; and John Major, *Prize Possession: The United States and the Panama Canal, 1903–1979* (Cambridge University Press, 1993), 130.

18. Ann L. Stoler, "Making Empire Respectable: The Politics of Race and Sexual Morality in 20th-Century Colonial Cultures," *American Ethnologist* 16, no. 4 (November 1989): 634–60; and Parker, "Empire's Angst," 188.

19. Parker, "Empire's Angst," 29.

20. Parker, "Empire's Angst," 197.

21. Parker, "Empire's Angst," 211.

22. Parker, "Empire's Angst," 202.

23. Stoler, "Making Empire Respectable."

24. Donoghue, *Borderland on the Isthmus*, 143.

25. Vernadette Vicuña Gonzalez, *Securing Paradise: Tourism and Militarism in Hawai'i and the Philippines* (Duke University Press, 2013), 4. See also Vernadette Vicuña Gonzalez and Jana K. Lipman, "Tours of Duty and Tours of Leisure," *American Studies* 68, no. 3 (September 2016): 507–21; and Cynthia Enloe, *Bananas, Beaches and Bases: Making Feminist Sense of International Politics*, 2nd ed. (University of California Press, 2014).

26. Vicuña Gonzalez, *Securing Paradise*, 12.

27. Greg Thomas, *The Sexual Demon of Colonial Power: Pan-African Embodiment and Erotic Schemes of Empire* (Indiana University Press, 2007), 130.

28. María del Carmen Barcia Zequeira, "Entre el poder y la crisis: Las prostitutas se defienden," in *Mujeres latinoamericanas: Historia y cultura, siglos XVI al XIX*, ed. Luisa Campuzano (Casa de las Américas, 1997), 263–73.

29. Barcia Zequeira, "Entre el poder y la crisis."

30. Tiffany A. Sippial, *Prostitution, Modernity, and the Making of the Cuban Republic, 1840–1920* (University of North Carolina Press, 2013); and Mayra Beers, "Murder in San Isidro: Crime and Culture During the Second Cuban Republic," *Cuban Studies* 34 (2003): 97–129.

31. Victoria González-Rivera, *Before the Revolution: Women's Rights and Right-Wing Politics in Nicaragua, 1821–1979* (Pennsylvania State University Press, 2011).

32. Andrew Grant Wood, *Revolution in the Street: Women, Workers, and Urban Protest in Veracruz, 1870–1927* (Scholarly Resources, 2001); and Andrew Wood, "Urban Rebels: The Mexican Tenant Movement in the 1920s," *The Latin Americanist* 54, no. 4 (December 2010): 121–42.

33. Lizabeth Paravisini-Gebert, "Decolonizing Feminism: The Home-Grown Roots of Caribbean Women's Movements," in *Daughters of Caliban: Caribbean Women in the*

Twentieth Century, ed. Consuelo López Springfield (Indiana University Press, 1997), 3–17.

34. Amalia L. Cabezas, "Latin American and Caribbean Sex Workers: Gains and Challenges in the Movement," *Anti-Trafficking Review*, no. 12 (April 2019): 37–56; and Amalia L. Cabezas, "Latin American and Caribbean Sex Workers: Gains and Challenges in the Movement" (video), Global Alliance Against Traffic in Women, YouTube, April 25, 2019, https://www.youtube.com/watch?v=iCDb29Hy6OY.

35. The fourteen countries are Argentina, Bolivia, Chile, Colombia, Costa Rica, the Dominican Republic, El Salvador, Guatemala, Honduras, Mexico, Nicaragua, Panama, Paraguay, and Peru.

36. Jorgelina Mariana Loza, "Putas feministas en América Latina: La RedTraSex y su vínculo con el feminismo latinoamericano," *Revista Argentina de Sociología* 12, no. 21 (2017): 6–21.

37. Jorgelina Loza, "Ideas nacionales en la escala regional: La experiencia de acción colectiva transnacional de la RedTraSex en América Latina," Facultad Latinoamericana de Ciencias Sociales, Universidad de Buenos Aires; Consejo Nacional de Investigaciones Científicas y Técnicas, 2012, http://web.isanet.org/Web/Conferences/FLACSO-ISA%20Buenos-Aires%202014/Archive/8886d0d9-3dd9-4693-9d10-aa1ac5c7320f.pdf.

38. Angelita Abad, Marena Briones, Tatiana Cordero, Rosa Manzo, and Marta Marchán, "The Association of Autonomous Women Workers, Ecuador, '22nd June,'" in *Global Sex Workers: Rights, Resistance, and Redefinition*, ed. Kamala Kempadoo and Jo Doezema (Routledge, 1998), 172–77.

39. Sonia E. Alvarez, "Advocating Feminism: The Latin American Feminist NGO 'Boom,'" *International Feminist Journal of Politics* 1, no. 2 (1999): 181–209.

40. RedTraSex, *La revolución de las trabajadoras sexuales: 20 años de organización de la RedTraSex de Latinoamérica y el Caribe*, 2017, https://biblioteca.redtrasex.org/handle/123456789/146.

41. Elena Reynaga, interview with the author, February 4, 2021.

42. Inter-American Commission on Human Rights, "IACHR Holds First Hearing on the Rights of Sex Workers in the Americas," press release no. 036/17, March 23, 2017, https://www.oas.org/en/iachr/media_center/preleases/2017/036.asp.

43. Inter-American Commission on Human Rights, "IACHR Holds First Hearing."

44. Achille Mbembe, *Necropolitics*, trans. Steven Corcoran (Duke University Press, 2019).

CHAPTER 8

Transnational Genealogies of Performance Against Gender Violence in Argentina and Chile

BRENDA WERTH

CREATED BY LASTESIS, A feminist collective from Valparaíso, Chile, the flash mob performance *A Rapist in Your Path* (*Un violador en tu camino*) went viral after it was performed in Santiago on November 25, 2019, to commemorate the International Day for the Elimination of Violence Against Women. Inspired by the writings of Argentine feminist scholar Rita Segato, the performance enacts a manifesto against victim shaming, sexual assault, and state violence.[1] Before the arrival of COVID-19, it was performed in hundreds of cities in countries across the globe, including Colombia, Mexico, India, France, the United States, and Turkey, where the attempt to stage the performance was broken up by police.[2] In New York City, about a hundred women gathered to perform the protest outside the Manhattan courthouse where film producer Harvey Weinstein was being tried for rape.[3] US congressional representative Alexandria Ocasio-Cortez tweeted the lyrics and declared her solidarity with her Chilean sisters. The performance's catchy, powerful chants and simple yet moving choreography have contributed to its transnational appeal and adaptability. In March 2020, lockdowns cleared the streets, and people spoke of twin pandemics— COVID-19 and gender violence—which were proliferating across Latin America at alarming rates. The massive outpouring of bodies on the streets in collective action to denounce gender violence were halted, creating frustration but also new opportunities for transnational activism across digital platforms.

In this chapter, I examine specific case studies from theater and performance protest that link contemporary gender violence to the legacy of state violence orchestrated as part of Operation Condor, a transnational alliance of South American military regimes created in the 1970s that coordinated cross-border intelligence operations and spread terror through the torture, execution, and disappearance of political opponents.[4] I begin my analysis by examining the transnational scope of two foundational theatrical works of democratic transition and postdictatorship: Ariel Dorfman's *Death and the Maiden* (*La muerte y la doncella*, Chile, 1990) and Eduardo Pavlovsky's *Pas de deux* (*Paso de dos*, Argentina, 1990). I then analyze how these works lend insight to contextualizing the explosion of contemporary feminist activist performances in Chile and Argentina in actions such as *A Rapist in Your Path* in Chile (2019), and the *siluetazos* of the NiUnaMenos movement (Not One Less, 2015) and La Marea Verde (the Green Tide) in Argentina. I consider how feminist movements in Chile and Argentina engage the body in activist performance in the constitution of new political subjects, and the extent to which they show awareness of genealogies of protest that inform their work through the borrowing of symbols, slogans, and embodied practices from the dictatorship period. And last, by identifying the rooted histories of performance practices originating in Chile and Argentina, this chapter also contests the notion that movements such as NiUnaMenos and the flash mob performance *A Rapist in Your Path* emerged solely as versions of the #MeToo movement in the United States. I thus highlight the development of crucial feminist perspectives and transnational activism from Latin America that are often overlooked in scholarly discussion and mainstream media accounts of global feminist action.

Toward a Geopolitics of Reception: *Death and the Maiden* and *Pas de deux*

Movements such as NiUnaMenos and the flash mob performance *A Rapist in Your Path* constitute powerful examples of transnational activism, both through their digital circulation as well as through their diverse choreographic adaptations in sites across the globe. *Death and the Maiden* and *Pas de deux*, often considered canonical plays exemplifying the national theater traditions of Chile and Argentina, respectively, also bear witness, in complex ways, to the aftermath of the terror and shared repressive practices of Operation Condor. These early works have unique transnational histories through their engagement with themes of dictatorship and democratic transition and in their restaging across borders since the 1990s.

Ariel Dorfman's *Death and the Maiden* and Eduardo Pavlovsky's *Pas de deux*, works exploring the relationship between a captor and his torture victim, at their premieres were praised for exposing the widespread practice of torture under dictatorship. Both plays highlight and to varying degree reinforce tropes of gender violence that have endured since the dictatorships in Chile (1973–1990) and Argentina (1976–1983). In *Death and the Maiden*, the main character, Paulina, a former political prisoner who had been held captive, tortured, and raped during the dictatorship, finds herself in a position of power vis-à-vis her former captor and rapist and threatens to kill him unless he confesses to his crimes. The satisfaction of seeing Paulina fighting for justice on her own accord, particularly in light of the lack of trials in Chile and the omission of survivors of torture in the Rettig Report (officially the National Commission for Truth and Reconciliation Report, 1991), is complicated by the fact that in the play Paulina is described by both her husband and her former captor as an unreliable witness who is mentally unstable and is trying to sabotage due process and the work of the truth commission.

Pavlovksy's *Pas de deux* is more problematic in its representation of torture and gender violence. In the play, a man and a woman, EL and ELLA (played by Pavlovsky and his wife, Susana Evans), wrestle in a tub of mud onstage. As the stage directions indicate, ELLA is near death. Over the course of the play, EL undresses her, and, by the end, she is naked and he is shirtless. EL overpowers her onstage physically, subjecting her to a choke hold, pulling her breasts, and throwing her down in the mud, while throughout she moans in anguish. ELLA has no lines in the play, though she speaks through a third character, seated in the audience. From this dislocated voice, we learn that ELLA resists EL by refusing to acquiesce to his desire to be named by her. Yet her resistance is complicated by the fact that she also desires him sexually.[5] Through the disjointed dialogue between EL and ELLA, it becomes clear over the course of the play that he had been her captor, and she his victim, under the dictatorship (implicitly alluded to). One of the many troubling aspects of this play is the fact that the victim's refusal to name her torturer is portrayed as an act of resistance. In the postdictatorship context, the act of not naming reinforces a culture of impunity surrounding the human rights violations committed during dictatorship as well as persisting patterns of gender violence in Argentina.[6]

Both plays usher in a new democratic era while at the same time revealing misogynistic gender attitudes and gender violence tropes that flourished under dictatorship. As Vannina Sztainbok and Teresa Macías note, "while the plays disturb the civilizational and gendered project of authoritarianism, they do not completely disavow it and continue to rely on liberal discourses of rationality, heteropatriarchy, and recognition."[7] Envisioned by the playwrights as agents of resistance, the characters in these plays nonetheless embody the gender stereotypes that had been cultivated by the military regimes: Paulina, an unreliable witness, crazed and unable to act rationally; and ELLA, a voiceless victim.

While *Death and the Maiden* was received favorably everywhere except for Chile, Pavlovsky's *Pas de deux* was praised solely by audiences in Argentina with some notable exceptions at the time of its premiere. Scholars Marguerite Feitlowitz and Diana Taylor have written extensively about their own personal responses to the staging in Buenos Aires. In conversation with Laura Yusem, the play's director, Taylor suggested that the performance "reproduced rather than dismantled the military's authoritarian discourse."[8] Likewise, Feitlowitz questioned why the violence had to take place on a woman's body, adding that "surely there were other theatrical recourses."[9] Feitlowitz's and Taylor's observations offer clues as to why *Pas de deux* did not export to international audiences as successfully as *Death and the Maiden*. While both plays explore themes of torture under dictatorship, *Pas de deux* reproduces acts of gender violence graphically onstage. The play also ends in femicide (though it wasn't referred to as such at the time of the premiere), which raises ethical questions pertaining to the representation of violence onstage and links the play to current feminist practices denouncing femicide in Chile and Argentina. Rita Segato's work on the pedagogy of cruelty addresses one of the main paradoxes of representations of gender violence, which also applies to Pavlovsky's play: it exposes violence ostensibly as a form of denunciation but essentially mimics and encourages its reproduction.[10]

Scholars have discussed the tension between the global and the local in *Death and the Maiden* in light of Dorfman's description of the setting of the play as "probably Chile though it could be about any country that has recently emerged from dictatorship."[11] Sophia McClennen writes, "What is of interest is the way that the setting of the play reasserts the national context of Chile while also speaking to a global audience."[12] Patricia Ybarra is more critical, stating: "Ultimately, setting a play in a generic Latin American setting was simply read as a mode of allegorizing Latin America rather than asking audiences to pay attention to Latin American formal tactics as a mode of understanding hemispheric political violence."[13] Ybarra's following statement is particularly relevant for this analysis: "Whatever their faults, these plays reveal the beginning of a transnational consciousness, buttressed by the dissemination of information about U.S. involvement in Southern Cone and Central American dictatorships in the mainstream press."[14] As I show throughout this analysis, both the formal arts and more grassroots activist performances play a significant role in developing this transnational consciousness and fostering cultural exchange and feminist mobilization within and across borders.

Genealogies of Patriarchy and Gender Violence in the Southern Cone

Scholars have documented extensively how Southern Cone authoritarian regimes reinforced conservative gender roles in order to consolidate the image of a patriarchal and heteronormative nation.[15] These images build and expand on nation-building narratives of family promoted through what Doris Sommer calls "the foundational fictions" of the nineteenth century in Latin America.[16] In colonial Latin America, the Catholic Church played a prominent role in reinforcing patriarchy and confining women to the private sphere through the "mapping of knowledge and gender."[17] Indigenous and Afro–Latin American women, trans women, and members of the LGBTQ+ community have been "trapped in bad scripts" imposed over centuries of colonial rule, nation building, and periods of state-orchestrated violence.[18] Taking into account the long history of patriarchy and gender violence in Latin America, here I am interested in exploring the continuing impacts of these overlapping and accumulating legacies of violence, focusing specifically on how tropes and practices of gender violence were deployed in Augusto Pinochet's Chile and by the junta in Argentina.[19]

Chile and Argentina were key members of Operation Condor.[20] In 1992, the discovery in Asunción, Paraguay, of an "Archive of Terror" containing official records documenting repression under Alfredo Stroessner's regime revealed important information about the functioning of Condor.[21] In 1999, 2002, and most recently in 2018, subsequent troves of documents were declassified, offering further confirmation that the CIA, the US State Department, and the US Defense Department were all well informed about the campaign.[22] Operation Condor has also received more attention both in Argentina and internationally due to the Operation Condor Trial, which ended in Buenos Aires in May 2016 after more than three years and convicted fifteen defendants of kidnappings and torture of more than a hundred victims of the campaign.[23] As Francesca Lessa notes, "this emblematic trial broke new ground in human rights and transitional justice, for prosecuting for the first time atrocities of a transnational nature."[24] In her analysis of the trial, Lessa emphasizes the importance of taking into account transnational approaches to the field of human rights and transitional justice, and she criticizes the tendency of scholars to continue to focus almost exclusively on the role of national actors operating in national frameworks.[25]

Lessa's critique dovetails with a dynamic body of scholarship on the transnational turn in Cold War studies in Latin America exploring how social and cultural actors disrupt and reinforce existing transnational frameworks and generate new transnational alliances through the creation of art and activism.[26] I focus on the transnational reframing of cultural production and activist performances as they engage with symbolic systems and discourses emerging within and across national borders during and after democratic transition. This transnational reframing encourages consideration not only of how gender and sexuality were deployed and interpreted within national frameworks but also of how Operation Condor, and particularly the network's emphasis on the concept of subversion, was instrumental in creating a culture of gender violence and oppression that was central to demonstrating authoritarian power and whose legacy continues to the present day.

A key record in the 2018 trove of declassified documents on Operation Condor titled "Text of the Agreement by Condor Countries Regulating Their Subversive Targets" provides guidelines for the operations, logistics, and everyday bureaucratic functions of the campaign and emphasizes the centrality of the concept of subversion in providing a rationale for the countries' actions.[27] Manuel Contreras Sepúlveda, former head of Chile's National Intelligence

Directorate (Dirección de Inteligencia Nacional, DINA), described Operation Condor as a "gentlemen's pact."[28] A vehicle of Cold War masculinity, the campaign played a significant role in framing nonconforming gender and sexuality as subversion. Participating countries cultivated links between communism and sexual subversion in their respective national frameworks. In Argentina, the military junta "constructed a link between youth, sexual deviancy and subversion, which they saw as the characteristics of the 'enemy within' that jeopardised the fabric of the national body."[29] In his study on gender, sexuality, and the subversive in the Escola Superior de Guerra in Brazil, Benjamin Cowan discusses how sexuality became one of the central discourses in conceptualizing subversion: "By the 1970s, national security theorists stressed degenerative, 'perverse' sex as a primary weapon of the 'subversive' and/or 'communist' enemy against which they so fanatically inveighed."[30] The bodies of political prisoners in both countries were codified sexually: "[P]olitical deviancy was also sexual deviancy," according to María Rosa Olivera-Williams in her study on sexual violence under dictatorship in the Southern Cone.[31]

The equation between immoral or threatening sexual practices and subversion consolidated by the military regimes under the framework of Operation Condor continued to shape attitudes toward gender and sexuality after the transitions to democracy. The well-known slogan "algo habrá hecho" (they must have done something) became common currency during Argentina's civic-military dictatorship, suggesting that individuals who were detained, tortured, or disappeared by the military must have done something to deserve it.[32] The slogan exemplifies the victim blaming that continues between past and present in Argentina, and it perpetuates the concept of subversion that operated during the dictatorship. In recent years, this saying has been recycled by the media to suggest that women who are victims of femicide or gender violence may have done something to deserve it. While the origins of gender violence in Argentina and Chile can be found in the authoritarian regimes of the 1970s and 1980s as well as in legacies of coloniality of gender and the patriarchal systems that preceded them, the continued refashioning of this slogan in the present offers one specific example of how, according to Barbara Sutton, "violence produced during the dictatorship and disseminated to the rest of society still survives in direct or subtle forms."[33]

Dorfman's and Pavlovsky's plays have most frequently been discussed as works about torture, yet they are also specifically works about rape.[34] The links they establish between state terror and rape are key to understanding the endurance of patterns of gender violence and the emergence of feminist movements across Argentina and Chile. In focusing on the depictions of rape in these plays specifically as examples of gender violence and not only as torture, I participate in "unraveling the cultural texts that have obsessively made rape both so pervasive and so invisible a theme."[35] I join efforts of Southern Cone scholars who are revisiting original survivor testimony from the 1980s to draw attention to the specifically gendered aspects of torture that took place under dictatorship.[36]

Recent scholarship highlighting gendered aspects of torture under dictatorship has emerged in Argentina and Chile at a moment characterized by a major shift in mainstream understanding and advocacy of gender and sexuality justice across Latin America. Beginning in the 1990s, landmark international events such as the Fourth World Conference on Women in 1995 in Beijing and the adoption of the Rome Statute establishing the International Criminal Court in 1998 contributed to this shift in perspective, as did the rise of the Pink Tide and progressive legislation on gender and sexuality rights in Latin America.[37] At the Fourth World Conference on Women, the idea of "gender perspective" was introduced as a crucial approach to achieving gender equality; it was seen as vital to the future transformation of "social institutions, laws, cultural norms and community practices that are discriminatory."[38] Artists and activists in feminist mobilizations and protests such as NiUnaMenos and *A Rapist in Your Path* have also continued to reinforce the importance of this gender perspective. While the idea of "gender perspective" described by the United Nations Entity for Gender Equality and the Empowerment of Women (UN Women) is presented as forward looking, in postdictatorship Southern Cone countries, the application of a gender perspective in a human rights context is also retrospective.[39] In Argentina, the reopening of human rights trials of repressors in 2005 had a significant effect on this turn toward reassessing gender violence occurring under dictatorship.[40] In Chile, a post-1998 revival of accountability seeking has also contributed to this reexamination.[41]

Since the return to democracy, Argentina and Chile have forged unique paths in coming to terms with the violence of dictatorship, though there are some notable parallels worth highlighting for the purposes of this chapter. In both countries, truth commissions were created with the objective of documenting human rights violations. Also in both countries, gender violence was overlooked in the first round of commissions.[42] Instead, the focus was limited to documenting cases of death and disappearance and proving that these cases took place in a repressive framework of systematic terror. The testimony offered by survivors often revealed personal experiences of sexual violence but was valued more for the information it could provide to illuminate what had happened to the disappeared.[43] Only later, due in part to breakthroughs in international law, would gender violence begin to be considered in this framework as well. Lawyers, scholars, activists, and journalists have recently urged a reassessment of the specifically gendered aspects of torture taking place in clandestine centers under dictatorship. This reassessment must be considered hand in hand with the trailblazing feminist activism that has mobilized hundreds of thousands of women in Argentina and Chile and around the world. These activist performances reembody and repurpose practices and symbols of gender violence that took place in Argentina and Chile during dictatorship. I seek to draw attention to the synergies and simultaneous emergence of movements and actions as an example of transversal feminisms mobilizing against the transnational practices and policies of Operation Condor.

Transnational Performances, Past and Present

Argentina and Chile have emerged as leaders in raising awareness of and denouncing gender violence through performance protest.[44] The examination of the gendered aspects of torture during dictatorship has produced a moment of reckoning in both countries and the lucid articulation of how unacknowledged forms of gender violence have persisted during transition and into the postdictatorship period. The choreography of recent street performances and flash mobs resignifies representations of gender violence staged during the transition and early postdictatorship period, as seen in *Death and the Maiden* and *Paso de dos*. The siluetazos that appeared in the first NiUnaMenos march in Buenos Aires in June 2015 and the performance *A Rapist in Your Path*, acted for the first time in November 2019 by the Chilean arts collective LASTESIS, borrow language, practices, and symbols from the dictatorship and adapt them to denounce gender violence and femicide in a context informed by a new gender perspective. In the framework of these vibrant feminist mobilization emerged La Marea Verde (the

Green Tide) in Argentina, symbolized by the green handkerchiefs donned by supporters of the Campaign for Legal, Safe, and Free Abortion. Sometimes referred to as the *revolución de las hijas* (revolution of the daughters), this young generation, including high schoolers, took to the streets and other public spaces, transforming social perceptions of abortion rights in Argentina.[45] Building on the long human rights tradition in Argentina pioneered by the Mothers and Grandmothers of Plaza de Mayo, activists argued that prohibition of access to legal and safe abortion constituted an act of gender violence. Through mass street protests and coalition building with politicians, activists were successful in generating widespread public support that influenced Congress to legalize abortion in Argentina in 2020.[46]

The *Siluetazos* of NiUnaMenos

The NiUnaMenos movement brought together hundreds of thousands of protesters in inaugural marches taking place simultaneously across Argentina, Chile, and Uruguay on June 3, 2015. The marches marked a watershed moment in generating awareness of gender violence in Argentina and across Latin America, long considered a private, family affair. Much like the Mothers of Plaza de Mayo did in the late 1970s while still under dictatorship, the NiUnaMenos demonstrators strove to combat the invisibilization of forms of violence unacknowledged or denied by the state. In both movements, demonstrators emphasized the victims' rights to bodily integrity and legal representation. Both movements denounced the impunity of the state and criticized the widespread notion that the victims must have done something to deserve the violence acted upon them. And both movements were founded and carried out publicly and largely by women. Las Madres de Plaza de Mayo used their role as mothers strategically as a way to carry out their activism in the public sphere during dictatorship. The military leaders had identified the heteronormative family as one of the cornerstone virtues of the nation and could hardly punish a group of women openly exercising their role as mothers.[47] Cecilia Palmeiro, one of the founders of NiUnaMenos, refers to the genealogy of "locas" who have intervened in public spaces reserved for men since the 1970s, including the Mothers of Plaza de Mayo, LGBTQ+ activists, and NiUnaMenos protesters.[48] The slogan "NiUnaMenos" comes from a line of a poem written by Mexican poet and activist Susana Chávez

Castillo, who witnessed the violence of femicide firsthand from her hometown, Ciudad Juárez, where she was murdered. Another popular slogan of the NiUna-Menos movement, "¡Vivas nos queremos! ¡Vivas las queremos!" (We want to be alive! We want them to be alive!) is a variation of a slogan chanted by the Mothers of Plaza de Mayo during the dictatorship, "Con vida los llevaron, con vida los queremos" (They took them alive; we want them back alive). In the original slogan, the Mothers confronted the military government's lack of acknowledgment of the practice of systematic disappearance. In the adaptation, NiUnaMenos activists confront the state's lack of acknowledgment of the structural violence enabling femicide.[49]

There are other notable continuities in the kinds of performative practices that protesters and artists have used to stage their activism in public spaces in the past and present in Argentina. The siluetazo, for example, has been used in both contexts, in 1983 to denounce the disappearances committed during dictatorship and more recently to draw attention to the women who have disappeared as a result of femicide. In 1983, the act of the siluetazo consisted of pasting line drawings of human-size silhouettes of bodies on white paper on building walls throughout Buenos Aires and other cities as a way of intervening in public urban space.[50] On each drawing was the name of the disappeared person and the date on which they disappeared. According to Ludmila da Silva Catela, the presence of these silhouettes in 1983 presented the new democratic government with an enormous question mark, prompting recognition of and response to the violation and erasure of identity of the disappeared.[51]

The silhouettes appeared again in March 2015, several weeks before the *NiUnaMenos* march. This time, the immediate impetus for the siluetazos was the murder of nineteen-year-old Daiana García, who had last been seen alive walking to a job interview. Once again, the media participated in perpetuating the "algo habrá hecho" discourse by pointing out that she had been wearing short shorts and that she was walking alone late at night at the time of her disappearance.[52] Rocío Collazo and Gato Fernández envision the mass siluetazo in Buenos Aires as a way of creating space for women to embody protest against femicide in the form of performative urban intervention. In an interview, Collazo stated: "We thought it was a way for them to be present in the streets, so that people might walk by and see those silhouettes and recognize them as those girls who are no longer here."[53] On March 21, 2015, more than a hundred people—mostly women, some children, and a handful of men—lay down on the streets and sidewalks of Buenos Aires at the corner of Acoyte and Rivadavia while others drew silhouettes around their bodies. Next to the silhouettes, protesters wrote some of the phrases commonly used to "explain" these murders, such as "she wore too much makeup," "she was cheating on her boyfriend," "she showed too much cleavage," "she stayed out dancing too late," and so on.[54] Another protester wore a shirt that said, "I am the dead woman in that bag." And another carried a sign that said, "Pardon the inconvenience but they're killing us."[55]

The siluetazos of NiUnaMenos highlight how gender violence, whether practiced systematically by a repressive regime or sustained by structural inequities, violates bodily integrity and reinforces a femicidal ecology.[56] The power of the silhouettes, rendered artistically on paper in murals across the city during the transition or traced around live bodies lying on the ground in solidarity, occupying the streets, reveals embodiment as a form of outcry, a rejection of impunity, a demand for accountability, and a commemoration of those who have been killed. In both contexts, the silhouettes participate in the artistic resurrection of bodies that had been labeled subversive by the military government or by conservative media.

A Rapist in Your Path

Since its debut in November 2019, the flash mob performance *A Rapist in Your Path*, created by the Chilean feminist collective LASTESIS, has been performed around the world to decry the role of the state and police in perpetuating gender violence. Hailing from Valparaíso, the collective's four members, Dafne Valdés, Paula Cometa, Sibila Sotomayor, and Lea Cáceres, work with a diverse range of genres and media, including theater, music, visual arts, and design.[57] The poem that they created synthesizes one of Rita Segato's key messages: that rape is not a sexual act but a political act of power and domination.[58] During the flash mob, participants chant the poem while performing choreographed body movements and poses together, in synchronous fashion. Participants around the world have adapted the text of the poem to speak to the specific contexts of gender violence in their respective countries.

Like the siluetazos that appeared during the NiUnaMenos protests, *A Rapist in Your Path* similarly draws on cultural texts, symbols, and practices of the dictatorship and resignifies them in the context of feminist mobilizations in the present. The poem identifies gender violence as "the violence that you don't see" and calls out the police, judges, the state, and the president specifically as agents of patriarchy. The title of the poem, "A Rapist in Your Path," is an explicit reference to the slogan "A friend in your path" implemented by the Chilean National Police during the late 1980s in an attempt to rehabilitate their image and eliminate associations with torture and brutality. The altered slogan in the context of the poem reinforces the continuity of violent practices of the Chilean police between past and present. The poem also cites verses from the institutional hymn of the Chilean police, "Sleep peacefully, innocent girl. [. . .] Your loving policeman watches over your sweet and smiling dreams." Preceding and following this intertext is the refrain, "The rapist was you. The rapist is you." In addition to textual references to the past, the flash mob also draws on a repertoire of bodily practices originating during the dictatorship that reveal the legacy of gender violence in Chile. When performers chant, "It's femicide; impunity for my murderer; it's disappearance; it's rape," participants put their hands behind their heads and squat down.[59] Here, participants allude to the cavity searches the police routinely carried out on women detainees during the dictatorship.

As Palmeiro observes, NiUnaMenos is more than a hashtag; "above all it's a cry that uses the hashtag and social networks to put bodies on the street."[60] Hashtags may be envisioned as a means to an end, in the service of performance and the choreography of bodies engaged in localized actions, but they also lend transnational resonance to the performative interventions of NiUnaMenos.[61] As Gabriel Giorgi notes, "This kind of struggle is no longer intelligible in a national framework."[62] The embodied actions and localized slogans that originate in the feminist mobilizations in Chile and Argentina are captured and disseminated instantly on smartphones, creating new transnational circuits and spectacles of activism that radiate outward from the Southern Cone. While the transnational exchange these performances have created is unprecedented in its reach, this chapter has shown a genealogy of cultural representations documenting gender violence that preceded them, that emerged in response to dictatorship in the transnational framework of Operation Condor. As troves of declassified documents continue to be released on the details of Operation Condor, the network's role in defining subversion in terms of nonconforming gender and sexuality acquires new relevance in an era characterized by a new gender perspective and in light of current attempts to reassess the gendered aspects of torture during dictatorship.

Notes

1. Sandra Cuffe, "Chile's 'A Rapist in Your Path' Chant Hits 200 Cities: Map," Al Jazeera, December 20, 2019, https://www.aljazeera.com/news/2019/12/20/chiles-a-rapist-in-your-path-chant-hits-200-cities-map.

2. Carolina A. Miranda, "How the Viral Protest 'A Rapist in Your Path' Became a Defiant Anthem for 2019," *Los Angeles Times*, December 10, 2019, https://www.latimes.com/entertainment-arts/story/2019-12-10/the-viral-protest-a-rapist-in-your-path-is-catchy-defiant-an-the-anthem-for-2019.

3. Lauren Aratani, "More Than 100 Women Protest Trump and Weinstein with Anti-Rape Anthem," *Guardian*, January 10, 2020, https://www.theguardian.com/us-news/2020/jan/10/more-than-100-women-protest-trump-harvey-weinstein-anti-rape-anthem-new-york.

4. Key members of Operation Condor included Argentina, Chile, Uruguay, Paraguay, Bolivia, and Brazil. Ecuador and Peru joined later. J. Patrice McSherry, "Tracking the Origins of a State Terror Network: Operation Condor," *Latin American Perspectives* 29, no. 1 (January 2002): 38–60, quoted at 38.

5. Ana Forcinito, "El nudo de consentimiento: Violencia sexual y nuevos paradigmas de interpretación en Argentina," in *Poner el cuerpo: Rescatar y visibilizar las marcas sexuales y de género de los archivos dictatoriales del Cono Sur*, ed. Ksenija Bilbija, Ana Forcinito, and Bernardita Llanos (Editorial Cuarto Propio, 2017), 188.

6. In this chapter, I defer to the definitions of sexual and gender-based violence used by the Office of the United Nations High Commissioner for Human Rights: "Sexual violence is a form of gender-based violence and encompasses any sexual act, attempt to obtain a sexual act, unwanted sexual comments or advances, or acts to traffic, or otherwise directed against a person's sexuality using coercion, by any person regardless of their relationship to the victim. [. . .] Gender-based violence is considered to be any harmful act directed against individuals or groups of individuals on the basis of their gender." www.ohchr.org/sites/default/files/Documents/Issues/Women/WRGS/OnePagers/Sexual_and_gender-based_violence.pdf.

7. Vannina Sztainbok and Teresa Macías, "Making Terror Intelligible: Narrating the Scene of Torture in the Southern Cone," *Canadian Journal of Women and the Law* 30, no. 3 (2018): 423–46, quoted at 425.

8. Diana Taylor, *Disappearing Acts: Spectacles of Gender and Nationalism in Argentina's "Dirty War"* (Duke University Press, 1997), 17.

9. Marguerite Feitlowitz, *A Lexicon of Terror: Argentina and the Legacies of Torture*, rev. ed. (Oxford University Press, 2011), 65.

10. Rita Segato, *Contra-pedagogías de la crueldad* (Prometeo Libros, 2018).

11. Ariel Dorfman, *La muerte y la doncella (Teatro I)* (Ediciones de la Flor, 1992), 14.

12. Sophia A. McClennen, "Torture and Truth in Ariel Dorfman's *La muerte y la doncella,*" *Revista Hispánica Moderna* 62, no. 2 (December 2009): 179–95, quoted at 180.

13. Patricia A. Ybarra, *Latinx Theater in the Times of Neoliberalism* (Northwestern University Press, 2018), 12.

14. Ybarra, *Latinx Theater in the Times of Neoliberalism*, 12.

15. Ximena Bunster-Burotto, "Surviving Beyond Fear: Women and Torture in Latin America," in *Women and Change in Latin America*, ed. June C. Nash and Helen I. Safa (South Hadley, MA: Bergin and Garvey, 1986), 297–325; Taylor, *Disappearing Acts*; Hillary Hiner, "Voces soterradas, violencias ignoradas: Discurso, violencia política y género en los Informes Rettig y Valech," *Latin American Research Review* 44, no. 3 (2009): 50–74; Elisabeth Jay Friedman, ed., *Seeking Rights from the Left: Gender, Sexuality, and the Latin American Pink Tide* (Duke University Press, 2019); and Elizabeth Jelin, *La lucha por el pasado: Cómo construimos la memoria social* (Siglo XXI Editores, 2017).

16. Doris Sommer, *Foundational Fictions: The National Romances of Latin America* (University of California Press, 1993).

17. Jean Franco, *Plotting Women: Gender and Representation in Mexico* (Columbia University Press, 1989), xvii.

18. Taylor, *Disappearing Acts*, 183.

19. Bunster-Burotto, "Surviving Beyond Fear," 300; Taylor, *Disappearing Acts*, x; Hiner, "Voces soterradas, violencias ignoradas," 57; and Julieta Kirkwood, *Ser política en Chile: Los nudos de la sabiduría feminista*, 2nd ed. (Editorial Cuarto Propio, 1990).

20. McSherry, "Tracking the Origins of a State Terror Network," 38.

21. McSherry, "Tracking the Origins of a State Terror Network," 40.

22. McSherry, "Tracking the Origins of a State Terror Network," 40; and Ernesto Londoño, "Declassified U.S. Documents Reveal Details About Argentina's Dictatorship," *New York Times*, April 12, 2019, https://www.nytimes.com/2019/04/12/world/americas/argentina-dictatorship-cia-documents.html.

23. Francesca Lessa, "Operation Condor on Trial: Justice for Transnational Human Rights Crimes in South America," *Journal of Latin American Studies* 51, no. 2 (May 2019): 410.

24. Lessa, "Operation Condor on Trial," 410.

25. Lessa, "Operation Condor on Trial," 414.

26. Gilbert M. Joseph and Daniela Spenser, eds., In from the Cold: Latin America's New Encounter with the Cold War (Duke University Press, 2008); Hal Brands, *Latin America's Cold War* (Harvard University Press, 2010); Greg Grandin and Gilbert M. Joseph, eds., *A Century of Revolution: Insurgent and Counterinsurgent Violence During Latin America's Long Cold War* (Duke University Press, 2010); Tanya Harmer, *Allende's Chile and the Inter-American Cold War* (University of North Carolina Press, 2011); Jessica Stites Mor, "Introduction: Situating Transnational Solidarity Within Critical Human Rights Studies of Cold War Latin America," in *Human Rights and Transnational Solidarity in Cold War Latin America*, ed. Jessica Stites Mor (University of Wisconsin Press, 2013), 3–20; Vanni Pettinà and José Antonio Sánchez Román, "Beyond US Hegemony: The Shaping of the Cold War in Latin America," *Culture and History Digital Journal* 4, no. 1 (2015): 15–32; Juan Poblete, ed., *New*

Approaches to Latin American Studies: Culture and Power (Routledge, 2018); Kerry Bystrom, Monica Popescu, and Katherine Zien, eds., *The Cultural Cold War and the Global South: Sites of Contest and Communitas* (Routledge, 2021); and Donald E. Pease, "Introduction: Re-Mapping the Transnational Turn," in *Re-Framing the Transnational Turn in American Studies*, ed. Winfried Fluck, Donald E. Pease, and John Carlos Rowe (University Press of New England, 2011), 1–46.

27. Londoño, "Declassified U.S. Documents Reveal Details."

28. Centro de Información Judicial, "Lesa humanidad: Difundieron los fundamentos de la sentencia por el 'Plan Cóndor,'" quoted in Lessa, "Operation Condor on Trial," 429.

29. Valeria Manzano, "Sex, Gender and the Making of the 'Enemy Within' in Cold War Argentina," *Journal of Latin American Studies* 47, no. 1 (2015): 1–29, quoted at 2.

30. Benjamin Cowan, "Sex and the Security State: Gender, Sexuality, and 'Subversion' at Brazil's Escola Superior de Guerra, 1964–1985," *Journal of the History of Sexuality* 16, no. 3 (September 2007): 462.

31. María Rosa Olivera-Williams, "Maldito cuerpo de mujer: Violencia de género y violencia sexual dentro del terrorismo de Estado en Argentina y Chile," in *Poner el cuerpo: Rescatar y visibilizar las marcas sexuales y de género de los archivos dictatoriales del Cono Sur*, ed. Ksenija Bilbija, Ana Forcinito, and Bernardita Llanos (Editorial Cuarto Propio, 2017), 65.

32. This saying was also referenced in speeches made at the NiUnaMenos march on June 3, 2015, in Buenos Aires.

33. María Lugones, "The Coloniality of Gender," in *Feminisms in Movement: Theories and Practices from the Americas*, ed. Lívia De Souza Lima, Edith Otero Quezada, and Julia Roth (Bielefeld, Germany: Transcript Verlag, 2024), 35; and Barbara Sutton, *Bodies in Crisis: Culture, Violence, and Women's Resistance in Neoliberal Argentina* (New Brunswick, NJ: Rutgers University Press, 2010), 136.

34. See excellent studies on the portrayal of torture in postdictatorship theater: Osvaldo Sandoval-León, "La tortura silenciada: La violencia sexual en el teatro posdictadura del Cono Sur," *Journal of Gender and Sexuality Studies / Revista de Estudios de Género y Sexualidades* 46, nos. 1–2 (Spring–Fall 2020): 151–72; Idelber Avelar, "Five Theses on Torture," *Journal of Latin American Cultural Studies* 10, no. 3 (2001): 253–71; Nancy J. Gates-Madsen, "Tortured Silence and Silenced Torture in Mario Benedetti's *Pedro y el capitán*, Ariel Dorfman's *La muerte y la doncella* and Eduardo Pavlovsky's *Paso de dos*," *Latin American Theatre Review* 42, no. 1 (Fall 2008): 5–31; and McClennen, "Torture and Truth."

35. Lynn A. Higgins and Brenda R. Silver, eds., *Rape and Representation* (Columbia University Press, 1991): 3.

36. Bárbara Soledad Bilbao, "Violencia de género en los juicios del pasado y del presente," *Question / Cuestión* 1, no. 31 (September 2011): n.p.; Cecilia Macón, "Illuminating Affects: Sexual Violence as a Crime Against Humanity; The Argentine Case," *Historein* 14, no. 1 (2013): 22–42; Lorena Balardini, Ana Oberlin, and Laura Sobredo, "Violencia de género y abusos sexuales en centros clandestinos de detención: Un aporte a la comprensión de la experiencia argentina," in *Hacer justicia: Nuevos debates sobre el juzgamiento de crímenes de lesa humanidad en la Argentina*, ed. Centro de Estudios Legales y Sociales and Centro Internacional para la Justicia Transicional (Siglo XXI Editores, 2011), 97–118; María

Sonderéguer, Violeta Correa, Miranda Cassino, and Amaranta González, "Violencias de género en el terrorismo de Estado en América Latina," Centro Cultural de la Memoria Haroldo Conti, Secretaría de Derechos Humanos, Buenos Aires, 2016, http://conti.derhuman.jus.gov.ar/2011/10/mesa_9/sondereguer_correa_cassino_gonzalez_mesa_9.pdf; Ksenija Bilbija, Ana Forcinito, and Bernardita Llanos, eds., *Poner el cuerpo: Rescatar y visibilizar las marcas sexuales y de género de los archivos dictatoriales del Cono Sur* (Editorial Cuarto Propio, 2017); Barbara Sutton, *Surviving State Terror: Women's Testimonies of Repression and Resistance in Argentina* (New York University Press, 2018); and Jelin, *La lucha por el pasado.*

37. Friedman, *Seeking Rights from the Left.*

38. "Incorporación de la perspectiva de género," ONU Mujeres, https://www.unwomen.org/es/how-we-work/un-system-coordination/gender-mainstreaming.

39. UN Women translates "perspectiva de género" as "gender mainstreaming": https://www.unwomen.org/en/how-we-work/un-system-coordination/gender-mainstreaming.

40. Balardini, Oberlin, and Sobredo, "Violencia de género."

41. Cath Collins, "Human Rights Trials in Chile During and After the 'Pinochet Years,'" *International Journal of Transitional Justice* 4, no. 1 (March 2010): 67–86.

42. The Rettig Report (1991) in Chile and the Comisión Nacional sobre la Desaparición de Personas (CONADEP, 1983) in Argentina.

43. Jelin, *La lucha por el pasado,* 227.

44. This chapter was written before Javier Milei was elected president of Argentina in December 2023. A self-professed anarcho-capitalist and member of Argentina's new libertarian party, La Libertad Avanza, Milei's open disregard and contempt for gender, sexuality, and reproductive rights will have a significant impact on feminist activism in the region. For excellent discussions of recent feminist mobilization in Chile and Argentina, see these chapters in Brenda Werth and Katherine Zien, eds., *Bodies on the Front Lines: Performance, Gender, and Sexuality in Latin America and the Caribbean* (University of Michigan Press, 2024): Vanessa M. Gubbins, "General Strike: Feminist Performance?," 59–78; Jennifer Joan Thompson, "'An Explosion of Feminism': Dramaturgies of Excess and Revolution in Chile's New Feminist Vanguard," 39–58; and Cecilia Sosa, "Between the White and the Green Scarves: Vibrant Assemblages of Feminist Insubordination," 327–49.

45. Barbara Sutton, "Intergenerational Encounters in the Struggle for Abortion Rights in Argentina," *Women's Studies International Forum* 82 (September–October 2020): 1–11.

46. Brenda Werth and Katherine Zien, "Latin America: Lessons Learned from Abortion Rights Struggle," AULABlog, Center for Latin American and Latino Studies, American University, June 9, 2022, https://aulablog.net/2022/06/09/latin-america-lessons-learned-from-abortion-rights-struggle/.

47. Taylor, *Disappearing Acts,* 184.

48. Cecilia Palmeiro, speaking at a panel moderated by Gabriel Giorgi at New York University. "Feminismo, cultura, política: #NiUnaMenos Argentina," *Esferas* (Department of Spanish and Portuguese, New York University), https://wp.nyu.edu/esferas/feminismo-cultura-politica-niunamenos-argentina/.

49. Some scholars make an important distinction between the terms "femicide" and "feminicide." Jill Radford, Diana Russell, Marcela Lagarde y de Los Ríos, and others have advocated

for the use of the term "feminicide" to signal the endemic nature of violence against women and to emphasize the role of the state in accountability for violence against women. While I agree with this definition of "feminicide," in this chapter I use "femicide" because *femicidio* is used widely in Argentina and Chile.

50. See Ana Longoni, "Photographs and Silhouettes: Visual Politics in the Human Rights Movement of Argentina," *Afterall: A Journal of Art, Context and Enquiry* 25 (Autumn 2010): 5–17.

51. Ludmila da Silva Catela, *No habrá flores en la tumba del pasado: La experiencia de reconstrucción del mundo de los familiares de desaparecidos* (La Plata, Argentina: Ediciones Al Margen, 2001), 134.

52. Marta Dillon, "Perder el miedo," *Página 12* (Buenos Aires), May 15, 2015, https://www.pagina12.com.ar/diario/suplementos/las12/13-9698-2015-05-15.html.

53. Natalia Rizzo and Lucía Simone, "Siluetazo de protesta contra los femicidios," *La Izquierda Diario*, March 25, 2015, http://www.laizquierdadiario.com/Siluetazo-de-protesta-contra-los-femicidios.

54. Rizzo and Simone, "Siluetazo de protesta."

55. Rizzo and Simone, "Siluetazo de protesta."

56. Karen Stout, "Intimate Femicide: An Ecological Analysis," *Journal of Sociology and Social Welfare* 19, no. 3 (September 1992): 29–50.

57. Sofía Boggia, "Un violador en tu camino: la simbología y la historia," *Actualidad a diario*, December 9, 2019, https://www.actualidadadiario.com/index.php/2019/12/09/un-violador-en-tu-camino-la-simbologia-y-la-historia/.

58. Mar Pichel, "Rita Segato, la feminista cuyas tesis inspiraron 'Un violador en tu camino': 'La violación no es un acto sexual, es un acto de poder, de dominación, es un acto político,'" BBC News Mundo, December 11, 2019, https://www.bbc.com/mundo/noticias-50735010.

59. Boggia, "Un violador en tu camino."

60. "Feminismo, cultura, política: #NiUnaMenos Argentina."

61. Marcela A. Fuentes, *Performance Constellations: Networks of Protest and Activism in Latin America* (University of Michigan Press, 2019).

62. Gabriel Giorgi, speaker and moderator at a panel at New York University. "Feminismo, cultura, política: #NiUnaMenos Argentina."

CHAPTER 9

Transnational Intersections

Latin American Feminist Counterpublics and Digital Technology

ELISABETH JAY FRIEDMAN

MAPPING THE INTERSECTIONS OF digital technology and social justice movements is a critical endeavor. The Internet simultaneously provides infrastructure for movements rebelling against oppressive social systems and enables the "surveillance capitalism" of tech firms that gorge on freely proffered data to predict, if not control, future behavior.[1] It disrupts attention spans and elections, and strengthens authoritarians' power.[2] Yet movements benefit from the direct communication, networks of cooperation, information sharing, hybrid protests, and other "affordances" of this transnational technology.[3]

In Latin America, the Internet's many applications have profoundly shaped contemporary feminist contentious politics, now larger, younger, more diverse, and more demanding than ever. Transnationally articulated movements focused on gender justice did not erupt because of the Internet; they can be traced back more than a century. Shaped as these efforts have been by alternative media, they were well positioned to integrate digital technologies.[4] Parsing the relative importance of context, history, ideology, and technology to the explosion of gender-focused and often women-led movements from Chile to Mexico may be futile. But a transnational perspective helps to reveal the distinct ways feminist counterpublics—the internal arenas of movements where women develop identities, build communities, and formulate strategies to affect larger publics—have encountered and interpreted the Internet.

This chapter begins by distinguishing among the social scientific terms for cross-border political action and showing why "transnational" best applies to both (gender-based) movements and Internet technology. It subsequently offers a survey of their intersections in Latin America. Although powerful "antigender ideology" countermovements are not the focus of this chapter, they also demonstrate regional articulation and deploy Internet technology; right-wing collectivities may in some cases make more effective use of it than their progressive counterparts.[5]

The Analytic Purchase of "Transnational" Approaches to Technology and Movements

Political studies offers interpreters of regional dynamics a framework to distinguish among the protagonists working across national borders. Given the many critical cross-border flows—of people and ideas, financial instruments and viruses, drugs and food, weapons and technology—illuminating the actors and institutions that help to determine their impact is equally critical. Rather than synonyms, the terms "global," "international," and "transnational" offer distinct analytic purchase.

Although "global" is often deployed to indicate "having to do with many countries," a more accurate definition limits it to phenomena that represent or affect all world regions.[6] For example, asserting the existence of a "global" movement against environmental destruction, for reproductive autonomy, or in defense of the heteronormative family implies finding evidence of at least ideational, if not organizational, worldwide connections among actors with these goals. Such a definition should not be taken to imply that all global phenomena have the same impact everywhere: in the global movement of people across borders, immigrants and refugees leave home for distinct reasons and receive disparate treatment where they are received; the global penetration of capitalist formations results in different impacts around the world; the global climate crisis results in distinctly devastating floods, freezes, and fires. "Global" indicates worldwide presence, but not homogeneous impact.

The term "international," frequently attached to any idea, actor, or institution associated with more than one national territory, more precisely identifies state-to-state relations. International relations are cross-border exchanges taking place among state decision makers, official representatives, or institutions. International organizations represent more than one nation-state; as perhaps the most well-known example, the United Nations General Assembly incorporates ambassadors formally appointed to represent national positions on, often, global issues. International interactions take place among states.

Finally, "transnational" refers to phenomena that cross national borders *and* involve nonstate actors but do not necessarily reach the demanding test of globality.[7] Early work on the "international activities of nongovernmental actors" centered economic relations and actors such as multinational corporations.[8] Influenced by the actions of noneconomic movements and organizations active across borders, later work takes into account how nongovernmental actors participate in the emergence, diffusion, and impact of shared norms.[9] In the sphere of contentious politics, cross-border movements, organizations, and alliances such as transnational advocacy networks, which may include state actors, offer ideational and material assistance for national movements; exert pressure on individual states; and organize protests against—or cooperation through—international institutions such as the World Trade Organization or the UN.[10] Transnational analysis that recognizes a range of nonstate actors has the most potential to apply to a wide range of cross-border phenomena.

These semantic distinctions map onto digital technology's reach and governance. Despite the potential for truly global coverage, the spread of the three "layers" of the Internet—the hardware, software, and content—is uneven.[11] The pathways of undersea cables, connectivity coverage, and the distribution of devices varies, reflecting and reinforcing deep-seated inequalities. Languages mediate access to and development of applications. With regard to governance, this technology clearly escapes international control. Authoritative governors and governing agreements include a geographically skewed mix of national institutions, nonprofits, and private actors.[12] Market actors, especially the "big five" (Alphabet [Google's parent company], Apple, Meta/Facebook, Microsoft, and Amazon), often escape democratic oversight, relying instead on self-regulation.[13] A transnational lens can fruitfully identify every aspect of digital technology.

Turning to the issue of gender-based organizing, particularly women's human rights struggles, activists have long reached across state borders for solidarity and support. They have done so to confront the national elites who have dismissed concerns about "private" issues such as reproduction, gender roles, and family structure as meddling with the "natural" social order and thus inappropriate for state action—despite states' routine regulation of such issues. Using this chapter's categorizations, such organizing is not international—that is, undertaken by state representatives. Gender-based movements exist in all world regions, and as such they are a global phenomenon, with occasional global eruptions. For example, the 2017 Women's March included nearly a thousand marches, with an estimated four and a half million participants, on every continent.[14] Earlier manifestations include the UN World Women's conferences, which movements around the world used as an opportunity to organize; tens of thousands also participated during the global conference processes.[15] Earlier movements for women's citizenship also crossed many borders.[16] Global movements have a robust history and present. However, more activity can be captured by lowering the high bar of global representation. Transnationally articulated movements may be found in particular regions or involve just a few countries. Prior to the contemporary cycles of mass mobilization, Latin American feminists engaged in transnational action on issues ranging from suffrage to the rights of Indigenous and Afro-Latin women.[17]

Transnational contentious politics have been tracked using a hegemonic logic whereby movement "innovations originate in the Western core and enter receptive communities on the non-Western periphery" through the actions of social elites.[18] But empirical research on practices such as Gandhian nonviolence and LGBT "coming out" repertoires reveals not only more complex pathways but also situated reinterpretations of extranational ideas. In Latin America, for example, LGBT activists have reworked ideas and strategies from elsewhere; and Latin American advocates have been sources of extraregional human rights innovation, including on women's human rights.[19] Latin American diffusion radiates in many directions.

Feminist analysts offer reasons to take a transnational perspective on activism. A focus on the national level effectively reifies the project of Western modernity, neglecting consequential cross-border economic, social, and political forces that affect the life chances of all people—and, as such, become organizing targets.[20] Variations among the demands and targets of women's activism within and across national borders refutes the idea that transnational activism always flows from the "West to the rest."[21] Capturing the dynamics of gender-based contention demonstrates that "transnationalism is always located somewhere."[22]

Previous research on movements and technology provides a springboard for this chapter's centering of Latin American feminist counterpublics and Internet technology. Analysts extol the benefits of the Internet's inexpensive, expansive reach for distributing information and facilitating exchange.[23] They also note its accessibility to the young and marginal.[24] And beyond "online" or "hashtag" movements, empirical study reveals how the technology can enhance place-based protest.[25] But Internet reliance presents challenges in the medium's (re)production and (re)configuration of colonial/ethnoracial, class-, gender-, and sexuality-based relations of power; in its market-relations bias; and in its deployment for disinformation, abuse, and repression.[26] Moreover, as remarkable as rapidly scaled up, Internet-fueled mass movements are, their "tactical agility" and sustainability may be compromised without attention to the critical human infrastructure that has undergirded previous movements.[27] As with all movement analysis, those that center technology must appreciate innovation while addressing obstacles.

The following exploration of the intersection of transnational technology and feminist counterpublics in Latin America uses a "sociomaterial" approach.[28] Sociomaterial analysis understands the Internet as an assemblage of coders, users, machines, protocols, applications, and content permeated by social ideas, experiences, and hierarchies. Like all technology, the Internet does not stand outside of society, as we commonly imply when we ask questions such as "what is the impact of the Internet on social movements?" Science and technology studies, with its insights concerning the "entangled" assemblages of social, cultural, human, and nonhuman subjects in media "ecologies," helps us to understand that movement actors and ideas are influenced by and influence the trajectories of digital technology.[29]

Mapping Latin American Transnational Feminist Counterpublics and the Internet

Transnational feminist organizing in Latin America has relied for well over a century on both face-to-face meetings and alternative media. One early marker of the cross-pollination of regional feminist advocacy came during the 1910

International Feminist Congress in Buenos Aires, which, despite the elite status of most participants, focused on issues ranging from women's employment to familial relations. There, congress attendees advocated for a regional movement.[30] Finding transnational articulation useful for domestic pressure, Latin American women founded regional organizations in the 1920s and engaged with transnational suffrage networks.[31] Moving into the mid-twentieth century, they collaborated through leftist, antifascist networks; prominent leaders targeted the new United Nations.[32] Even when military-backed authoritarian regimes repressed feminism alongside other liberal and progressive movements in the 1970s and 1980s, exiles in North America and Europe continued to engage in transnational exchange. They brought insights home when the region democratized.[33] Meanwhile, the UN Decade for Women (1976–1985) and world conferences brought inspiration and resources.[34]

Of critical importance as a counterpublic space, the Latin American and Caribbean feminist "Encuentro" (Encuentro Feminista de Latinoamerica y del Caribe, or EFLAC), first held in 1981, became a venue for exchange and networking. From the challenges of working with leftist "allies," other movements, state institutions, and philanthropic foundations, to the inclusion of a range of female-identified persons—across differences of class, race, ethnicity, gender identity, and sexuality—and their demands, EFLAC reflected and charted regional feminisms.[35] In part due to a deliberate attempt to make sure the Encuentro moved around the region, activists from Brazil to El Salvador have been able to engage in this transnational space.

Regional counterpublic organization takes the shape of issue- or identity-based networks. The 28th of September Campaign to decriminalize abortion in Latin America and the Caribbean came together at the fifth EFLAC in 1990. Seeking the "recognition and broadening of rights, territories, and natural resources, [and] sustainability and protection of ancestral knowledge," the Continental Link of Indigenous Women of the Americas, created in 1995, represents Indigenous women from twenty-three countries; the subregional Alliance of Indigenous Women of Central America and Mexico was founded in 2004.[36] Foregrounding intersections among racism, sexism, and poverty, Afrodescendant women established the Network of Afro–Latin American and Caribbean Women in 1992.[37] Lesbian feminists have articulated regionally since 1987; in 2012, those who insist on a wider spectrum of gender and sexuality identities began to meet at the LesBiTransInter feminist encounter.[38] Networks focused on a range of economic justice issues include the Network of Women Transforming the Economy, the Latin American chapter of the International Gender and Trade Network, and the Marcosur Feminist Articulation.[39] Regional feminist and women's activism has also been manifest in the global 2017 Women's March and "sidestreamed" into other transnational (and global) venues for social justice activism, such as the World Social Forum.[40] And "femocrats," women's rights–oriented representatives and policy makers in state institutions, have constituted regional networks to support work in legislatures, courts, and executive branches.

Such regional articulation has been complex and often fraught. Degrees of institutional access—whether political, civic, or educational—translate into privileges for lighter-skinned, urban, middle- and upper-class, cis/hetero women in terms of representation and resources. Fierce struggles over the meaning of feminism and its arenas and types of action continue to characterize regional relationships.[41] Language differences present foundational obstacles to communication, solidarity, and strategizing, given the dominance of Spanish in regional forums.[42] But strong transnational connections have been forged over time.

Alternative media have been central to feminist counterpublic communications since the beginning, when intellectuals excluded from the male-dominated press circulated their own publications across geographic borders, winning elite and middle-class adherents. Activists a century later founded hundreds of women's magazines. Influential regional publications such as *Mujer/fempress* and *fem* helped to build Latin American feminist identities and a sense of community. Well-networked feminists have had significant experience with building their own communications platforms.[43]

As part of broader leftist communities, many feminist counterpublics were well positioned to take advantage of the early Internet. Within the Association for Progressive Communications (APC), a global network constructing and enabling access to the precommercial Internet, the Women's Networking Support Programme (WNSP) introduced women's organizations and feminist movements from the Global South to the digital environment. In preparing for the 1995 Fourth World Conference on Women in Beijing, communicators in Latin America founded the regional WNSP-LA. They collaborated with Latin American APC nodes to get feminist and women's organizations networked online. Prior to the commercialization and massification of the Internet in Latin America, these efforts "sought to enable women at the grassroots to gain access to an elite-oriented organizing and advocacy space" through communications, information, and action.[44]

Drawing on the WNSP-LA's lessons, first adopters integrated the Internet to enhance national and regional counterpublics. Mindful of the region's inequalities, some targeted digital exclusions, creating "chains of access" through hardware, training, and content for marginalized communities. Email distribution lists proved key for the consultative processes prized by the region's feminists. Combining online, community, and mass media to take into account the media ecology of the time, they adapted campaigns and applications to the needs and demands of women's and feminist movements focused on development and ending violence.

Internet/Counterpublic Entanglements in the Contemporary Cycle of Contention

These networked counterpublics continue to integrate new digital technologies, particularly social media, in a contemporary cycle of protest. Across the region, mass movements have focused on making visible, and repudiating, the gender-based violence that has resulted in an estimated one-third of all partnered women in the Americas suffering from domestic violence,[45] and Latin America and the Caribbean occupying nearly every spot in the top twenty countries in global femicide rankings.[46] Such rankings have led to a diagnosis of gendered violence as going far beyond traumatic interpersonal relations. Given the structural violence of a range of oppressions with colonial roots and branches in authoritarian politics and neoliberal economics; the cultural manifestations that uphold male privilege alongside ethnoracial, class, cis-heteronormative, and other hierarchies; and the routine impunity, whether of domestic abusers, organized crime, or public security forces—it is perhaps not surprising that in the twenty-first century, "the struggle against gender violence has become the minimum common denominator of all the feminisms."[47] The following sets out a necessarily schematic and suggestive genealogy of this antiviolence activism before examining its Internet entanglements.

Although mass movements against feminicide and other forms of gender violence exploded in the second half of the 2010s, women's and feminist antiviolence protests—and their expanding conceptual underpinnings—came to the fore during the authoritarianism of the 1970s. Responding to widespread human rights abuse, mothers' and grandmothers' movements sought to expose and resist state security policies that had resulted in the murder, torture, and disappearance of family members. Feminist thinkers developed insights about the parallels between violence exerted by authoritarian men in public and private, demanding "democracy in the street—and in the home."[48] The very first EFLAC, held in Bogotá, called for a "Day to End Violence Against Women" on November 25 (which is now observed globally, having been recognized by the UN General Assembly in 1999). The date commemorates the lives of the Dominican Mirabal sisters, killed on that day in 1965 for their role in the opposition to the misogynistic dictator Rafael Trujillo.

Thus, Latin American activists had already honed their ideas and strategies when, in the early 1990s, a transnational movement to insert women's rights into the human rights "orbit" took shape around the 1992 UN Human Rights Conference process. Latin Americans were at the forefront of efforts to foreground violence against women (VAW) as the paradigmatic example of the routine, yet overlooked, violation of women's human rights. Despite the physical and psychological torture it manifested, VAW had not been included on human rights agendas due to the masculinist assumptions embedded in an approach centered on defending the rights of (male) political prisoners. Demanding that states take action to end impunity about VAW—whether in public or private—activists expanded human rights frameworks.[49]

Such transnational action also resulted in the Americas becoming the first region to adopt a VAW treaty, which became the norm for domestic activism. Regional advocacy through two inter-American women's rights organizations led the Organization of American States to adopt the 1994 Inter-American Convention on the Prevention, Punishment, and Eradication of Violence Against Women, based on the feminist definition that VAW includes "any act or conduct, based on gender, which causes death or physical, sexual or psychological harm or suffering to women, whether in the public or the private sphere" and holds states as well as individuals accountable.[50] Advocates pressured governments to uphold convention principles. With often arduous, multilevel strategic lobbying, they not only succeeded in having nearly every country sanction some form of legislation against VAW, but also insisted on the revision of a first wave of laws that entrenched conservative values with a second that built from the regional norm.[51]

As the forgoing attests, the struggle against gendered violence is not new; as horrific examples have continued under democratic conditions, so has Latin American women's protagonism. The current cycle of such protests can be dated to the Ni Una Más (Not One More) anti-feminicide movement of northern Mexico, which stretched from the mid-1990s until 2005. Notorious cases on the US/Mexico border, where hundreds of factory workers and students were kidnapped, abused, and killed, sparked protests by family members, communities, and feminist organizations, joined by transnational campaigns.[52] Deepening regional analytic insights, the term *feminicidio* (feminicide) was coined "not just [to be] the female equivalent of homicide, but [to] reveal the misogynist grounds of the crime, the authorities' negligence, and the cultural and sociopolitical conditions normalizing gender violence."[53]

The regional has not been the only transnational vector of the contemporary cycle. In the 2010s, Latin Americans offered their own translations of the "Slut Walk," sparked by students in Toronto to simultaneously protest a "blame the victim" mentality within the public security sector and assert their freedom to choose their physical expression. The Marchas de Putas/Vadias brought together young feminists and transfeminists alongside sex workers in a vividly embodied protest against gendered violence; in Brazil, marches took place in twenty-three cities in every region of the country. Alongside mass movements of rural women workers to demand land and water rights in the face of environmentally destructive agrobusiness; the fifty-thousand-strong Black Women's March Against Racism and Violence and in Favor of Living Well; and students honing skills through school occupations to protest poor public school quality and school closures, by 2015 Brazil was experiencing a "feminist spring": "a contemporary feminist boom that is a dynamic mix of women—old, young, black, indigenous, white, Asian, rural, urban, trans, LGBT, disabled—that aggregates theory and praxis."[54] The diversity within this "boom" in terms of subject position and demands widened feminist understandings of violence.

The growing momentum of feminist protest was influenced by the regional oscillation of left-wing to right-wing governance. The so-called Pink Tide of left-leaning governments gave way in some countries to illiberal or rights-repressive administrations seeking to undo even the limited progress of a decade of struggle against inequality while relying on neoliberal austerity to replace a fading commodity boom. A new generation of activists often steeped in the ideas imparted to them by popular movements, gender and ethnic studies programs, and the leftist rhetoric of progressive governments were primed to put their bodies on the line.

The transnational cycle took on explosive force beginning on June 3, 2015, when hundreds of thousands of people across Argentina took to the streets to protest the murder of young women and demand state action in the "NiUnaMenos" (Not One Less) protests. Even as this protest spread to Mexico, Peru, and Brazil, other commemorations on the "gender calendar," such as the International Day for the Elimination of Violence Against Women, took on new life. Inspired by the Polish "Black Protest" Women's Strike against a total ban on abortion and outraged by yet another young woman's murder, NiUnaMenos organizers called for the October 2016 Women's Strike. Picking up energy from the first global Women's March in January 2017, another strike was called on International Women's Day (IWD), taking place in "nearly 110 cities, becoming the largest mass protest in Latin America and Europe." In 2018, IWD saw "a massive wave of protest. [. . .] Millions of women in more than 500 cities across the globe protested against violence and in favour of women's rights."[55] This cycle reverberated in viral protests such as the powerful 2019 performance *Un violador en tu camino* (A Rapist in Your Path), written and choreographed by Chile's LASTESIS collective. Building on Chile's own "feminist spring" in 2018, when younger activists occupied schools and universities, and the 2019 nationwide protests against inequality, the protests echoed the decades-old call against state impunity. Across the region and beyond, women chanted: "The oppressive state is a macho rapist." Although the COVID-19 shelter-in-place orders initially quieted street protests, movements rose up against the upsurge of gendered violence during the lockdown. Their actions prompted government responses.[56]

The mass movements of this cycle have depended on a digital infrastructure ever more integrated into each counterpublic element: generating identity, building community, and developing strategic actions. Elements such as hashtags "do things in the world rather than merely describe what exists. [. . .] [They] shape feminist publics, help disseminate counter-pedagogies seeking to debunk patriarchal pedagogies of cruelty, and ultimately, usher in utopian futures."[57] For example, with regard to the mass marches in Brazil, "the speed with which the march spread across the country and mobilized the youth is inseparable from the possibilities that new communication technologies offer political activism."[58] Social media platforms cannot be disentangled from movement meanings and movement expansion.

In terms of shaping feminist publics (or counterpublics) from the ground up, the massive and transnational circulation of personal testimonies has contributed to the development of feminist identities while blurring the boundary between on- and off-line engagement. Sharing such experiences through a range of digital applications is "redefining the function of testimony in terms of agency" across the region.[59] In October 2015, Juliana de Faria, founder of the feminist Think Olga collective, launched the #PrimeiroAssédio: Você não está mais só (#FirstHarrassment: You are no longer alone) campaign in response to the viral circulation of sexually harassing comments directed at a twelve-year-old girl participant on the popular Master Chef Junior TV program. This "ground breaking" moment when Brazilian women took to Twitter to share their own stories of childhood harassment resulted in sixty-five thousand tweets in two days; an analysis of them revealed that the average age at which women were first harassed was just under ten years old.[60] Ultimately, "[t]he hashtag would be retweeted more than 100,000 times, culminating in 11 million searches and being the highlight of Google in 2015."[61] Translated into Spanish as #MiPrimerAcoso, the hashtag took off again around the region, spurred by Mexican antiviolence protests in April 2016.[62] Whether through tweets, Facebook posts, WhatsApp group texts, or other digital modalities, users help themselves, and each other, to feel empowered as feminists. The ease of sharing across geographical and linguistic borders has translated into an immediate—and widespread—diffusion of feminist ideas.

Internet-based activism bridges personal growth and street-based strategy through the development of feminist community and, within it, the expansion of feminist thought—and the proliferation of feminist thinkers. Across the region, activists deploy various applications to establish a "locus of action and reflection of feminist groups in the construction of a new epistemology of feminist knowledge, more reticulated, fluid and multivariate—and no longer guided by a split between watertight categories" such as academic-theoretical versus militant-pragmatic, offline versus online, or mature versus young.[63] These epistemological insights reroute the early "sidestreaming" flows, when feminists sought to bring their insights into other progressive spaces and movements.

As suggested above, a new generation understands gender relations as inherently linked to a range of intersecting relations of power: "[A]bortion, femicides, and austerity measures [are] different but interrelated forms of violence towards women and bodies marked as feminine."[64] Such insights have resulted in the multiple subject positions and issues of the mass mobilizations that have captured the region. For example, expansive frames championed by feminist actors led them to spark the #EleNão (NotHim) movement against the presidential candidacy of the extreme right-wing former military officer Jair Bolsonaro. This slogan was originally the motto of the group Women United Against Bolsonaro, created during the presidential campaign season in 2018 to oppose his disparaging comments about women and Indigenous peoples, and other reactionary rhetoric. The group grew to two million members in two weeks. Despite cyberattacks (abetted by Bolsonaro himself), it spawned other Facebook pages and groups; the hashtag was circulating thousands of times an hour by mid-September, and ultimately #EleNão became the encompassing demand of "the largest women-led demonstrations in Brazilian history."[65] Similarly, the Argentine NiUnaMenos movement expanded its focus and publics in its second year, "[m]oving beyond identitarian multiculturalism and linking violence against women and feminized bodies to forms of labor exploitation, police violence, and the business offensives against common resources."[66] The thoroughly transnational Women's Strike continued this demonstration of heterogeneity.

Agenda expansion links to a distinct mode of decentralized massification that refuses the online/offline binary in thoroughly hybridized transnational counterpublics. Unlike earlier protest cycles of protest, these mass mobilizations have been less deliberately coordinated[67] and have instead flowed through capillary, digitized networks: "[D]igital and non-digital media disobediently appropriated by feminist activists acquire a self-propelling vitality [. . .] as they move through human and computer networks and formats, being re-used, re-signified and re-shared."[68] Some instantiations, such as the Marchas de Putas/Vadias, rely on social media in order to be "'horizontal,' disconnected from any formal leadership."[69] Many build on the affective results of testimonial sharing but are also anchored in real-time encounters: "Digital enthusiasm and online emotional contagion play a pivotal role in fostering mass protest participation" in which there is a "virtuous exchange between physical [. . .] and online meetings."[70] The combination of the Internet and "conventional means of mobilization" results in "large and rapid diffusion, internalization, externalization, appropriation, and reappropriation of ideas and methods" across as well as within regions.[71]

The entwining of online and offline engagement comes alive through new actions, such as the digital and physical mapping of where women have been murdered and the performances that characterize nearly every mass mobilization. Social media inspires and (re)transmits the widespread, body-focused activities. Younger activists proudly present themselves in all their glory—barebreasted, decorated with slogans and glitter, of every shape, hue, and gender identity—simultaneously rejecting traditional gender norms and insisting on their right to be foundationally free. By exercising bodily autonomy, they refuse to be subjected to a range of gender-based violences oriented at controlling them.[72] Their body politics also implicitly and explicitly reference the female and feminized bodies whose deaths have been fundamental to inspiring the fierce fight for the right to live free from violence. The resonance of digital engagements sounds loudly in public spaces, as feminist activists make their claims and commemorations audible and tangible.

Conclusion

At the multiple intersections of the Internet and feminist organizing in Latin America, a transnational lens furthers our understanding of their development, dissemination, and mutual constitution. In particular, it reveals the organizational and conceptual taproots of the contemporary cycle of antigender violence mass mobilization, including the historical twining of alternative media and counterpublic growth across the region and beyond. Using an assemblage of dynamic knowledges and digital resources, feminists firmly located in their own contexts demonstrate and denounce gender-based violence, spreading ideas and actions for local, national, and transnational mobilization. Given the vertiginous rise of opposition to their demands and achievements, it is more important than ever to witness and understand their resistance.

Notes

1. Zeynep Tufekci, *Twitter and Tear Gas: The Power and Fragility of Networked Protest* (New

Haven, CT: Yale University Press, 2017); and Shoshana Zuboff, *The Age of Surveillance Capitalism: The Fight for a Human Future at the New Frontier of Power* (PublicAffairs, 2019).

2. Ronald J. Deibert, "The Road to Digital Unfreedom: Three Painful Truths About Social Media," *Journal of Democracy* 30, no. 1 (January 2019): 25–39; and Manuel Meléndez-Sánchez, "Latin America Erupts: Millennial Authoritarianism in El Salvador," *Journal of Democracy* 32, no. 3 (July 2021): 19–32.

3. Manuel Castells, *Networks of Outrage and Hope: Social Movements in the Internet Age* (Polity Press, 2012); Bruce Bimber, "Three Prompts for Collective Action in the Context of Digital Media," *Political Communication* 34, no. 1 (2017): 6–20; and Raymond H. Brescia, "The Strength of Digital Ties: Virtual Networks, Norm-Generating Communities, and Collective Action Problems," *Dickinson Law Review* 122, no. 2 (Winter 2018): 479–549.

4. Elisabeth J. Friedman, *Interpreting the Internet: Feminist and Queer Counterpublics in Latin America* (University of California Press, 2017), 57–88.

5. Maximiliano Campana, *Políticas antigénero en América Latina: Argentina* (Rio de Janeiro: Observatorio de Sexualidad y Política, 2020), https://sxpolitics.org/GPAL/uploads/Ebook-argentina_20200203.pdf; Sonia Corrêa and Isabela Kalil, *Políticas antigénero en América Latina: Brasil—¿La catástrofe perfecta?* (Rio de Janeiro: Observatorio de Sexualidad y Política, 2020), https://sxpolitics.org/GPAL/uploads/Ebook-Brasil%2020200204.pdf; and Jen Schradie, *The Revolution That Wasn't: How Digital Activism Favors Conservatives* (Harvard University Press, 2019).

6. Elisabeth Jay Friedman, Kathryn Hochstetler, and Ann Marie Clark, *Sovereignty, Democracy, and Global Civil Society: State-Society Relations at UN World Conferences* (State University of New York Press, 2005), 32.

7. Thomas Risse-Kappen, ed., *Bringing Transnational Relations Back In: Non-State Actors, Domestic Structures and International Institutions* (Cambridge University Press, 1995).

8. Sidney Tarrow, "Transnational Politics: Contention and Institutions in International Politics," *Annual Review of Political Science* 4, no. 1 (June 2001): 4.

9. Margaret E. Keck and Kathryn Sikkink, *Activists Beyond Borders: Advocacy Networks in International Politics* (Cornell University Press, 1998); and Thomas Risse, Stephen C. Ropp, and Kathryn Sikkink, eds., *The Power of Human Rights: International Norms and Domestic Change* (Cambridge University Press, 1999).

10. Keck and Sikkink, *Activists Beyond Borders*; and Tarrow, "Transnational Politics."

11. Yochai Benkler, *The Wealth of Networks: How Social Production Transforms Markets and Freedom* (New Haven, CT: Yale University Press, 2006).

12. Robert J. Domanski, *Who Governs the Internet? A Political Architecture* (Lexington Books, 2015).

13. Tarleton Gillespie, "Platforms Are Not Intermediaries," *Georgetown Law Technology Review* 2, no. 2 (July 2018): 198–216; and Nicolas Suzor, "Digital Constitutionalism: Using the Rule of Law to Evaluate the Legitimacy of Governance by Platforms," *Social Media + Society* 4, no. 3 (July 2018).

14. Erica Chenoweth and Jeremy Pressman, "This Is What We Learned by Counting the Women's Marches," *Washington Post*, February 7, 2017, https://www.washingtonpost.com/

news/monkey-cage/wp/2017/02/07/this-is-what-we-learned-by-counting-the-womens-marches/.

15. Jocelyn Olcott, *International Women's Year: The Greatest Consciousness-Raising Event in History* (Oxford University Press, 2017); and Elisabeth Jay Friedman, "Gendering the Agenda: The Impact of the Transnational Women's Rights Movement at the UN Conferences of the 1990s," *Women's Studies International Forum* 26, no. 4 (July–August 2003): 313–31.

16. Nitza Berkovitch, *From Motherhood to Citizenship: Women's Rights and International Organizations* (Johns Hopkins University Press, 2002); and Katherine M. Marino, *Feminism for the Americas: The Making of an International Human Rights Movement* (University of North Carolina Press, 2019).

17. Marino, *Feminism for the Americas*; Francesca Miller, *Latin American Women and the Search for Social Justice* (University Press of New England, 1991); and Marisa Revilla Blanco, "Del ¡Ni una más! al #NiUnaMenos: Movimientos de mujeres y feminismos en América Latina," *Política y Sociedad* 56, no. 1 (May 2019): 47–67.

18. Sean Chabot and Jan Willem Duyvendak, "Globalization and Transnational Diffusion Between Social Movements: Reconceptualizing the Dissemination of the Gandhian Repertoire and the 'Coming Out' Routine," *Theory and Society* 31, no. 6 (December 2002): 700.

19. Rafael de la Dehesa, *Queering the Public Sphere in Mexico and Brazil: Sexual Rights Movements in Emerging Democracies* (Durham NC: Duke University Press, 2010); Elisabeth Jay Friedman, "Constructing 'The Same Rights with the Same Names': The Impact of Spanish Norm Diffusion on Marriage Equality in Argentina," *Latin American Politics and Society* 54, no. 4 (Winter 2012): 29–59; Omar Guillermo Encarnación, *Out in the Periphery: Latin America's Gay Rights Revolution* (Oxford University Press, 2016); Kathryn Sikkink, "From Pariah State to Global Protagonist: Argentina and the Struggle for International Human Rights," *Latin American Politics and Society* 50, no. 1 (Spring 2008): 1–29; and Elisabeth Jay Friedman, "Women's Human Rights: The Emergence of a Movement," in *Women's Rights, Human Rights: International Feminist Perspectives*, ed. Julie Peters and Andrea Wolper (Routledge, 1996), 18–35.

20. Inderpal Grewal and Caren Kaplan, *Scattered Hegemonies: Postmodernity and Transnational Feminist Practices* (University of Minnesota Press, 1994).

21. Marianne H. Marchand, "Engendering Transnational Movements/Transnationalizing Women's and Feminist Movements in the Americas," *Latin American Policy* 5, no. 2 (December 2014): 180–92; Janet M. Conway, "Troubling Transnational Feminism(s): Theorising Activist Praxis," *Feminist Theory* 18, no. 2 (August 2017): 205–27; and Yvonne A. Braun and Michael C. Dreiling, "Networking for Women's Rights: Academic Centers, Regional Information Networks, and Feminist Advocacy in Southern Africa," *International Feminist Journal of Politics* 21, no. 1 (2018): 89–110.

22. Almudena Cabezas González and Gabriela Pinheiro Machado Brochner, "The New Cycle of Women's Mobilizations Between Latin America and Europe: A Feminist Geopolitical Perspective on Interregionalism," in *Critical Geopolitics and Regional (Re)Configurations: Interregionalism and Transnationalism Between Latin America and Europe*, ed. Heriberto Cairo and Breno Bringel (Abingdon, Oxon., England: Routledge, 2019), 179.

23. Jennifer Earl and Katrina Kimport, *Digitally Enabled Social Change: Activism in the Internet Age* (MIT Press, 2011); and Christina Neumayer and Jakob Svensson, "Activism and Radical Politics in the Digital Age: Towards a Typology," *Convergence* 22, no. 2 (April 2016): 131–46.

24. Jeffrey Scott Juris and Geoffrey Henri Pleyers, "Alter-Activism: Emerging Cultures of Participation Among Young Global Justice Activists," *Journal of Youth Studies* 12, no. 1 (2009): 57–75; Henry Jenkins, Sangita Shresthova, Liana Gamber-Thompson, Neta Kligler-Vilenchik, and Arely M. Zimmerman, *By Any Media Necessary: The New Youth Activism* (New York University Press, 2016); and Jessica K. Taft, *Rebel Girls: Youth Activism and Social Change Across the Americas* (New York University Press, 2011).

25. Castells, *Networks of Outrage and Hope.*

26. Lisa Nakamura, *Cybertypes: Race, Ethnicity, and Identity on the Internet* (Routledge, 2002); Lisa Nakamura, *Digitizing Race: Visual Cultures of the Internet* (University of Minnesota Press, 2008); Jessie Daniels, "Race and Racism in Internet Studies: A Review and Critique," *New Media and Society* 15, no. 5 (August 2013): 695–719; Safiya Umoja Noble, *Algorithms of Oppression: How Search Engines Reinforce Racism* (New York University Press, 2018); Ruha Benjamin, *Race After Technology: Abolitionist Tools for the New Jim Code* (Polity Press, 2019); Marie Segrave and Laura Vitis, eds., *Gender, Technology and Violence* (Abingdon, Oxon., England: Routledge, 2017); Zuboff, *The Age of Surveillance Capitalism*; and Deibert, "The Road to Digital Unfreedom."

27. Tufekci, *Twitter and Tear Gas.*

28. Robert Latham and Saskia Sassen, "Digital Formations: Constructing an Object of Study," in *Digital Formations: IT and New Architectures in the Global Realm*, ed. Robert Latham and Saskia Sassen (Princeton University Press, 2005), 1–34.

29. Karen Barad, *Meeting the Universe Halfway: Quantum Physics and the Entanglement of Matter and Meaning* (Duke University Press, 2007); Jane Bennett, *Vibrant Matter: A Political Ecology of Things* (Duke University Press, 2010); and Bonnie A. Nardi and Vicki L. O'Day, *Information Ecologies: Using Technology with Heart* (MIT Press, 1999), 49–58.

30. Marino, *Feminism for the Americas*, 16.

31. Miller, *Latin American Women*, 95.

32. Marino, *Feminism for the Americas*, 120–28.

33. Alicia Frohmann and Teresa Valdés, "Democracy in the Country and in the Home: The Women's Movement in Chile," in *The Challenge of Local Feminisms: Women's Movements in Global Perspective*, ed. Amrita Basu (Westview Press, 1995), 276–301.

34. Olcott, *International Women's Year*; and Friedman, "Gendering the Agenda."

35. Sonia E. Alvarez et al., "Encountering Latin American and Caribbean Feminisms," *Signs* 28, no. 2 (Winter 2003): 537–79; Revilla Blanco, "Del ¡Ni una más! al #NiUnaMenos"; and Friedman, *Interpreting the Internet*, 41–45.

36. Revilla Blanco, "Del ¡Ni una más! al #NiUnaMenos," 56–57.

37. Agustín Laó-Montes, "Afro–Latin American Feminisms at the Cutting Edge of Emerging Political-Epistemic Movements," *Meridians: Feminism, Race, Transnationalism* 14, no. 2 (2016): 1–24.

38. Revilla Blanco, "Del ¡Ni una más! al #NiUnaMenos," 59.

39. Almudena Cabezas, "Transnational Feminist Networks Building Regions in Latin America," *Latin American Policy* 5, no. 2 (December 2014): 207–20.

40. Janet M. Conway, "Activist Knowledges on the Anti-Globalization Terrain: Transnational Feminisms at the World Social Forum," *Interface: A Journal For and About Social Movements* 3, no. 2 (November 2011): 33–64; and Sonia E. Alvarez, "Para além da sociedade civil: Reflexões sobre o campo feminista," *Cadernos Pagu* 43 (July–December 2014): 13–56.

41. Alvarez et al., "Encountering Latin American and Caribbean Feminisms."

42. See Alvarez et al., "Encountering Latin American and Caribbean Feminisms," 567–69; and Cabezas, "Transnational Feminist Networks," 216.

43. Friedman, *Interpreting the Internet*, 27–56.

44. Friedman, *Interpreting the Internet*, 77.

45. Sarah Bott, Alessandra Guedes, Ana P. Ruiz-Celis, and Jennifer Adams Mendoza, "Intimate Partner Violence in the Americas: A Systematic Review and Reanalysis of National Prevalence Estimates," *Revista Panamericana de Salud Pública* 43 (2018).

46. UN Office on Drugs and Crime, International Homicide Statistics Database, "Intentional Homicides, Female (per 100,00 Female)," 1990–2021, World Bank Group, https://data.worldbank.org/indicator/VC.IHR.PSRC.FE.P5?most_recent_value_desc=true.

47. Revilla Blanco, "Del ¡Ni una más! al #NiUnaMenos," 48.

48. Marysa Navarro, "The Personal Is Political: Las Madres de Plaza de Mayo," in *Power and Popular Protest: Latin American Social Movements*, updated ed., ed. Susan Eckstein (University of California Press, 2001), 241–58; and Julieta Kirkwood, *Ser política en Chile: Los nudos de la sabiduría feminista*, 2nd ed. (Editorial Cuarto Propio, 1990).

49. Friedman, "Women's Human Rights"; and Niamh Reilly, *Women's Human Rights: Seeking Gender Justice in a Globalizing Age* (Polity Press, 2009).

50. Organization of American States, "Inter-American Convention on the Prevention, Punishment, and Eradication of Violence Against Women (Convention of Belém Do Pará)," 1994, https://www.oas.org/en/mesecvi/docs/BelemDoPara-ENGLISH.pdf.

51. Elisabeth Jay Friedman, "Re(gion)alizing Women's Human Rights in Latin America," *Politics and Gender* 5, no. 3 (September 2009): 349–75. For work on the resistance to implementation of anti-VAW policies, see Cheryl O'Brien and Shannon Drysdale Walsh, "Women's Rights and Opposition: Explaining the Stunted Rise and Sudden Reversals of Progressive Violence Against Women Policies in Contentious Contexts," *Journal of Latin American Studies* 52, no. 1 (February 2020): 107–31.

52. Julia Monárrez Fragoso, "Feminicidio sexual serial en Ciudad Juárez: 1993–2001," *Debate Feminista* 25 (April 2002): 279–305; and Melissa W. Wright, "Necropolitics, Narcopolitics, and Femicide: Gendered Violence on the Mexico-U.S. Border," *Signs* 36, no. 3 (March 2011): 707–31.

53. Francesca Belotti, Francesca Comunello, and Consuelo Corradi, "*Feminicidio* and #NiUnaMenos: An Analysis of Twitter Conversations During the First 3 Years of the Argentinean Movement," *Violence Against Women* 27, no. 8 (2021): 1035–63.

54. Cara K. Snyder and Cristina Scheibe Wolff, "The Perfect Misogynist Storm and the Electromagnetic Shape of Feminism: Weathering Brazil's Political Crisis," *Journal of International Women's Studies* 20, no. 8 (October 2019): 96–97.

55. Cabezas González and Machado Brochner, "The New Cycle of Women's Mobilizations," 178.

56. UN Women and the United Nations Development Programme, *Government Responses to COVID-19: Lessons on Gender Equality for a World in Turmoil* (UN Women, 2022), 27.

57. Marcela A. Fuentes, "#NiUnaMenos (#NotOneWomanLess): Hashtag Performativity, Memory, and Direct Action Against Gender Violence in Argentina," in *Women Mobilizing Memory*, ed. Ayşe Gül Altınay, María José Contreras, Marianne Hirsch, Jean Howard, Banu Karaca, and Alisa Solomon (Columbia University Press, 2019), 180.

58. Carla Gomes and Bila Sorj, "Corpo, geração e identidade: A marcha das vadias no Brasil," *Revista Sociedade e Estado* 29, no. 2 (May 2014): 437.

59. Belotti, Comunello, and Corradi, "*Feminicidio* and #NiUnaMenos," 8; and Valentina Errázuriz, "A Digital Room of Their Own: Chilean Students Struggling Against Patriarchy in Digital Sites," *Feminist Media Studies* 21, no. 2 (2021): 281–97.

60. Carolina Matos, "New Brazilian Feminisms and Online Networks: Cyberfeminism, Protest and the Female 'Arab Spring,'" *International Sociology* 32, no. 3 (2017): 428.

61. Matos, "New Brazilian Feminisms," 428.

62. Elizabeth Rivera, "#MiPrimerAcoso: Fuertes testimonios de acoso cotidiano a las mujeres," Global Voices, April 24, 2016, https://es.globalvoices.org/2016/04/24/miprimer-acoso-fuertes-testimonios-de-acoso-cotidiano-a-las-mujeres/.

63. Mariela Méndez, "Operación Araña: Reflections on How a Performative Intervention in Buenos Aires's Subway System Can Help Rethink Feminist Activism," *Revista Estudos Históricos* (Rio de Janeiro) 33, no. 70 (May–August 2020): 282.

64. Méndez, "Operación Araña," 283; see also Marina Larrondo and Camila Ponce Lara, "Activismos feministas jóvenes en América Latina: Dimensiones y perspectivas conceptuales," in *Activismos feministas jóvenes: Emergencias, actrices y luchas en América Latina*, ed. Marina Larrondo and Camila Ponce Lara (Consejo Latinoamericano de Ciencias Sociales, 2019), 21–40.

65. Luisa Cruz Lobato and Cristiana Gonzalez, "Embodying the Web, Recoding Gender: How Feminists Are Shaping Progressive Politics in Latin America," *First Monday* 25, no. 5 (2020), https://firstmonday.org/ojs/index.php/fm/article/view/10129.

66. Verónica Gago, "#WeStrike: Notes Toward a Political Theory of the Feminist Strike," *South Atlantic Quarterly* 117, no. 3 (2018): 663.

67. Cabezas González and Machado Brochner, "The New Cycle of Women's Mobilizations," 190.

68. Helena Suárez Val, "Vibrant Maps: Exploring the Reverberations of Feminist Digital Mapping," *Inmaterial: Diseño, Arte y Sociedad* 3, no. 5 (2018): 118.

69. Snyder and Wolff, "The Perfect Misogynist Storm," 96.

70. Belotti, Comunello, and Corradi, "*Feminicidio* and #NiUnaMenos," 7.

71. Cabezas González and Machado Brochner, "The New Cycle of Women's Mobilizations," 178.

72. Natália Maria Félix de Souza, "When the Body Speaks (to) the Political: Feminist Activism in Latin America and the Quest for Alternative Democratic Futures," *Contexto Internacional* 41, no. 1 (April 2019): 89–112; Snyder and Wolff, "The Perfect Misogynist Storm"; and Gomes and Sorj, "Corpo, geração e identidade."

CHAPTER 10

Multilateral Transnationalism

Gang Stories from the Latino Atlantic

CARLES FEIXA

THE STARTING POINT OF this text is a trio of concepts linked to transnational studies: "grassroots transnationalism,"[1] "minor transnationalism,"[2] and "subaltern transnationalism."[3] From that point, I rely on the data and reflections resulting from fifteen years of investigating transnational youth gangs, specifically a street youth organization present on both sides of the Atlantic—the Latin Kings and Queens—who currently circulate between four "homelands": the original "motherland" in Chicago, the "second homeland" in some Latin American cities (mainly in Ecuador), the "third homeland" of the European exodus—in this case in Spain—and the "fourth homeland" established in cyberspace.[4]

Starting from the life stories of three leaders of this organization in the United States, Ecuador, and Spain, I analyze how transnationalism affects the gang phenomenon on three levels. First, as transnationalism "from above": as a circulation of visual imagery rooted in cinema, television series, and YouTube videos; as a circulation of "zero tolerance" policies toward street youth groups, translated into police exchanges and encounters with the neoliberal penal state; and as a circulation of models of institutional racism that turn young migrants into precarious workers and scapegoats for "moral panic" campaigns. Second, as transnationalism "from below": as a circulation of symbols, identities, and myths among the youth of a quasi-clandestine organization; as a feeling of brotherhood and mutual aid practices among the victims of globalization; and as an exchange of "knowledge of resistance" and "resilience" that allows subaltern people to survive in a hostile environment. Finally, as "multilateral transnationalism": as the circulation of intercultural experiences within and outside the group that demonstrate the agency of its members in their capacity to lead a transnational life without dying in the attempt.

The Four Homelands of the Latin Kings and Queens

The usual policy of boys' work agencies has been to redirect the activities of existing gangs into wholesome channels by some sort of supervision. While this method is difficult and not always successful, its usefulness has been conclusively demonstrated by many Chicago agencies.

—FREDERIC M. THRASHER, *THE GANG:*
A STUDY OF 1,313 GANGS IN CHICAGO

The Almighty Latin Kings and Queens Nation (ALKQN) is the official name of a transnational youth street organization sometimes considered a criminal gang and on other occasions a resistant brotherhood. It has at least four homelands. The first is Chicago, the "motherland," according to the terminology of the group's own literature,[5] the same place where the first serious study about gangs was published: *The Gang*, by Frederic M. Thrasher.[6] Some accounts maintain that the Latin Kings emerged in the 1940s as a defense of the second generation of Latino immigrants against the dominance of Afro-American gangs. Other accounts claim that they appeared in the 1960s, within the framework of the civil rights movement (which also gave rise to groups like the Black Panthers and the Young Lords).[7] They first emerged as a street gang in the Latin quarter of Chicago (first at Lincoln Park and later around Humboldt Park), and the gang was then officially formed in a jail, where some of the leaders who drafted the King's Manifesto Constitution (KMC) were serving sentences. In the 1970s, the Latin Kings expanded among the Latino community in other cities in the United States, mainly on the East Coast, where Puerto Rican and Caribbean immigration was predominant. In the 1990s, the New York chapter of the Latin King and Queens underwent a process of politicization and commitment thanks to new leadership and the support of intellectuals and religious people. As part of this process, the group began to deploy hip-hop, coming together in the concept of *nation* (drawing inspiration from the "Zulu Nation" founded in 1973 by Kevin Donovan, a.ka. Afrika Bambaataa, a pioneer of rap), specifically a mestiza nation—the "coffee nation" in the heart of the "wasp nation." A female branch (the Queens) was also incorporated. The result was the official creation of the Almighty Latin Kings and Queens Nation. The process ended abruptly in 1996 when Rudolph Giuliani, the then mayor of New York, promoted Operation Corona, which took the most combative ALKQN leaders to jail.[8]

The second homeland of the Latin Kings and Queens is Ecuador. In the 1990s, as a result of a change in US deportation policies (which, as a side effect, implanted gangs in Central America), several *hermanitos* arrived in Ecuador and tried to "plant the flag" there. After the ephemeral precedent of King Juice, who had arrived in Quito in 1992, King Boy Gean arrived in Guayaquil from New York in 1994 and King Lucky arrived in Quito from Chicago in 1996. The difference between the gang cultures of the cities of origin and those of the destination, as well as the rivalry between the two leaders, caused a division that lasted over time and did not cease to provoke conflicts. The dominant faction, led by King Boy Gean, later relieved by King Majesty, took the name Sacred Tribe Atahualpa Ecuador (STAE), after the last Inca emperor to resist the Spanish conquistadors, and obtained written authorization from King Bishop in New York in 1996. The ground was fertilized: in a country in permanent crisis and with thousands of street gangs, the Nation grew quickly in the neighborhoods of Guayaquil and Quito, inaugurating the process of globalization of the Latin Kings. In 2007, the Ecuadorian government of Rafael Correa, following the path opened in Barcelona (see below), legalized the Corporation of Latin Kings and Queens of Ecuador, initiating a mediation process, which significantly reduced crime. A similar process occurred in other Latin American countries such as Mexico, the Dominican Republic, and Colombia, where *little brothers* deported from the United States tried to implant the Nation, although without as much success as they achieved in Ecuador.[9]

The third homeland of the Latin Kings and Queens is Spain (and other European countries, like Italy). In the year 2000, an Ecuadorian leader, King Wolverine, emigrated to Spain and "planted the flag" in a new territory, founding the Sacred Tribe America Spain (STAS), which was independent of the previous group. In 2003, after appearing on a TV show, King Wolverine was arrested and convicted of rape. During these years, which coincided with a profound economic and political crisis in Ecuador and an economic boom in Spain, other Ecuadorian Latin Kings emigrated to Madrid and then to Barcelona and Murcia and refounded the Ecuadorian branch of the Latin Kings (STAE). In 2006, the Catalan branch was officially constituted as the Cultural Organization of Latin Kings and Queens of Catalonia, with the support of the Barcelona City Council, the Catalan leftist coalition government, and the regional police. This process was replicated in other places such as Alicante, Mallorca, and Navarre, although it failed in Madrid when that city's conservative community president and top official, Esperanza Aguirre, blocked any official recognition by thwarting the attempts at dialogue pursued by Pedro Núñez Morgades, ombudsman and advocate for children, who had opted for dialogue. In 2007, the Madrid faction of the Latin Kings (STAS), under the leadership of King Wolverine but never given official recognition, was put on trial for unlawful association. In 2011, after the return of the conservative party to the Catalan government, the Catalan police replaced their leadership with new managers who were advocates of criminalization. This had a negative impact on Latin American immigrants, some of whom chose to return to their countries, while others lost their jobs and still others started criminal careers.[10]

The fourth and last homeland of the Latin Kings and Queens is cyberspace. Since its transnationalization to Europe, the members of the Nation started to use the Internet, social networks, and smartphones to communicate among themselves: first, among friends living in the same locality or country; second, among emigrated youngsters and brothers who stayed in Ecuador; third, between the local factions of the Nation in Europe and Ecuador and the group's leaders in the United States; and finally, among all the hermanitos living on both sides of the Atlantic. Through this process, they created private virtual communities but also public cybercorners where current media and external social stigmas were transformed into internal group icons through the circulation of texts, emoticons, images, and videos that became objects of self-recognition and pride.[11]

Today, Latin Kings are present in most Latin American countries and in many European and even Asian countries. At the international level, there is no single leadership structure due to the persistent rivalry between Chicago and New York. In Ecuador, the group is still legal (they even have a deputy in the parliament); in Catalonia, it has still not been declared illegal, although members are not very active; and in Madrid, STAS is an illegal association, but there are other groups that, although also not legal, act openly with the support of NGOs who work with Ecuadorian immigrants in Spain.

The Five Chronotopes of the Crown

The chronotope makes narrative events concrete, makes them take flesh, causes blood to flow in their veins. [. . .] It is the chronotope that provides the ground essential for the [. . .] representativity of events. And this is so thanks precisely to the special increase of density and concreteness of time markers—the time of human life, the time of history—that occurs within well-delineated spatial areas. [. . .] Thus the chronotope, functioning as the primary means for materializing time in space, emerges as a center for concretizing representations.

—MIKHAIL BAKHTIN, *THE DIALOGIC IMAGINATION*

The autobiographical narrative can be read as an "open work";[12] that is, subject to different readings, so the reader becomes (co)author and the interpretation is polysemic and polyphonic. My reading of autobiography is inspired by the "dialogic imagination" proposed by Mikhail Bakhtin,[13] specifically by the concept of "chronotope," which we have tried elsewhere to apply in the study of youth cultures.[14] In *The Dialogic Imagination*, Bakhtin shows that an understanding of the space and time of a novel depends on *heteroglossic* ability (that is, on the ability to make other voices echo; to interpret not only depending on the text but also on the context). This capacity arises from a double dialogue: the "internal dialogue," fruit of the interaction of the subject with their own memory, and the "external dialogue," fruit of the interaction with the social environment represented by the audience (or by the researcher who asks, transcribes, and interprets what is spoken).

Here, I propose to follow Bakhtin and compare the life stories of three members of ALKQN who live in three different cities on two continents: King Manaba, an Ecuadorian who migrated to Barcelona; King Kannabis, a friend of his still living in Quito; and King Mission, an American king with Puerto Rican ancestors living in the United States. The three kings have been in contact with each other since the early part of the twenty-first century—online and offline—and have experienced transnationalism in different ways. I will analyze the spaces and times of these three kings through five central *chronotopes*: the Nation, the nation, the border, the corner, and the coffee brown force. These five chronotopes are the same for all the three kings but are lived and interpreted according to their own national and biographical experiences.

Barcelona: King Manaba

César Andrade was born twice. The first time was in Manabí, on the coast of Ecuador, in 1976, in a poor family. The second time was in Santo Domingo, a city in the interior of Ecuador, at age twenty, in 1996, when he was crowned a Latin King and took King Manaba as a new name, the only name by which he was known by most of the hermanitos. After a few years of commitment to the Ecuadorian section of the Nation (STAE), during which he came to be an "official," conflicts with other gangs, especially the Ñetas, motivated him to emigrate. He arrived in Madrid in 2003, where two years earlier the first European section of the Latin Kings, known as Sacred Tribe America Spain, had been founded. In early 2005 he transferred to Barcelona with the aim of expanding the Nation, and in June of that year we met and began our collaboration. This led to the establishment of the Cultural Organization of Latin Kings and Queens of Catalonia in August 2006.[15] After three intense years in which he became involved in countless cultural projects, in 2009 he was sentenced to five years in prison for a crime against public health (drug trafficking). After serving his sentence, he was released back into civil life and proceeded to take multiple jobs in the underground economy (during his prison stay he had been unable to renew his papers; in 2020 he completed his second regularization process, and in January 2025 he finally obtained Spanish citizenship—on that day, he sent me a photo of his first Spanish ID—and after that he could reunify with his son). In 2015 he was arrested again in a macro-raid that had the explicit aim of dismantling the legal sector of the Latin Kings. Although there were no serious crimes behind the accusations, the objective of the new Catalan police leaders and the Prosecutor's Office was to set a precedent and condemn the group as a criminal organization. What they wanted was to prove that King Manaba was a leader, although there was no material evidence of who was involved in crimes, and the evidence was based on contradictory statements by former members (some allegedly threatened with deportation if they did not cooperate with the police). The trial took place in December 2018, and I acted as an expert. In January 2020, a day before we submitted the manuscript for King Manaba's life story, which we had written together, the court declared King Manaba not guilty on all charges.[16]

For King Manaba, the first chronotope, the *Nation* (capitalized), is the space-time of the Almighty Latin King and Queen Nation, with their myths of origin, their rites of passage, their three states (Primitive King, Conservative King, and New King), their four phases (Observation, Five Alive, Probation, and Coronation), their five points (Love, Honor, Obedience, Sacrifice, and Rectitude), the five precious rocks of the royalty (white rock, golden amber, green emerald, red ruby, and black onyx), their formal organization in chapters, sectors, *and* tribes (and their informal organization in *factions, clans,* and *generations*), their annual calendar of local and universal meetings, and their culmination in the 360 (the hermeneutic and social circle of the imagined community, which some interpret as the circle of pain in which neophytes must bear the blows of the initiated):

[A Nation is] a group of people governed by a single government, race, constitution, laws. We live here a Nation in which we have a president, vice president, a secretary, a treasurer, a counselor, a war chief, teachers who teach, our policies, regulations, we have a supreme court, judges. [. . .] Within our organization, we live a Nation within the other nation, which is Spain. (King Manaba, July 30, 2005)

The second chronotope, the nation (in lowercase), is the transnational space-time that connects the identity of origin (Ecuador) and the identity of destination, also binational (Spain-Catalonia), which is expressed in the concept of "Nation of nations" and is a constant in the story:

When we say: "My king's love forever and ever on both continents," it means the American continent and the European continent, that the cry of the king reaches those always dark corners, which we say. I was born in Ecuador, but we always respect our motherland, our mother earth that is Chicago, where the Latin Kings were born in the 1960s. So, we hierarchically come from Chicago and from there it extends to New York, to all the states of the USA, Latin America, Central America. From Ecuador kings are born to come here for Europe. Right now, I am Catalan, I am a king from here. (King Manaba, January 8, 2019)

The third chronotope, the border, refers to the physical, legal, and symbolic barriers that separate continents, countries, neighborhoods, and rival gangs, as well as the instances (political, police, media) that build walls and justify exclusion:

We are a little afraid of being bullied by the police. On Friday we went to a meeting [at the parish] to pray for our deceased brothers. That day new kings are born, new queens, a work plan for the year is given and all that. Everything was normal in the meeting and then we went out and the police were waiting for us outside and they made an intervention to all of us. In this way we are not helping anything because what they are doing is for young people to become more rebellious. (King Manaba, January 15, 2012)

The fourth chronotope, the corner, refers to the connections and alliances that allow these borders to be crossed or mitigated, as well as to the refuge-places (parks, youth centers, parishes, discos, etc.) where fraternal and friendship ties can be made:

When we established ourselves as a legal association here in Barcelona, many things changed: young people were no longer afraid of being on the streets, because previously they saw a group of four or five people in a park or on the street and the police were probably going to ask them for documentation, but then they also mistreated you either verbally or physically. When we were established, all that decreased; from that moment the "hermanitos" gave themselves the opportunity to occupy the youth centers, receive training workshops, and many of the young people now have their jobs, are professionals and some continued studying. In those days it was positive. (King Manaba, October 24, 2019)

Finally, the fifth chronotope, the coffee brown force, refers both to the third phase of the protagonist's biography (that of the New King) and to the experiences of cultural hybridization and mediation in which he has participated: his commitment to the process of constituting the association, including his task as a peacemaker between different factions of the group and between rival groups:

> These [tattoos], every season I have been doing them. I have a phoenix on my right leg. It means that all the kings rise from the ashes to continue fighting. One resurfaces little by little. When one is in the ash, it is when one is in difficult situations. And when it resurfaces is when you go out. And every day, when you get out of something, or get something, you are making a comeback; that is, you can resurface every day. (King Manaba, March 9, 2016)

The story of King Manaba, as drawn from a dozen conversations I have had with him over fifteen years, is organized from the present through the three states into which the life of a king is divided: the state of "primitive king," which corresponds to an adolescent and immature attitude of fighting and street life; the state of "conservative king," which corresponds to maturation through happy experiences (such as his commitment to the legalization process) and also painful experiences (such as his time in prison); and the state of "new king," which corresponds to overcoming difficulties and becoming aware of a hybrid identity that converges in the so-called brown force. The coffee brown force is the magic potion that, after a period of hardship and deprivation of liberty, allows everyone to be reborn as a king, according to the classic phoenix bird metaphor, the bird resurfacing from its own ashes. In this case, it coincides with Manaba's work as a research assistant in the Transgang Project, culminating in the publication of a book in which he exposes his memoirs, and in his return trip to Ecuador, after twenty years of absence, to present it.[17]

Quito: King Kannabis

King Kannabis is one of the "little brothers" King Manaba most appreciated, whom he crowned as king and who later led one of the factions of the Nation in Ecuador, and with whom King Manaba has kept in contact during all these years, first by letter and later online. Kannabis breaks several stereotypes about the gang member: he does not come from a poor social sector but rather from a wealthy one ("I do not come from a dysfunctional family"), and he is currently the manager of a company with more than fifty employees. He received his pseudonym from his adolescent taste for marijuana, a habit he abandoned when he became king ("I stopped smoking many years ago. And do you know who took marijuana from me? The Nation"). He was crowned in 1996, shortly after his eighteenth birthday, in the same city as King Manaba: Santo Domingo, Ecuador. From that time until 2002 he established a close relationship with King Manaba and with Queen Melody, Manaba's companion at that time. When the latter pair emigrated in 2002, Kannabis felt like an orphan, but he decided to oversee several chapters, reaching a position of power but suffering splits and clashes with other groups. When the Corporation of Latin Kings and Queens of Ecuador was established in 2007, Kannabis's group did not want to participate, so they were labeled "crooked" by King Majesty, leader of the dominant faction. I interviewed Kannabis for the first time in Quito in 2019, after a day at Central University of Ecuador, where I met King Majesty and members of the Corporation. And I saw him again in 2022, this time accompanied by King Manaba, in a context of great violence due to the massacres in prisons by drug cartels, which a week after our visit tragically ended Majesty's life.

In the case of King Kannabis, the first chronotope—the Nation—represents the strength of Love, the first of the five points of the crown, which motivated his entry into the group in his youth and his permanence in it twenty-five years later, and which evokes the arrival of the Latin King to Ecuador in 1992 by the hand of a little brother deported from New York. The original antiracist rhetoric voiced in multiethnic US cities was transformed into antihypocrisy discourse in the allegedly more homogeneous Ecuadorian cities, even if in fact more subtle racial/ethnic differences were evident:

> This grew out of love, let alone lies, grew out of love inside or outside wherever it has been, in prison or on the streets. [...] Here we do not fight against racism [but] so that there is no hypocrisy among us, that is one of the purposes set by Boy Gean, the founder of the organization here in Ecuador in 1992. (King Kannabis, June 16, 2018)

The second chronotope—the nation—alludes to Ecuador as the "cradle of kings," a crucial stage in the globalization of the Nation after the departure from its North American "motherland," but it also refers to the Ecuadorian exodus to Spain, which left the Nation decimated:

The Nation began in Chicago and that is mother earth. Ecuador is the cradle, it is the cradle of kings because from here came all those *manes* [men] who are forming kings in Italy, in Spain, in Sweden, in Belgium, in Switzerland, in Chile, in Argentina, there in Peru, from here they left. I have contacts with everyone: with Chile with Peru with Argentina with Bolivia, with Sweden, with Switzerland, with Spain. [...] The US has already lost respect worldwide over the Latin Kings, it lost the leadership, the mandate, the strength they had. [...] Look how small the world is, my friends went there to Spain, they were the bosses and here also a person who left the organization. [...] [T]hey're living there, it's another pod, it's another life, it's another continent, it's another culture, it's other people . . . (King Kannabis, June 16, 2018)

The third chronotope—the border—evokes conflicts inside and outside the Nation, those arising from the complicated legalization process, which involved the split of the organization into four opposing factions:

There are so many people who were left behind, and today I must go visit them at a grave and bring them a flower and tell them and cry with them because that's when I vent, I cry and cry and go out, thank you brother, I get up and I don't want it to happen again, honestly, I don't want it to happen again. [...] That's where [King Majesty, leader of the dominant faction] cataloged those who left their circle to be *torcidos* [crooked], the little brothers who regrouped among themselves, even those who were no longer reported. That's where they looked for me. (King Kannabis, June 16, 2018)

The fourth chronotope—the corner—alludes to everyday encounters in the neighborhood and attempts at mediation with other gangs in prison or on the street:

We no longer do meetings in parks, and the regional official knows that he has to manage the request for a neighborhood house or an activity center of the prefecture, or we talk to the mayor or without, as well. Sometimes we also organize a walk, we go to a pool, too, we always try to mix that issue, a meeting of knowledge and of talking and of discussing and of praying, to pray is to speak with God, to pray is to repeat, we pray, we ask that we all do well.

[. . .] It also happened in Guayaquil with the Ñetas, and with the Masters in Duran, I had to go talk to them and of course: "Who is this *man* this skinny you want here?" I was going: "Hey, *brother* they had a problem with the Latin Kings, I am a king. What happens now? How can we fix it?" And now I have to make calls to jail to mediate, the same for the contacts I have. (King Kannabis, June 16, 2018)

The fifth and final chronotope—the coffee brown force—symbolizes the personal maturation that belonging to the group entails, faith supported by the spiritual strength of the collective:

When I entered, I was a childish child, of good school, I was even afraid, the typical skinny, white. Everyone was like, "What is he doing here?" I always wanted to be me like you [he addresses King Manaba]. You were the Inca: "Someday I'm going to be like this." And I mentalized. But who found the strength in me? The *Nación*. Your fist, his embrace, Erika's kiss, Chibolo's push, the problems, the enemies, those options or opportunities in which the Nación confronts you in the street, that is what brought out the outside of me, that leadership was taken out by the Nación. [. . .] Definitively has evolved the human being, the king, and the Nación. I as a human being have evolved, as a king I have evolved, and as the bearer of my crown I have evolved. I had meetings with the president of the assembly here in Ecuador, at that time when there were the *correistas* [followers of President Correa], I had meetings with Vice President Lenín [Moreno], we did the campaign to Lenín when he was president with a political party that we promoted: COS, Coalition of Social Organizations. We did [that] at the national level with the kings. That does allow you to evolve, change your vision, and somehow the leadership that the Nación takes from you as a person. (King Kannabis, April 6, 2022)

The story of King Kannabis, drawn from two meetings I had with him four years apart, has the alliances and ruptures between the different factions of the Nation in Ecuador as its guiding thread; the story is organized around his assessment of the process of transnationalization from the point of view of the kings who did not emigrate, but who kept in touch with those who left for other countries. He is currently a successful small businessman, and unlike King Manaba, he has not gone through the prison experience. However, instead of renouncing his identity as king, which has brought him many personal troubles, he makes an emblem of it, which gives him strength to progress individually and collectively.

New York and Chicago: King Mission

The third of our Latin kings is also a friend of King Manaba and has had contacts with King Kannabis, but he does not come from Ecuador but rather the United States. Quentin Ross, a.ka. King Mission, was born in New York in 1979 into a family of Puerto Rican origin. His mother was a member of the Young Lords, a former gang transformed into a political organization—the Latin version of the Black Panthers—which grew in the wave of the civil rights movement of the 1960s. His pseudonym comes from his origins as a poet, being accepted within the Nation for its connotations of a religious mission—he is also considered a *santero*.[18] Mission was crowned king in 1996—the same year as King Manaba and King Kannabis—when he was only sixteen years old, by King Tone, who was leading the reform process for New York's Latin Kings and Queens. I met him in 2006 in Genoa, Italy, at the first transnational meeting of Latin Kings and Ñetas in Europe, and that same year I invited him to a day at the University of Lleida in Catalonia. In that first interview, we reviewed the history of the Nation and the dilemmas of the "constitution of association" that had just been successfully completed in Barcelona. A second interview took place in 2007 in New York and focused on the process of globalization of the Nation. In 2019, we incorporated King Mission as a local researcher of the Transgang Project in Chicago, conducting two long formal interviews, the first in Barcelona in 2019, focused on the effects of the legalization process in Spain and Ecuador, and the second in 2022 in Chicago, focused on the history of gangs in the "mother country."

In the case of King Mission, the first chronotope—the Nation—represents the official and apocryphal history of the Latin Kings and Queens in their place of origin: the United States and specifically the city of Chicago, the motherland:

Carles Feixa: Where does the term "Nation" come from?
King Mission: The Nation, why we live in a government that oppresses the

people. [...] We are a Nation because we have our rules, to govern ourselves, ourselves. (King Mission, October 25, 2006)

The original meaning of the term "Nation," however, comes into question when the "little brothers" move to other territories, either by deportation or by migratory processes, which provokes a reflection not free of contradictions on the part of the American leaders on the way to manage the process of globalization:

Chicago had not thought of being a mother country, because they had not thought of leaving Chicago. [...] When they realized that there were nations in different parts of the world, then they would say, "Here is literature, it is for the whole Nation." [...] As Americans, we [got] proud: "We are everywhere in the world!" But we're not communicating with them, you are not under any other brother. Although the Nation began here, we are not higher than you, your brothers, one beside the other. [...] The United States in their mind is the center of the world; Americans do not understand which countries are recognized because they are only concerned about this country. And that's why we're here, that's why I've gone to Chicago several times to make sure everything is okay and, honestly, we're already at a historic point to give permission to represent the Nation to someone who isn't from Chicago. [...] There are many things that are changing globally that have to do with respect for immigrants in the United States and different countries. (King Mission, November 2, 2007)

The second chronotope—the nation—evokes the family origins of King Mission in Puerto Rico and his identification with the Latino community in the United States, which converges in a foundational space/time: the Puerto Rican Parade of January 20, 1996, a festive moment in the public space of New York. The protagonist identifies a group of young people dressed in yellow and black and decides to join them:

The thing about Puerto Ricans is that we can never feel at home, we are a mixture of Taíno, Indian, Spanish, African. [...] That pride of being Latino has to do with the Black civil rights movement, saying, "We're Latinos right now in the United States!" [...] The Latin stays in the middle, we are not white, but sometimes we are not Black enough, sometimes we are *caramelito*, we lack two or three drops of being darker, that's why there are groups like the Young Lords, because we needed a Latin voice. (King Mission, October 19, 2019)

The third chronotope—the border—refers to surveillance systems on a local and global scale, and ultimately to the transnational panopticon that persecutes gangs everywhere and criminalizes their members:

In every school, in the city of Chicago, which is from the Black and Latino community, in every corner of that school, there is a police camera, recording twenty-four hours, seven days a week, because they say they are gang members, that they are criminals. In every neighborhood, where there is a lot of Latino and Black, they are recording. (King Mission, October 25, 2006)

In the case of Spain, Italy, they have different problems from Ecuador. First, we are a foreign country; they're seeing us as immigrants first, [as] gang members second: Aren't you from here? It's already wrong. Do you belong to a gang? Even worse. (King Mission, October 25, 2006)

The fourth chronotope—the corner—alludes to the exchanges and hybridizations in the "transition zone" of the original gangland in Chicago, but also of the new gangland in transnational space. Through the phases to become a king, the corner becomes a domesticated, familiar, intimate space:

In Chicago, if there are four corners, there are four chapters. But there is no division, every corner is its world: "You there, I here; you have your thing, I have mine." (King Mission, November 2, 2007)

Antonio Fernández, who is King Tone, was the one who crowned me, but everything in the Nación takes its process, of course there is a time of observation, there is a time of probation that has been different in each chapter, in my case they never put me, I was in observation because they knew me, they put me on probation and for example today and in two weeks I had gone to a universal. (King Mission, October 19, 2019)

The fifth and final chronotope—the coffee brown force—symbolizes the ethnogenesis of the King identity from the fusion of previous subcultural traditions, expressed through the cult of ancestors, which allows one to differentiate the experience from mere belonging and which is theorized through holistic belief ("everything is connected"):

> It is one thing to live the Nation and another thing to belong to the Nation. [. . .] It's something we have, it's called coffee force or brown force. [. . .] Everything is connected, everything. Why we have tattoos, how we dress, the clothes we wear, how we speak, how we cut hair, what we eat, when we eat. Everything is connected, everything . . . (King Mission, October 25, 2006)

The story of King Mission, drawn from four discontinuous conversations over fifteen years, is organized as digressions around the pros and cons of the globalization of the Nation. Starting from the subaltern position of the Latino community in the United States, he assumes the role of mediator in the process of transnationalization of the Latin Kings in Ecuador and Spain, through his contacts with little brothers like King Manaba and King Kannabis. On the one hand, he is proud that the coffee brown force is expanding throughout the world with positive results; on the other hand, he is concerned about the lack of control this implies in the organization, as well as about the consequent greater visibility of the kings of Chicago and New York, which can draw greater police and criminal control. His trips to Europe place him between the two continents, presenting himself as a mediator between communities and worlds of life.

Internet: Three Kings

The chronotopes of the lives of these three kings converge in a hyper-chronotope that connects them personally, socially, and emotionally and that allows the transnational to pass from power to action: the Internet. In the interviews, they constantly allude to the transformation of the ways of communicating within the Nation, a process through which the space/time of gang members passes from the street to the networks. Five dialogic forms of this hyper-chronotope can be distinguished: the meeting, the letter, the literature, the chat, and the meet.

When the three kings entered the Nation in the second half of the 1990s, communication took place face-to-face within the local chapter in meetings or "mirings." This is how King Mission recalls his initiation into the New York Nation in 1996:

> I decided to get into the Nativity scene, I say to [King] Tone, "I want a king." Because I went to a Puerto Rican parade in the Bronx as a guest without knowing anything, with a blue shirt and black pants, totally wrong. I get in the middle, the whole yellow and black world: "Hey, this is cool! These tastes are good! They are so funny!" (King Mission, October 19, 2019)

The informal verbal and nonverbal communication of the meetings is combined with the official textual communication (notes, writings, messages) and visual (logos, T-shirts, tattoos) with which neophytes in Latin King culture are socialized. When communication crosses the local level, especially when it crosses a national border, it must be formalized in the form of a letter, which is also an instrument of power to give orders or authorize colonizing new territories ("planting the flag"). The implantation of the Nation in Spain also involved epistolary conflicts. The first king to "plant a flag" in the new territory, King Wolverine (a leader from Ecuador), did so without authorization from his mother tribe (STAE), so he had to invent a new tribe (STAS), which was legitimized by a specific founding act in December 2000. And my ethnographic contact with the Nation in Barcelona in June 2005 was made possible thanks to a letter of introduction from researchers who had written about the Nation in New York, which I then forwarded to King Manaba.

The most important form of textual communication is "literature." This refers to a compilation of sacred texts, often apocryphal, written by leaders from prison or at foundational or refounding moments and then disseminated among "little brothers" who are in the process of formation (in "phases"), who must memorize the texts as the catechism. The most important is the King's Manifesto Constitution (KMC), also known as the Latin King Bible:

> We decided to make a constitution, because we had to find a way to separate ourselves from the other groups. How are you going to have such a powerful name as Kings and be the same as the others? [...] It is like reading the Bible, which has pieces of different religions, of different parts, different histories.

The constitution of us has been part of different manifestos of different organizations, even Confucius has [his] piece in the constitution, but the most important piece of the constitution is the stages of being king, they are the most important because it's there where you find what's the thought of the book. (King Mission, October 19, 2019)

The Latin Kings in the '40s gather in the streets, but they were founded as the Latin Kings Organization in the year '62, then they gave each other their name. From '62 onward literature is written: the KMC and other texts. [The KMC is] the only text that is supposed to be universally recognized by all parties, by all factions and in all groups, because there is no literature written in [all places]. (King Manaba, January 19, 2019)

The KMC has a halo of secrecy—supposedly only crowned kings and queens can know it. But in the age of the Internet, secrets don't exist. On the other hand, the process of globalization of the Nation implies rethinking literature so that the local can encompass the transnational, without this implying distorting the original creed or promoting independent kingdoms in which each Inca imposes his rules.

After 2005, coinciding with the expansion of the Latin kings in Europe, communication within the Nation also began to be virtual. The first space of exchange between the "little brothers" was the chat: initially the virtual corner was a relatively small platform preponderant in Ecuador—Hi5—then Facebook and WhatsApp, and finally Instagram. The networks serve to maintain contact between kings and queens who have emigrated and know each other from yesteryear, but also to establish new contacts between US kings and those in other countries. As happened among the general population, at first there was a digital divide that can be read as a generation gap.

Chat is just a transitional form of asynchronous online communication that prepared the terrain for synchronous communication (videoconferencing), which consolidated the evolution of the meeting toward Meet, completed during the COVID-19 pandemic, when the street was reduced or disappeared in the life of the gangs. The Internet 3.0 allows leaders of several countries to establish agreements and to carry out internal trials of dissidents—such as the trial of an Ecuadorian leader in which the three protagonists of this essay participated—but it also feeds rumors, conflicts, and factionalism.

If we smell a fart in Europe, we must smell it here in the United States. So, that's why we must have more organization. (King Mission, November 15, 2007)

The members of the Nation are ambivalent about the impact of the Internet. On the one hand, it undoubtedly facilitates the process of globalization and democratization of the Nation, which can thus become more open and transparent. On the other hand, it is a fundamentally playful and recreational tool, which instead of promoting open-mindedness and relationships with other groups and factions runs the risk of encapsulating participants in closed and self-referential groups, and facilitates panoptic control by the electronic surveillance of transnational police:

> With [the] Internet . . . what's going on? In '95, '96, out there, there was communication with Ecuador. [. . .] Now that they have a very easy opportunity to speak worldwide, they only talk to themselves. They don't talk outside their group, because they don't want to break that image, that if they break it, they must think, pussy. [. . .] Remember that we are Americans, and we think with a lot of paranoia: if the world finds out, it starts talking in different conversations. What's going on? The crimes if they are done here affect there. Now, every time something happens using this name, it affects us. The feds here have us as terrorists on their website. (King Mission, November 2, 2007)

The stories of the three kings converge in cyberspace, understood as technology and culture.[19] As technology, the Internet offers the infrastructure that allows interpersonal communication between kings and queens separated by national borders. As culture, the Internet regenerates the coffee brown force, facilitating decentralization and horizontality in an originally centralized and vertical nation. The cybernetic hyper-chronotope reconstructs a Nation beyond borders, building bridges between individuals and between nations.

Conclusion: Multilateral Transnationalism

While there have always been gangs, today's urbanized world is producing them faster and in countless forms. High levels of violence by "non-state actors" such as gangs or terrorists have been a disturbing aspect of globalization. [. . .] [G]angs are not going to disappear, no matter what we do.

—JOHN HAGEDORN, *A WORLD OF GANGS:*
ARMED YOUNG MEN AND GANGSTA CULTURE

The life stories of King Manaba, King Kannabis, and King Mission have numerous parallels: the three were crowned the same year—1996—and profess the same faith, expressed in the KMC; all three assumed leadership positions in the organization and were involved in internecine conflicts; all three participated in mediation and association-building experiences; the three lived in their own flesh the expansion of the Nation and the recognition of its limits; and all three experienced the process of transitioning to a digital society. Their stories contain numerous lessons about globalization: for better or worse, gangs have become (trans)gangs—which does not necessarily mean that they are transnational gangs in a geographical sense, according to the model of international corporations or franchises, or that they behave as compact and centralized structures; it may even be that some of them have accentuated their local dimensions. If the gangs are today (trans)gangs, it is because three different and complementary processes of transnationalization converge in them: transnationalism from above, transnationalism from below, and multilateral transnationalism.[20]

Transnationalism from above—or major transnationalism—includes processes driven by states, international bodies, transnational corporations, and the mass media, as a response to the expansion of gangs.[21] I will highlight five main processes. (1) Economic and political *neoliberalism* dismantles the industrial economy, a labor alternative for young people of the working class or of migrant origin, and replaces it with an economy of services and information based on laissez-faire, to which these sectors do not have access. This coincides with the expansion of the drug market as the only alternative of self-employment, as well as with the dismantling of the remnants of the welfare state, which disappears from many marginal enclaves. (2) Some of these gangs have expanded territorially because of *deportation* policies pushed by the US government since 1996, as evidenced by the emblematic case of Salvadoran gangs. (3) *Security*, intelligence, repressive, and police policies—especially those of a *mano dura*—are exercised today on a global level, using strategies short of warfare including lawfare and prison fare, promoted by transnational security agencies or by private antigang

Figure 10.1. Gangs and
transnationalism.

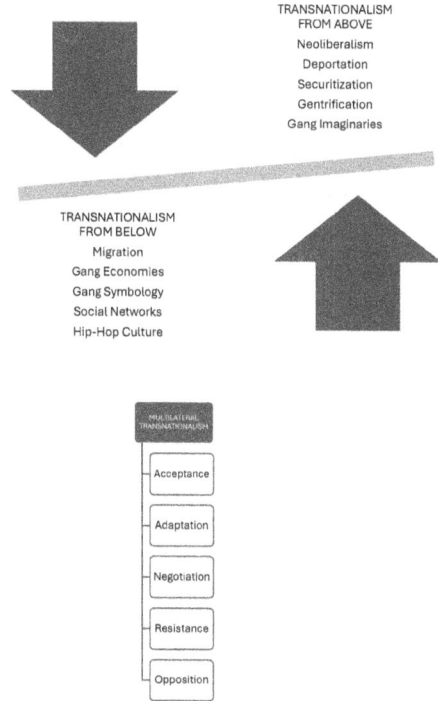

TRANSNATIONALISM
FROM ABOVE
Neoliberalism
Deportation
Securitization
Gentrification
Gang Imaginaries

TRANSNATIONALISM
FROM BELOW
Migration
Gang Economies
Gang Symbology
Social Networks
Hip-Hop Culture

MULTILATERAL
TRANSNATIONALISM

Acceptance

Adaptation

Negotiation

Resistance

Opposition

advisory agencies. (4) Strong urban segregation and *gentrification* drive gang members out of their original territories and move them to marginal ghettos, where invisible borders or new forms of surveillance and control impede or limit mobility, but at the same time drive a criminal economy that relies on large-scale smuggling. (5) *Gang imaginaries* are built in a transnational space, of which movies and television series about gangs or narcos are a by-product.

Transnationalism from below—or minor transnationalism—includes processes that occur at the initiative of grassroots social actors, whether they are the gang members themselves, their families, their social environments, or the formal or informal organizations with which they interact.[22] I will highlight five main processes. (1) *Migrations* constitute an origin, a context, or a possibility of expansion of the gangs themselves, following three complementary directions: translocal (from the countryside to the city, or from war zones to refuge zones), transnational (from the Global South to the United States in the Global North by land, sea, and air), or transoceanic (from the Americas to Europe, as a return journey from the original Columbian voyage, crossing the Atlantic Ocean). (2) As an effect of these migratory processes, the collaborative *gang economies* become an alternative or complement to the market economy, based on remittances, the informal economy, barter, and the nonmonetary exchange of goods and services, turning gangs into a suprafamilial space of mutual support and labor insertion. (3) *Gang symbology* and the lifestyles related to it, based on face-to-face or epistolary personal exchanges as well as the dissemination of the literature of the most important gangs, are transnationalized while en route from the United States to Europe through Latin America. (4) *Social networks* have facilitated the "flow space" for contacts, exchanges, and decision making among the different nodes of the gangs, but they have also generated a transnational "gang branding," as evidenced by the interactions of the Latin Kings and Queens from beyond the seas. (5) *Hip-hop culture*, with its four components—rap, DJ, break dancing, and graffiti—in its different local versions, constitutes the expression of the transnational space built into the "Latino Atlantic,"[23] a counterpart of the "Black Atlantic,"[24] extended in recent times with the globalization of reggaeton and trap.

Finally, *multilateral transnationalism* includes processes of adaptation, interaction, opposition, and mediation between transnationalisms from above and below, in each of the ten processes outlined above and in any other process involving gangs.[25] I will highlight five possible types of response. (1) *Acceptance* implies the conscious participation of gang members or their environments in the creation of delimited transnational spaces, such as corrupt links between state agencies and criminal groups or collaborative projects to prevent violence between international organizations, gang leaders, and academic actors. (2) *Adaptation* implies the exploitation by gangs or their members of the loopholes offered by major transnational activity, such as the creation of an informal collaborative economy or the conversion of ghettos into self-managed protected spaces. (3) *Negotiation* involves different forms of intercultural mediation such as attempts at a truce, the formation of associations based on gangs, or preventive and rehabilitative work with prisoners or ex-prisoners. (4) *Resistance* implies conscious actions to boycott major transnationalism, such as mutual support networks to overcome barriers to emigration or to confront "iron fist" policies. (5) *Opposition* implies the convergence of gangs with broader social movements fighting for minority rights or contesting through illicit or clandestine means.

The accounts of the three kings according to the five dialogical chronotypes that I have analyzed contain numerous lessons on the so-called process of globalization. Although the forces that animate the transnational are powerful, it cannot impose itself unequivocally on individuals: even if they are devoid of economic and political capital, people can use their social and symbolic capital to oppose, resist, negotiate, adapt, or accept their subaltern position. Changes in offline and online forms of communication are both the consequence and the cause of such a process, transforming the nation-state into a nation of nations where stigmatized minorities—especially youth nations—can open transnational spaces to negotiate and defend their own identity. Through such negotiation, *resistance* can be transformed into *resilience*—and vice versa—turning the dualistic playing field of hegemonic transnationalism, up versus down, into a multilateral playing field where subordinates have more options to consider.[26]

Notes

1. Arjun Appadurai, ed., *Globalization* (Duke University Press, 2001).

2. Françoise Lionnet and Shu-mei Shih, eds., *Minor Transnationalism* (Duke University Press, 2005).

3. Gayatri Chakravorty Spivak, "Can the Subaltern Speak?," in *Marxism and the Interpretation of Culture*, ed. Cary Nelson and Lawrence Grossberg (University of Illinois Press, 1988), 271–316; and Edward Piñuelas, "Transnationalism in Postcolonial and Subaltern Studies," Oxford Bibliographies, July 26, 2017, https://doi.org/10.1093/OBO/9780190221911-0047.

4. This text is an outcome of the Transgang Project, which investigates transnational gangs as agents of mediation in twelve cites of southern Europe, North Africa, and the Americas. See Carles Feixa, José Sánchez-García, Eduard Ballesté, Ana Belén Cano, Maria-Jose Masanet, Margot Mecca, and Maria Oliver, *The (Trans) Gang: Notes and Queries on Youth Street Group Research* (Universitat Pompeu Fabra; Brussels: European Research Council, 2019), http://dx.doi.org/10.31009/transgang.2019.wp02.1. For the Transgang Project, see www.upf.edu/web/transgang. This project has received funding from the European Research Council under the European Union's Horizon 2020 research and innovation program (H2020-ERC-AdG-742705), and from the Spanish Ministry of Science, Innovation, and Universities under the R+D+I National Plan (PID2019-110893RB-I00).

5. The "literature" is the compilation of the canonic readings of ALKQN.

6. Frederic M. Thrasher, *The Gang: A Study of 1,313 Gangs in Chicago*, 2nd ed. (University of Chicago Press, 1936). Thrasher's work was first published in 1927 and was reprinted in 2013.

7. Wikipedia gives the official founding date as 1954; the official constitution of the group, the King's Manifesto Constitution (KMC), known as the Latin King Bible, says that the group was born in 1962. See https://en.wikipedia.org/wiki/Latin_Kings.

8. David C. Brotherton and Luis Barrios, *The Almighty Latin King and Queen Nation: Street*

Politics and the Transformation of a New York City Gang (Columbia University Press, 2003); David Conquergood, "How Street Gangs Problematize Patriotism," in *After Postmodernism: Reconstructing Ideology Critique*, ed. Herbert W. Simons and Michael Billig (Sage, 1994), 200–221; and Louis Kontos, "Between Criminal and Political Deviance: A Sociological Analysis of the New York Chapter of the Almighty Latin King and Queen Nation," in *The Post-Subcultures Reader*, ed. David Muggleton and Rupert Weinzierl (Berg, 2003), 133–50.

9. David C. Brotherton and Rafael Gude, *Social Inclusion from Below: The Perspectives of Street Gangs and Their Possible Effects on Declining Homicide Rates in Ecuador* (Inter-American Development Bank, 2018); and Carles Feixa and César Andrade, *El Rey: Diario de un Latin King* (NED Ediciones, 2020).

10. Carles Feixa, Laura Porzio, and Carolina Recio, *Jóvenes "latinos" en Barcelona: Espacio público y cultura urbana* (Anthropos Editorial; Ajuntament de Barcelona, 2006); and Luca Queirolo Palmas, "Gangs in the Latino Atlantic: *La Raza Latina*, Transnationalism and Generations," in *Youth, Space and Time: Agoras and Chronotopes in the Global City*, ed. Carles Feixa, Carmen Leccardi, and Pam Nilan (Brill, 2016), 85–114.

11. Ariadna Fernández-Planells, Enrique Orduña-Malea, and Carles Feixa, "Gangs and Social Media: A Systematic Literature Review and an Identification of Future Challenges, Risks and Recommendations," *New Media and Society* 23, no. 7 (July 2021): 2099–124.

12. Umberto Eco, *The Open Work*, trans. Anna Cancogni (Harvard University Press, 1989).

13. Mikhail Bakhtin, *The Dialogic Imagination: Four Essays*, ed. Michael Holquist, trans. Caryl Emerson and Michael Holquist (University of Texas Press, 1981).

14. Carles Feixa, Carmen Leccardi, and Pam Nilan, eds., *Youth, Space and Time: Agoras and Chronotopes in the Global City* (Brill, 2016).

15. I actively participated in this process, alongside representatives of the Barcelona City Council, the Institute of Human Rights of Catalonia, and the ombudsman of Catalonia.

16. Feixa and Andrade, *El Rey*.

17. Feixa and Andrade, *El Rey*. In April 2022, I traveled with King Manaba to Ecuador. He met his son (whom he had left, when the child was just a baby, in the care of his two grandmothers), his fellow students (one of whom had become a senior police officer), and his hermanitos from the Nation, including King Kannabis. At the presentation of the book, Ecuador's two primary newspapers, *El Comercio* (Quito) and *El Universo* (Guayaquil), published interviews.

18. A *santero* is a priest of Santería, an Afro-American religion.

19. Christine Hine, *Virtual Ethnography* (SAGE Publications, 2000).

20. Carles Feixa and José Sánchez-García, "Global Gangs? Beyond Marginalization and Resilience," *Youth and Globalization* 3, no. 2 (2022): 255–64.

21. Appadurai, *Globalization*; and Loïc Wacquant, *Punishing the Poor: The Neoliberal Government of Social Insecurity* (Duke University Press, 2009).

22. Lionnet and Shih, *Minor Transnationalism*; and Saskia Sassen, *Los espectros de la globalización* (Fondo de Cultura Económica, 2003).

23. Queirolo Palmas, "Gangs in the Latino Atlantic."

24. Paul Gilroy, *The Black Atlantic: Modernity and Double Consciousness* (Harvard University Press, 1993).

25. Ulf Hannerz, *Transnational Connections: Culture, People, Places* (Routledge, 2010); and Feixa and Sánchez-García, "Global Gangs?"

26. The situation has changed since the interviews and the first version of this chapter, especially in Ecuador and the United States, due to political changes in both countries and the subordination of youth gangs to criminal and prison gangs in Ecuador.

CHAPTER II

Transnationalism and the German Diaspora in Latin America

Content, Form, and the Revenge of the Nation-State

MAX PAUL FRIEDMAN

FOR MANY MIGRANTS, THE persistence of nationalism and ethnic self-identification across space (beyond national boundaries) and across time (years or generations spent in emigration) has produced diasporic or transnational communities maintained through cultural practices, communicative networks, and the education of children, perhaps especially when coupled with forms of exclusion in the new country. The surge in international migration in the decades following World War II and decolonization yielded such communities on an unprecedented scale: Indians in London and Durban, Haitians in Santo Domingo and Quebec, Vietnamese in Paris and Los Angeles, Palestinians in Tegucigalpa and Amman. Many of these refugees and emigrants retained strong cultural, political, and economic ties to a remote homeland, and identified themselves primarily as scattered members of the homeland nation rather than as new members of the country in which they happened to reside and that often treated them with suspicion.

Migrants have always carried emotional attachments to their homeland. What distinguishes a diasporic community is the centrality of the affective ties to the homeland and its tenacity in persisting over a lifetime or even across generations, as well as, frequently, continued political engagement with the sending country and diaspora members. Transnationalism here potentially represents a decoupling, whether of people from territory or of the nation from the state. Receiving states often see this as a threat. Allegations of dual loyalty and the danger of ethnic influence over US foreign policy have been raised with increasing frequency, from Louis Gerson's 1964 charge that ethnic groups in America felt "duty-bound to act in the interest of their ancestral land" to Charles S. Maier's warnings of the "tides of fragmentation [. . .] lap[ping] at Western democracies" and Samuel Huntington's apocalyptic predictions of a transnational threat from diasporic loyalties to "kin-country" that could lead to the "de-Americanization" of the United States.[1] The Donald Trump era has only intensified the political conflict over migration and transnational identity, even as some Latin American states have quietly worked to make "transnationalism and transnational citizenship mutually beneficial to migrants and the state" by promoting the integration of diasporic citizens into the political life of the home country, advocating for the rights of migrants abroad regardless of legal status, and encouraging—indeed, often relying on—their remittances.[2]

Scholars of the postnational, often writing in the idiom of postcolonial studies, do not share Huntington's or Trump's political views, but they may share certain assumptions. Most tend to cast and exalt the rise of diasporic communities in terms of subaltern resistance; many believe that this phenomenon heralds the last gasp of the nation-state and may even have already caused its demise. They describe reimagined communities, updating Benedict Anderson's concept of "imagined communities."[3] Where Anderson posited national communities unified by a common language and common reading materials, scholars of diasporas describe communities still unified by common national symbols but no longer confined within artificial political borders. And whereas theories of nationalism emphasize the theoretical contiguity between the nation (community of people) and state (supreme political unit),[4] in practice there are few such states; neat contiguity depends on comprehensive systems of exclusion and often violence, and postnationalists argue that contiguity is in any case disappearing.

The various terms used to describe this evaporation of the nation-state's monopoly on nationality reflect different thinking about causes and consequences. For Michael Kearney, writing on the Mixtecs of Mexico and the southwestern United States, "transnational" migrants are nation-state destroy-ers. Since they commute between two countries and become absorbed in neither, contemporary migrants are replacing the model of assimilation with one of "indigestion," as they "escape the power of the nation-state to inform their sense of collective identity."[5] For Kearney, this is a new and irreversible fact with sweeping implications: "'Transnationalism,'" he writes, "implies a blurring, or perhaps better said, a reordering of the binary cultural, social, and epistemo-logical distinctions of the modern period. [. . .] [H]istory and anthropology have entered a post-national age."[6]

Arjun Appadurai, an early postnational theorist, argues that people of a dias-pora continue to identify themselves as a national group, but that nation has become "deterritorialized"—cut loose from its territorial anchor, freed from confinement within artificial borders:

> [The nation-state is not] yet out of business. It is certainly in crisis, and part of the crisis is an increasingly violent relationship between the nation-state and its postnational others. [. . .] [N]either popular nor academic thought in this country [the United States] has come to terms with the difference between being a land of immigrants and being one node in a postnational network of diasporas.[7]

Other writers joined Appadurai and Kearney in viewing the proliferation of dia-sporic communities as a growing (and welcome) antagonist of the nation-state system.[8] Linda Basch, Nina Glick Schiller, and Cristina Szanton Blanc depart from this conclusion, arguing that nation-states, paradoxically, will be strength-ened by the "new nationalism" of the diasporas—at least in the states that *send* the migrants.[9] These authors represent the main currents of thinking among postnational scholars of migration who shaped the emerging field in the 1990s. They may disagree on whether the nation-state is disappearing or merely radi-cally changing in character, but surprisingly, none of them dwell on the implica-tions for the receiving states of the growth in power and scope of the diasporic or transnational or deterritorialized communities.

Historical shifts of such sweeping proportions rarely happen without major repercussions. If the Basch, Glick Schiller, and Szanton Blanc model is correct, and postcolonial nations are strengthening their hold on their nationals who are abroad, is it likely that the receiving states will benevolently play host to the "newly nationalistic" transnational citizens of another state residing within their borders? Or will these migrants be declared "alien enemies" and deported, as were Palestinians in Kuwait in 1991 and thousands of Arabs and Muslims of many nationalities in the United States after September 11, 2001; and as happened to Latin American immigrants also in the United States in recurring cycles of state repression including our own time? And if Kearney and Appadurai are correct, and the nation-state is coming apart under the pressure of so many diasporas, can we expect it to slink away without a fight? Appadurai hints darkly at the "increasingly violent relationship between the nation-state and its postnational others," without elaboration. Kearney recognizes in the English-only movement and racialized public discourse in the United States "new forms of discipline [that] correspond to a movement from an offensive jingoist nationalism to a nationalism on the defensive."[10] And all of this only prefigured the Trumpian backlash and its right-wing nationalist counterparts in Australia, Hungary, Italy, India, the United Kingdom, and elsewhere.

History and today's news headlines provide us with concrete examples of nationalism defending itself from its transnational others. One forgotten but illuminating case is explored in this chapter: migrants from Germany who made their homes in Latin America while maintaining transnational connections with their natal or ancestral country as well as other German communities in the region. By focusing on a period when global events put this diasporic identity under extreme pressure, this chapter considers a troubling aspect of transnationalism: the way that war and security concerns can turn transnational identities into perceived threats, a problem that states prefer to resolve by forcefully containing transnational people into national groups and subjecting them to discipline. Nation-states in crisis, whether real or manufactured for political ends, remain afflicted by this particular form of what we might be tempted to call (were the term not already in use for another grim form of anxious hostility) transphobia.

The fate of German residents of the Americas offers an illustrative case. Large-scale German migration to Latin America began in the middle of the nineteenth century, following the failed liberal revolutions of 1848; a larger wave followed in the last two decades of that century. Of all European immigrants to Latin America, Germans received perhaps the warmest welcome. The influential writer and future Argentine president Domingo Sarmiento in 1860 praised "their proverbial honesty, their tireless devotion to work, and their pacific character."[11] Latin American politicians tended to embrace European immigrants in general for bringing "sobriety" and "culture" as a necessary corrective to local "creole indolence"—a kind of racial flattery that would make some German expatriates receptive to twentieth-century racist appeals.[12]

A vast array of separate cultural institutions reinforced the immigrants' sense of their difference. "The first thing that two Germans do when they meet overseas is to found three associations," wrote an observer, and the Germans of Latin America proved this with enthusiasm, creating a profusion of *Vereine*, clubs or associations for recreational, educational, cultural, and charitable purposes. There were singing clubs, sports clubs, beer-drinking clubs, mutual aid societies, volunteer fire brigades. The *Vereine* were sanctuaries of familiarity and the focal points of community. The emigrants' direct contact with the homeland tended to wane over time, vitiating any truly aggressive nationalism on their part. They knew where their own interests lay: in maintaining friendly relations with their Latin American neighbors, governors, and customers. Most German immigrants ultimately occupied an in-between space, loyal but apart, welcomed but unincorporated, in Latin America but not of it.[13] This nuanced positioning reflects the complexity of the human experience, but states are not good at seeing or managing complex identities.

Small, isolated Nazi groups sprouted in several Latin American capitals after 1929. Most German emigrants tried at first to ignore these coarse, noisy upstarts. It was not merely their grating style that kept the Nazis from making many early converts. The conservative German expatriates abhorred the disorder, the acid partisan rivalries that hobbled the Weimar government and regularly spilled onto the streets of Germany's cities. Shrill local Nazis now threatened to import the same conflicts to the staid overseas communities. Extolling the supremacy of German culture and calling for defending the purity of German blood seemed to many emigrants to be in extremely poor taste where maintaining respectful relations with Latinos was crucial to their continued social and financial success.

The specificities of the Latin American context worked for and against the spread of Nazi ideology. Those immigrants whose worldview rested on the then-fashionable social Darwinist, positivist, and racial determinist assumptions often had their prejudices reinforced by the stratification of the Latin American societies they joined. They took their places in the *pigmentocracia*, the pigmentocracy, a hierarchy in which those with a lighter skin tone advanced further up the social ladder. Some Germans managed rapidly to create sizeable plantations or thriving businesses, tangible achievements that some of them—and not a few of their Latino neighbors—interpreted in racial terms, overlooking the advantages of education, technical skill, and access to German capital and markets that they brought along with their legendary work ethic.

Those Germans who intermarried or had close social ties with Latin Americans were far less likely to welcome an ideology based on racial supremacy. The Nazis explicitly rejected a large segment of the German population—those who married non-Aryans, those who did not speak German in daily life, or those who adopted Latin American citizenship. For this reason, the early Nazis alienated many Germans and wound up becoming not the unifying force they aspired to be, but a corrosive and divisive faction.[14]

Hitler's rise to power in 1933 changed the equation, and the influence of the Nazi Party in Latin America began to grow.[15] Germans living outside the Third Reich were included in the Nazi vision of a *Volksgemeinschaft*, a German ethnonational or, in the language of the era, "racial" community. The Nazi Party (NSDAP) undertook to enlist them in its ranks via its *Auslandsorganisation* (AO, or Foreign Organization). Substantial open resistance in the first few years was rapidly stamped out as the Nazi Party moved to back up its transnational organizing efforts with the machinery of the state.[16] The first targets were, naturally enough, the *Vereine*, the centers of community life. In country after country, NSDAP officials marched into meetings with the boards of directors of German schools and German clubs to demand control as the true representatives of the Führer. These schools were central to the life of the German community, shaping the character of what H. Glenn Penny has called "diaspora nationalism."[17] Since Germanness was undefined, it could be contested, and the prime sites of the shaping of German identity in Latin America were the focal points of an increasingly desperate struggle.[18]

By 1937, the disputes over control of the Vereine in the largest countries had largely been resolved in favor of the local Nazi Party groups. Only about 10 of the 350 German-Brazilian societies in Rio Grande do Sul were free of Nazi control. The hundreds of highly regarded German schools across Latin America were dependent on Berlin for their budgets. Only one of them, the Pestalozzi-Schule in Buenos Aires, managed to avoid the Nazification of its faculty and curriculum.[19]

Since party and state had fused, Germans who lacked the courage or political commitment to express their patriotism via acts of resistance now embraced national symbols that had become Nazi symbols. If they attended embassy functions or German Club events, the speeches at those events now were tinged with Nazi overtones. If they flew the German flag, that flag now bore a swastika. The party cleverly used the state to try to capture potential outlets for patriotic expression and in this fashion achieved significant surface-level compliance even among Germans abroad who did not share the expected ideological fanaticism.

In the context of a world war, of course, such subtleties were far less compelling than the images of Nazis in brownshirts marching through Latin American towns. Therefore, in December 1941, the US government, facing war on two fronts and hoping to avoid a third front to the south, moved quickly to eliminate the apparent menace. On President Franklin D. Roosevelt's orders, the FBI and military intelligence worked with US diplomatic missions to identify suspected Nazis throughout Latin America. Through a combination of enticements and threats, Washington prevailed upon fifteen Latin American countries to hand over their German residents suspected of subversive potential. More than four thousand were arrested, deported, and interned at US Army bases, prisons, and later in specially prepared internment camps in the Texas desert.[20]

We can readily appreciate the nuances of the transnational condition in hindsight from the comfort of libraries, archives, and relaxed conversations with elderly participants in this forgotten episode. At the time, however, such nuances were not dispositive to nation-states frantically engaged in total war. US officials pressed Latin American governments to hand over any German nationals suspected of Nazi sympathies, often on the slimmest of evidence. Washington met with the most cooperation from authoritarian regimes and the most resistance from democracies that tried to defend the rights of their residents. Dictators such as Anastasio Somoza of Nicaragua and Jorge Ubico of Guatemala took advantage of the US desire for the expulsion of German residents as an opportunity to seize their property for personal enrichment. Democratic governments such as those of Costa Rica and Chile, more responsive to their populations and their constitutions, were less keen to sacrifice their sovereignty and hand over legal residents against whom Washington, relying excessively on badly flawed intelligence and hearsay, provided little or no proof of dangerousness. Chile refused to participate in the deportation program, applying a system of police investigation and judicial prosecution to individual cases where warranted. Costa Rica, where Germans had intermarried with the governing elite, insisted on following the laws of due process until US diplomats sent a blunt message: seize German properties and deliver German residents on the embassy's lists, or the United States would cease all purchases of Costa Rican coffee and sugar. That threat of economic devastation brought a rapid end to Costa Rica's principled stance.[21]

The US decision to ignore complex transnational identities led to the creation of highly diverse microcommunities inside the internment camps, where Latin American deportees mingled with other Germans from the United States. The much more selective domestic process applied to the German population of the United States required real evidence of pro-Nazi sympathies or activities. When twenty-nine-year-old Gunter Lisken arrived at Camp Crystal City in Texas from Ecuador in 1944, a burly German American man approached him and growled, "Listen up, kid. In this camp we're all Nazis and anyone who doesn't agree, we'll break his skull." On April 20, Hitler's birthday, Lisken and some of the other deportees from Latin America were shocked to see some fellow inmates, mostly longtime US residents, parading through the camp in brownshirts and singing Nazi songs all the way to the assembly hall, where they held a celebration under a huge portrait of Adolf Hitler.[22]

It struck many observers at the time as odd that internees should be allowed to display Nazi symbols in American camps. As a result of the broad spectrum of political beliefs among the internees (rather than the unanimity proclaimed by Lisken's greeter), the camps were riven by the same conflicts that had divided the communities from which they came. Nazi Party members, the largest politically organized group among the internees, tried as they had done in Latin America to seize control of all available community institutions, to extend the transnational reach of the Nazi state into the German communities created inside the camps. When camp authorities asked the internees to select an internal leadership, party members quickly captured the influential posts and used them to reward their supporters and punish their opponents. Nazi camp leaders controlled the distribution of Red Cross packages and scrip for the canteen, as well as aid money sent by the German government. Nazi teachers in camp schools, deported and interned to prevent them from propagandizing in Latin America, now carried on their efforts, literally before a captive audience.[23]

But the struggle for control was contested and always incomplete. Divisions among the internee population were most starkly clear in the cases of physical violence against dissident prisoners. Otto Kugler, a dentist arrested in Honduras and interned in Camp Kenedy, Texas, performed dental work for the other inmates for free. Camp commander Ivan Williams estimated that Kugler thereby saved the US taxpayer $16,767 in medical costs. Williams also noted that Kugler's "anti-Nazi attitude led to active persecution from the camp Nazis. On one occasion he was saved by the guards after he had been dragged from the hospital and was being beaten. It became necessary to give him a room in the hospital and to escort him to meals under guard for a period of three months. Nevertheless his attitude did not change."[24]

Kugler's was not an isolated case.[25] Fritz Sauter, a nineteen-year-old Costa Rican–born son of German parents, was deported to the United States for allegedly shouting "Heil Hitler" on July 4, 1943, according to an informant. The embassy labeled him a Nazi. Postwar investigators from the Justice Department reached a different conclusion. Sauter so tenaciously defended his allegiance to Costa Rica that friction with the pro-Nazi group in Camp Kenedy "finally culminated in a fight in which a considerable number of the pro-Nazis attacked him." For his own safety, he was transferred to Camp Algiers, Louisiana, where most of the inmates were German Jews or non-Nazis caught up in the Latin American deportation sweeps and segregated for their own safety after a year of pleading and protest by themselves and American Jews who had learned of their plight. "At that camp [Sauter] was reported as well behaved, studious, a Catholic, with anti-Nazis as his closest friends, and not known to have engaged in political discussions." The report concluded with a telling indication of Sauter's sympathies: "He enlisted in the U.S. Army in January 1945."[26] Sauter represents the kind of erosion of intense identification with the country of origin that is one of several paths open to members of the second generation.

At the opposite end of the spectrum from the organized Nazis, at least eighty German Jews seized in Latin America thanks to shoddy US intelligence languished in the same camps designed for their enemies, even though those who had migrated from Germany or Austria had been rendered stateless by Nazi decree—yet another level of complexity to identifying their national belonging.

At Stringtown, a run-down, overcrowded former state prison in Oklahoma, eighteen Jewish refugees seized in Latin America as suspected "dangerous enemy aliens" were relegated to a steam-filled room in the basement leading to the camp showers. Other prisoners trooped through their quarters from morning to night on their way to bathe, some taking the opportunity to call them "Jewish swine" and "dirty Jews." After Lieutenant Colonel Bertram Frankenberger, himself Jewish, took over as camp commander, they were moved to more private quarters and interviewed one by one by an officer. Their testimony is revealing, not only of their Kafkaesque predicament but because it provides some indication of the diversity among the rest of the German group.[27] Interestingly, several of the Jewish prisoners made statements that confirm the picture of a German internee group divided between a coercive Nazi faction and a passive majority. "A lot of internees would be nice but do not associate with us because they are afraid of the Nazi element," said Erwin Klyszcz. Emil Loewenthal's statement is especially intriguing: "I have heard them [the Nazis] say that there are not enough of them to fight us but they are hoping that more will come and then they will take care of us." Since there were only 18 Jews, mostly older men, among a total internee population of 531 German adult males at Stringtown, Loewenthal's comment is a further sign that the number of fervent Nazis was actually quite modest, that their influence inside the camps rested on intimidation and seizing key positions in the internal hierarchy rather than on numerical strength. Despite the nominal Nazi Party membership of a minority of prisoners, Nazi activists could not draw on large numbers of adherents to carry out their schemes.[28]

The microcosm of German expatriate society inside the camps, then, reflected the communities in Latin America whence the internees had come: a small number of fanatics used appeals to patriotism or access to state-sponsored goods to get others to sign up as party members, and applied coercive measures to bring still more into line. But a popular readiness to take concrete action, and face the possible consequences, was quite another matter.

From 1942 to 1944, a series of prisoner exchanges reduced the population of internees from Latin America by three-fourths, as many chose a return to an uncertain fate in Germany over the certainty of lengthy confinement behind barbed wire. Some of them, like Emil Prüfert, leader of the Nazi organization in Colombia, were eager and impatient to go. Others made the decision after realizing that the bleak alternative was indefinite incarceration. "I said yes," recalled Juan Niemann, deported from Guatemala to Texas, "because liberty is better than prison. [. . .] We didn't know what state Germany would be in—we thought the war would be over soon."[29] Walter Sommer, expelled from Colombia, considered staying in the camp but then thought, "Why shouldn't I go visit my old mother?"[30] Gotthold Busch-Beckemeyer, an employee of Standard Oil who had been a resident of Chile since 1914 and a Chilean citizen since 1920, was picked up while on business in Haiti and deported for internment in the United States. When Camp Kenedy authorities asked him whether he would volunteer for repatriation to Germany, the following exchange ensued:

Q: Do you desire that you be repatriated to Germany?
A: I thought not to go back. I do not know why I go back, and I like to go back to Chile. [. . .]
Q: If you are unable to return to Chile or some other South American country, had you rather remain in detention, or be repatriated to Germany?
A: Then I had better go back to Germany before I would stay in the camp. If I can't get freedom in the United States, then I would go.
Q: You understand, do you not, that you have made a statement that if you are unable to return to a country in Central or South America, that you prefer to be repatriated to Germany than remain in detention in the United States. Is that right?
A: No. I didn't understand it properly what it meant. [. . .] My opinion is always I want to get freedom, never mind where. At the last I would go to Germany, but if I could get freedom here or at Chile or somewhere else—if I could get freedom here, I go to work here and do something. I am Chilean. I like Chile. That's the reason the last time I stayed there. I like to get freedom. That's the most important for me.[31]

US officials interpreted that attempt to explain the transnational condition of a German emigrant as his consent to repatriation, and Busch-Beckemeyer was sent to Germany in January 1945.[32]

The end of the war in May 1945 brought the first organized US government effort to evaluate the internees on the basis of their commitment to Nazism. About a thousand German deportees remained in the camps, half of them "cases" (individuals selected for internment) and the other half accompanying family members. The State Department attempted to deport all these internees to occupied Germany and ban them from ever returning to the Americas, but immediately ran into trouble. Internees filed *habeas corpus* suits in federal court, contending that shipping people off to the ruined cities of Germany was unjustified cruelty, especially since they had not been shown to have done anything unlawful. The courts ruled that there was no legal basis to treat them as illegal immigrants subject to deportation, since they had been brought to the United States involuntarily.[33] The Department of State therefore formed a hearing board, the Alien Enemy Control Section (AECS), to collect and review all evidence held by any government agency or embassy post regarding those Germans from Latin America still in internment at the end of the war. The AECS rated the internees "A" if they were dangerous Nazis, "B" if they were "small fry" or if the evidence against them was unclear, and "C" if they were probably harmless. All "A" Germans were to be deported to the US occupation zone in Germany. "B" internees would be deported as well, unless they had mitigating family ties in Latin America. Germans rated "C" would be released.[34]

Of the 531 cases, 413 were summarily released after a preliminary review of their files without a hearing indicated no compelling reason to hold them. The AECS hearing board then released more than half of the remaining 118, and recommended deportation for a hard core of about 50 cases. Members of the hearing board concluded that some of the Germans it set free may have been interned legitimately as potential supporters of the German war effort, but they expressed shock and outrage at other cases of individuals detained with no apparent justification.[35] Wartime urgency and disorganization had brought a broad collection of Germans into the camps. Peacetime reflection, though, identified less than 10 percent who might be considered sufficiently devoted to Nazism to warrant special concern, even among a group in which pro-Nazi sympathies might be expected to have been especially prominent, since they had been selected for seizure and internment.

The evidence from inside the camps and from German communities in Latin America shows that acceptance of the Nazis among these German residents of Latin America may have been broad, but it did not go deep. Had more of them been more enthusiastic, they would have expressed it not merely with occasional symbolic acts, which can be read in different ways, but through the concrete commitment of time and resources—such as joining the party and working for its goals. Large majorities of Germans in Latin American countries were unwilling to do so, with party membership in most countries ranging from 3 to 9 percent of German citizens.[36] If, as has been speculated, there was a particular inclination toward fanaticism among "ordinary Germans" that, inside Germany, led them to embrace Nazi ideology and enable the crimes of the dictatorship, that inclination does not seem to have been especially pronounced among this group of Germans abroad.

Nonetheless, more than four thousand paid with the seizure of their homes and businesses, expulsion from their adopted countries often after decades of residence, and several years of their lives spent behind barbed wire. It was a high price for their failure to wholly integrate into the host countries, even if in the context of the Second World War there were certainly worse fates for people caught up in the massive violence unfurling around the world—especially for civilians on the receiving end of the ideology that claimed to have won the allegiance of the transnational German communities.

This episode illustrates the perils of transnationalism in a world of nation-states, at least in times of perceived emergency. Vicious movements that take over nation-states may seek to mobilize the diaspora for their purposes, even if, in this case, they did so rather ineffectively. In fact, most Germans in Latin America were able to maintain productive cultural and economic ties to their country of origin without ever becoming a threat to their host countries. But the appearance of Nazification of the diaspora, coupled with national thinking, which is so often racialized, catalyzed an overreaction by a rival nation-state seeking to defend itself from a serious international threat that appeared to be manifesting itself in the Western Hemisphere.

For liberal humanists writing about migration, when it comes to transnationalism, what should matter is the content, not the form. States expect humans to be loyal to nations and in times of crisis want those loyalties to reach a level of unambiguous performance that migration often complicates. History does not repeat itself, as they say, but sometimes it rhymes, and the words "internment" and "deportation" are now part of a familiar refrain. Whatever the merits of any particular case, the triumphant academic discourse surrounding transnationalism as the harbinger or catalyst of the nation-state's demise may not necessarily serve the interests of the transnational humans who embody it. The nation-state has not yet come to terms with its encounter with transnationalism.

Notes

1. Louis L. Gerson, *The Hyphenate and Recent American Politics and Diplomacy* (University of Kansas Press, 1964), 235; Charles S. Maier, "Unsafe Haven," *New Republic*, October 14, 1992, 21; Samuel P. Huntington, *The Clash of Civilizations and the Remaking of World Order* (Simon and Schuster, 1996), 272–91; and Samuel P. Huntington, *Who Are We? The Challenges to America's National Identity* (Simon and Schuster, 2004). A more moderate view comes from Alexander DeConde, whose *Ethnicity, Race, and American Foreign Policy: A History* (Northeastern University Press, 1992) points out that the most successful ethnic lobbying group in influencing US foreign policy has been the Anglo-Americans, in control for more than two hundred years.

2. Gregory Weeks and John Weeks, "Immigration and Transnationalism: Rethinking the Role of the State in Latin America," *International Migration* 53, no. 5 (October 2015): 122–34.

3. Benedict Anderson, *Imagined Communities: Reflections on the Origin and Spread of Nationalism* (Verso, 1983).

4. Ernest Gellner, *Nations and Nationalism* (Blackwell, 1983).

5. Michael Kearney, "Borders and Boundaries of State and Self at the End of Empire," *Journal of Historical Sociology* 4, no. 1 (March 1991): 70, 59.

6. Kearney, "Borders and Boundaries," 55.

7. Arjun Appadurai, "Patriotism and Its Futures," *Public Culture* 5, no. 3 (Spring 1993): 411–29, quoted at 421, 423.

8. Yasemin Nuhoğlu Soysal, *Limits of Citizenship: Migrants and Postnational Membership in Europe* (University of Chicago Press, 1994); Roger Rouse, "Mexican Migration and the Social Space of Postmodernism," *Diaspora: A Journal of Transnational Studies* 1, no. 1 (Spring 1991): 8–23; and Michel S. Laguerre, *Diasporic Citizenship: Haitian Americans in Transnational America* (Palgrave Macmillan, 1998).

9. Linda Basch, Nina Glick Schiller, and Cristina Szanton Blanc, *Nations Unbound: Transnational Projects, Postcolonial Predicaments, and Deterritorialized Nation-States* (Gordon and Breach, 1994), 45–46.

10. Kearney, "Borders and Boundaries," 60.

11. Jean-Pierre Blancpain, "Des visées pangermanistes au noyautage hitlérien: Le nationalisme allemand et l'Amérique latine (1890–1945)," *Revue Historique* 281, no. 2 (1990): 433–82, quoted at 437.

12. H. Glenn Penny, "Latin American Connections: Recent Work on German Interactions with Latin America," *Central European History* 46, no. 2 (June 2013): 362–94; Jean-Pierre Blancpain, *Migrations et mémoires germaniques en Amérique latine* (Presses Universitaires de Strasbourg, 1994), 70–72; Benjamin Bryce, *To Belong in Buenos Aires: Germans, Argentines, and the Rise of a Pluralist Society* (Stanford University Press, 2018); Thomas

Schoonover, *Germany in Central America: Competitive Imperialism, 1821–1929* (University of Alabama Press, 1998), 149; Horst Nitschack, "La recepción de la cultura de habla alemana en *Amauta*," in *Encuentros y desencuentros: Estudios sobre la recepción de la cultura alemana en América Latina*, ed. Miguel A. Giusti and Horst Nitschack (Pontificia Universidad Católica del Perú, 1993), 231–60; and Jürgen Buchenau, "Blond and Blue-Eyed in Mexico City, 1821 to 1975," in *The Heimat Abroad: The Boundaries of Germanness*, ed. Krista O'Donnell, Renate Bridenthal, and Nancy Reagin (University of Michigan Press, 2005), 85–110.

13. On the persistence of German identity in these communities, see H. Glenn Penny, "Reflections: German Polycentrism and the Writing of History," *German History* 30, no. 2 (June 2012): 265–82.

14. Marionilde Brepohl de Magalhães, *Pangermanismo e Nazismo: A trajetória alemã rumo ao Brasil* (Campinas, Brazil: Editora da Unicamp; São Paulo: Fundação de Amparo à Pesquisa do Estado, 1998), 158.

15. Hitler himself evinced almost no interest in Latin America. In contrast to his usual micromanagement of foreign policy toward nations that did interest him, Hitler and his top aides left policy making toward Latin America to the Foreign Ministry—an agency so often cut out of important decisions—and the Foreign Ministry left it to minor department heads. When Hitler did make a rare reference to Latin America in a late edition of *Mein Kampf* and in his so-called Second Book, it was merely to dismiss the region as the epitome of degenerate racial mixing; he did not even remark upon the large German presence in South America—a telling omission, given his fervent interest in the ethnic Germans of eastern Europe and the Soviet Union, and his vision of a worldwide *Volksgemeinschaft*.

16. Olaf Gaudig and Peter Veit, *Der Widerschein des Nazismus: Das Bild des Nationalsozialismus in der deutschsprachigen Presse Argentiniens, Brasiliens und Chiles 1932–1945* (Wissenschaftlicher Verlag, 1997); and Jürgen Müller, *Nationalsozialismus in Lateinamerika: Die Auslandsorganisation der NSDAP in Argentinien, Brasilien, Chile und Mexiko, 1931–1945* (Verlag Hans-Dieter Heinz, 1997). See also Uwe Lübken, *Bedrohliche Nähe: Die USA und die nationalsozialistische Herausforderung in Lateinamerika, 1937–1945* (Franz Steiner Verlag, 2004).

17. H. Glenn Penny, "Diversity, Inclusivity, and 'Germanness' in Latin America During the Interwar Period," *Bulletin of the German Historical Institute* 61 (Fall 2017): 85–108; and H. Glenn Penny, "Material Connections: German Schools, Things, and Soft Power in Argentina and Chile from the 1880s Through the Interwar Period," *Comparative Studies in Society and History* 59, no. 3 (July 2017): 519–49.

18. Frederik Schulze, "Von verbrasilianisierten Deutschen und deutschen Brasilianern: 'Deutschsein' in Rio Grande do Sul, Brasilien, 1870–1945," *Geschichte und Gesellschaft* 41, no. 2 (April–June 2015): 197–227.

19. Gaudig and Veit, *Der Widerschein des Nazismus*, 484.

20. See Max Paul Friedman, *Nazis and Good Neighbors: The United States Campaign Against the Germans of Latin America in World War II* (Cambridge University Press, 2003).

21. Friedman, *Nazis and Good Neighbors*, 172–76.

22. Gunter Lisken, interview with the author, Guayaquil, February 17, 1998.

23. Kurt P. Biederbeck to Schulz (an official in the Rechtsabteilung, or Legal Department,

of the German Foreign Office), April 7, 1944, "Amerikanische Zivilinternierte in Deutschland," R41570, Rechtsabteilung, Politisches Archiv des Auswärtigen Amtes, Berlin (hereafter PAAA); Kurt P. Biederbeck to Schulz, May 12, 1944, R41879, Deutsche Zivilgefangene in den V. St. v. Am., Rechtsabteilung, PAAA; Hermann Egner to Swiss Legation Washington, *Camp Kenedy, Texas*, June 27, 1942, R41562, Zivilgefangenen-Austausch-Vereinigten Staaten von Amerika, Rechtsabteilung, PAAA; P. W. Herrick, *Supplemental Report on Civilian Detention Station Kenedy, Texas*, October 13–14, 1942, "Kenedy '42," Inspection Reports on War Relocation Centers, 1942–1946, box 20, Special War Problems (hereafter SWP), RG59, National Archives, College Park, Maryland (hereafter NA); M. A. Cardinaux (IRC), *Camp Kenedy*, "Kenedy '43–'44," Inspection Reports on War Relocation Centers, 1942–1946, box 20, SWP, RG59, NA; Otto Luis Schwarz, interview with the author, Guayaquil, February 16, 1998; and John Karl, telephone interview with the author, June 15, 1997.

24. *Justice Department Summary*, 1946, "Kugler, Otto Berthold," Name Files of Interned Enemy Aliens from Latin America, 1942–1948, box 42, SWP, RG59, NA.

25. Friedrich Karl Kaul recounts the same thing happening to him in his novelized memoir, *Es wird Zeit, dass du nach Hause kommst* (Das Neue Berlin, 1959), 266; see also Glover, "Confidential: Richard Ernst Ressel (Colombia)," February 1, 1946, "Ressel, Richard Ernst, Colombia," Name Files of Interned Enemy Aliens from Latin America, 1942–1948, box 46, SWP, RG59, NA; and John Christgau, *Enemies: World War II Alien Internment* (Iowa State University Press, 1985), 35.

26. Tenney, "Confidential: Fritz Sauter, Jr. (Costa Rica)," February 5, 1946, folder S, Name Files of Interned Enemy Aliens from Latin America, 1942–1948, box 34, SWP, RG59, NA.

27. Colonel Bryan to Gufler, September 14, 1942, 740.00115EW1939/4525, RG59, NA.

28. Colonel Bryan to Gufler, September 14, 1942, 740.00115EW1939/4525, RG59, NA; and Max Habicht to Swiss Foreign Ministry, *Report on the Visit to Detention Stations for Civilian Internees in the United States of America*, August 18, 1942, vol. 1, E2200 Washington/15, Schweizerisches Bundesarchiv, Bern.

29. Juan Niemann, interview with the author, Guatemala City, May 30, 1996.

30. Walter Sommer, interview with the author, Bogotá, March 13, 1998.

31. Gotthold Heinrich Carl Busch-Beckemeyer, "Statement," May 26, 1942, "146-13-2-0 Section 16," Closed Legal Case Files, box 6, Alien Enemy Control Unit, War Division, Department of Justice, RG60, NA.

32. *German Nationals Deported by the Other American Republics Who Were Deported by the United States*, in folder of same name, subject files 1939–1954, box 121, SWP, RG59, NA.

33. Von Heymann v. Watkins, 159 F.2d 650; and Citizens Protective League v. Clark, App. D.C. 1946, 155 F.2d 290.

34. Summary by George Gray, February 9, 1948, 710.62115/10-246, RG59, NA; and author analysis of AECS records in Name Files of Interned Enemy Aliens from Latin America, boxes 31–50, SWP, RG59, NA.

35. Author analysis of AECS records in Name Files of Interned Enemy Aliens from Latin America, boxes 31–50, SWP, RG59, NA.

36. Statistics on Nazi membership in Latin American countries vary, partly according to sources used; the most reliable are Senate Committee on Military Affairs, *Nazi Party Membership Records*, Senate Committee Prints 79/2/46, part 2, March 1946, and part 3, September 1946, S1535–S1538 (US Government Printing Office, 1946); and Hans-Adolf Jacobsen, *Nationalsozialistische Außenpolitik 1933–1938* (Frankfurt am Main: Alfred Metzner Verlag, 1968), 662–63.

CHAPTER 12

Ghost Transnationalisms

Embodied Transborder Histories in Music and Dance
in the Dominican Republic and the United States

SYDNEY HUTCHINSON

TRANSNATIONAL PRACTICES AND PROCESSES are old news in world cross-roads like the Caribbean. Contested terms like creolization, *créolité, mestizaje, métissage*, hybridity, syncretism, and transculturation[1] have been used at different times to refer to various aspects of transnational culture, identities, and exchanges in this region, while cross-cultural studies of diaspora, globalization, cosmopolitanism, and deterritorialization also overlap significantly with "transnationalism." In this chapter I use the term "transnationalism" to refer to *the processes, practices, and beliefs people use to build and maintain imagined communities that transcend the geographic and conceptual limits of the nation.*

This definition differs in some ways from the well-known one by Nina Glick Schiller, Linda Basch, and Cristina Blanc-Szanton, who define transnationalism as "the processes by which immigrants build social fields that link together their country of origin and their country of settlement,"[2] emphasizing migration and countries. My definition eliminates these terms in order to include transnationalisms created and practiced by those without migration backgrounds and also to emphasize the fact that so-called transnational linkages are often much more local and specific than country-to-country. When using my definition, it becomes clear that it is particularly in its emphasis on elective community maintenance that transnationalism differs from related concepts. It is important to remember that even though transnationalism is widespread, belonging to a transnational community is still somewhat of a privilege, and the politics of transnationalism can be rather suspect—for instance, Leela Fernandes sees it as "a device of the [expanding] security state" since 9/11/2001.[3] We should neither take transnationalism for granted nor celebrate it unquestioningly.

Music and dance—the subjects of my study as an ethnomusicologist—figure among some of the tools most frequently used in the building of nations, both inside and outside their geographic borders. They are also among the practices that most freely travel across borders, both with migrating people and through media technologies, globe-spanning or otherwise. The embodied, expressive nature of music and dance helps to illuminate transnationalisms (a word I use in the plural to underline its many forms) in a more intimate way than is possible using many other tools. Studying transnationalism as an embodied practice helps us to see that transnationalisms are intersectional, because border-crossing practices, like nations themselves, are experienced by and available to different people differently. Acknowledging embodiment also demonstrates that transnationalisms are often contested. Whether people and communities engage in transnational practices by choice or necessity, contradictory impulses will also enter into play.

My primary aim in this chapter is to explain a new concept I introduce here: "ghost transnationalisms," my term for transborder practices that are deliberately covered up ex post facto but that continue to haunt present-day people and culture. The term also echoes the recently coined word "ghosting," popularly used to describe the termination of a relationship by ignoring all subsequent attempts at contact; in this case, nationalist musicians, music scholars, and listeners "ghost" or ignore an entire community, culture, or country with which they once had a close relationship.

When I write of "music" I am also writing about dance, as throughout Latin America the two are generally inseparable. The North Atlantic impulse to separate the two, related perhaps to Cartesian dualism, creates an artificial division of conjoined practices into different categories and even academic disciplines. Such a separation does not fit the way music/dance is used or even conceived of and labeled in most of the world. Ethnomusicologists have long loved to point out that many African languages use one word to cover music, dance, and ritual. But even in Latin American Spanish, terms like "merengue," "bachata," "tango," and others refer to dance as well as music.

I begin this chapter with a brief review of scholarship on transnational music aimed at readers from outside (ethno)musicology,[4] and then I summarize my own ethnographic observations and analyses of the interplay of transnationalism with national musics, regional imaginaries, gender, tradition, and neoliberalism in the field of music/dance. Finally, I focus in on a specific example from my research into Dominican music history and compare it with a seemingly quite different case, that of US American country music. Throughout, I will highlight how transnationalisms are embodied and show how attention to ghost transnationalisms can bring alternative histories to light, with the caveat that they should be viewed intersectionally: race, class, gender, and other identity categories play important roles in both the original transnational practices and in their later ghosting. Investigating ghost transnationalisms also entails taking an antinationalist stance by working to deconstruct and dismantle national mythologies, as I do here.

Transnationalism in Ethnomusicological Literature

The development of the transnational framework in ethnomusicology was roughly coeval with its use in other fieldwork-based disciplines. As in other fields, it provided a useful corrective to the fixation on nations, which in my husband Maurice Mengel's colorful phrasing often serve as "blindness machines"—apparatuses that hide or render invisible other forms of identification and organization. The ties of music as well as musicology to nationalism go back to the nineteenth century and possibly earlier, but perhaps it was not until the early 1990s that most ethnomusicologists came to recognize that people's musical experiences and practices could not be explained without a frame both larger and smaller than the nation.

A first group of transnational music scholars focused on the popular music industry and products like "world music." Already in 1984, Roger Wallis and Krister Malm assembled ethnographic data on the development of a transnational music industry in "small countries," viewing the development of transnational music businesses and cultures as an ominous portent of cultural grayout.[5]

In the next decade, Veit Erlmann turned attention to "world" musics; he found these transnational genres to be unified by a shared aesthetic based on pastiche and nostalgia wherein the global and the local may be translated into the conceptual pair of "modernity" versus an often romanticized idea of "tradition" in which "locality itself becomes a fetish which disguises the globally dispersed forces of production."[6] At the same time, Reebee Garofalo described the decentralization of musical production and consumption in the transnational music industry, with findings similar to Erlmann's: he believed that insistence on the "preservation" of traditional musics in contrast to the transnational musics produced through transculturation showed that popular understandings of "authenticity" had not kept pace with technological developments.[7]

Multisited ethnographic studies of music in transnational communities also proliferated beginning in the 1990s. Examples include Gage Averill's social history of Haitian popular music and politics, which attends to the incorporation of transnational Haitians into island dialogues;[8] Paul Austerlitz's work on the modern, hybrid merengue he saw as representative of Dominican transnational identities;[9] Cathy Ragland's examination of the transnational social spaces produced by *sonideros* (deejays) at Mexican dances in New York City, which both affirmed a cosmopolitan, transnational Mexican identity and cemented bonds with fans' homes in Central Mexico;[10] and Helena Simonett's study of Mexican *banda* music as a transnational style linking Sinaloa, Guadalajara, and Los Angeles.[11] Digital fieldwork developed into a useful tool for studying transnational music by the end of the century, for instance in Dan Lundberg's description of how a fictive Assyrian "nation" and an invented Assyrian "national music" were created on the Web through the electronic activities of diasporic Christian Turkish, Syrian, and Lebanese in Sweden and elsewhere.[12]

In the twenty-first century, the promise of multisited, transnational music research continues to bear fruit. Edited volumes place attention on the "transnational encounters" characteristic of border areas,[13] on the valuation of transnational musics,[14] and on the transnational circulation of particular genres;[15] new monographs focus on the transnational flows of popular music prior to economic globalization,[16] or on how national identities circulate in transnational musics;[17] some articles work to better theorize transnational music activities in music, including fusions and appropriations.[18] More recent scholarly trends include a network approach to studies of transnational music and communities,[19] the related use of hub theory,[20] and analyses of music with no single definitive home-land, like reggaeton, hip-hop, and salsa.[21] Larger-scale projects on transnational digital music cultures emerged in the 2010s, for instance through the large "Music, Digitisation, Mediation" project headed by Georgina Born from 2010 to 2015.[22] As was true earlier, the term "transnational" is still most often used to describe the workings of the popular music industry, or else the musics created by and circulated among migratory communities, with a few new topics taking hold among such studies—for instance, how second-generation immigrants build new kinds of transnational networks through music,[23] how new transna-tional musics emerge through neoliberal/late capitalist policies and pressures,[24] and what constitutes the workings of transnational musical activism.[25]

Ethnomusicologists have also employed other concepts related to transna-tionalism, including syncretism, hybridity, and globalization, and each has been the subject of critique: syncretism emphasizes the merging of traditions or beliefs from disparate origins, but may leave out the violence inherent in the imposition of culture, particularly in colonial contexts; hybridity similarly focuses on mixture but carries echoes of biological determinism and essential-ism. In earlier studies, globalization was used to highlight economic aspects of transborder practices, and scholars who applied the concept to culture under-lined its tendency to homogenize culture and eliminate difference; later, more scholars followed Arjun Appadurai in viewing cultural globalization in a more differentiated way, as the interaction of various "scapes."[26] Scholars who choose instead to employ the transnational framework may do so to counter the baggage of these earlier terms while still, like Appadurai, highlighting inequalities, exam-ining the interplay between local and global politics, focusing on individual agency, or analyzing the emergence of new forms of culture and difference. My own multisited in-person and digital field research has long focused on cross-border migratory networks and how the people within them think about and employ music and dance genres that belie the primacy of the nation in everyday life, including Mexicano/Chicano *quebradita*, *pasito duranguense*, and *norteño*;[27] Dominican *merengue típico*;[28] and multiethnic salsa.[29] In each of these cases, an affective imagined community has coalesced around a particular musical or cho-reographic genre, albeit in quite different ways. More recently, I have focused instead on researching cross-border practices outside capitalism, like socialist internationalism; the relationship between transnationalisms, late capitalism, and expressive culture still requires further theorization though is outside the scope of this chapter.

In music and dance studies, we also need more research on transnationalism as an embodied, intersectional practice. The discussion on transnational feminism has now been underway for over two decades;[30] moving it into the #MeToo era means working to eradicate structural sexism from our fields and to combat it in our training.[31] Scholarship on transnational Indigenous movements is of the same vintage and indeed suggests different readings of the term trans*national* (Chadwick Allen, for instance, proposes the alternate term "trans-indigenous"[32]); moving it into the post–Standing Rock era means contending with the links between the struggle for Indigenous sovereignty and global environmental and anticapitalist movements.[33] Meanwhile, the intersection of race with transnationalism is at the heart of Black transnationalist studies;[34] taking it into the era of Black Lives Matter means being more proactive about acknowledging and countering racism in academia and its study objects, including music. The roles of music, dance, and the body in each of these current transnational protest movements suggest fruitful areas of study, both for those who write and analyze culture and for those who strive for a more praxis-based, activist form of scholarship.

Transnational Regionalisms

My early field research in transnational communities showed that the concept of transnationalism was not yet as nuanced as it needed to be. While one reason for this was the need for more intersectional analysis, another reason was the concept's failure to account for communities whose practices linked places, spaces, and identities much more specific than the "national" of transnationalism might imply. In my research on the Chican@/x or Mexican American[35] youth cultural dances quebradita and pasito duranguense as well as on (neo)traditional, accordion-based Dominican merengue típico, I found that first- and second-generation migrant communities often identify more with a particular region in the sending country rather than with the nation as a whole. This narrower identification could be observed in musical/choreographic practices, embodied experiences, and practitioners' discourses. Quebradoras and quebradores (female and male quebradita dancers) singled out their connections with the Mexican states of Sinaloa and Jalisco, pasito dancers with Durango, and merengue típico fans and musicians with the Dominican Republic's northern Cibao region. Notably, participants in each scene either did not identify with the musics typically held up as "national" symbols—namely mariachi for Mexico or *orquesta* (big-band) merengue for the Dominican Republic—or they did so only to a limited degree. Participation in a transnational music-dance network of aficionados often intensified ties to very specific places and markers of regional (not national) culture, while causing participants to reimagine "tradition" through bodily practice in inventive new ways.[36] More broadly, one might say that the intimate, bodily nature of lived experience and emotional ties also work at a more intimate geographic level than the broad one of "nation." I proposed the term "transnational regionalism"[37] to explain the intensification of regional ties in diaspora.

Transnational regional musics have particular gendered and racial dynamics. Outsiders often assume that when they observe more progressive attitudes toward gender or racial equality among migrant groups, it must be the result of interactions with international feminism or civil rights movements, but this assumption is frequently false. Transnational communities may react to their new experiences by becoming open to new ideas and beliefs, but equally often they may retrench traditional gender roles or racial hierarchies. At the same time, "tradition" itself may not be as unequal, conservative, or prejudicial as outsiders believe; instead, "Western" (or perhaps better, North Atlantic) capitalist culture may be the one that better fits that description.

Over the past two decades, I observed how new Dominican popular music styles like *merengue de calle*, *merengue con mambo*, and *merengue urbano*[38] arose through (or amid) the interplay of transnational life experiences and neoliberal economic pressures. They are intimately tied to new conceptions of gender and race that are part of a border-crossing youth culture I term "transnational *tigueraje*," since it is centered on the *tíguere* or urban, hustling, hypermasculine "tiger" figure as well as its more recently developed feminine counterpart, the *tíguera*. As the Spanish term *género* means both gender and genre, merengue con mambo and tigueraje are both *géneros nuevos* that build contemporary Black Atlantic connections even as they draw on local traditional music like merengue típico, regional Afro-Caribbean historical resonances, and culture-specific gender archetypes as sources for creativity and authenticity. Frequently, these earlier layers of culture also provided local, alternative models for feminist action and

Dominican Blackness. For example, in contrast to most popular music genres worldwide, a number of women play instruments in merengue típico and lead otherwise all-male bands, a curiosity I trace in part to the existence of a cultural framework for strong women like the tíguera and the roles tíguera-like figures have played in the music's and the country's history. The fact that *dominicanas* could inhabit the tíguera role even before transnational migration became a defining factor of Dominican life should decenter the feminism of the Global North in any narrative of women's liberation. Meanwhile, the Afro-Dominican folk religions practiced mainly by the lower classes provided a less heteronormative and more Afrocentric sphere for music making and bodily performance than did the Hispanic Catholicism of the Dominican upper classes. For these reasons, some musicians use local and regional Afro-Dominican religious sounds to create queer musical performances, for instance in the work of Rita Indiana, or antiracist ones, as in the work of Xiomara Fortuna, José Duluc, Concón Quemao, Batey Cero, Vicente García, and others. These musicians use little-known Dominican traditions to make local statements while connecting sonically with transnational activist communities. When people dance or play along to such recordings, they embody and reproduce those connections. The decolonial turn in the humanities pushes us to engage seriously with the critical potential of these once (and too frequently still) devalued forms of knowledge, decentering and pluralizing the knowledge(s) we have inherited through our academic training.[39]

Ghost Transnationalisms: A Dominican Example

My later historical research pushed me to define another kind of transborder culture: ghost transnationalisms, which provide evidence both of close cross-border relationships and of their later concealment. Like transnational regionalisms, ghost transnationalisms can arise from disidentification with national projects; sometimes, they even cause it. They appear frequently in border cultures, as transnational practices are a constant feature of border areas—even if (later) nationalists frequently erase their traces. They, too, are embodied practices, just as border crossing is not only a metaphor but a physical movement. For example, my research into nineteenth- and early twentieth-century merengue between Haiti and the Dominican Republic uncovered shared, border-crossing rhythms, vocabulary, and dances still embedded in the so-called Dominican national music in spite of nearly a century of (pseudo)scholarly and journalistic attempts to write them away. One specific case is that of the *pambiche*, a beloved rhythm at the heart of the repertoire of merengue típico, the accordion-based tradition considered the progenitor of the nationalized and internationally popular big-band merengue.[40] Oral histories tell that the pambiche rhythm was brought to the central Cibao region in the early twentieth century by Monguita Peralta, an accordionist from the border town of Dajabón, and that the dance came from Haitian workers who had moved to Santiago de los Caballeros in the 1930s. Musically, it is very similar to rhythms used in Haitian *petwo* and Cuban *changüí*, a rhythm from Cuba's Oriente Province itself influenced by migrants from Saint-Domingue (the French colony that preceded Haiti). Etymologically, it seems related to *bamboche*, a Haitian Kreyol term for rural parties in which dances like merengue are played. Nonetheless, a set of myths arose around the pambiche that explained away signs of difference in the term, dance style, and rhythm, for instance connecting the name to the "Palm Beach" fabric worn by US troops when they occupied the Dominican Republic from 1916 to 1924, or attributing the dance style to a general who had a wounded leg. These myths continue to circulate in popular discourse, providing nationalistic camouflage for Haitian or border roots.

Pambiche is not the only Dominican music with a border-crossing history; many other traditional genres like *tumba, mangulina, carabiné,* and even merengue fit this description as well. The tumba, which preceded merengue as the Dominican Republic's first "national" dance, is a contradance variant said to have entered the country in 1822,[41] the same year the Haitian government took control of the whole island. While it gradually lost favor among Dominicans, the similar *tumba francesa* is still practiced in eastern Cuba by descendants of migrants from Saint-Domingue. Mangulina, carabiné, and merengue are all considered distinct, separate dances today, but as late as 1963 these names were used interchangeably and inconsistently for lively rural dances.[42] The mangulina is a partner dance proposed in 1929 as a more suitable national dance than merengue specifically because of the latter's perceived Haitian ties—this even though *mangouline* is also a Haitian folk dance that Haitian scholars believe was exported eastward in 1822. The first Dominican national anthem was reportedly a mangulina. Still today, it is performed in the Dominican Southwest in a set with a carabiné, another contradance-style choreography of the nineteenth century that conventional wisdom says was named for the carbines Haitian soldiers carried on their shoulders; in Haiti, *carabinier* or *karabinye* is a partner dance believed a forerunner of the Haitian Kreyol *mereng* (French *méringue*) music. In contrast to the current framing of Haitian-Dominican relations as eternally antagonistic, the adoption by Dominicans of Haitian music/dance in the nineteenth century was not then seen as politically problematic; in fact, Dominicans at the time likely saw Haiti as a modernizing influence due to its liberal revolution and well-developed urban musical culture, much as Black Americans in the United States did.[43] In this light, mangulina/mangouline, carabiné/karabinye, and tumba appear as a nineteenth-century form of embodied cosmopolitanism. Merengue itself was reported in Puerto Rico and Cuba before the Dominican Republic, and different styles of merengue today exist in those three countries as well as in Venezuela, Colombia, and Curaçao; in Haiti, *mereng* now has multiple meanings, running from peasant songs to parlor music or a section within a *kontradans* (contradance). Only in the Dominican Republic did merengue become nationalized, a process that entailed covering up and forgetting the transnational origins and cosmopolitan circulation of earlier national dances as well as of merengue itself.

This cover-up can be attributed to the Rafael Trujillo dictatorship (1930–1961), under which Haitians and Dominicans of Haitian descent were the targets of both state violence and historical/musicological erasure. While in 1936 Trujillo signed historic border accords with Haitian president Sténio Vincent and proudly claimed his own Haitian ancestry through his maternal grandmother, in October 1937 he unleashed the brutal Parsley Massacre in the northwest border area, purportedly to deal with the "problem" of cattle rustling. (The massacre receives its name from the practice of forcing people to pronounce the Spanish word *perejil*, parsley, to determine who was Haitian; native speakers of Kreyol or French often could not properly pronounce the Spanish word.) After tens of thousands of Haitian or Haitian-appearing people were murdered at the hands of their civilian neighbors, retroactive justification was provided by a group of Trujillist intellectuals, most of whom had been educated abroad.[44] They constructed political myths explaining the massacre as a necessary measure to secure Dominican borders; they also rewrote music history to "prove" the Hispanic descent of Dominican music, often attributing sounds that couldn't be traced to Spain instead to Taíno (Indigenous) ancestry.

Philologist Andrés Mateo has effectively dismantled the myths that long propped up Trujillo's power,[45] and historian Richard Lee Turits has shown that the now-dominant Dominican national identity constructed around "an essentialized opposition between Haiti and the Dominican Republic" depends upon the erasure of pre-massacre transnationalism and cultural pluralism.[46] Yet the post-massacre musicological myths that asserted merengue's exceptionality as well as the essential Dominicanness and whiteness attributed to both merengue and pambiche still stand and continue doing their ideological work even today.[47] It is vital to subject these musical myths to the same treatment as the better-known rhetorical Trujillist myths and thus to reveal the ghosts hiding in the walls of the Dominican national edifice. Rather than exorcising them, however, we should invite them in to tell us their stories: if we did, merengueros and merengueras could once again feel choreographic connections and hear auditory links with their kin across the border. Because just as the ghosts of vanished Haitian and Dominico-Haitian neighbors continue to haunt the borderlands, so, too, do the phantoms of border-crossing dances continue to inhabit the bodies of merengue dancers and musicians to this day.

Some Dominican musicians are engaged in just this sort of séance. Since the 1970s, Dominican *fusión*/fusion music—an amorphous "alternative" popular music movement that mixes North American sounds like rock with Dominican roots genres (Dominican music blogger Rossy Díaz terms it MAD, *música alternativa dominicana*[48])—has taken a left-leaning and Afro-centric stance. Today, artists like Xiomara Fortuna and José Duluc continue this tradition, while members of the next generation like Rita Indiana and Vicente García bring an ever-wider array of global sounds into their socially conscious music. For example, on García's 2016 Grammy-winning album *A la mar*, the track "Zafra negra" (Black Harvest) incorporates sounds and rhythms from Afro-Dominican *palos* long drums, *salve* singing, *ali-babá* percussion bands, and Dominico-Haitian *gagá* as well as Afrobeat and international singer-songwriter music. The focus on Black Dominican sounds complements lyrics that refer to Black labor, suffering, and government corruption, going on to claim, "We came from the same place. [. . .] Africa was confiscated and they stuck us on a boat. [. . .] The palm grove is everyone's; it belongs to people, sand and sea." Over the sound of the ali-babá drums now played at carnivals around the Dominican Republic but based on the traditions of *cocolos*, Black migrants from the Anglophone islands, a climactic section of "Zafra negra" calls for "More justice! More freedom! More equality!" just before segueing into a quieter salve or sung prayer dedicated to Gran Bua, a powerful wilderness deity of the rural Dominican "vodú"[49] pantheon, protector of trees, positioned here as an antidote to the ills of corruption.

The lyrics of "Zafra negra" were penned not by García but by Rita Indiana, a queer Dominican singer-songwriter and novelist who was residing in Puerto Rico when she wrote the lyrics. Haitian-Dominican relations and the exclusions of Dominican national identity are ongoing concerns throughout her work in different media, and she addressed them on her own critically acclaimed 2010 album *El juidero* (The Getaway). The track "Da pa lo do" does so most explicitly, using fusions similar to Vicente's (congos, gagá, and Haitian-Dominican sacred music) with the significant addition of merengue, symbolic of the Dominican nation. The lyrics tell of two brothers fighting and the father telling them to stop because, as the title states, "there's enough for two"; they also suggest that the sons' absent mother birthed the *balsié*, a traditional drum used in Afro-Dominican religious music as well as in border-crossing dances like the carabiné. At the song's climax, Rita sings a vodou verse in Kreyol, asking Saint Jacques to have mercy on his "horse," or the person he possesses. Finally a lengthy merengue section carries the piece to its end with Rita repeating, "We are siblings." For both Rita and Vicente, the lyrical "we" is as inclusive as the "we" implied by their musical sound, spanning the island's border and looking to revive the pre-massacre transnational ghosts.

Ghost Transnationalisms: A US American Example

Ghost transnationalisms are not limited to the divided island of Quisqueya (the precolonial name of Hispaniola), of course; they can be observed in many other nationalized or patriotic musics. The Mexican influence on US country and western music, for example, is substantial but scarcely acknowledged. Through the border-crossing cowboy/vaquero culture of the US Southwest/Mexican Northwest, Spanish-derived terms like lariat, lasso, ranch, buckaroo, chaps, canyon, and chaparral entered their occupational language; clothing and work implements also traveled from south to north. Numerous characteristics of Mexican *ranchera* can also be found in US country music, from its "crying" vocal quality and pathos to its rural imagery, while the corrido ballad form influenced folk singers like Woody Guthrie and country songwriters like Marty Robbins. In his 1959 Grammy-winning country hit "El Paso," Robbins—who was born in rural Arizona and had an early interest in cowboy music—uses numerous corrido conventions including Mexican-style waltz accompaniment played on guitar, a second voice harmonizing above the lead, narrative structure, four-line strophic form, and an ABCB rhyme scheme. One Guthrie composition based on corridos is "Deportee"—a song that remains sadly relevant today: Guthrie wrote it in protest of newspapers' racist coverage of a plane crash that killed, among others, twenty-eight Mexican migrant farm workers. George Lewis provides numerous additional examples of Mexican influence in country music, some speculative and some well documented, such as cowboy yodeling and Jimmie Rodgers's "blue yodels" (perhaps based on or influenced by northeastern Mexican *huapango/huasteco* vocal style), Texas swing versions of Mexican two-step dances, twelve-string guitar playing that resembles the sound of the Mexican *bajo sexto*, mariachi-style trumpets, and duet singing by country artists.[50] Much as I do, Lewis also describes this Mexican presence as ghostly, taking inspiration from Mexican writer Octavio Paz's words upon visiting Los Angeles.[51] While Paz expected to see obvious Mexican influences in the city, instead he found a "Mexicanism" that "floats" above the city, never appearing fully in view.[52]

To this day, many Texas Mexicans are avid listeners of both rancheras and country music, a fact implicitly recognized by some country musicians. For example, "King of Country" George Strait's 2009 album *Twang* closed with the track "El Rey," a mariachi/ranchera classic by José Alfredo Jiménez and a favorite for macho[53] types to sing along to, especially at moments of heartbreak. In a 2010 performance, Strait could hardly be heard above the audience when he performed the song in front of fifty-five thousand at the Alamo Dome,[54] the San Antonio arena named after the iconic battle won by the Mexican side during the Texas Revolution ("Remember the Alamo"), a centerpiece in white Texans' anti-Mexican foundational mythology. In a converse case, Las Eréndiras de San Antonio performed Gretchen Wilson's country hit "Redneck Woman" at the 2009 Northwest Mariachi Festival in Wenatchee, Washington, and audience members can be heard enthusiastically shouting the "hell, yeah" responses the song requires.[55]

In spite of this performance of country music's transnationalism and the success of genre-crossing projects like the Texas Tornados, however, country's

Mexican roots have largely been written out of its history and forgotten by much of its large listening public (at least outside of Texas) in the process of turning the music into a symbol of right-wing US American patriotism—as well as a valuable commercial product. Mexican corridos and rancheras continue to haunt country but can only be heard by those equipped to pick up on their auditory signals.

In both Dominican merengue and US American country, we see that transborder practices were later forgotten or purposely erased in order to invent an ostensibly unique, exclusive national culture. It is possible, however, that some ghost transnational musics may have been appropriated as national symbols precisely because of their transnational, even cosmopolitan origins. After all, as Thomas Turino notes, nationalism itself is a "cosmopolitan ideology and political project."[56] Racial mixture (*mestizaje* or *mulataje*) and its connotations were frequently a reason for such music's nationalization in Latin America, in part because independence movements needed to solicit the support of the crucial swing group of mixed-race people,[57] but also because of the symbolic importance of new national identities based on mixture. While John Charles Chasteen implies that importance lay in the actual genetic makeup of the national populations,[58] Belinda Edmondson locates it in colonialist hierarchies of race. She finds that whiteness connotes modernity in the Caribbean and that the symbolic positioning of mixed-race (brown or *mulata*) women thus reveals "how the nationalist project has attempted to fuse the indigenous and 'primitive' with visions for national progress in the postindependence era."[59] Nationalists have emphasized the mixed heritage of numerous national (or quasi-national) musics around the Caribbean and Latin America such as Mexican mariachi, Venezuelan joropo, Colombian cumbia, Brazilian samba, Dominican merengue, and many others. Following Edmondson's proposition, we can interpret such hybrid musics (or musics strategically portrayed as such) as attempts to "modernize" Indigenous, local, and Afro-diasporic forms by merging them with white ones, making them suitable for projecting the nation to an international, cosmopolitan audience.

This explanation still doesn't fully account for the ghost transnationalisms I have just outlined, however. In the US American case, the music industry's influence likely contributed to the ghosting of country music's Mexican ties. From the beginning, music labels divided and marketed along racial lines, a practice that still haunts the music business today: the early twentieth-century "race" and "hillbilly" categories morphed respectively into "rhythm and blues" and "country and western" by the 1950s, which today have been replaced by "R&B/hip-hop," "Latin," and "country."[60] Such practices encouraged listeners to hear music as monoethnic rather than multiethnic and artificially segmented a public that had formerly been less exclusive and more omnivorous.

In the Dominican case, as we have seen, merengue's transnational history was ghosted mainly because of the racist and anti-Haitian politics of the Trujillo era, which themselves built upon US American racism imported by visiting North American officials.[61] The country's idiosyncratic racialization also played a role. Ambivalence about Black heritage among Dominicans today is still tied to anti-Haitianism and the typical views equating Haiti with Blackness and with Africa. Since the Trujillo era, dark-skinned Dominicans have been euphemistically categorized as "indio" rather than "negro,"[62] and the same occurred with many cultural practices that seemed too Black. But even before that time, both Dominicans and outside observers had difficulty assigning the country's mixed-heritage population to a recognized racial category. The lack of a plantation economy since the seventeenth century, the resulting majority population of free Blacks, and the growth of the mixed-race population in the eighteenth century are reasons for what Silvio Torres-Saillant terms a "deracialized social consciousness" and the failure to develop a "discourse of black affirmation."[63] In the nineteenth century, when merengue, mangulina, and the like first appeared, it was common for both Dominicans and outside observers to insist upon the essential "whiteness" of Dominicans, even those of mixed heritage.[64] By the early twentieth century, as merengue began to be nationalized, Dominicans saw themselves as a people united by culture and language, not race.[65] All of these factors helped the nationalist mythologies of merengue to take root, turning all other narratives into phantoms.

The transnational existences of Dominicans and Haitians in the 1800s thus have a phantasmic afterlife in the present, and their ghosts are tinged with gendered and racialized ideologies. As previously noted, women like Monguita Peralta played roles in creating and transmitting Haitian-Dominican border culture like the pambiche around the island, while the more recent presence of numerous female accordionists in merengue típico and male cross-dressing performances points toward a longer history of gender transgressions in the "national" music, some of which draw on local and transnational Afro-Caribbean culture.[66] If the understanding were to become mainstream that Dominican national identity was not always and inherently anti-Haitian but rather built on cosmopolitan ideals; if we could consider that that national identity also included feminine masculinities and masculine femininities; if we could dance merengue while being conscious of its history—in other words, if ghost transnationalisms could be widely recognized, embodied, and thereby reanimated—not only could intercultural and international relations be repaired, but so could Dominican Blackness and local traditions of gender inclusivity be recognized and celebrated.

Ghost transnationalisms are echoes of prior national configurations, archives of vanished politics and relations, or even evidence of past violence. They are also carried in the body, causing gut-level reactions and intersecting with racial and gender identities that themselves are read upon the body. In the Quisqueyan case, ghost gestures[67] might haunt the Dominican and Haitian present by recalling the Parsley Massacre and embodying ongoing racism—but ghost transnationalisms can also recall a more distant past, one in which Dominicans and Haitians were more comrades than antagonists. Through consciously embracing narratives of Haitian-Dominican cooperation and enacting them through bodily cooperation including co-musicking and dancing, it may be possible to rebuild more ethical and empathetic intra-island relations.

Beyond Transnationalisms

In this chapter, I have shown that transnational musicians, dancers, and listeners relate to the nation in complex ways, sometimes disidentifying with national projects by participating in local or regional expressive culture at a distance and thus contributing to or creating transnational regional cultures. They can also embody, carry, and transmit knowledge of earlier national identities and transborder practices, even while they may be complicit in erasing those earlier formations. Literary scholar Lorgia García Peña argues that practitioners of Afro-Dominican religion embody an alternative history of past traumas like the US occupation through the practices of palos drumming and salve singing, as well as through literature that contradicts hegemonic narratives.[68] I believe that merengue dancers and musicians similarly embody an alternative history of the early Dominican nation, but unlike salve singers, who often sing explicitly about historical injustices, that history is more deeply buried in the merengue (as well as in pambiche, carabiné, mangulina, and other "apolitical" folk dances). Coun-try music recordings may do the same for US-Mexico border history, selectively revealing hints of earlier cooperation and cohabitation. None of this bodily or sonic evidence negates the violence against marginalized populations either at the time of the genres' creation or today, but it does offer hints of another way of being and coexisting.

This chapter nevertheless represents only a small intervention into a poten-tially broader field of embodied, intersectional transnational studies. Recogniz-ing that our work is political in any case, many scholars are now moving toward more activist forms of scholarship and even rethinking the very foundations of our disciplines. Just as not being racist or sexist is no longer enough, and we strive instead to be antiracist and feminist, perhaps our research on nationalism also needs to take a more explicit and activist stand. If it is no longer enough just to explain nationalisms and their workings, is there a way for us to be antinational-ist (as well as, perhaps, anticolonial and anticapitalist) in our scholarship? Can a transnational perspective help with the decolonization of our disciplines, or has its moment passed? Has the long-predicted postnational moment actually turned into a renationalizing one? Are we now moving away from globalization as well, with worldwide movements toward reinforcing borders, renationalizing corporations, and the like? If the answer to these questions is "yes," perhaps Purnima Mankekar's term "unsettled"[69] might better describe many current migrations and communities. At the same time, during the COVID-19 pan-demic, all sorts of communities found new ways to enhance connectivity, even when travel was prohibited; such actions help build and maintain transborder communities and thus are transnational more than they are unsettled. The "trans" in transnationalism implies *action* that reaches "across" boundaries, and that "trans" prefix is useful not only for academics wanting to work against nationalism, but also for the broader society. Anything that builds bridges rather than walls is sorely needed in the current moment.

Notes

1. The term "transculturation" was proposed by Cuban scholar Fernando Ortiz to describe the uneven "process of transition from one culture to another," which involves both loss and new creation and which he saw as characteristic of Caribbean cultures. *Cuban Counterpoint: Tobacco and Sugar*, trans. Harriet de Onís (Duke University Press, [1947] 1995), 102–3.

2. Nina Glick Schiller, Linda Basch, and Christina Blanc-Szanton, eds., *Towards a Transnational Perspective on Migration: Race, Class, Ethnicity, and Nationalism Reconsidered* (New York Academy of Sciences, 1992), 1.

3. Leela Fernandes, *Transnational Feminism in the United States: Knowledge, Ethics, Power* (New York University Press, 2013), 192. In this work, I follow Alejandro L. Madrid, ed., *Transnational Encounters: Music and Performance at the U.S.-Mexico Border* (Oxford University Press, 2011) in employing Benedict Anderson's concept of imagined communities beyond national borders. I also follow Peggy Levitt, *The Transnational Villagers* (University of California Press, 2001), 8, in observing vast differences among transnational actors with differing levels of privilege, ranging from refugees and postcolonial subjects to transmigrant professionals (the latter not discussed in Levitt's typology).

4. While my field is known as "ethnomusicology," meaning more or less the study of music of groups of people (*ethnos*), many ethnomusicologists have long contended that the unprefixed term "musicology" more rightfully belongs to ethnomusicologists than to "musicologists," because (ethno)musicologists study musics of all the world's peoples while "musicologists" study only one music culture, that of Western art music. When I put the prefix inside parentheses, I do so to include both ethnomusicology and Western art or "historical" musicology (itself a problematic addition, given that many ethnomusicologists also study history and many Western art musicologists study contemporary music).

5. Roger Wallis and Krister Malm, *Big Sounds from Small Peoples: The Music Industry in Small Countries* (Constable, 1984), 96.

6. Veit Erlmann, "The Politics and Aesthetics of Transnational Musics," *World of Music* 35, no. 2 (1993): 3–15.

7. Reebee Garofalo, "Whose World, What Beat: The Transnational Music Industry, Identity, and Cultural Imperialism," *World of Music* 35, no. 2 (1993): 16–32, quoted at 23.

8. Gage Averill, *A Day for the Hunter, a Day for the Prey: Popular Music and Power in Haiti* (University of Chicago Press, 1997).

9. Paul Austerlitz, *Merengue: Dominican Music and Dominican Identity* (Temple University Press, 1997); and Paul Austerlitz, "From Transplant to Transnational Circuit: Merengue in New York," in *Island Sounds in the Global City: Caribbean Popular Music and Identity in New York*, ed. Ray Allen and Lois Wilcken (University of Illinois Press, 1998), 44–60.

10. Cathy Ragland, "Mexican Deejays and the Transnational Space of Youth Dances in New York and New Jersey," *Ethnomusicology* 47, no. 3 (Autumn 2003): 338–54.

11. Helena Simonett, *Banda: Mexican Musical Life Across Borders* (Wesleyan University Press, 2001).

12. Dan Lundberg, "Welcome to Assyria—Your Land on the Cyber Space: Music and the Internet in the Establishment of a Transnational Assyrian Identity," *Etnomusikologian Vuosikirja* 10 (1998): 13–28.

13. Madrid, *Transnational Encounters*.

14. Glaucia Peres da Silva and Konstantin Hondros, eds., *Music Practices Across Borders: (E)Valuating Space, Diversity and Exchange* (Bielefeld, Germany: Transcript Verlag, 2019).

15. See, for example, Héctor Fernández L'Hoeste and Pablo Vila, eds., *Cumbia! Scenes of a Migrant Latin American Music Genre* (Duke University Press, 2013); and Raquel Z. Rivera,

Wayne Marshall, and Deborah Pacini Hernández, eds., *Reggaeton* (Duke University Press, 2009).

16. See, for example, David F. García, *Arsenio Rodríguez and the Transnational Flows of Latin Popular Music* (Temple University Press, 2006); and Alejandro L. Madrid and Robin D. Moore, *Danzón: Circum-Caribbean Dialogues in Music and Dance* (Oxford University Press, 2013).

17. Nabeel Zuberi, *Sounds English: Transnational Popular Music* (University of Illinois Press, 2001).

18. See, for example, Juniper Hill, "'Global Folk Music' Fusions: The Reification of Transnational Relationships and the Ethics of Cross-Cultural Appropriations in Finnish Contemporary Folk Music," *Yearbook for Traditional Music* 39 (2007): 50–83.

19. See, for example, Michael Frishkopf, "Forging Transnational Actor Networks Through Participatory Action Research: Responsibility to Protect via Musical Rehumanisation in Post-War Liberia," *World of Music* 7, nos. 1–2 (2018): 107–34; and Lonán Ó Briain, "'Happy to Be Born Hmong': The Implications of a Transnational Musical Network for the Vietnamese-Hmong People," *Journal of Vietnamese Studies* 8, no. 2 (Spring 2013): 115–48.

20. Tenley Martin, *Transnational Flamenco: Exchange and the Individual in British and Spanish Flamenco Culture* (Cham, Switzerland: Palgrave Macmillan, 2020).

21. Juan Flores, "Bring the Salsa: Diaspora Music as Source and Challenge," in *The Diaspora Strikes Back: Caribeño Tales of Learning and Turning* (Routledge, 2009), 151–72; Rivera, Marshall, and Pacini Hernández, *Reggaeton*; and Pancho McFarland, *The Chican@ Hip Hop Nation: Politics of a New Millennial Mestizaje* (Michigan State University Press, 2013).

22. Alexandrine Boudreault-Fournier, "The Fortune of Scarcity: Digital Music Circulation in Cuba," in *The Routledge Companion to Digital Ethnography*, ed. Larissa Hjorth, Heather Horst, Anne Galloway, and Genevieve Bell (Routledge, 2017), 344–53; and Georgina Born and Christopher Haworth, "Mixing It: Digital Ethnography and Online Research Methods; A Tale of Two Global Digital Music Genres," in *The Routledge Companion to Digital Ethnography*, ed. Larissa Hjorth, Heather Horst, Anne Galloway, and Genevieve Bell (Routledge, 2017), 70–86.

23. Melissa Castillo Planas, *A Mexican State of Mind: New York City and the New Borderlands of Culture* (New Brunswick, NJ: Rutgers University Press, 2020); Teresita D. Lozano, "'It's a Coptic Thing': Music, Liturgy, and Religious Identity in an American Coptic Community," *World of Music* n.s. 4, no. 2 (2015): 37–56; and Eun-Young Jung, "Transnational Migrations and YouTube Sensations: Korean Americans, Popular Music, and Social Media," *Ethnomusicology* 58, no. 1 (Winter 2014): 54–82.

24. Timothy D. Taylor, *Music and Capitalism: A History of the Present* (University of Chicago Press, 2015); and JoAnne Hoffman, "Diasporic Networks, Political Change, and the Growth of Cabo-Zouk Music," in *Transnational Archipelago: Perspectives on Cape Verdean Migration and Diaspora*, ed. Luís Batalha and Jørgen Carling (Amsterdam University Press, 2008), 205–20.

25. Jacob Rekedal, "Martyrdom and Mapuche Metal: Defying Cultural and Territorial Reductions in Twenty-First-Century Wallmapu," *Ethnomusicology* 63, no. 1 (Winter 2019):

78–104; and Reebee Garofalo, Erin T. Allen, and Andrew Snyder, eds., *HONK! A Street Band Renaissance of Music and Activism* (Routledge, 2019).

26. Arjun Appadurai, *Modernity at Large: Cultural Dimensions of Globalization* (University of Minnesota Press, 1996).

27. Field research in 1999 and 2004; digital research in 2009 and 2015. See Sydney Hutchinson, *From Quebradita to Duranguense: Dance in Mexican American Youth Culture* (University of Arizona Press, 2007); Sydney Hutchinson, "Breaking Borders/*Quebrando fronteras*: Dancing in the Borderscape," in *Transnational Encounters: Music and Performance at the U.S.-Mexico Border*, ed. Alejandro L. Madrid (Oxford University Press, 2011), 41–66; and Sydney Hutchinson, "Norteño Corporeality: Body, Gender, Sound, and Economy in Commercialized Norteño Music Videos," *Popular Music and Society* 45, no. 3 (July 2022): 317–40.

28. Field research ca. 2001–2009; digital research, 2013–2018. See also Sydney Hutchinson, "*Merengue Típico* in Santiago and New York: Transnational Regionalism in a Neo-Traditional Dominican Music," *Ethnomusicology* 50, no. 1 (Winter 2006): 37–72; Sydney Hutchinson, "Entangled Rhythms on a Conflicted Island: Digging Up the Buried Histories of Dominican Folk Music," *Resonancias: Revista de Investigación Musical* 20, no. 39 (July–November 2016): 139–54; Sydney Hutchinson, *Tigers of a Different Stripe: Performing Gender in Dominican Music* (University of Chicago Press, 2016); and Sydney Hutchinson, *Focus: Music of the Caribbean* (Routledge, 2019).

29. Field research, 2000–2003; digital research in 2015, 2017, and 2020. See Sydney Hutchinson, ed., *Salsa World: A Global Dance in Local Contexts* (Temple University Press, 2013); and Sydney Hutchinson, "On Social Dancing and Social Movements: Salsa and Resistance," in *Rhythm and Power: Performing Salsa in Latino Communities*, ed. Derrick León Washington, Priscilla Renta, and Sydney Hutchinson (Centro Press, 2017), 17–30.

30. See, for example, Inderpal Grewal and Caren Kaplan, eds., *Scattered Hegemonies: Postmodernity and Transnational Feminist Practices* (University of Minnesota Press, 1994).

31. See, for example, Catherine M. Appert and Sidra Lawrence, "Ethnomusicology Beyond #MeToo: Listening for the Violences of the Field," *Ethnomusicology* 64, no. 2 (Summer 2020): 225–53.

32. Chadwick Allen, *Trans-Indigenous: Methodologies for Global Native Literary Studies* (University of Minnesota Press, 2012).

33. See, for example, Michelle L. Cook, "Striking at the Heart of Capital: International Financial Institutions and Indigenous Peoples' Human Rights," in *Standing with Standing Rock: Voices from the #NoDAPL Movement*, ed. Nick Estes and Jaskiran Dhillon (University of Minnesota Press, 2019), 103–57.

34. See Quito Swan, "Transnationalism," in *Keywords for African American Studies*, ed. Erica R. Edwards, Roderick A. Ferguson, and Jeffrey O. G. Ogbar (New York University Press, 2018), 209–13; and Kia M. Q. Hall, "A Transnational Black Feminist Framework: Rooting in Feminist Scholarship, Framing Contemporary Black Activism," *Meridians: Feminism, Race, Transnationalism* 15, no. 1 (2016): 86–105.

35. The youth I interviewed at the time did not (yet) identify as Chican@, which is typically a politicized identity, and so in my book that resulted from this research I maintained the,

for them, more common term "Mexican American." The latter term also has the advantage of encompassing both immigrants and US-born people of Mexican heritage, while Chican@ typically includes only the US-born population; the dancers I interviewed came from both groups. "Chicanx" is one current term for including all genders, but it can be polarizing because it is unpronounceable in Spanish, so Spanish speakers often feel it to be a foreign imposition. More recently, Spanish speakers have proposed a gender-neutral -es ending for adjectives.

36. Such was particularly the case for merengue típico: understanding the music and participating in the community entailed knowing specific Cibao villages and local Cibao celebrities, and having a Cibaeño accent. A sometimes uncanny sense of geographic overlap emerged between Brooklyn or Queens restaurants on the one hand and sites where típico was played in the northern Dominican city of Santiago de los Caballeros on the other, as the frequent travel of fans and musicians alike caused the quick spread of transnational gossip, while visual-architectural imagery and sonic markers of Cibaeño identity were much the same in either place. These sites were invisible, inaccessible, or undesirable for those from other Dominican regions (as well as for many elite urban Santiagueros), meaning that the network was circumscribed by geographic and social factors as well as by musical taste.

37. Hutchinson, "*Merengue típico* in Santiago and New York."

38. These are all terms for a very fast, hard-driving, riff-based form of merengue that uses the truncated *maco* rhythm, controversial lyrics (due to explicitness, violence, misogyny, or other factors), occasionally rapped vocals, and sensual dancing, often in back-to-front position. See Hutchinson, *Tigers of a Different Stripe*, chap. 5.

39. Claire Gallien, "A Decolonial Turn in the Humanities – المنعطف المقوّض للاستعمار في الإنسانيات," *Alif: Journal of Comparative Poetics*, no. 40 (2020): 28–58, 31; and see Lorgia García Peña, *The Borders of Dominicanidad: Race, Nation, and Archives of Contradiction* (Duke University Press, 2016), for an excellent revaluation and analysis of Afro-Dominican forms of knowledge.

40. Hutchinson, "Entangled Rhythms on a Conflicted Island."

41. Contradances (also known as country dances, *contredanses* in French, *contradanzas* in Spanish) were wildly popular around western Europe and its colonies in the seventeenth and eighteenth centuries. They involve two lines of male and female dancers who change partners and carry out sequences of moves following a caller.

42. Isabel Aretz and Luis Felipe Ramón y Rivera, "Reseña de un viaje a la República Dominicana," *Boletín del Instituto de Folklore* 4, no. 4 (1963): 15–204, esp. 181–83.

43. In the 1810s–1820s, many residents of Santo Domingo admired Haiti as a "revolutionary example, [with a] relatively sturdy economy and governance," but these meanings "have been erased by the tremendous weight of subsequent historiography." Anne Eller, "'All Would Be Equal in the Effort': Santo Domingo's 'Italian Revolution,' Independence, and Haiti, 1809–1822," *Journal of Early American History* 1, no. 2 (July 2011): 105–41, quoted at 140. In the eighteenth century, Saint-Domingue was a center for European concert music performance; after independence in 1860, Haiti established a national music conservatory where students followed a Parisian curriculum. Michael Largey, *Vodou Nation: Haitian Art Music and Cultural Nationalism* (University of Chicago Press, 2006), 4–5. If the musical traditions

Santo Domingo and Haiti shared might once have served as symbols of modernity and liberalism, it is all the more tragic that those cross-border histories and revolutionary meanings were forcibly extracted from musical narratives for no other reason than racism and lust for power.

44. See Andrés L. Mateo, *Mito y cultura en la era de Trujillo*, 2nd ed. (Editora Manatí, 2004).

45. Mateo, *Mito y cultura en la era de Trujillo*.

46. Richard Lee Turits, "A World Destroyed, a Nation Imposed: The 1937 Haitian Massacre in the Dominican Republic," *Hispanic American Historical Review* 82, no. 3 (August 2002): 589–635, quoted at 635.

47. Hutchinson, "Entangled Rhythms on a Conflicted Island."

48. See Rossy Díaz, *Diez años blogueando música* (Luna Insomne Editores, 2018).

49. "Vodú" is a term used by Dominican scholars to show the close ties between this folk religion and Haitian vodú. Practitioners themselves do not use this term, though, instead speaking of "La 21 División" or *devoción a los misterios* (devotion to the mysteries, i.e., spirits).

50. George H. Lewis, "Ghosts, Ragged but Beautiful: Influences of Mexican Music on American Country-Western & Rock 'n' Roll," *Popular Music and Society* 15, no. 4 (1991): 85–103, esp. 88–93.

51. Lewis, "Ghosts, Ragged but Beautiful," 85.

52. Octavio Paz, *The Labyrinth of Solitude and Other Writings*, trans. Lysander Kemp, Yara Milos, and Rachel Phillips Belash (Grove Press, 1985), 13.

53. I use this term here with a touch of irony. In Spanish, *macho* simply means "male," but the term has entered English to mean a hypermasculine Latin American male. The construct of "machismo" is problematic because it reduces Latin American masculinities to a stereotypical, essentialized, monolithic one when the reality is far more complex and multifaceted (Hutchinson, *Tigers of a Different Stripe*, 8–20). In fact, Rafael Ramírez believes machismo not to be Latin American at all, but rather an invention of northern social scientists gazing southward. Rafael L. Ramírez, *What It Means to Be a Man: Reflections on Puerto Rican Masculinity*, trans. Rosa E. Casper (New Brunswick, NJ: Rutgers University Press, 1999). In Spanish, *machista* is roughly equivalent to the English "male chauvinist." Here, my use of the term *macho* is intended to point out the stereotypically "macho" behavior described in the lyrics to "El Rey" and enacted by those singing along to it.

54. Straitfever, "George Strait: 'El Rey' in San Antonio," YouTube, May 11, 2010, www.youtube.com/watch?v=jzToWKm86L8.

55. Rail17, "2009 Northwest Mariachi Festival: Redneck Woman," YouTube, May 27, 2009, www.youtube.com/watch?v=lQqJs4ImcN4.

56. Thomas Turino, "Nationalism and Latin American Music: Selected Case Studies and Theoretical Considerations," *Latin American Music Review / Revista de Música Latinoamericana* 24, no. 2 (Autumn–Winter 2003): 169–209, quoted at 171.

57. John Charles Chasteen, *National Rhythms, African Roots: The Deep History of Latin American Popular Dance* (University of New Mexico Press, 2004), 140.

58. Chasteen, *National Rhythms, African Roots*, 163.

59. Belinda Edmondson, "Public Spectacles: Caribbean Women and the Politics of Public Performance," *Small Axe: A Caribbean Journal of Criticism* 7, no. 1 (March 2003): 1–16, quoted at 5.

60. Barry Shank, "From Rice to Ice: The Face of Race in Rock and Pop," in *The Cambridge Companion to Pop and Rock*, ed. Simon Frith, Will Straw, and John Street (Cambridge University Press, 2001), 256–71, quoted at 261.

61. Silvio Torres-Saillant, "The Tribulations of Blackness: Stages in Dominican Racial Identity," *Latin American Perspectives* 25, no. 3 (May 1998): 126–46, quoted at 129.

62. Torres-Saillant, "The Tribulations of Blackness," 139.

63. Torres-Saillant, "The Tribulations of Blackness," 134, 136.

64. Torres-Saillant, "The Tribulations of Blackness," 128–29.

65. Torres-Saillant, "The Tribulations of Blackness," 137. However, the country still had features of a *pigmentocracia*, a term coined by Chilean researcher Alejandro Lipschutz for a social system with a hierarchy based on skin color.

66. Hutchinson, *Tigers of a Different Stripe*.

67. Elizabeth A. Behnke, "Ghost Gestures: Phenomenological Investigations of Bodily Micromovements and Their Intercorporeal Implications," *Human Studies* 20, no. 2 (April 1997): 181–201.

68. García Peña, *The Borders of Dominicanidad*.

69. Purnima Mankekar, *Unsettling India: Affect, Temporality, Transnationality* (Duke University Press, 2015).

CHAPTER 13

"Without an Image, There Is No Story"

The Indigenous and the Transnational Turn in Latin American Cinema and Video

JEFFREY ROMERO MIDDENTS AND NÚRIA VILANOVA

THE 2009 FILM *ALTIPLANO* finds an Andean Indigenous woman named Saturnina beset with grief because her fiancé—and her community—have been poisoned from mercury spills resulting from irresponsible mining practices by a transnational corporation. She positions a small, handheld video camera and records herself, delivering a message to those who will find her, those responsible for this poisoning, in an uninterrupted take: "I will not die in silence, invisible. Your poison will not kill me slowly." A pause, and then: "Without an image, there is no story." She reaches under a pillow to grab a vial of mercury and continues her condemnation: "Mother Earth will never forgive your greed. Amongst the stones, my blood will run forever like a warrior. In the water, my shadow will run like a warrior." She drinks the mercury and, still in an uninterrupted shot, we watch her body convulse as she dies.

This use of the video camera is not documenting a real image, nor one that is entirely Peruvian. The woman in the video is Magaly Solier, an actress whose starring role in the same year in another film, *La teta asustada* (The Milk of

Sorrow) by Claudia Llosa, won the Golden Bear at the Berlin Film Festival and brought her international attention. *Altiplano* was a Belgian-French-Dutch-Peruvian coproduction and the first fiction film by Belgian documentarians Peter Brosens and Jessica Woodworth. The very next shot of the film confirms the fiction: Saturnina lies down on the bed, is still for a moment, and then all four walls of the house she is in slowly fall away, revealing an arid environment bathed in bright sunlight, with symphonic, nondiegetic music announcing the most transcendent—and unreal—moment of the film.

This method of using a video camera to fight the oppression of a mining company, specifically because of mercury poisoning, has been used by Indigenous filmmakers beyond the world of fiction. The 2002 documentary *Choropampa: El precio de oro* (Choropampa: The Price of Gold), directed by Peruvian Ernesto Cabellos and Canadian Stephanie Boyd, follows the revolt against the Yanacocha mining project, which was responsible for a mercury spill in a small community, bringing together archival footage of the spill and raw, cinema verité images of the popular revolt against the company that followed. The film won awards at film festivals in Europe and the United States and brought international attention to Indigenous communities in the Andean region. Through these examples, we can identify two patterns that have grown only since the 1990s: the proliferation of digital video cameras and, more recently, smartphones;[1] and the flourishing of transnational productions, that is, productions that are joint ventures between different countries. This chapter analyzes the transnational turn in Latin American cinema, paying special attention to fiction films and documentaries engaging with Indigeneity and often directed by Indigenous filmmakers.

What might be termed "critical transnationalist film studies" comes after a relatively robust period of national film studies throughout the 1970s and 1980s. In an article tracing the trajectory of the field for the inaugural issue of *Transnational Cinemas* (now *Transnational Screens*) in 2010, Will Higbee and Song Hwee Lim warn of the tempting binary between the "national" and the "transnational," especially since cinema studies has been resistant to ideas of hybridity. They call for transnational film studies to understand "the potential for local, regional and diasporic film cultures to affect, subvert and transform national and transnational cinemas. It may also wish to pay attention to the largely neglected question of the audience and to examine the capacity of local, global and diasporic audiences to decode films as they circulate transnationally (not only in cinema theatres but also on DVD and online), constructing a variety of meanings ranging from adaptation and assimilation to more challenging or subversive readings of these transnational films."[2] Latin American cinema in particular provides a rich source with which to confront Eurocentric and nationalist cinematic considerations, particularly as Indigenous contexts naturally confront colonial boundaries and perspectives.

We understand transnationalism as taking place across geopolitical borders or involving more than one nation-state, precisely because the concept of the Indigenous nation conflicts with and resists the colonialist idea of the contemporary nation-state. Thus, the transnational dimension of Indigenous cinema is multilayered, since it echoes the transitioning across tangible national borders as well as the crossing of intangible but existing boundaries between Indigenous nations vis-à-vis the nation-state. It is also the hegemonic view of the nation as the grounding for "national" cinema that the very concept of transnationalism, applied to filmic productions, challenges in the protected space where filmmaking emerges and flourishes. In Latin America, particularly, it connotes the idea of submission and dependence, and it "is precisely the political and cultural displacement of the nation that the use of the term transnational suggests which is at the core of some Latin American film scholars' objections to it."[3]

As pointed out by Dolores Tierney,[4] transnationalism has been attached to Latin American cinematic productions since the mid-twentieth century and has become increasingly important with the proliferation of films, and with the scarcity of state funds in most countries. When addressing Indigenous cinema, cinematic transnational networks intensify. Transnationalism also permeates cinematic aesthetics, in particular in those films that aspire to succeed in the global circuits of film festivals. The proliferation of digital media and the increase in transnational production are two consequential phenomena that have gone hand in hand with the consolidation of new technologies of communication. Cinema is a costly art, and neither state nor private financing in Latin America has been consistent since the economic crises of the 1990s. The ability to disseminate films nationally and internationally using social media and the Internet without incurring the expensive costs of distribution, as well as the partnership of international producers, has had a deep impact on Latin American filmmaking, providing a broader economic grounding that has enabled a more diverse and technically more sophisticated cinematic portfolio. Tamara Falicov, for example, has written extensively about how transnational funding[5] and the film festival circuit[6] have enabled the global reach of Latin American filmmaking, but a reach that has become more complex as demands for certain kinds of films and filmmaking are presented abroad.

Indigenous filmmaking is, as has been since the outset, an explicitly transnational practice, with a constant exchange of ideas and initiatives between cultures. Most Indigenous communities in Latin America were only bounded by national borders as a result of colonization and corollary independence since the nineteenth century. Therefore, if transnational cinema is that which transcends national (nation-state) boundaries, Indigenous filmmaking should be considered transnational at its most basic level.

Filmmaking engaging with Indigeneity has mainly resulted in two different venues that parallel Latin American filmmaking in the first quarter of the twenty-first century. On the one hand, the rise of film festival aesthetics in world cinema fiction production has resulted in a dominant story structure and visual palette that dictates much of the storytelling and presentation of the Indigenous; this is particularly true of productions with transnational funding. On the other hand, the rise of digital filmmaking has lowered the high costs involved in film production and democratized cinema production, mostly in the form of documentaries by Indigenous individuals and communities. What is now known as "Indigenous Media," closely linked to social and political Indigenous activism, presents a new, decolonized approach to Indigeneity in which Indigenous individuals take the camera and move from being the object of the filmic lens to becoming their own subject. Our chapter addresses both main aspects of this transnational turn with a specific focus on how Indigenous subjects are represented—and how they represent themselves—in Latin American filmmaking.

Cinema, Indigeneity, and the Transnational Film Festival

In discussing the transnational turn of Latin American filmmaking, a brief history of the continental project (to borrow Zuzana Pick's term[7]) needs to first be addressed. Although most countries produced films in the early part of the twentieth century, these were largely local productions designed for local audiences. The coming of World War II and the subsequent rationing of celluloid nitrate by the United States led to the demise of most Latin American film industries with the exception of Mexico, where Hollywood assistance was part of a larger, strategic "soft power" move by the US government to promote a more unified Latin American identity. The dissemination of Mexican cinema (and *radionovelas*) throughout Spanish-speaking América can be seen as the first deliberate transnationally mediated move. After cinemas started redeveloping in individual countries throughout the 1940s, 1950s, and 1960s, a counternarrative—equally deliberate and transnational—began with the 1967 Viña del Mar International Film Festival in Chile, which invited filmmakers from around Latin America. Over the next decade, filmmaking that was militant in both content and form would coalesce around the "New Latin American Cinema," articulated as part of what Argentinean filmmakers and theorists Fernando Solanas and Octavio Getino termed "Third Cinema." Embraced and further theorized in manifestoes by Glauber Rocha from Brazil and Julio García Espinosa and Tomás Gutiérrez Alea from Cuba, politicized cinema became the defining characteristic of cinema from Latin America in the late 1960s and early 1970s, championed by films—and their often exiled filmmakers—screened at European film festivals. Most significant for our purposes are the works of Jorge Sanjinés from Bolivia, who formed the collective Grupo Ukamau (in Aymara, "It's like this"). After writing and filming his own scripts for his first features, Sanjinés turned to collaborative writing and filmmaking as he and Grupo Ukamau moved into the twenty-first century. Interviewed by Ignacio Ramonet about his critical book *Teoría y práctica de un cine junto al pueblo* (Theory and Practice of a Cinema of the People, 1979), Sanjinés articulated that beauty should be appreciated in New Latin American Cinema by recognizing how it differs as an Indigenous concept from the Western one:

> The artist in a revolutionary society must be a means and not an end, and beauty must play the same role. Beauty must have the same function that it has in the Indigenous community, where everyone has the capacity to create beautiful objects: each person makes cloth, and this cloth, which is used for clothing, is simultaneously an art object that is expressing the spirituality of the community. [. . .] We repeat that a beautiful film can be more efficiently revolutionary because it doesn't stay at the level of a leaflet. A cinema that is like a weapon, like a filmic expression of a people without cinema, needs to

concern itself with beauty, because beauty is a necessary element. We strive for beauty among our people, a beauty that imperialism today tries to destroy, degrade, and subjugate.[8]

While this militant politics lost momentum by the end of the 1970s, Latin American filmmaking has continued to depend on exhibition at international film festivals, particularly the European ones, as a vehicle for international distribution and recognition, whether they be in Cannes (France), Berlin (Germany), San Sebastián (Spain), or Tashkent (the Soviet Union, now Uzbekistan).

This broad overview covers how Latin American cinema developed as a historically transnational project. Locating the Indigenous in this larger project, however, proved to be difficult until recent years, precisely because most filmmaking has been concentrated in metropolitan areas where power (even artistic) was (and largely remains to this day) concentrated among a handful of mostly white, male directors. However, these dynamics have gradually changed, and increasingly Indigenous cinema, by both Indigenous and non-Indigenous filmmakers, has seen a significant rise in production and interest at film festivals and among international audiences. A trajectory of the Indigenous in Latin American fiction filmmaking can be traced by looking specifically at contemporary Peruvian film history, which begins with the 1961 release of the feature length *Kukuli*, crafted by several non-Indigenous filmmakers (Luis Figueroa, Eulogio Nishiyama, and César Villanueva) known as the Cuzco School. The film loosely follows the myth of an *ukuku*, an Andean bear, who kidnaps a young woman before being transformed into a llama. While created locally and spoken entirely in Quechua, the film is voiced over (in Spanish) by *limeño* author Sebastián Salazar Bondy, rendering a reading of the film as "authentically Andean" complex at best. While Peru's 1972 Law for the Promotion of the Film Industry created a wave of short film production, the majority of filmmakers were geographically concentrated in the capital, and thus, even when films featured Indigenous themes or actors, the narrative reflected the largely white, upper-class, male perspective that dominated filmmaking in Lima. One of the country's most successful feature films of the late 1980s, Francisco Lombardi's 1988 *La boca del lobo* (The Wolf's Den), emblematically references this aspect. Following a band of young, naïve army recruits trying to fight against members of the Sendero Luminoso (Shining Path) terrorist group, the film conspicuously chooses not to show any of the terrorists themselves, using shots of the landscape to substitute for the otherwise unknown and missing faces. The townspeople themselves are condensed into a single female character, who is raped by one of the soldiers; otherwise, the locals have no real presence at all, with the focus of the film on the outsiders. The film was wildly successful both at home and abroad, perhaps because it reflects the positionality of the largely white metropolitan filmmakers and festival audiences.

This is not to say that there were no Indigenous perspectives in filmmaking at the time, but these films were very localized at both the production and exhibition levels and thus resist the transnationality we are examining here. As such, in contrast to Lombardi's films, these perspectives have been largely ignored in broader examinations of transnational Latin American filmmaking. Pablo Salinas writes eloquently about Juan Carlos Torrico's 1986 film *Los Shapis en el mundo de los pobres* (Los Shapis in the World of the Poor), which capitalizes on the popularity of the Peruvian *chicha* musical group by conveying a fictionalized version of their rise to fame in Lima. Tellingly, the movie ends with a series of pictures of the group posing in front of the Eiffel Tower as a recognizable sign of their international fame; the movie itself, however, did not play outside Peru. Similar feature film efforts by the collective Grupo Chaski took a critical and more political approach to urban migration following the gritty trials of teenagers in *Gregorio* (1984) and *Juliana* (1989). Grupo Chaski's efforts differ significantly from those of others, however, in being more explicitly transnational, in part due to their efforts at the distribution level as much as at the production level. Two of the original five members of Grupo Chaski were not Peruvian (Stefan Kaspar from Switzerland and Alejandro Legaspi from Uruguay), and, as Sophia McClennen has noted, the collective borrows strongly from other politically active filmmakers throughout the region associated with New Latin American Cinema, such as Grupo Liberación in Argentina and Grupo Ukamau in Bolivia.[9] Their first feature, the documentary *Miss Universo en Perú* (Miss Universe in Peru, 1982), juxtaposes images from the 1982 pageant held in Lima with Indigenous women watching the competition, directly combating an "international" white, Western concept of beauty. Unlike many other Peruvian filmmakers of this period working with Indigenous topics, Grupo Chaski explicitly worked with international distribution efforts, and thus their films have wide international exposure.

The prominence of the work of Claudia Llosa marks a major shift to the figure of Native women in Latin American cinema. Her first feature, 2006's *Madeinusa*, privileges the full perspective of a young Quechua woman (played by Magaly Solier) whose village is unexpectedly visited by an outsider during their main religious festival. White, Lima-based Salvador (whom Llosa has endowed with an iconic name, which means "Savior" in Spanish), ignorant of the ways of the town he has stumbled into, finds himself immersed in a world he neither comprehends nor is able to navigate. The film's screenplay development and subsequent screening at the Sundance Film Festival brought significant attention to the film and filmmaker. Both internationally and nationally, the film was criticized for stereotyping Indigenous Peruvians, despite the feminist stance predominating through the actions of the Quechua protagonist, Madeinusa (another iconic name). It is worth noting that large segments of the film are in Quechua but, unlike *Kukuli*, this dialogue was left unsubtitled in the original screenings in Peru. Llosa's *La teta asustada* then extends the protagonist female role, bringing an Indigenous family to Lima. In *La teta*, Solier plays a young woman named Fausta who is traumatized by the stories her mother has sung to her of rape at the hands of military and terrorist figures in the mountains during the war between Sendero and the Peruvian state. Fausta struggles to form her own identity and (literally) find her own voice, fearful of both the city at large and men in particular; the private songs she sings while working as a domestic are appropriated by her older white employer, a musician who has lost inspiration. Throughout the entire film, the narrative focus stays squarely on Fausta.

La teta asustada is of major importance for this chapter because of its transnational profile. The film became the first Peruvian film to be screened at one of the "Big Three" film festivals when it premiered at Berlin in 2009—and subsequently took home the top prize as the Golden Bear; it then became the first film from Peru to be nominated for the Academy Award for Best Foreign Film.[10] This successful work adheres to what Cindy Hing-Yuk Wong terms a "film festival aesthetic," which characterizes much transnational filmmaking in the early twenty-first century.[11] Wong notes that "festival films" are serious and austere in a careful, precise manner, both on the visual level as well as the narrative: this usually means careful compositions with long takes, often using nonprofessional actors. As Jeffrey Middents describes Latin American cinema on the festival circuit:

These films are specifically designed for international distribution at the level of the art film, particularly to be screened at international film festivals. Such films need to be readily identifiable as from their countries of origin to international audiences that may not be familiar with the subtleties a national audience might. Such films also may latch onto stereotypes, either visual or narrative, that are embraced by audiences overseas. The "made for export" films play fantastically well to international audiences, and recognition abroad then circles back to affirm status as higher art among upper-class audiences at home.[12]

Tamara Falicov further writes about how international film festivals provide direct funding that promotes a depiction of poverty that is cloaked in beautiful aesthetics, often defined by emphasis on cinematography.[13] In 2023, for example, the mission statement on the Berlin Film Festival's website describes its funding source, the World Cinema Fund, as one that supports "films that stand out with an *unconventional aesthetic approach*, that tell powerful stories and transmit an *authentic* image of their *cultural roots*" (our emphasis).[14]

In essence, films that successfully compete for funding sources like the World Cinema Fund are simultaneously local (through "authentic" stories) and transnational (through the "aesthetic approach"). Maria Chiara D'Argenio classifies these films as "Indigenous plots": "By this, I refer to inter/cultural feature films [mainly] made by non-Indigenous directors [. . .]—in varying degrees of collaboration with Indigenous actors—which tell Indigenous stories, played by Indigenous actors and spoken in Indigenous languages, and [. . .] made for global (mostly non-Indigenous) consumption."[15] D'Argenio aptly points out that films like *La teta asustada* do not just travel to Berlin, where they are consumed by international audiences: these films then travel back and change the context in the countries of origin as well. This is a very meaningful aspect of the dynamics between the local and the transnational and how they reciprocally impact one another. Extensive portions of *La teta asustada* are spoken entirely in Quechua, which speaks volumes regarding the "authenticity" of these Indigenous characters, who, while living in the metropole, are from the rural Andes. In Spanish-language screenings, however, these sections are subtitled to be comprehensible to more cosmopolitan audiences. We find the transnational elements of these films, however, in their aesthetic representations, geared largely toward the "festival film" style articulated earlier. In *La teta asustada*, the city of Lima is treated as landscape in a similar way that the Andes had earlier been treated by other filmmakers. Llosa and cinematographer Natasha Braier make extensive use of wide shots that frame the city low on the horizon, often with strong diagonals reflecting walking paths, making the city both otherworldly and familiar at once, reflecting Fausta's introverted life experience. These shots are often juxtaposed with Steadicam shots of relatively long duration to follow Fausta, the camera gliding either in front of or behind her at medium range, or closer to establish a lyrical visual pace.

Many films featuring these "Indigenous plots" have been released in the early twenty-first century from around Latin America to great international success, especially at film festivals, including *El abrazo de la serpiente* (Embrace of the Serpent, 2015), by Ciro Guerra from Colombia; *Ixcanul* (2015) and *La Llorona* (The Weeping Woman, 2019), by Jayro Bustamante from Guatemala; and *Retablo* (2017), by Álvaro Delgado Aparicio, and *Wiñaypacha* (Eternity, 2017), by Óscar Catacora, both from Peru. The most widely seen and distributed (and celebrated) of these films is the black-and-white opus *Roma* (2018), by Alfonso Cuarón of Mexico. Ostensibly about a middle-class family in early 1970s Mexico City, the film actually privileges the perspective of the family's young maid, Cleo (played by Yalitza Aparicio), with a good portion of her dialogue delivered in (subtitled) Mixtec. The film was supposed to premiere at Cannes but was removed from the lineup due to the financier's negotiated mode of distribution: the streaming service Netflix. Cuarón's status as an auteur and the worldwide simultaneous distribution of the film on the platform brought attention to the film—and subsequent Oscar nominations that resulted in Aparicio becoming the first Indigenous woman to be nominated in the Best Actress category. Netflix's own status as a transnational media entity and the attention it brought to *Roma* is perhaps the most prominent example of how Indigenous narratives have acquired a prominent place in the dissemination of Latin American fictional narratives.

A contemporary film that offers an alternative to D'Argenio's "Indigenous plots" while simultaneously being explicitly transnational in its intentions is the insouciant Bolivian comedy *¿Quién mató a la llamita blanca?* (Who Killed the White Llama?, 2007). Credited to Rodrigo Bellott, the film was shot entirely on video as a semicollaborative effort with film school students and rejects festival aesthetics in favor of frantic pastiche editing that yields a rougher result. An Indigenous everyman narrator explains the very "Bolivian" situation and dialogue to viewers clearly coded as "outsiders," and affirms an idea that fiction filmmaking can introduce the more challenging aesthetics and practices that Indigenous media presents, perhaps even beating them at their own game. The diversity of films that have proliferated since the turn of the twenty-first century is a testament to the increasing role played by Indigenous communities and individuals across Latin America and the world.

"Close-by" Indigeneity, Self-Representations, and Transnational Popular Exhibition

Digital media emerged at a moment when Indigenous activism was being internationally echoed and the resistance to oppression and exploitation was once again at the forefront. In 1992, the Nobel Peace Prize was awarded to Mayan K'iche' Rigoberta Menchú; her testimonial book *Me llamo Rigoberta Menchú y así me nació la conciencia* (I, Rigoberta Mechú: An Indian Woman in Guatemala), written with Elizabeth Burgos and published in 1983, narrates the hardship of Mayans in Guatemala amid the bloody civil war in which 83 percent of the two hundred thousand murdered Guatemalans or *desaparecidos* were Mayan. In 1994, the Ejército Zapatista de Liberación Nacional (EZLN; Zapatista Army of National Liberation) took up arms against the Mexican government in the Lacandon Jungle in the southern state of Chiapas. Among demands for social and economic justice for the Indigenous population, the EZLN denounced the government's neoliberal policies that had led to the signing of the North American Free Trade Agreement (NAFTA) with Mexico's northern neighbor countries, Canada and the United States. It was also at the beginning of the 1990s when the conflict between the Shining Path and the Peruvian army reached its peak, catching thousands of highlander Quechuas in between. These struggles, among others, and their aftermaths were captured by audiovisual testimonials and documentaries, many produced by Indigenous individuals. Established toward the end of the twentieth century, Indigenous media enabled Indigenous individuals and communities to use cinematic tools and techniques to take into their own hands their own representation. This important development emerged amid an increasing presence of Indigenous movements across the Americas and worldwide, with a strong transnational component. Chilean anthropologist and filmmaker Juan Francisco Salazar notes that "the term Indigenous Media itself invokes a series of social relations that lie beyond a television program, a You-Tube video, or any other product of information and communication. It demands the consideration of a formal socio-technical assemblage of technologies, resources, social organizations, legal frameworks and bureaucracies, and cultural principles, into a representational and performative form embodied in processes that extend beyond the completed product."[16] Indigenous media has incorporated a transnational dimension that is embedded in Indigeneity itself and has been transferred into its work and mission since its outset, with a constant exchange of ideas and initiatives among the different projects and filmmakers across the Americas. We argue that this transcendental aspect mirrors the collective spirit embedded in Indigenous practices and is key to thinking about Indigenous media as an intrinsically transnational endeavor.[17]

Freya Schiwy notes in her book *Indianizing Film: Decolonization, the Andes, and the Question of Technology* (2009) that two organizations pioneered Indigenous media in Latin America. Centro de Información y Realización Cinematográfica (CEFREC; the Center for Information and Filmmaking) was founded in Bolivia in 1989 and provided the tools and infrastructure for Indigenous cinematic production, epitomizing Jorge Sanjinés's main goal to move audiovisual technology closer to Aymara and Quechua communities and individuals as a tool of resistance. Sanjinés's early fiction work, such as *Yawar mallku* (The Blood of the Condor, 1968) through his collaborative work *La nación clandestina* (The Secret Nation, 1989), serves as a testament to CEFREC's mission. The center's undertaking has two main pillars: Indigenous cinematic self-representation, namely the production of films that are not mediated by Spanish, nor by a hegemonic gaze or prevalent aesthetics, and thus by an external perspective; and filmmaking as a tool to denounce the marginality, injustice, and exploitation to which most Indigenous communities and individuals have been subjected since colonial times.

CEFREC has worked alongside another pioneering group, the multinational Coordinadora Latinoamericana de Cine y Comunicación de los Pueblos Indígenas (CLACPI), in a clear transnational enterprise. Launched in 1985, CLACPI organized and promoted Indigenous media and cinema festivals in Latin America and across the world as well as playing a key role in organizing workshops and training sessions for Indigenous individuals and communities. The group's founders come from across the continent. Marta Rodríguez (Colombia) has established a groundbreaking career beginning in the late 1960s, with the documentary *Chircales* (The Brickmakers, 1972), created with her husband Jorge Silva, denouncing the exploitation and marginalization suffered by many Indigenous individuals in rural and urban areas.[18] Ecuadorian Gustavo Guayasamín has also produced important documentaries, such as *Los hieleros del Chimborazo* (Chimborazo Ice Collectors, 1980). Although these filmmakers do not identify as Indigenous, their work, alongside that of Claudio Menezes (Brazil), Jeannette Paillán (Chile), Ana Piñó Sandoval and Juan Francisco Urrusti (Mexico), Alejandro Camino (Peru), and Iris Sánchez D. (Venezuela), has contributed to the expansion and proliferation of a media created by Indigenous individuals and communities and has been fundamental in establishing CLACPI as a transnational initiative.[19] More Indigenous filmmakers joined the organization's leadership in the early twenty-first century. In 2004, the non-Indigenous director of CLACPI, Iván Sanjinés (Bolivia), was replaced by Zapotec Juan José García.[20]

In 1985, Kichwa Alberto Muenala launched the Corporación Rupai as a platform for the creation of cultural and visual projects. Muenala, alongside Iván Sanjinés and Marta Rodríguez, organized audiovisual workshops and training to promote Indigenous audiovisual education.[21] In 1994, Muenala, in collaboration with the Confederación de Nacionalidades Indígenas del Ecuador (CONAIE), launched the first cinema festival of Abya Yala (the term used by Indigenous people to refer to the Americas), aimed at integrating a broad variety of projects while reaching out to rural and isolated communities; from 2006 to 2008, Muenala led CLACPI. The transnational scope of Indigenous media is partly due to the contributions of Guillermo Monteforte (Ojo de Agua, Mexico) and Vincent Carelli (Video de las Aldeas, Brazil), who have been key in fostering and consolidating Indigenous media projects across Latin America.

Both CEFREC and CLACPI have facilitated collaboration between Indigenous and non-Indigenous filmmakers. Juan Francisco Salazar and Amalia Córdova, in their book chapter "Imperfect Media and the Poetics of Indigenous Video in Latin America" (2008), note the tensions that have emerged at times, as expressed by P'urhepecha director Dante Cerano, who, at the Second International Film Festival in Morelia, Mexico, in 2004, stated that any non-Indigenous documentalist engaging with Indigeneity had unavoidably an *indigenista* approach; in other words, their perspective was impacted by an external, condescending, and paternalistic gaze.[22] Cerano's allusion has a long history in Latin American politics, cultures, arts, and literature. Its impact cannot be underestimated, particularly in the Andean region and in postrevolutionary Mexico. Originated at the end of the nineteenth century by intellectuals who denounced in their works the exploitation and oppression suffered by Indigenous individuals and communities since colonial times, indigenismo became a movement, a tendency, an ideology, and a perspective among non-Indigenous, mainly white criollos (those of European descent) who recognized the long-standing marginalization and abuses that Indigenous peoples had experienced from the authorities, the church, and society in general.[23] Indigenismo was usually permeated with a condescending view that did not see Indigenous subjects as having agency, power, or will; instead, they were approached as helpless individuals, unable to fight for themselves. That view, commonly seen in fiction writing and other artistic expressions such as painting and photography, is translated to cinema. Many non-Indigenous filmmakers, mostly in Ecuador, Peru, and Mexico, who engaged with Indigeneity throughout most of the twentieth century are influenced by this perspective. We might view Francisco Lombardi's 1989 film *La boca del lobo* (The Wolf's Den) as following this tradition; when the village depicted in the film is besieged by terrorists, the townspeople's perspective is subjugated to that of the army, consisting mostly of individuals from Lima, who arrived there to fight Sendero.

That said, some non-Indigenous filmmakers favor a decolonial approach that advocates the open denunciation of exploitation and oppression but more importantly articulates a clear goal to influence structural change. In the 1980s, both Jorge Sanjinés and Marta Rodríguez were already developing their work "close-by" the Indigenous people who had become the main subjects of that work. Trinh T. Minh-ha describes "working close-by" as the strategy of a filmmaker who does not identify exactly with the subject of their film but nevertheless successfully presents perspectives that are closer to the world represented.[24] If we consider the stereotyped representations of Indigeneity that once predominated in Latin American cinema, particularly those that were broadly disseminated and seen by many in successful Mexican films from the late 1930s through the mid-1950s, Sanjinés's cinematic proposal does represent an important step forward in dismantling demeaning and discriminatory imaginaries that had rarely been challenged since colonial times. Many of the well-known films of the 1940s Golden Age of Mexican cinema, such as *María Candelaria* (1943) and *Maclovia* (1948) by Emilio Fernández, included Indigenous characters who were acted by well-known white actors and actresses like Dolores del Río, María Félix, and Pedro Armendáriz, made up with Indigenous-looking makeup and costumes.[25] Films such as *Kukuli* (1961), mentioned above, are also performed by white non-Indigenous actors disguised as Indigenous. This was a common trait well into the second half of the twentieth century, when filmmakers like Sanjinés and Rodríguez began introducing nonprofessional Indigenous actors in their films, a collaboration that has proven very fruitful, as reflected by the actor protagonist of *La nación clandestina*, Reynaldo Yujra, a major player in Bolivian Indigenous media.[26] This veered away from the traditional mainstream indigenista approach and gaze. Sanjinés's film brings cinema "close-by" by keeping the film almost entirely in the Aymara and Quechua languages and using filmic techniques that do not cater to an outside point of view. The exploration and implementation of new techniques has been essential to representing Indigeneity more faithfully from within.

Indigenous media in the twenty-first century has developed a vast array of projects explored by groundbreaking scholarship.[27] Indigenous audiovisuals have been used to address matters related to the communal, social, and individual dimensions of life, mostly connected to advocacy and activism. Indigenous media has indeed been a window to represent and self-represent a long history of oppression and marginalization, centering Indigeneity at its core, across Latin America. Hence, a decolonial gaze is not compartmentalized or reserved to films, mostly documentaries, ascribed to emancipatory proposals that are codified within social parameters. Instances of decoloniality are found also in films by non-Indigenous filmmakers, many times intertwined with recurrent clichés and stereotypes. "Indigenous plots" such as those of *El abrazo de la serpiente* and *Madeinusa* speak to this unresolved tension.[28]

A transnational approach to Indigenous filmmaking recognizes the significance of genre fiction films, which go by various names in different countries— "regional cinema" in Peru and "Bajo Tierra" (underground) cinema in Ecuador, for example. Our transnational approach to these films follows Song Hwee Lim's expansive view of what constitutes transnationalism in cinema,[29] ten years after his and Will Higbee's publication discussed above. Lim incorporates new cinematic categories in response to current worldwide political, economic, and social dynamics mirrored in filmmaking. Alongside slow cinema and the new genre of ecocinema, poor cinema is a useful tool to examine Peru's regional cinema and Ecuador's Bajo Tierra, since the low budget and precarity of resources echo Lim's argument. In Peru, these films emerged mostly in places where the war between the Shining Path and the Peruvian state had been most severe, such as Ayacucho and Puno. As noted by Emilio Bustamante, a clear correlation exists between cinema as a form of art and entertainment and the ordeal experienced during the war. Most of the cinematic genres developed and the topics addressed are both directly and indirectly impacted by those violent years. For the most part, these films are distributed locally and only on rare occasions travel to Lima to be seen in the commercial multicinemas where more mainstream movies are released and shown. The concept of "regional," as acknowledged by Bustamante, singles out this filmography as belonging to a marginal subcategory of Peruvian cinema,[30] running the risk of making a division between a "national" cinema, in reference to a filmography mainly produced in Lima with broader domestic and international projection, and a "regional" cinema, circumscribed to the margins of Peruvian cinematography.

Without sharing the experience of war with Peru, Ecuador nevertheless has seen the emergence of a similar phenomenon in what is known as Bajo Tierra films to describe low-budget, popular films that range from romantic melodramatic stories to action thrillers and evangelical Christian proselytizing accounts. What all these films have in common is very low-budget production, mostly supported by family and friends, and extensive circulation underground in parallel to the official and regular channels of distribution, foremost through the extended national and international pirate market.[31] Among the lively and multifaceted Bajo Tierra films, the popular productions by the Kichwa group Sinchi Samay stand out, appealing to many who have experienced stories of migration and abandonment similar to those re-created in the group's fictional films.[32] Gabriela Alemán has explored the connection of these films with exploitation cinema,[33] while Carolina Sitnisky has addressed this phenomenon, reassessing the concept of precarity to highlight the creativity and independence involved in these projects, considering that their production literally takes place at the margins of mainstream Ecuadorian cinema.[34] Many of the thrillers this cinema has produced are known as *cine guerrilla* or "Chonewood"—an allusion to the coastal town of Chone, where many of them have emerged—which also serves to desta-bilize the position of Quito as the country's cinematic capital.[35] Amid the multi-faceted cinematic "underground" proposals, a significant number of films have been produced by Indigenous filmmakers. These are mostly spoken in Kichwa, starring nonprofessional Kichwa actors trained in acting workshops.[36]

Exhibition strategies have changed dramatically. As filmmaking across Latin America expanded at the end of the twentieth century, most filmmaking could not get beyond very local confines without first going through the metropolitan areas where cultural capital was concentrated; even there, support from transna-tional funding sources like Ibermedia or the World Cinema Fund was crucial for getting films seen at all. Local and inexpensively made films would thus stay local, often distributed on street corners and viewed in small, makeshift venues; Indigenous material in particular would rarely be distributed outside these very local channels. These same materials have more recently circulated through the Internet, acquiring a transnational dimension in their exhibition and becoming more available to migrant communities both in metropolitan areas in-country as well as abroad. Perhaps the most entertaining example of the kind of transna-tional crossings that the Internet has engendered is *El último guerrero Chanka* (The Last Chanka Fighter, 2011), directed by Victor Zarabia, a kung-fu movie set in the Peruvian province of Apurímac and featuring dialogue in Spanish and Quechua; in 2020, during the COVID-19 pandemic, the film was redistributed with English voice-over commentary by Ugandan V. J. Emmie, who himself had gained international fame by providing similar commentary for the microbudget action movie *Who Killed Captain Alex?*[37] In this way, the images and the story of Indigenous populations throughout Latin America find an audience far beyond what they would through more traditional distribution methods, and have that much more influence.

As seen in these pages, in many different and creative ways, transnationalism crosses cinema that engages with Indigeneity. From glamorous film festivals, with an increase of related aesthetics in world cinema fiction production, resulting in dominant narrative and visual structures that guide much of the production addressing Indigenous peoples, to the rise of digital filmmaking with its lower costs, fostering more democratized cinema production mostly in the form of doc-umentaries by Indigenous communities, transnationalism permeates the fabric of Indigenous cinema and media, combating colonialist notions of the nation-state.

Notes

1. See Eduardo Ledesma's chapter in this volume.

2. Will Higbee and Song Hwee Lim, "Concepts of Transnational Cinema: Towards a Critical Transnationalism in Film Studies," *Transnational Cinemas* 1, no. 1 (January 2010): 18.

3. Dolores Tierney, *New Transnationalisms in Contemporary Latin American Cinemas* (Edinburgh University Press, 2018), 6.

4. Tierney, *New Transnationalisms*, 2.

5. Tamara Falicov, "Programa Ibermedia: Co-Production and the Cultural Politics of Constructing the Ibero-American Audiovisual Space," *Spectator* 27, no. 2 (Fall 2007): 21–30.

6. Tamara Falicov, "Migrating from South to North: The Role of Film Festivals in Funding and Shaping Global South Film and Video," in *Locating Migrating Media*, ed. Greg Elmer, Charles H. Davis, Janine Marchessault, and John McCullough (Lexington Books, 2010), 3–22.

7. Zuzana M. Pick, *The New Latin American Cinema: A Continental Project* (University of Texas Press, 1993).

8. Jorge Sanjinés and Grupo Ukamau, *Teoría y práctica de un cine junto al pueblo* (Siglo XXI Editores, 1980), 156–57. Our translation.

9. Sophia A. McClennen, "The Theory and Practice of the Peruvian Grupo Chaski," *Jump Cut*, no. 50 (Spring 2008), https://www.ejumpcut.org/archive/jc50.2008/Chaski/.

10. In 2019, the name of the award changed to Best International Feature Film.

11. Cindy Hing-Yuk Wong, *Film Festivals: Culture, People, and Power on the Global Screen* (Rutgers University Press, 2011), 74–93.

12. Jeffrey Middents, "The First Rule of Latin American Cinema Is You Do Not Talk About Latin American Cinema: Notes on Discussing a Sense of Place in Contemporary Cinema," *Transnational Cinemas* 4, no. 2 (2013): 155.

13. Falicov, "Migrating from South to North."

14. Institute of Documentary Film, "World Cinema Fund: Production and Funding," https://dokweb.net/database/organizations/about/2c50f142-2fae-4920-8a59-ca50ef3a0296/world-cinema-fund-production-and-distribution-funding.

15. Maria Chiara D'Argenio, *Indigenous Plots in Twenty-First Century Latin American Cinema* (Palgrave Macmillan, 2022), 1.

16. Juan Francisco Salazar, "Indigenous Media in Latin America," *Miami Rail*, https://miamirail.org/performing-arts/indigenous-media-in-latin-america/.

17. See Andrew Canessa's chapter in this volume; and Alcida Rita Ramos, "Cutting Through State and Class: Sources and Strategies of Self-Representation in Latin America," in *Indigenous Movements, Self-Representation, and the State in Latin America*, ed. Kay B. Warren and Jean E. Jackson (University of Texas Press, 2002), 251–79.

18. Hugo Chaparro Valderrama, *Marta Rodríguez: La historia a través de una cámara* (Alcaldía Mayor de Bogotá; Secretaría de Cultura, Recreación y Deporte, 2015).

19. Freya Schiwy, *Indianizing Film: Decolonization, the Andes, and the Question of Technology* (Rutgers University Press, 2009), 65. See also CLACPI's website at https://clacpi.org/.

20. Schiwy, *Indianizing Film*, 67.

21. Christian León, *Reinventando al otro: El documental indigenista en el Ecuador* (Consejo Nacional de Cinematografía del Ecuador, 2010), 29–30.

22. Juan Francisco Salazar and Amalia Córdova, "Imperfect Media and the Poetics of Indigenous Video in Latin America," in *Global Indigenous Media: Cultures, Poetics, and Politics*, ed. Pamela Wilson and Michelle Stewart (Duke University Press, 2008), 40–41.

23. *Aves sin nido* (Birds Without a Nest, 1889), by Clorinda Matto de Turner, is considered the first indigenista novel, denouncing the abuse of the Andean villagers of the fictitious community of Kíllac by its ecclesiastical and local authorities.

24. Trinh T. Minh-ha, *Woman, Native, Other: Writing Postcoloniality and Feminism* (Indiana University Press, 1989).

25. Mónica García Blizzard, *The White Indians of Mexican Cinema: Racial Masquerade Throughout the Golden Age* (State University of New York Press, 2022).

26. Gabriela Zamorano Villarreal, *Indigenous Media and Political Imaginaries in Contemporary Bolivia* (University of Nebraska Press, 2017).

27. Valerie Alia, *The New Media Nation: Indigenous Peoples and Global Communication* (Berghahn Books, 2010); Verónica Córdova, "Cine boliviano: Del indigenismo a la globalización," *Revista Nuestra América*, no. 3 (July 2007): 129–45; Erica Cusi Wortham, *Indigenous Media in Mexico: Culture, Community, and the State* (Duke University Press, 2013); Charlotte Gleghorn, "Indigenous Filmmaking in Latin America," in *A Companion to Latin American Cinema*, ed. Maria M. Delgado, Stephen M. Hart, and Randal Johnson (Wiley Blackwell, 2017), 167–86; Salazar and Córdova, "Imperfect Media"; Schiwy, *Indianizing Film*; Freya Schiwy, *The Open Invitation: Activist Video, Mexico, and the Politics of Affect* (University of Pittsburgh Press, 2019); and Zamorano Villarreal, *Indigenous Media and Political Imaginaries*.

28. D'Argenio, *Indigenous Plots*.

29. Song Hwee Lim, "Concepts of Transnational Cinema Revisited," *Transnational Screens* 10, no. 1 (2019): 1–12.

30. Miguel Alvear and Christian León, *Ecuador Bajo Tierra: Videografías en circulación paralela* (Ochoymedio, 2009), 60–63; and Emilio Bustamante and Jaime Luna-Victoria, "El cine regional en el Perú," *Contratexto*, no. 22 (2014): 189–212.

31. Gabriela Alemán, "At the Margin of the Margins: Contemporary Ecuadorian Exploitation Cinema and the Local Pirate Market," in *Latsploitation, Exploitation Cinemas, and Latin America*, ed. Victoria Ruétalo and Dolores Tierney (Routledge, 2009), 261–74.

32. Alvear and León, *Ecuador Bajo Tierra*.

33. Alemán, "At the Margin of the Margins," 261–74.

34. Carolina Sitnisky, "Rethinking Contemporary Ecuadorian Cinema," in *The Precarious in the Cinemas of the Americas*, ed. Constanza Burucúa and Carolina Sitnisky (Cham, Switzerland: Palgrave Macmillan, 2018), 191–92.

35. Diana Coryat and Noah Zweig, "New Ecuadorian Cinema: Small, Glocal and Plurinational," *International Journal of Media and Cultural Politics* 13, no. 3 (September 2017): 276.

36. Alvear and León, *Ecuador Bajo Tierra*, 60–64.

37. Official Wakaliwood, "Special Message from VJ Emmie," YouTube, April 6, 2020, https://www.youtube.com/watch?v=HeFl8wWvS4M/.

CHAPTER 14

Pocket Cinema and the Transnational Turn

Cell Phone Films as Global(ized) Counter-Cinema

EDUARDO LEDESMA

Where Is Cell Phone Cinema in Transnational Film Studies?

The phenomenon of transnational cinema, or the transnational turn in cinema studies, has been widely theorized since the turn of the twenty-first century, with a significant number of books flooding the market in recent years.[1] The definition of the elusive term remains contested, although one approximation, according to Tim Bergfelder, delineates the transnational as

> an umbrella that encompasses a range of historically mutable activities and movements between national cinemas and also between nations [that . . .] include economic exchanges, movement of labor, co-production practices, instances of cross-national distribution and reception, cross-national aesthetic influences in terms of imitations, adaptations, and transformations of visual style and narrative (genre); and finally, the on-screen representation of actual transnational processes and experiences of migration and exile.[2]

Regardless of the definition or the facet of the phenomenon adopted, the transnational is here to stay as a leading category for film criticism. Beyond numerous monographs and edited volumes, another marker indicating the prominence of this critical approach is the 2010 creation of a film studies journal dedicated exclusively to transnationalism, and aptly named *Transnational Cinemas*. Or the burgeoning symposia, conferences, and workshops about transnational cinema, and research groups such as the Transnational Cinemas Scholarly Interest Group created by Austin Fisher and Iain Smith in 2013 for the Society for Cinema and Media Studies. Finally, we might point to the flourishing of university courses exploring transnationality in film (one need only Google "Syllabus" + "Transnational Cinema" to become convinced). Despite their heterogeneity, what many of these volumes, conferences, and scholarly efforts show is that the field, well into its second decade, is evolving from its original emphasis on defining what the "transnational" means toward a second phase in transnational cultural studies that is applying the transnational as an analytical tool for various cinemas and contexts.[3] It is to that second phase that I add my own contribution by bringing attention to an eminently transnational new modality of filmmaking, cell phone cinema, focusing on its production in Latin America and Spain as case studies representative of global trends toward a so-called Silicone Screen. The stakes are high when it comes to this emerging cinematic format, its proponents making broad claims that the widespread global availability and ease of creating, distributing, and archiving movies shot with cell phones has democratized filmmaking and fostered a renewal in audiovisual creativity. But this technological utopianism often neglects a darker side resulting from the ubiquity of cell phone filming, including the threat of widespread surveillance, cyberstalking, and a simplification of social issues through a superficial engagement with images.

Despite the growing body of research on transnational cinema, scant attention has been paid to the phenomenon of cell phone cinema, also known as pocket cinema, mobile cinema, and cell filmmaking. But although this research may be lagging, it is imminent, as signaled by the renaming of *Transnational Cinemas* to *Transnational Screens*, to account for a seismic shift in how movies are created, distributed, and consumed, as we progressively rely on the silicone screen for our media consumption. Digital media content is now mainly mobile and transnational, as it displaces static and nation-centric formats such as television and national film industries. Evidently there is a growing awareness that filmic modes of production, distribution, and consumption are undergoing a radical transformation, but one of the cultural by-products and indicators of this shift—cell phone cinema—is not yet on the radar of film critics, not even for those who focus on transnational filmmaking. There is a lag between praxis and theory, since the number of amateur and professional filmmakers who have taken to handheld communication devices to make their movies is expanding, as is the viewership of cell phone films.

The neglect by scholars of transnational cinema is surprising given the constitutive nature of mobile media and cell phone video as eminently global, diasporic, interconnected, and polycentric as well as culturally hybrid in both refreshing and problematic ways—and therefore ideally suited to be studied under the umbrella of the transnational. The low-budget amateur filmmaking scene in Spain and Latin America is using cell phones to forge a common audiovisual space; filmmakers are creating works that are transnational by virtue of their shared characteristics and cultural affinities, their joint presence in international film festivals, and their immediate and global online distribution, as well as the mobility and exchanges between filmmakers and crews across national boundaries. The interplay between these elements makes Ibero-American mobile cinema a fascinating case study to interrogate the very concept of the transnational, and of the persistence of the national as a remainder or trace within global trends.[4] Without losing sight of the specificity of these films, similar observations may apply to other world regions (Africa, Asia, North America, and Europe) that are tapping into the cell phone's movie-making capabilities. There are also questions of ideology vis-à-vis the transnational that require sorting out within cell phone cinema practices as the national is redefined, abandoned, subsumed, elided, or deliberately performed, or as the films themselves are posited as "overcoming" the national so as to (perhaps) incorrectly suggest the existence of "an unproblematic, idealizing and seamless sameness across nations and industries."[5]

The aim of this chapter is to illuminate cell phone cinema as an emergent transnational film format and as a body of global movies that might at times function as a counter-cinema to the commercial film industry, while avoiding celebratory discourses about transnationalism that presume that any hybridity (material or cultural) is automatically a positive factor. Moreover, when considering cell phone cinema, which, as I argue, can be a democratizing and leveling format, a certain built-in unevenness in power relations needs to be accounted for, including questions of accessibility to training, to funding, to equipment, to distribution platforms, and to festivals—although the ubiquity and affordability of cell phones is making access easier, as is the intuitive quality of filming with mobile devices. Scholars of transnational film such as Lúcia Nagib caution against the binary that automatically sets Hollywood as the (exclusive) foil of other global cinemas, exhorting researchers to resist this reductive formula.[6] Cell phone cinema defies this simplified opposition, at times presenting itself as a counter-cinema not only to Hollywood but also to European art cinema and to other types of commercial filmmaking, but often also openly emulating Hollywood aesthetics and its commercial ideology.

Mobile films from Spain and Latin America also oscillate between undercutting and emulating transnational coproductions. These might include, for example, coproductions between the Spanish media conglomerate Ibermedia, or the Spanish telecommunications corporate giant Telefónica, and smaller Latin American production companies—resulting in highly visible transnational productions such as *Amores perros* (Alejandro González Iñárritu, 2001) or *Nueve reinas* (Fabián Bielinsky, 1999), which often perform a certain idea of Latin Americanness for foreign audiences.[7] Other transnational megaproductions encompass collaborations between Hollywood companies and Latin American filmmakers, including many recent blockbusters by Mexican director Guillermo del Toro, to name but one such iconic transnational filmmaker. Despite analogous claims to transnationalism (by virtue of their online availability or their presence in festivals, for example), there is little else in common between large commercial coproductions and typically low-budget cell films except that the latter, at times, emulate the sleek stylistics of the former, but other times opt for an underground aesthetic instead. Unlike transnational blockbusters, cell films are not typically internationally financed nor expected to portray the Latin America imagined by North American and European festival and arthouse cinephiles, or to satisfy the expectations of global film distributors; films do not need to adjust to that foreign imaginary by depicting poverty and crime, political turmoil, immigration, or narcotrafficking but can instead embrace a broader diversity of topics and approaches, focusing on both local and global issues, or on the personal interests of the filmmaker. Eschewing these mega coproductions with multi-million-dollar budgets, cell phone cinema, either by choice or by necessity, aligns/allies instead with do-it-yourself cultural practices (selfie-movies, home movies, coming-out YouTube videos, nonprofessional music videos) and may approximate an experimental or underground style. Cell phone filmmaking therefore joins a lengthy history of alternative and amateur filmic practices such as Super 8 in the 1960s and 1970s, or VHS home videos in the 1980s and 1990s. Like cell phone films, these now obsolete formats related to participatory and anticommercial youth culture and to underground art practices—that is, to practices that focus on the marginalized, the peripheral, the bizarre; on the fringe and artisanal aspects of global culture.

In fact, a significant portion of fiction pocket cinematic production also falls within the category of "genre cinema" (horror, sci-fi, noir, soft-core, etc.), itself seen as on the margins of the mainstream and as such rife with counter-cinematic potential. Many of these styles were adapted from American models, and common genre traits (such as in sci-fi or horror) might be more salient than national or regional elements, engendering global trends in amateur and DIY cell films. Similarly, the technical affordances of cell phone cinema establish important links between cinemas created in different national contexts and directly influence the emergence of shared aesthetic affinities. In other words, the aesthetic choices respond to what filmmakers can or cannot do with cell phones, understanding that these affordances change over time. Cell phone cinema therefore stages a tension between the desire to retain cultural and linguistic specificity, and "a recognition of the movable, unstable nature of national identities and outlooks on the other."[8]

In an overview of the format as a transnational phenomenon, I analyze two paradigmatic cell phone cinema examples in genre film, one from Spain and one from Chile, to consider the following questions: Are these films part of a trans-atlantic and, indeed, transnational cinema? How do methods of distribution (international, regional, and local festivals; online streaming) determine their transnational character? How do genre characteristics and expectations play into their shared transnationality? And is online self-distribution part and parcel of the global, intermedial, and materially impure nature of the films themselves? Will these films eventually be co-opted by market forces and lose their DIY quality? Or could they become a (legitimate) counter-cinema with a transnational reach?

An Approximate Definition of Cell Phone Cinema

Cell phone cinema is, simply put, films (shorts or full-length features, of any category or genre) shot with a cell phone or tablet. It is an ideal format for independent filmmakers in the Global South, given its low cost and ease of distribution, although it is being adapted everywhere as a discrete, portable method for making cinema, whether documentary, fiction, or hybrid genres. Sometimes described as a "mode of minor cinema,"[9] the cell phone has been referred to by prominent filmmakers of the ilk of Christopher Nolan and Steven Soderbergh as the twenty-first-century equivalent of Super 8 in terms of its capacity to reinvent film aesthetics, level access, and reinvigorate cinema in the (not so) new millennium. To this end, several mainstream movies by these and other well-known directors have been filmed with cellular phones. But Hollywood, with its drive toward seamless perfection, large-screen projection, and megadistribution, is not necessarily the most suitable industry for cell phone films. With easy-to-use technology and low production costs as well as open and free distribution via online streaming, cell phone cinema has the potential to democratize access to filmmaking for many who lack access to costly cameras and to the commercial industry. Liberated from the rules and expectations of the commercial industry, cell phone filmmakers can experiment freely and follow their creative impulses, but the same limitations might sideline their work and present it as marginal, deeming it, as scholar Gavin Wilson argues, as a transient or minor cinema.[10] This marginalization, according to Wilson, is made manifest by the fact that "phone films face difficulties in appropriating the industrial and economic/commercial benefits that are often enjoyed by mainstream cinema, placing them fundamentally in a delegitimized position."[11] This position is at times claimed as a badge of authenticity, conferring a counter-cinematic aura to the rough and do-it-yourself nature of the format. To that extent, since cell phone cinema's arrival in the early 2000s, filmmakers across the globe seem to fall into two (sometimes overlapping) camps: those who embrace making films that are low budget, roughly styled, transgressive, and independent; and those who strive for higher production quality to compete with commercial cinema. At times, the same film seems caught in between these poles, between becoming a genuine counter-cinema and wanting to "go mainstream." That is, filmmakers may embrace the DIY ethos but also seek to monetize the films or gain admittance to the larger festivals and mainstream distribution networks. Case in point, Aryan Kaganof's *SMS Sugar Man* (South Africa, 2006) is a DIY first-generation cell film that was initially promoted by its director as a radical low-budget work well suited to the African continent, an example of how to democratize filmmaking (admittedly, the claim of technology's potential to "democratize" is often suspect). Later, the film was transferred to 35 mm for theatrical distribution in order to monetize it.[12] Efforts to reconcile these seemingly opposing tendencies have profound repercussions in the content and aesthetics of cell phone films—works that are made close to the body and that are increasingly intermedial and hybrid (mixing digital and analog elements) and often characterized by a transnational post-digital aesthetic of glitch, digital errors, flickering, pixelation, and other visual distortions. These imperfections have become a stylistic mark of cell phone moviemaking worldwide that distinguishes the mode from its more polished commercial counterparts, regardless of national origin. However, this seemingly antithetical position toward commercial cinema has often wavered, and as the capabilities of cell phones have improved, cell phone cinema has also adopted many aspects of mainstream cinema in terms of its aesthetics, production, and/ or distribution.

No doubt, cell phone films have become profoundly transnational in charac-ter, as the filmmakers submit (and target) them to international festivals and share them on public websites with global audiences, with the aim of reaching the largest possible public—with success measured both by number of hits to their videos and by the enthusiasm of viewer comments. Another evident aspect of their transnational nature is that the movies themselves are frequently the product of cross-cultural themes and collaborations; they are about global con-cerns and feature transnational subjects. Focusing on films made in Spain and Latin America, I note that these works share additional affinities linguistically, culturally, historically, and stylistically. United by a common language (the films are in Spanish, or often in English if not subtitled) and by a shared cultural tra-dition, contemporary Spanish and Latin American cell phone films inform and influence each other. Such transnational and transatlantic mutual impact is also visible in commercial cinema, but in that case the relationship can be fraught with questions of domination and coloniality, as influence seems to flow pre-dominantly from Spain to Latin America, duplicating old patterns of metropole/ colony in terms of the movement of films, money, and technology, granting that

Spanish ascendancy has long been dwarfed by US cultural hegemony in the region. Mainstream feature films by acclaimed directors Guillermo del Toro, Alejandro González Iñárritu, and Alfonso Cuarón come immediately to mind—to mention three eminently transnational Mexican filmmakers who operate within the nexus Mexico–United States–Spain, and who are featured in Deborah Shaw's *The Three Amigos: The Transnational Filmmaking of Guillermo del Toro, Alejandro González Iñárritu, and Alfonso Cuarón* (2013). Such transnationalist tendencies are also present in the DIY productions of cell phone cinema subgenres (predominantly fantasy, horror, and sci-fi) by amateur and virtually unknown filmmakers. Strong affinities and stylistic commonalities notwithstanding, I am not arguing here for the existence of a flattened cell phone cinema that is the same across the Atlantic or even within each country or region, as national elements and local particularities always persist, giving rise to "glocal" works. As Chris Perriam, Isabel Santaolalla, and Peter Evans have suggested, it would be a troubling gesture "to indicate an unproblematic, idealizing and seamless sameness across nations and industries. [...] [Cinematic hybridity...] is not necessarily a breaking free of the boundaries and binds of the national construct."[13] Transnationalism, in other words, coexists with regional distinctiveness and specificity in cell phone cinema—just as it does in other kinds of cinema. In cell phone filmmaking, however, this tension between the transnational and the local is enhanced or further complicated by many other competing impulses, such as the apparent antagonism between amateurism and professionalism or the disjunct between large public screens (festival projection) and small private silicone screens (mobile viewing).

Cell Phone Cinema as a Global, Transnational, and Collective Phenomenon

In Latin America, as in much of the Global South, obtaining access to high-quality digital cameras or to 35 mm equipment is difficult without economic and institutional support. While in Spain such access to technology has been relatively easier, the effects of the global financial crisis in the first decade of the twenty-first century, as well as the recent worldwide industry slowdown during the COVID-19 pandemic, also drove aspiring Spanish filmmakers to use affordable equipment and pursue online distribution. For economic and aesthetic or cultural reasons, especially in Africa, Asia, and Latin America, cell phone cinema has grown in volume and popularity since the 2010s.[14] Film festivals exclusively dedicated to cell phone movies proliferate, with visible venues in places like Paris (the Mobile Film Festival), Barcelona (the Cinephone International Smartphone Short Film Festival), Lisbon (the Super 9 Mobile Film Fest), and San Diego (the International Mobile Film Festival), among others. These festivals promote themselves as global events, encourage entries from all countries, and identify films by national origin, although they compete in the same categories. Global participation is possible at low cost to filmmakers, since the films are typically submitted online, with winners projected at the festival venues and ultimately uploaded to the festival websites. From those websites they are also republished on YouTube and other video platforms, where the movies gain a second life and wider exposure than in their in situ festival screenings. Increasingly, and as another form of reducing cost and encouraging participation, cell phone festivals are taking place fully online.

Despite its evident growth, and in part due to a dearth of research and to the rapid changes in the medium, it is difficult to ascertain the exact quantity of cell phone films in actual numbers, as there is scant statistical information available.[15] There is, however, some anecdotal information about the recent rise of cell phone films, mostly rough counts of films uploaded to YouTube and Vimeo, and the increase in festival submissions. Jan Simons links the single largest increase in cell phone filmic production to the 2005 launching of YouTube and the advent of 3G cell phones equipped with video cameras, so that "DIY movies, many of which are made with cameras built-in to mobile devices or computers, seem to constitute the bulk of YouTube's supply."[16] While Latin America and Spain have not experienced the phenomenon on the scale of Asia or parts of Africa (Nigeria and South Africa are prime examples), it is evident (albeit also anecdotal) that more cell phone cinema is being made in Ibero-America, especially in the Southern Cone and Spain, where most Spanish-language phone film festivals are currently based, but also in Mexico, Brazil, and Colombia.

Each global region has established a distinct relationship with the dominant Hollywood and European cinematic styles, just as aesthetic quality and links to the commercial industry vary. For example, in Asian countries such as South Korea and Japan, the technical quality of cell phone films has reached levels that place it well beyond the typically DIY approaches seen in Latin America, as evidenced by Park Chan-wook's highly polished *Night Fishing* (2011), awarded a

Berlin Golden Bear for short features and shot on the then newly released iPhone 4. Most global cell phone films, however, still privilege narrative concerns over technical proficiency.[17] Filmmakers prefer distribution through online streaming or via participation in film festivals rather than through mainstream production companies, involvement with which is perceived as "selling out."

Case 1: Chilean Cell Phone Found-Footage Horror

Although many early cell phone films from Latin America, dating back to the earliest ones in 2004, displayed a rough style that identified them as low-budget DIY productions, recent works approximate commercial feature quality. This question of style has repercussions in relation to Hollywood cinema, positioning cell films as counter-cinematic or derivative. The film *09 La película* (2014) places the cell phone directly in its title, since 09 is the prefix for dialing cell phones in Chile. Besides itself being made with cell phones, *09* captures the cultural uses cell phones have had throughout the continent, especially regarding their ability to document, to communicate, and, no less important for this film, to entertain. Moreover, the film, distancing itself from DIY cell phone films that reject commercial trappings, adopts many transnational marketing strategies in its efforts to break into the mainstream industry (in effect embracing rather than challenging Hollywood dominance). The film was tactically advertised in Chile as the first feature film made with cell phones anywhere, which is patently false given that the earliest cell phone films appeared in the region a decade earlier, but the claim to originality was used to attract younger audiences looking for novel approaches and to entice investors.

The filmmakers also opted for a subgenre that is attuned to younger audiences and particularly suited for the cell phone, the found-footage horror film. The popularity of the subgenre exploded in the twenty-first century, in part due to a renewed ability to make horror seem more immediate to viewers.[18] This proximity to horror was quite possibly a mass posttraumatic reaction to 9/11 and the War on Terror, or more recently financial crises and global pandemics, tragic events with transnational consequences, which, according to Kevin Wetmore Jr., are the most visually reproduced events in history—especially the disturbing images of the collapsing twin towers. According to Wetmore's *Post-9/11 Horror in American Cinema* (2012), the found-footage aesthetic also tapped into "terrorist-made, internet-dispersed videos of real torture,"[19] which displayed the same characteristic low-grade images that would also become synonymous with cell phone horror, so that reality and fiction blurred.

Similarly, *09* shows the ease with which cell phone cinema can blend with related twenty-first-century popular (global) cultural forms and with the found-footage horror film. The alliance with a highly popular (if trashy) genre combined with an aggressive marketing campaign propelled this cell phone film into mainstream cinemas, although only for a short run on a limited number of screens. Exhibitors were only willing to take a limited chance on a film that remained, despite its commercial intents, on the margins.

Indeed, the filmmaker's intent for *09* had been to create a mainstream commercial film with transnational potential, a product of the easily translatable and placeless horror genre. Rather than uploading a free online version to YouTube or some other streaming venue (a common practice for cell phone cinema, especially shorts), access was restricted to the film's original screening run to bolster theater attendance and a potential DVD deal, which never materialized. Arguably, that failure to enter the mainstream underscores the point that, perhaps, the ideal distribution method for an indie cell film is the Internet, which can still be monetized through advertising but offers free viewing to users. With no DVD distributor and unavailable online, after a short theatrical run, *09* faded from circulation and is now all but forgotten. The film's attempt to bridge amateur and commercial circuits resulted in a double failure, reaching neither audience, sparking only minimal interest within Chile and none abroad. This lack of success perhaps underscores the risk of not fully embracing a DIY ethos that encourages sharing films online to broaden viewership transnationally.

From a technical standpoint, *09* innovated by enlisting its lead actresses to also be camerapersons, each armed with an identical cell phone. Despite its commercial aspirations and professional cast drawn from Chilean soaps, not having designated professional camera technicians allowed *09* to masquerade as a selfie film, a film made by true amateurs. This device predetermined the rough appearance of the film but was well aligned with found-footage genre expectations. Each of the three main characters uses her own phone to film events from a singular perspective, edited into a nonlinear plot that is reminiscent of, but less sophisticated than, films like *Memento* (Christopher Nolan, 2000) or, earlier, *Rashomon* (Akira Kurosawa, 1950). To make sense of the disjointed narrative, the spectator needs to reorder all three cell phone threads, which are presented sequentially so that with each additional perspective we approximate a more complete picture, but only at the film's end do we possess all the information needed to reorganize the disjointed events into a coherent story.

To increase the spectator's disorientation, each actress or cameraperson used a different filming style, so that each point of view could be identified with a particular character—some more restrained (slower and deliberate camera motion), others more risqué (quicker pans, swishes, even abrupt camera rotations and drops). Regardless of whose point of view we experience, however, filming becomes more unreliable, shakier, and less focused as narrative events reach their horrific climax. The first-person POV, which is a staple in transnational found-footage horror filmmaking from any nation and which has become even more prevalent in cell phone movies, is further bolstered by a technique that strengthens spectators' identification with the characters holding the cameras, as well as accentuating a sense of realism, as Xavier Aldana Reyes suggests:

> Found footage horror may further exploit its peculiar aesthetics to bolster this corporeal interaction, for example by including damaged stock that simulates the effects of external attacks on the camera holder or the recording [apparatus]. Destabilization, skipping frames, white squares over a black screen that precedes an immediate and syncopated jump to a [later] scene, bouts of white noise, loud deafening rings accompanying impacts, and degraded or water-damaged images are all utilized to create this sensation and to heighten realism.[20]

But despite its relatively adept recourse to these and other strategies representative of the transnational found-footage subgenre, *09* is noticeably formulaic, even for a film from a genre that often relies on formulas to appeal to global audiences. To briefly summarize, Carolina, Andrea, and Florencia are three college friends spending the weekend at Carolina's parents' secluded vacation home to celebrate her birthday while the parents are away. Although we can ascertain that the place is somewhere in the Chilean countryside, the locale is generic enough to allow for the necessary ambiguity of place that marks another element in transnational found-footage and cell phone horror flicks more broadly; it also connects to the sorts of undefined spaces and places that characterize transnational narratives.

Shortly after arriving, the three friends learn from a news report that a couple has been murdered in a nearby wood, and police are asking locals to hunker down at home until the unknown killers are apprehended. This is where another feature of the transnational found-footage genre is deployed, the need to justify the existence of the found-footage material itself. In this case, Carolina has to complete a project for her journalism class and suggests that the three friends use their cell phones to collectively document the unfolding events. Although initially the women do not expect anything to happen, soon things begin to go awry. Gripping their phones, they record the tense atmosphere and disquieting events that occur in the home and its wooded environs. These include a blend of transnational horror genre classics: strangers arriving and pleading for help as they flee an undisclosed threat, terrifying noises and manifestations of the supernatural in the middle of the night, and eventually several violent murders by unseen and ghostly assailants, all of it set in an undefined location. The transnational appeal of the film resides in these tried-and-true genre devices, which are recognized across the globe and fulfill audience expectations.

More captivating than the anemic storyline is the film's cinema verité aesthetic. The postproduction editing retains the rough, trial-and-error filming style of the three protagonists. In fact, the rough appearance is in part a by-product of the now dated phone technology, but also a deliberate effect. The actresses were *trained* to use their phones so the filming looks spontaneous and amateur-like, and in postproduction the raw material was further manipulated to enhance the appearance of spontaneity, to induce a kind of "reality" effect. The seemingly unrehearsed (but carefully scripted) dialogue also constructs the illusion of immediacy and authenticity, as though the spectators were seeing actual footage from a crime investigation. The production of authenticity is not only predetermined by the cell phone aesthetic but also dovetails with the twenty-first-century transnational horror genre, which Aldana Reyes identifies as having a "documentary treatment" that in turn shapes narrative structure.[21] In 09, this documentary or reality effect is salient in scenes that favor the capture of a supposedly unmediated reality over a more polished finished appearance.

The sense of falsified authenticity is also achieved, for example, by underscoring the illusion that cell phones are neutral, objective tools that record and archive real-time events without altering them; thus, we see footage from a phone that fell on the floor, strange angles as phones are held while running, and generally a close correspondence between subject and phone. Given the phone's shared context as a tool also used for citizen reportage during national events (a strategy deployed in various global conflicts, from the Arab Spring to the George Floyd protests and the Chilean student marches), the cell phone fiction flick can help us realize how easy it is to manipulate recorded material, and it illustrates how the aesthetic of glitch and pixilation itself can serve to authenticate manipulated narratives. The films show that cell phones are not in any way an essential technology for truth telling any more or less than other video-capturing devices. While cell phone video can prove useful in documenting real-life events (human rights abuses, police brutality, political scandals, etc.), there are concerns regarding deepfakes and other less sophisticated forms of video tampering. That said, video authentication is possible, and the ubiquity and proliferation of cell phones have also meant that events are often captured from multiple perspectives, approximating them to eyewitness testimony in terms of evidentiary value. Of course, presenting an event from multiple perspectives can also cast doubt on the absolute reliability of interpreting recorded images, even when they are not tampered with. In *09*, the suggestion of an unmediated reality before the spectator is also at odds with the subjective POV perspective offered by the individual segments filmed by each of the protagonists. Despite the conflict between objective and subjective camera use, a deliberately roughened style continues to act as a certification of reality, precisely because it diverges from the polished aesthetic of fictional Hollywood cinema and is seen as closer to surveillance footage, home videos, and citizen journalism.

Emphasizing the transnational framework of cell phone horror cinema as well as its antecedents in found footage, Javier Aguirrezábal, who directed *09*, enumerates as precursors independent horror films such as *The Blair Witch Project*, the Spanish franchise *[·REC]* (Jaume Balagueró and Paco Plaza, 2007), and the Uruguayan film *La casa muda* (The Silent House, Gustavo Hernández, 2010). Made with cheap recording equipment (video and photo cameras, cell phones, tablets), these films rely on shaky handheld camerawork, display a glitchy and degraded aesthetic motivated by the found nature of their footage, and purport to have been filmed by untrained amateurs, often the protagonists themselves— all of it in an effort to blur the line between reality and fiction. In these global genre movies, the protagonists insist that they are not actors but just people recording events from their daily lives—a stipulation that is made more plausible in the case of cell phone cinema when the films are housed at streaming sites such as YouTube and not clearly labeled as fictional narratives.

Found-footage films, regardless of how they are distributed and filmed, share stylistic traits that cross national boundaries and emulate the mediation of real life, reflecting the presence of violence in contemporary media.[22] Moreover, the films prominently feature and justify the recording devices within the narratives, to make clear how the recording came about and to assert the very real existence of the protagonists, purported to be real people who may or may not be alive as spectators watch the footage later. Interestingly, these transnational films present an ambiguous temporality in which the action seems to take place at once in real time (providing a sense of immediacy) while at the same time patently after the fact (as the footage predates its viewing). These films are also related to the snuff genre, which depicts disturbing violence (including murder, torture, suicide, and the like) while presenting the material as authentic (but unconfirmed as such), fulfilling our fascination with the macabre and grotesque. Both the availability of cell phones and the existence of video sharing platforms like YouTube, and now the brevity afforded by TikTok, have accelerated the proliferation of horror and snuff, since, as film critic Mary Beth McAndrews observes, "the short-form video app [TikTok] is all about the mobile experience, making micro horror films accessible wherever, whenever."[23] While every film genre attempts to immerse spectators in a convincing fantasy world, these particular transnational horror films rely on the titillating ambiguity, in the potential crossover between the real and the fictional worlds, between the simultaneity and the belatedness of their temporality. In cell phone cinema, this crossover effect will be exploited with full force (as we will see in *iMedium*, the next film I analyze) once the films activate the communication capabilities of the phone, going as far as sending text messages, images, or videos to the viewers.

Although *09* sought (unsuccessfully) to position itself as a commercially viable film, rather than embracing an amateur distribution approach (like the next film I examine), it nevertheless partook of many of the elements of the transnational cell phone cinema ethos. It did not reach a transnational audience (barely a Chilean one), but it is, undoubtedly, a transnational horror cell film in its aesthetics and its mode of address. The film also demonstrates that cell phone cinema retains a perceived (if not actual) connection to the real, one that aligns with the generalized belief that today everything is being filmed and surveilled, and indeed the unsettling acceptance that only mediation makes an event readable as reality. If we cannot view something through our phones, if it is not recorded or, better yet, live-streamed on a social media or video sharing site, it does not seem immediate, proximate, or real—even when that sense of immediacy, presence, and nowness is wholly manufactured. Furthermore, the persistence of the grainy and pixelated image that somehow authenticates what is on screen can also be associated with the very tangible and evidentiary violence that is being captured by mobile devices across the globe today, from the by now historical 9/11 videos, to filmed abuses against pro-democracy activists during the Arab Spring, to the horrors of the Syrian conflict and the Ukraine war, to the Chilean student demonstrations, to recent videos capturing police violence toward people of color in the United States, and a long list of other amateur cell phone videos documenting everyday violence. The cell phone horror genre is a reflection and a symptom of these more authentic horrors.

Case 2: *iMedium*, Haunted Apps, and the Spanish (Global) Horror Cell Film

Cell phone cinema production in Spain, as in Latin America, has attained remarkable quality since the 2010s, with outstanding filmmakers such as Conrad Mess, Carlos J. Marín, and Alfonso García López, among others. To establish a contrast with *09 La película*, I focus on a self-referential film that is representative of the global panorama of mobile horror cinema, *iMedium* (2018), a short by Alfonso García López (b. 1974, Madrid) and scriptwriter Vicente Rubio (b. 1975, Tarragona, Spain). As with *09*, there is a trend in horror films that focus self-reflexively on technology as a locus for the uncanny. Kimberly Jackson refers to self-aware films as meta-horror and attributes their proliferation to the near exhaustion and predictability of horror genre plots, coupled with contemporary concerns "with the relationship between media and message."[24] *iMedium* signals its self-reflexive imbrication with smartphones from its title, with its conspicuous lowercase *i* that subverts the Apple branding scheme in a not-so-subtle anticorporatist gesture. The *i* indicates the Internet but also mocks the cult-like brand loyalty that enabled Apple's near-monopoly grip over the tech industry and over a media culture it shapes after its own image.[25] Turning toward technoskepticism and resistance, García López's film sabotages this fiction of sleek perfection and seamless integration between human and device. Ironically, García

López renders his critique of out-of-control technology with the (then) latest iPhone. The contradiction is not lost on the filmmaker, whose films repeatedly stage the theme of technology gone awry or becoming self-aware, a fear enhanced by popular fictions about sentient AI. García López's critique of technocapitalism incorporates a resigned acknowledgment of the inescapable commercialization of everything, even the afterlife. Resistance to transnational capitalism, he suggests, is futile.

Shot mostly in first-person point of view, the six-minute short opens as its protagonist, middle-aged Luz, is accessing a phone app that allows users to contact the dead. The film dizzyingly alternates between three types of subjectivity: Luz's first-person subjective POV, a second POV located within the phone screen (from the ghostly perspective of Alicia, Luz's missing daughter), and objective "cheat" shots that are not associated with any characters or motivated by the phone but that provide contextual information. The initial images show the distraught Luz searching for Alicia, absent from home for several days. Fearing the worst, Luz initiates a digital séance by clicking on the iMedium app. A soothing Siri-like voice reassures the protagonist that she will shortly establish contact with the beyond. The uncanny robotic voice reinforces a recurring filmic trope that genders horrifying technologies as female. Connecting with Alicia through the app, Luz realizes that her daughter is dead. The scene's jumpy and unfocused framing reflects Luz's terrified state. In a characteristic handheld cell phone sequence, fragmented, off-kilter, and extreme close-ups of Luz's face alternate with dizzying swish pans of her daughter's poorly lit bedroom. The frantic, unsteady framing, consistent with the cell phone horror genre, echoes Luz's distress and obstructs a full view of what is happening onscreen. Instead, García López makes the most of off-screen space to trigger the spectator's fears. Through the app, Alicia, amid horrifying screams, begins to recount her abduction. Just at that critical moment, Luz's husband enters the room and the app goes silent. As Luz disjointedly explains to her spouse what happened, he accuses her of having gone insane. The situation is complicated, therefore, by the possibility of an unreliable first-person narrator (Luz). The scene cuts to Luz wielding a knife, suddenly covered in blood, perhaps from slicing herself off-screen. Luz then threatens her husband and flees from the house to search for her daughter. The disorienting scene is rendered more dizzying by the uncomfortable proximity of the images to Luz's body and the sudden shifts of focus and framing—this close-to-the-body style a staple of global cell phone films. The iMedium app eventually leads Luz to a secluded forest, where she discovers Alicia's body. In yet another deranged twist, Alicia, still speaking through the app, accuses her father of having sexually abused and murdered her. In the film's grizzly conclusion, Luz's husband arrives at the scene and, confronted with his deeds, kills and buries his wife next to his daughter. In the closing scene we see him accessing the app to ask the deceased Luz for forgiveness, providing a sense of macabre circularity to the film and suggesting a new cycle of technohorror to come.

Beyond its disturbing narrative, iMedium is a skillfully accomplished short that nevertheless maintains a roughened surface style. Not a newcomer to amateur film, García López is the director of several award-winning sci-fi and horror cell phone shorts, showcased at transnational festivals like the fantasy and horror Mórbido in Mexico City (established in 2007) and the International Sitges Film Festival near Barcelona (operating since 1967).[26] García López's work shares much, aesthetically and thematically, with Latin American cell phone horror films, underscoring the transnational characteristics of the modality and the cross-pollination that comes from sharing films online. Almost all of García López's films combine sci-fi and horror, integrating the device of the cell phone and related technologies within the storyline itself, at times either as the apparatus that is conspicuously filming what is happening—as a live-streaming version of found footage—or as the technology that precipitates the unhappy end. García López typically rigs the cell phone with auxiliary devices that approximate its standards closer to commercial cinema but also expose the experimental and precarious assemblage he is working with. The filmmaker attaches special lenses, stabilizers, batteries, lights, and sound equipment, using common household items such as duct tape or screws to fasten these makeshift recording peripherals to the cell phone and thus creating a Franken-camera, which he sometimes attaches to roller skates to facilitate traveling shots.[27]

Returning to iMedium, its strong point is how closely the film's storyline ties with its decidedly mobile, shifting, and almost low-grade aesthetic, with its constant changes of location, perspective, and lighting. iMedium's sinister storyline about a mobile phone app that can connect us directly with the dead is also fully consistent with the technohorror subgenre, broadly defined as "those artworks exploring the potentially disquieting negotiations humans enter into with our tools, machines and social structures."[28] Bringing an app into the narrative foregrounds another function of cellular phones we did not see in the *09* example, one that investigates the capacity for mobile software to develop sentience, become evil, or simply malfunction. The mobile dimension associated with these apps enhances the sensation of an evil that is unescapable since it is, quite literally, in our pockets, or even prosthetically attached to us.

The transnational nature of these plots is patent. The idea of centering a horror film around an app is not original to *iMedium*, since the Dutch full-length feature *App* (2013) by Bobby Boermans (b. 1981, Eindhoven, Netherlands) plays with a similar concept. In this thriller, an AI interface app called Iris (in reference to Siri) becomes sentient and malevolent, thus emulating a long line of uncanny precursors and exploiting the psychosocial dread of the vanishing boundaries separating humans and technology. *App* has an additional gimmick, however, which is that, when viewed at a movie theater (or in DVD format), semipersonalized messages (supposedly) from Iris and synchronized with the film are sent to the spectators who downloaded the app designed for this purpose. The strategy serves to recruit a second interactive screen, creating a form of expanded cinema that combines the theater screen with the silicone one. The app is meant to further enhance the sensation of horror and the immediacy of the evil presence, now reaching into the spectator's pocket and speaking to them individually, provided the user has enabled geolocation and entered their name into their device (thus ensuring their own demise). As with social media horror in general, these films elicit, through their recourse to a second screen, a sensation of vulnerability that is linked to the proximity of the device to our bodies, and possibly to our minds (and perhaps less dramatically, gestures to issues of privacy loss).

Although *iMedium* does not reach *App*'s level of technical sophistication, with the addition of a Facebook page that promotes the (fictional) *iMedium* app as if it were a real application, the filmmakers broadened the universe of the film beyond its original cinematic space—or that of its online uploaded version—in a sense disrupting the linearity of the film by introducing paratextual materials that the viewer can choose to interact with before, during, or after seeing the short. The Facebook page provides a social dimension, since it includes comments from viewers and readers, many of them in Spanish and written by members of global diasporic communities (Spanish abroad, but also Latin Americans and others). The global circulation of cultural materials from "home" adds a sense of cultural connection to these Facebook users. In addition to whatever goal the paratextual material may fulfill in terms of enhancing the viewing experience, including its added social dimension, it serves additional purposes. On the Facebook page, one can view several promotional videos for the fake application, including a realistic-looking advertisement and some faux reaction videos portraying people speaking with their dead loved ones. While some of this extra material may function as a marketing ploy to engage interest among those who have not yet seen the film, it also serves as a not-so-veiled critique against the predatory proliferation of psychic mediums, fortune-tellers, and card readers in the Spanish mediascape, most conspicuously seen on television but also present in radio and on the Internet.

In sum, *iMedium* reflects a transnational trend in mobile films that critique the self-centered individualism and commodification not only of personal relations but even of the human subject, paradoxically exacerbated by the penetration of digital technologies into every aspect of our lives. These symptoms are on display in social media practices, from the intrusiveness of social and messaging apps to the self-absorbed obsession with selfie videos and the contrived manufacture of a virtual self for public consumption in online platforms, all to the detriment of a direct engagement with the physical world and its material problems.

In these technohorror films, cell phone communications become disrupted, apps malfunction, and subservience to technology often leads to self-destruction. Internet and social media technologies, along with cell phones, are presented not as assets that link us together and bring us into closer contact but as destabilizing and alienating tools that dehumanize us, pushing us toward greater anonymity and loneliness rather than collectivity. As phone apps such as *iMedium* become haunted, rather than connecting us with a spiritual beyond or with each other, these "cursed" technologies lead to death, despair, and isolation, underscoring the irony of our affective separation from each other in a virtually interconnected yet artificial reality. These are, of course, global problems related to connectivity and the lack thereof, not between devices but between humans— something the pandemic brought to the fore. I would argue that these films oscillate wildly between the optimism of creating with a malleable device, one that allows for greater intimacy and immediacy between filmmaker and subject filmed, and a sense of horror at the dangers such technologies may represent as they replace other forms of interpersonal associations.

The Future(s) of Transnational Cell Phone Cinema in Latin America and Spain

As these films show, cell phone cinema raises utopian expectations of access and distribution for all, of media democratization, and of unleashed creative potential, but it also reflects dystopian concerns about surveillance, criminality, and technological determinism. The format has a global reach and transnational implications. It has helped to revitalize amateur filmmaking in Latin America and Spain, providing a new tool for fiction, documentary, experimental, animation, and other uncategorized types of filmmaking. It has also facilitated an exchange of ideas and styles across national boundaries, as the films themselves are most often distributed online or at international festivals. Such transnational trends, however, have not erased the presence of national elements in the films. At a time when mainstream commercial Spanish-language cinema has become fully transnational and tapped into major international festivals (Berlin, New York, Toronto) and global markets, cell phone cinema, with its preference for subgenres like horror and sci-fi, still maintains some, if limited, ties to local cultural practices (smaller film festivals, cult viewership, home projections) even as, in some cases, it aspires toward greater access to commercial screens. Not all films are successful in being innovative; some, like *09 La película*, are mostly imitative of established formats and genres, failing to take full advantage of the possibilities offered by the cell phone camera or by online distribution platforms. Others, such as *iMedium*, seek to expand beyond a single screen and redefine the idea of cinematic space. Cell phone cinema therefore balances a set of transnational and local features, negotiating them at the level of form—by deliberately promoting or rejecting a roughened cell phone style—and at the level of content, by returning time and again to questions related to the emergence of cell phones as documentation devices, to the presence of surveillance technologies, and to the precarious status of amateur filmmakers.

Notes

1. To name a few of the more salient volumes dedicated exclusively or in part to cinema in a transnational context, we might mention Hamid Naficy, *An Accented Cinema: Exilic and Diasporic Filmmaking* (Princeton University Press, 2001); Stephanie Dennison and Song Hwee Lim, eds., *Remapping World Cinema: Identity, Culture and Politics in*

Film (Wallflower Press, 2006); Nataša Ďurovičová and Kathleen Newman, eds., *World Cinemas, Transnational Perspectives* (Routledge, 2010); Stephanie Dennison, *Contemporary Hispanic Cinema: Interrogating Transnationalism in Spanish and Latin American Film* (Woodbridge, Suff., England: Boydell and Brewer, 2013); Manuel Palacio and Jörg Türschmann, eds., *Transnational Cinema in Europe* (Münster, Germany: LIT Verlag, 2013); Samuel Amago, *Spanish Cinema in the Global Context: Film on Film* (Routledge, 2013); Steven Rawle, *Transnational Cinema: An Introduction* (Palgrave, 2017); Sophia A. McClennen, *Globalization and Latin American Cinema: Toward a New Critical Paradigm* (Cham, Switzerland: Palgrave Macmillan, 2018); Elizabeth Ezra and Terry Rowden, eds., *Transnational Cinema: The Film Reader* (Abingdon, Oxon., England: Routledge, 2006); Dolores Tierney, *New Transnationalisms in Contemporary Latin American Cinemas* (Edinburgh University Press, 2018); Robert Stam, *World Literature, Transnational Cinema, and Global Media: Towards a Transartistic Commons* (Abingdon, Oxon., England: Routledge, 2019); Cecilia Enjuto-Rangel, Sebastiaan Faber, Pedro García-Caro, and Robert Patrick Newcomb, eds., *Transatlantic Studies: Latin America, Iberia, and Africa* (Liverpool University Press, 2019); and Armida de la Garza, Deborah Shaw, and Ruth Doughty, eds., *Transnational Screens: Expanding the Borders of Transnational Cinema* (Abingdon, Oxon., England: Routledge, 2020); and the more recent *Cinema and Soft Power: Configuring the National and Transnational in Geo-Politics*, edited by Stephanie Dennison and Rachel Dwyer (Edinburgh University Press, 2021), or my own *Expanding Cinemas: Experimental Filmmaking Across the Luso-Hispanic Atlantic Since 1960* (State University of New York Press, 2024).

2. Austin Fisher and Iain Robert Smith, "Transnational Cinemas: A Critical Roundtable," *Frames Cinema Journal*, no. 9 (2016): 27.

3. Austin Fisher and Iain Robert Smith, "Second Phase Transnationalism: Reflections on Launching the SCMS Transnational Cinemas Scholarly Interest Group," *Transnational Screens* 10, no. 2 (2019): 114.

4. Scholarship on film festival networks has not picked up on cell phone movies, either. For example, in Marijke de Valck, Brendan Kredell, and Skadi Loist's edited volume *Film Festivals: History, Theory, Method, Practice* (Abingdon, Oxon., England: Routledge, 2016), there is not a single mention, although several chapters dwell on the transnationalism of the festival circuits and the festival space.

5. Chris Perriam, Isabel Santaolalla, and Peter W. Evans, "The Transnational in Iberian and Latin American Cinemas: Editors' Introduction," *Hispanic Research Journal* 8, no. 1 (2007): 4.

6. Lúcia Nagib, "Towards a Positive Definition of World Cinema," in *Remapping World Cinema: Identity, Culture and Politics in Film*, ed. Stephanie Dennison and Song Hwee Lim (Wallflower Press, 2006), 32.

7. Programa Ibermedia (or just Ibermedia) is a collective coproduction film fund and funding mechanism financed primarily by Spain (where it is housed), but also by Portugal, Italy, Puerto Rico, and a group of fifteen Latin American nations as of 2022. See their website at https://www.programaibermedia.com/el-programa/. For an in-depth analysis, see Tamara

Falicov, "Programa Ibermedia: Co-Production and the Cultural Politics of Constructing an Ibero-American Audiovisual Space," *Spectator* 27, no. 2 (Fall 2007): 21–30.

8. Fisher and Smith, "Second Phase Transnationalism," 118.

9. Gavin Wilson, "Film Festival Participation and Identity Formation: Non-Professional Creativity and the Pleasures of Mobile Phone Filmmaking," in *Discourses of (De)Legitimization: Participatory Culture in Digital Contexts*, ed. Andrew S. Ross and Damian J. Rivers (Routledge, 2019), 289.

10. Gavin Wilson, "Cell/ular Cinema: Individuated Production, Public Sharing and Mobile Phone Film Exhibition" (PhD thesis, University of Leeds, 2015), 89, http://etheses.whiterose.ac.uk/8475/.

11. Wilson, "Film Festival Participation," 289.

12. Christopher de Jager, "Helmer Phones It In with Cell-Shot Feature," *Variety*, February 13–19, 2006, 26.

13. Perriam, Santaolalla, and Evans, "The Transnational in Iberian and Latin American Cinemas," 4.

14. Roger Odin, "Spectator, Film and the Mobile Phone," in *Audiences: Defining and Researching Screen Entertainment Reception*, ed. Ian Christie (Amsterdam University Press, 2012), 162.

15. To the best of my knowledge, there are no significant statistical studies tracking the production of cell films. That includes research accounting for number of releases, video site views or downloads, sold copies (rare, since most films are freely distributed), box office sales (rarer still, since outside of festivals, commercial screening is highly unusual), or any such data that is available for mainstream films.

16. Jan Simons, "Between iPhone and YouTube: Movies on the Move?," in *Video Vortex Reader II: Moving Images Beyond YouTube*, ed. Geert Lovink and Rachel Somers Miles (Institute of Network Cultures, 2011), 95.

17. Wilson, "Film Festival Participation," 3.

18. Xavier Aldana Reyes, "Reel Evil: A Critical Reassessment of Found Footage Horror," *Gothic Studies* 17, no. 2 (November 2015): 123.

19. Kevin J. Wetmore Jr., *Post-9/11 Horror in American Cinema* (Continuum, 2012), 59.

20. Aldana Reyes, "Reel Evil," 130.

21. Aldana Reyes, "Reel Evil," 123.

22. Aldana Reyes, "Reel Evil," 124.

23. Mary Beth McAndrews, "Horror TikTok Solidifies Found Footage's Evolution into Digitally Discovered Horror," *Paste*, January 6, 2021, https://www.pastemagazine.com/movies/horror-movies/tiktok-digitally-discovered-horror.

24. Kimberly Jackson, *Technology, Monstrosity, and Reproduction in Twenty-First Century Horror* (Palgrave Macmillan, 2013), 2.

25. As such, the *i* prefix is synonymous with the latest gadgets and sleekest designs but also with unbounded corporate interest and a vast tech empire, reflected by the specular and infinite multiplication of the *i* (iMac, iPod, iBook, iPhone, iPad, iCloud, iOS, and so on).

26. Javier Cabrera, "Alfonso García: 'Tan respetable es hacer una película con móvil como con 35 mm,'" El Taller Audiovisual, October 21, 2014, https://eltalleraudiovisual.com/alfonso-garcia-entrevista/.

27. "Monográfico de geofilms," La Sala Tarambana, February 17, 2017, https://www.tarambana.net/espectaculos/monografico-de-geofilms/.

28. Daniel Powell, *Horror Culture in the New Millennium: Digital Dissonance and Technohorror* (Lexington Books, 2018), 22.

Bibliography

Akhtar, Salman. *Immigration and Identity: Turmoil, Treatment, and Transformation.* Jason Aronson, 1999.

Akhtar, Salman. "A Third Individuation: Immigration, Identity, and the Psychoanalytic Process." *Journal of the American Psychoanalytic Association* 43, no. 4 (August 1995): 1051–84.

Alba, Francisco. "Comercio, migración y esquemas de integración económica: Los casos de la CEE y el TLCAN." *Foro Internacional* 41, no. 2 (April–June 2001): 299–308.

Alba, Richard D., and Victor Nee. *Remaking the American Mainstream: Assimilation and Contemporary Immigration.* Harvard University Press, 2003.

Albó, Xavier. "And from Kataristas to MNRistas? The Surprising and Bold Alliance Between Aymaras and Neoliberals in Bolivia." In *Indigenous Peoples and Democracy in Latin America,* edited by Donna Lee Van Cott, 55–81. Palgrave Macmillan, 1994.

Albó, Xavier. "Making the Leap from Local Mobilization to National Politics." *NACLA Report on the Americas* 29, no. 5 (March–April 1996): 15–20.

Albó, Xavier. "El retorno del indio." *Revista Andina* 9, no. 2 (1991): 299–345.

Albro, Robert. "The Indigenous in the Plural in Bolivian Oppositional Politics." *Bulletin of Latin American Research* 24, no. 4 (October 2005): 433–53.

Alemán, Gabriela. "At the Margin of the Margins: Contemporary Ecuadorian Exploitation Cinema and the Local Pirate Market." In *Latsploitation, Exploitation Cinemas, and Latin America,* edited by Victoria Ruétalo and Dolores Tierney, 261–74. Routledge, 2009.

Alia, Valerie. *The New Media Nation: Indigenous Peoples and Global Communication.* Berghahn Books, 2010.

Allen, Chadwick. *Trans-Indigenous: Methodologies for Global Native Literary Studies.* University of Minnesota Press, 2012.

Alvarez, Sonia E. "Advocating Feminism: The Latin American Feminist NGO 'Boom.'" *International Feminist Journal of Politics* 1, no. 2 (1999): 181–209.

Alvarez, Sonia E. "Para além da sociedade civil: Reflexões sobre o campo feminista." *Cadernos Pagu* 43 (July–December 2014): 13–56.

Alvarez, Sonia E., Elisabeth Jay Friedman, Ericka Beckman, Maylei Blackwell, Norma Stoltz Chinchilla, Nathalie Lebon, Marysa Navarro, and Marcela Ríos Tobar. "Encountering Latin American and Caribbean Feminisms." *Signs* 28, no. 2 (Winter 2003): 537–79.

Alvear, Miguel, and Christian León. *Ecuador Bajo Tierra: Videografías en circulación paralela.* Ochoymedio, 2009.

Amago, Samuel. *Spanish Cinema in the Global Context: Film on Film.* New York: Routledge, 2013.

Amaral, Aiko Ikemura. "Making Money and Ends Meet: Racialization, Work, and Gender Among Bolivian Market Vendors." In *Urban Indigeneities: Being Indigenous in the 21st Century*, edited by Dana Brablec and Andrew Canessa, 93–118. University of Arizona Press, 2023.

Anderson, Benedict. *Imagined Communities: Reflections on the Origin and Spread of Nationalism.* Verso, 1983.

Anderson, Benedict. *Long-Distance Nationalism: World Capitalism and the Rise of Identity Politics.* Centre for Asian Studies, 1992.

Aparicio, Frances R. "Reading the 'Latino' in Latino Studies: Toward Re-Imagining Our Academic Location." *Discourse* 21, no. 3 (Fall 1999): 3–18.

Appadurai, Arjun, ed. *Globalization.* Duke University Press, 2001.

Appadurai, Arjun. *Modernity at Large: Cultural Dimensions of Globalization.* University of Minnesota Press, 1996.

Appadurai, Arjun. "Patriotism and Its Futures." *Public Culture* 5, no. 3 (Spring 1993): 411–29.

Appiah, Kwame Anthony. "Cosmopolitan Patriots." In *Cosmopolitics: Thinking and Feeling Beyond the Nation*, edited by Pheng Cheah and Bruce Robbins, 91–114. University of Minnesota Press, 1998.

Appiah, Kwame Anthony. *The Ethics of Identity.* Princeton University Press, 2005.

Ardao, Arturo. *Génesis de la idea y el nombre de América Latina.* Centro de Estudios Latinoamericanos Rómulo Gallegos, 1980.

Ari, Waskar. *Earth Politics: Religion, Decolonization, and Bolivia's Indigenous Intellectuals.* Duke University Press, 2014.

Ashcroft, Bill. "Chicano Transnation." In *Imagined Transnationalism: U.S. Latino/a Literature, Culture, and Identity*, edited by Kevin Concannon, Francisco A. Lomelí, and Marc Priewe, 13–28. Palgrave Macmillan, 2009.

Austerlitz, Paul. "From Transplant to Transnational Circuit: Merengue in New York." In *Island Sounds in the Global City: Caribbean Popular Music and Identity in New York*, edited by Ray Allen and Lois Wilcken, 44–60. University of Illinois Press, 1998.

Austerlitz, Paul. *Merengue: Dominican Music and Dominican Identity.* Temple University Press, 1997.

Avelar, Idelber. "Five Theses on Torture." *Journal of Latin American Cultural Studies* 10, no. 3 (2001): 253–71.

Averill, Gage. *A Day for the Hunter, a Day for the Prey: Popular Music and Power in Haiti.* University of Chicago Press, 1997.

Bakhtin, Mikhail. *The Dialogic Imagination: Four Essays.* Edited by Michael Holquist. Translated by Caryl Emerson and Michael Holquist. University of Texas Press, 1981.

Bal, Mieke. *Travelling Concepts in the Humanities: A Rough Guide.* University of Toronto Press, 2002.

Balardini, Lorena, Ana Oberlin, and Laura Sobredo. "Violencia de género y abusos sexuales en centros clandestinos de detención: Un aporte a la comprensión de la experiencia argentina." In *Hacer justicia: Nuevos debates sobre el juzgamiento de crímenes de lesa humanidad en la Argentina*, edited by Centro de Estudios Legales y Sociales and Centro Internacional para la Justicia Transicional, 97–118. Siglo XXI Editores, 2011.

Barrera Enderle, Víctor. "Entradas y salidas del fenómeno literario actual o la 'alfaguarización' de la literatura hispanoamericana." In *Ensayos sobre literatura y culturas latinoamericanas*, 91–111. LOM Ediciones, 2002.

Barth, Fredrik, ed. *Ethnic Groups and Boundaries: The Social Organization of Culture Difference*. Universitetsforlaget, 1969.

Basch, Linda, Nina Glick Schiller, and Cristina Szanton Blanc. *Nations Unbound: Transnational Projects, Postcolonial Predicaments, and Deterritorialized Nation-States*. Gordon and Breach, 1994.

Bassnett, Susan, and Harish Trivedi, eds. *Postcolonial Translation: Theory and Practice*. Routledge, 1999.

Bayly, Christopher A., Sven Beckert, Matthew Connelly, Isabel Hofmeyr, Wendy Kozol, and Patricia Seed. "*AHR* Conversation: On Transnational History." *American Historical Review* 111, no. 5 (December 2006): 1441–64.

Behnke, Elizabeth A. "Ghost Gestures: Phenomenological Investigations of Bodily Micromovements and Their Intercorporeal Implications." *Human Studies* 20, no. 2 (April 1997): 181–201.

Bell, Christopher. *East Harlem Remembered: Oral Histories of Community and Diversity*. McFarland, 2013.

Belotti, Francesca, Francesca Comunello, and Consuelo Corradi. "*Feminicidio* and #NiUnaMenos: An Analysis of Twitter Conversations During the First 3 Years of the Argentinean Movement." *Violence Against Women* 27, no. 8 (2021): 1035–63.

Benjamin, Ruha. *Race After Technology: Abolitionist Tools for the New Jim Code*. Polity Press, 2019.

Benkler, Yochai. *The Wealth of Networks: How Social Production Transforms Markets and Freedom*. Yale University Press, 2006.

Bennett, Jane. *Vibrant Matter: A Political Ecology of Things*. Duke University Press, 2010.

Berkovitch, Nitza. *From Motherhood to Citizenship: Women's Rights and International Organizations*. Johns Hopkins University Press, 2002.

Besserer, Federico. *Topografías transnacionales: Hacia una geografía de la vida transnacional*. Universidad Autónoma Metropolitana, Iztapalapa; Plaza y Valdés Editores, 2004.

Bilbao, Bárbara Soledad. "Violencia de género en los juicios del pasado y del presente." *Question / Cuestión* 1, no. 31 (September 2011): n.p.

Bilbija, Ksenija, Ana Forcinito, and Bernardita Llanos, eds. *Poner el cuerpo: Rescatar y visibilizar las marcas sexuales y de género de los archivos dictatoriales del Cono Sur*. Editorial Cuarto Propio, 2017.

Bimber, Bruce. "Three Prompts for Collective Action in the Context of Digital Media." *Political Communication* 34, no. 1 (2017): 6–20.

Biron, Rebecca E. "It's a Living: Hit Men in the Mexican Narco War." *PMLA* 127, no. 4 (October 2012): 820–34.

Blancpain, Jean-Pierre. *Migrations et mémoires germaniques en Amérique latine*. Presses Universitaires de Strasbourg, 1994.

Blancpain, Jean-Pierre. "Des visées pangermanistes au noyautage hitlérien: Le nationalisme allemand et l'Amérique latine (1890–1945)." *Revue Historique* 281, no. 2 (1990): 433–82.

Blumenthal, Edward. "Droit d'asile, droit d'expulsion et représentations de l'exilé en Amérique du Sud au XIXe siècle." *Diasporas: Circulations, Migrations, Histoire*, no. 33 (2019): 91–103.

Blumenthal, Edward. *Exile and Nation-State Formation in Argentina and Chile, 1810–1862*. Palgrave Macmillan, 2019.

Bodnar, John. *The Transplanted: A History of Immigrants in Urban America*. Indiana University Press, 1985.

Boehm, Deborah A. *Intimate Migrations: Gender, Family, and Illegality Among Transnational Mexicans*. New York University Press, 2012.

Boggia, Sofía. "Un violador en tu camino: La simbología y la historia." *Actualidad a Diario*, December 9, 2019. https://www.actualidadadiario.com/index.php/2019/12/09/un-violador-en-tu-camino-la-simbologia-y-la-historia/.

Bott, Sarah, Alessandra Guedes, Ana P. Ruiz-Celis, and Jennifer Adams Mendoza. "Intimate Partner Violence in the Americas: A Systematic Review and Reanalysis of National Prevalence Estimates." *Revista Panamericana de Salud Pública* 43 (2018).

Bourdieu, Pierre. *The Rules of Art: Genesis and Structure of the Literary Field*. Translated by Susan Emanuel. Stanford University Press, 1996.

Bourdieu, Pierre. *The State Nobility: Elite Schools in the Field of Power*. Translated by Lauretta C. Clough. Polity Press, 1996.

Bourdieu, Pierre, and Abdelmalek Sayad. *Le déracinement: La crise de l'agriculture traditionnelle en Algérie*. Éditions de Minuit, 1964.

Bourdieu, Pierre, and Loïc Wacquant. "The Organic Ethnologist of Algerian Migration." *Ethnography* 1, no. 2 (December 2000): 173–82.

Bourne, Randolph S. "Trans-National America." *Atlantic Monthly* 118, no. 1 (July 1916): 86–97.

Brablec, Dana, and Andrew Canessa, eds. *Urban Indigeneities: Being Indigenous in the 21st Century*. University of Arizona Press, 2023.

Brands, Hal. *Latin America's Cold War*. Harvard University Press, 2010.

Braun, Yvonne A., and Michael C. Dreiling. "Networking for Women's Rights: Academic Centers, Regional Information Networks, and Feminist Advocacy in Southern Africa." *International Feminist Journal of Politics* 21, no. 1 (2018): 89–110.

Brepohl de Magalhães, Marionilde. *Pangermanismo e Nazismo: A trajetória alemã rumo ao Brasil*. Editora da Unicamp; São Paulo: Fundação de Amparo à Pesquisa do Estado, 1998.

Brescia, Raymond H. "The Strength of Digital Ties: Virtual Networks, Norm-Generating Communities, and Collective Action Problems." *Dickinson Law Review* 122, no. 2 (Winter 2018): 479–549.

Briggs, Laura. *Reproducing Empire: Race, Sex, Science, and U.S. Imperialism in Puerto Rico*. University of California Press, 2002.

Briggs, Laura, Gladys McCormick, and J. T. Way. "Transnationalism: A Category of Analysis." *American Quarterly* 60, no. 3 (September 2008): 625–48.

Brotherton, David C., and Luis Barrios. *The Almighty Latin King and Queen Nation: Street
Politics and the Transformation of a New York City Gang.* Columbia University Press,
2003.

Brotherton, David C., and Rafael Gude. *Social Inclusion from Below: The Perspectives of Street
Gangs and Their Possible Effects on Declining Homicide Rates in Ecuador.* Inter-American Development Bank, 2018.

Brubaker, Rogers. *Ethnicity Without Groups.* Harvard University Press, 2004.

Bryce, Benjamin. *To Belong in Buenos Aires: Germans, Argentines, and the Rise of a Pluralist
Society.* Stanford University Press, 2018.

Brysk, Alison. *From Tribal Village to Global Village: Indian Rights and International Relations
in Latin America.* Stanford University Press, 2000.

Buchenau, Jürgen. "Blond and Blue-Eyed in Mexico City, 1821 to 1975." In *The Heimat
Abroad: The Boundaries of Germanness,* edited by Krista O'Donnell, Renate Bridenthal, and Nancy Reagin, 85–110. University of Michigan Press, 2005.

Bunster-Burotto, Ximena. "Surviving Beyond Fear: Women and Torture in Latin America."
In *Women and Change in Latin America,* edited by June C. Nash and Helen I. Safa,
297–325. Bergin and Garvey, 1986.

Burton, Julianne. *Cinema and Social Change in Latin America: Conversations with Filmmakers.* University of Texas Press, 1986.

Burton, Julianne, ed. *The Social Documentary in Latin America.* Pittsburgh University Press,
1990.

Bustamante, Emilio, and Jaime Luna-Victoria. "El cine regional en el Perú." *Contratexto,* no.
22 (2014): 189–212.

Bystrom, Kerry, Monica Popescu, and Katherine Zien, eds. *The Cultural Cold War and the
Global South: Sites of Contest and Communitas.* Routledge, 2021.

Cabañas, Miguel Ángel. "El narcocorrido global y las identidades transnacionales." *Revista
de Estudios Hispánicos* 42, no. 3 (2008): 519–42.

Cabezas, Almudena. "Transnational Feminist Networks Building Regions in Latin America." *Latin American Policy* 5, no. 2 (December 2014): 207–20.

Cabezas, Amalia L. "Latin American and Caribbean Sex Workers: Gains and Challenges in
the Movement." *Anti-Trafficking Review,* no. 12 (April 2019): 37–56.

Cabezas González, Almudena, and Gabriela Pinheiro Machado Brochner. "The New Cycle
of Women's Mobilizations Between Latin America and Europe: A Feminist Geopolitical Perspective on Interregionalism." In *Critical Geopolitics and Regional (Re)Con-
figurations: Interregionalism and Transnationalism Between Latin America and Europe,*
edited by Heriberto Cairo and Breno Bringel, 178–96. Routledge, 2019.

Calderwood, Eric. "Spanish in a Global Key." *Journal of Spanish Cultural Studies* 20, nos. 1–2
(2019): 53–65.

Calhoun, Craig J. "The Class Consciousness of Frequent Travelers: Toward a Critique of
Actually Existing Cosmopolitanism." *South Atlantic Quarterly* 101, no. 4 (Fall 2002):
869–97.

Calhoun, Craig J. "For the Social History of the Present: Bourdieu as Historical Sociologist." In *Bourdieu and Historical Analysis*, edited by Philip S. Gorski, 36–66. Duke University Press, 2013.

Calhoun, Craig J. "Habitus, Field, and Capital: The Question of Historical Specificity." In *Bourdieu: Critical Perspectives*, edited by Craig J. Calhoun, Edward LiPuma, and Moishe Postone, 61–88. University of Chicago Press, 1993.

Calhoun, Craig J. "Pierre Bourdieu and Social Transformation: Lessons from Algeria." *Development and Change* 37, no. 6 (2006): 1403–15.

Campana, Maximiliano. *Políticas antigénero en América Latina: Argentina*. Rio de Janeiro: Observatorio de Sexualidad y Política, 2020. https://sxpolitics.org/GPAL/uploads/Ebook-argentina_20200203.pdf.

Campoy-Cubillo, Adolfo, and Benita Sampedro Vizcaya. "Entering the Global Hispanophone: An Introduction." *Journal of Spanish Cultural Studies* 20, nos. 1–2 (2019): 1–16.

Canessa, Andrew. "Conflict, Claim and Contradiction in the New 'Indigenous' State of Bolivia." *Critique of Anthropology* 34, no. 2 (2014): 151–71.

Canessa, Andrew. "Indigenous Conflict in Bolivia Explored Through an African Lens: Towards a Comparative Analysis of Indigeneity." *Comparative Studies in Society and History* 60, no. 2 (April 2018): 308–37.

Canessa, Andrew. *Intimate Indigeneities: Race, Sex, and History in the Small Spaces of Andean Life*. Duke University Press, 2012.

Canessa, Andrew, and Manuela Lavinas Picq. *Savages and Citizens: How Indigeneity Shapes the State*. University of Arizona Press, 2024.

Cano, Gustavo, and Alexandra Délano. "The Mexican Government and Organised Mexican Immigrants in the United States: A Historical Analysis of Political Transnationalism (1848–2005)." *Journal of Ethnic and Migration Studies* 33, no. 5 (2007): 695–725.

Castañeda, Ernesto. *Building Walls: Excluding Latin People in the United States*. Lanham, MD: Lexington Books, 2019.

Castañeda, Ernesto. "The Indignados of Spain: A Precedent to Occupy Wall Street." *Social Movement Studies* 11, nos. 3–4 (2012): 309–19.

Castañeda, Ernesto. "Introduction to 'Reshaping the World: Rethinking Borders.'" *Social Sciences* 9, no. 11, article 214 (2020). https://www.mdpi.com/2076-0760/9/11/214.

Castañeda, Ernesto. "Living in Limbo: Transnational Households, Remittances and Development." *International Migration* 51, no. 1 (July 2013): 13–35.

Castañeda, Ernesto. *A Place to Call Home: Immigrant Exclusion and Urban Belonging in New York, Paris, and Barcelona*. Stanford University Press, 2018.

Castañeda, Ernesto. "Transnationalism in the Lives of Migrants: The Relevance of Thomas and Znaniecki's Work to Understand Migration." In *Contemporary Migrations in the Humanistic Coefficient Perspective: Florian Znaniecki's Thought in Today's Social Science Research*, edited by Jacek Kubera and Łukasz Skoczylas, 171–86. Peter Lang, 2017.

Castañeda, Ernesto. "Understanding Inequality, Migration, Race, and Ethnicity from a Relational Perspective." In *Immigration and Categorical Inequality: Migration to the City and the Birth of Race and Ethnicity*, edited by Ernesto Castañeda, 1–25. Routledge, 2018.

Castañeda, Ernesto, and Lesley Buck. "A Family of Strangers: Transnational Parenting and the Consequences of Family Separation Due to Undocumented Migration." In *Hidden Lives and Human Rights in the United States: Understanding the Controversies and Tragedies of Undocumented Immigration*, vol. 2, edited by Lois Ann Lorentzen, 175–202. Praeger, 2014.

Castañeda, Ernesto, and Lesley Buck. "Remittances, Transnational Parenting, and the Children Left Behind: Economic and Psychological Implications." *The Latin Americanist* 55, no. 4 (December 2011): 85–110.

Castañeda, Ernesto, Maria Cristina Morales, and Olga Ochoa. "Transnational Behavior in Comparative Perspective: The Relationship Between Immigrant Integration and Transnationalism in New York, El Paso, and Paris." *Comparative Migration Studies* 2, no. 3 (2014): 305–34.

Castañeda, Ernesto, and Amber Shemesh. "Overselling Globalization: The Misleading Conflation of Economic Globalization and Immigration, and the Subsequent Backlash." *Social Sciences* 9, no. 5, article 61 (May 2020). https://www.mdpi.com/2076-0760/9/5/61.

Castells, Manuel. *Networks of Outrage and Hope: Social Movements in the Internet Age*. Polity Press, 2012.

Celaya, Lori, and Sonja S. Watson, eds. *Transatlantic, Transcultural, and Transnational Dialogues on Identity, Culture, and Migration*. Lexington Books, 2021.

Chabot, Sean, and Jan Willem Duyvendak. "Globalization and Transnational Diffusion Between Social Movements: Reconceptualizing the Dissemination of the Gandhian Repertoire and the 'Coming Out' Routine." *Theory and Society* 31, no. 6 (December 2002): 697–740.

Chanan, Michael. "Latin American Documentary: A Political Trajectory." In *A Companion to Latin American Cinema*, edited by Maria M. Delgado, Stephen M. Hart, and Randal Johnson, 117–32. Wiley Blackwell, 2017.

Chasteen, John Charles. *National Rhythms, African Roots: The Deep History of Latin American Popular Dance*. University of New Mexico Press, 2004.

Chávez, Sergio R. *Border Lives: Fronterizos, Transnational Migrants, and Commuters in Tijuana*. Oxford University Press, 2016.

Childers, William, *Transnational Cervantes*. University of Toronto Press, 2006.

Clastres, Pierre. *Society Against the State: Essays in Political Anthropology*. Translated by Robert Hurley and Abe Stein. Zone Books, 1987.

Cohn, Deborah N. *History and Memory in the Two Souths: Recent Southern and Spanish American Fiction*. Vanderbilt University Press, 1999.

Collins, Cath. "Human Rights Trials in Chile During and After the 'Pinochet Years.'" *International Journal of Transitional Justice* 4, no. 1 (March 2010): 67–86.

Conquergood, David. "How Street Gangs Problematize Patriotism." In *After Postmodernism: Reconstructing Ideology Critique*, edited by Herbert W. Simons and Michael Billig, 200–221. SAGE Publications, 1994.

Consolim, Marcia. "Circulação de intelectuais e recepção das novas ciências do homem francesas no Brasil: 1908–1932." *Tempo Social* 33, no. 1 (January–April 2021): 17–51.

Conversi, Daniele. "Irresponsible Radicalisation: Diasporas, Globalisation and Long-Distance Nationalism in the Digital Age." *Journal of Ethnic and Migration Studies* 38, no. 9 (2012): 1357–79.

Conway, Janet M. "Activist Knowledges on the Anti-Globalization Terrain: Transnational Feminisms at the World Social Forum." *Interface: A Journal For and About Social Movements* 3, no. 2 (November 2011): 33–64.

Conway, Janet M. "Troubling Transnational Feminism(s): Theorising Activist Praxis." *Feminist Theory* 18, no. 2 (August 2017): 205–27.

Coraza de los Santos, Enrique, and Soledad Lastra, eds. *Miradas a las migraciones, las fronteras y los exilios.* Consejo Latinoamericano de Ciencias Sociales, 2020.

Córdova, Verónica. "Cine boliviano: Del indigenismo a la globalización." *Revista Nuestra América*, no. 3 (July 2007): 129–45.

Corona, Ignacio, and Alejandro L. Madrid. *Postnational Musical Identities: Cultural Production, Distribution, and Consumption in a Globalized Scenario.* Lexington Books, 2007.

Coronado, Jorge. *The Andes Imagined: Indigenismo, Society, and Modernity.* University of Pittsburgh Press, 2009.

Coryat, Diana, and Noah Zweig. "New Ecuadorian Cinema: Small, Glocal and Plurinational." *International Journal of Media and Cultural Politics* 13, no. 3 (September 2017): 265–87.

Cresswell, Tim. *On the Move: Mobility in the Modern Western World.* Routledge, 2006.

Cruz Lobato, Luisa, and Cristiana Gonzalez. "Embodying the Web, Recoding Gender: How Feminists Are Shaping Progressive Politics in Latin America." *First Monday* 25, no. 5 (2020). https://firstmonday.org/ojs/index.php/fm/article/view/10129.

Daniels, Jessie. "Race and Racism in Internet Studies: A Review and Critique." *New Media and Society* 15, no. 5 (August 2013): 695–719.

D'Argenio, Maria Chiara. *Indigenous Plots in Twenty-First Century Latin American Cinema.* Palgrave Macmillan, 2022.

Da Silva Catela, Ludmila. *No habrá flores en la tumba del pasado: La experiencia de reconstrucción del mundo de los familiares de desaparecidos.* Ediciones Al Margen, 2001.

Deibert, Ronald J. "The Road to Digital Unfreedom: Three Painful Truths About Social Media." *Journal of Democracy* 30, no. 1 (January 2019): 25–39.

De la Dehesa, Rafael. *Queering the Public Sphere in Mexico and Brazil: Sexual Rights Movements in Emerging Democracies.* Duke University Press, 2010.

De la Garza, Armida, Ruth Doughty, and Deborah Shaw. "From Transnational Cinemas to Transnational Screens." *Transnational Screens* 10, no. 1 (January 2019): i–vi.

Dennison, Stephanie, ed. *Contemporary Hispanic Cinema: Interrogating Transnationalism in Spanish and Latin American Film.* Boydell and Brewer, 2013.

Dennison, Stephanie, and Song Hwee Lim, eds. *Remapping World Cinema: Identity, Culture and Politics in Film.* Wallflower Press, 2006.

Deutschmann, Emanuel. *Mapping the Transnational World: How We Move and Communicate Across Borders, and Why It Matters.* Princeton University Press, 2021.

Devine Guzmán, Tracy. *Native and National in Brazil: Indigeneity After Independence.* University of North Carolina Press, 2013.

D'haen, Theo, and Reindert Dhondt, eds. *International Don Quixote*. Amsterdam: Rodopi, 2009.

Dhondt, Reindert. "Tríptico de la infamia de Pablo Montoya como cuadro barroco." *Mitologías Hoy: Revista de Pensamiento, Crítica y Estudios Literarios Latinoamericanos* 16 (2017): 307–19.

Dhondt, Reindert, Monica Jansen, and Maria Bonaria Urban, eds. *Transatlantic Practices of Fascism(s) and Populism(s) from the Margins: The Cultural Politics of "Us" Versus "Them."* Routledge, 2025.

Dhondt, Reindert, and Dagmar Vandebosch, eds. *Transnacionalidad e hibridez en el ensayo hispánico: Un género sin orillas*. Brill, 2017.

Dietz, Joshua, Bulin Li, and Ernesto Castañeda. "Keeping in Motion or Staying Put: Internal Migration in the United States and China." *Societies* 13, no. 7, article 162 (July 2023). https://www.mdpi.com/2075-4698/13/7/162.

Dobson, Kit, and Áine McGlynn. *Transnationalism, Activism, Art*. University of Toronto Press, 2013.

Domanski, Robert J. *Who Governs the Internet? A Political Architecture*. Lexington Books, 2015.

Doña-Reveco, Cristián. "The Unintended Consequences of Exile: The Brazilian and Chilean Cases in Comparative Perspective, 1964–1990." Latino/Latin American Studies Faculty Publications no. 11, Fall 2012. University of Nebraska Omaha. https://digitalcommons.unomaha.edu/cgi/viewcontent.cgi?article=1010&context=latinamstudfacpub.

Donoghue, Michael E. *Borderland on the Isthmus: Race, Culture, and the Struggle for the Canal Zone*. Duke University Press, 2014.

Dorfman, Ariel. *La muerte y la doncella (Teatro I)*. Ediciones de la Flor, 1992.

Dunkerley, James. *Rebellion in the Veins: Political Struggle in Bolivia, 1952–1982*. Verso, 1984.

Ďurovičová, Nataša, and Kathleen Newman, eds. *World Cinemas, Transnational Perspectives*. Routledge, 2010.

Dutrénit Bielous, Silvia, ed. *El Uruguay del exilio: Gente, circunstancias, escenarios*. Ediciones Trilce, 2006.

Earl, Jennifer, and Katrina Kimport. *Digitally Enabled Social Change: Activism in the Internet Age*. MIT Press, 2011.

Eco, Umberto. *The Open Work*. Translated by Anna Cancogni. Harvard University Press, 1989.

Encarnación, Omar Guillermo. *Out in the Periphery: Latin America's Gay Rights Revolution*. Oxford University Press, 2016.

Enjuto-Rangel, Cecilia, Sebastiaan Faber, Pedro García-Caro, and Robert Patrick Newcomb, eds. *Transatlantic Studies: Latin America, Iberia, and Africa*. Liverpool University Press, 2019.

Erlmann, Veit. "The Politics and Aesthetics of Transnational Musics." *World of Music* 35, no. 2 (1993): 3–15.

Escárcega, Sylvia. "Authenticating Strategic Essentialisms: The Politics of Indigenousness at the United Nations." *Cultural Dynamics* 22, no. 1 (March 2010): 3–28.

Esponda Fernández, Jaime. *La tradición latinoamericana de asilo y la protección internacional de los refugiados*. Siglo XXI Editores, 2003.

Ette, Ottmar. *Literature on the Move*. Translated by Katharina Vester. Rodopi, 2003.

Ezra, Elizabeth, and Terry Rowden, eds. *Transnational Cinema: The Film Reader*. Routledge, 2006.

Falicov, Tamara. "Migrating from South to North: The Role of Film Festivals in Funding and Shaping Global South Film and Video." In *Locating Migrating Media*, edited by Greg Elmer, Charles H. Davis, Janine Marchessault, and John McCullough, 3–22. Lexington Books, 2010.

Falicov, Tamara. "Programa Ibermedia: Co-Production and the Cultural Politics of Constructing an Ibero-American Audiovisual Space." *Spectator* 27, no. 2 (Fall 2007): 21–30.

Feitlowitz, Marguerite. *A Lexicon of Terror: Argentina and the Legacies of Torture*. Rev. ed. Oxford University Press, 2011.

Feixa, Carles, and César Andrade. *El Rey: Diario de un Latin King*. NED Ediciones, 2020.

Feixa, Carles, Carmen Leccardi, and Pam Nilan, eds. *Youth, Space and Time: Agoras and Chronotopes in the Global City*. Brill, 2016.

Feixa, Carles, Laura Porzio, and Carolina Recio. *Jóvenes "latinos" en Barcelona: Espacio público y cultura urbana*. Anthropos Editorial; Ajuntament de Barcelona, 2006.

Feixa, Carles, and José Sánchez-García. "Global Gangs? Beyond Marginalization and Resilience." *Youth and Globalization* 3, no. 2 (2022): 255–64.

Feixa, Carles, José Sánchez-García, Eduard Ballesté, Ana Belén Cano, Maria-Jose Masanet, Margot Mecca, and Maria Oliver. *The (Trans) Gang: Notes and Queries on Youth Street Group Research*. Universitat Pompeu Fabra; Brussels: European Research Council, 2019. http://dx.doi.org/10.31009/transgang.2019.wp02.1.

Fernandes, Leela. *Transnational Feminism in the United States: Knowledge, Ethics, Power*. New York University Press, 2013.

Fernández L'Hoeste, Héctor, and Pablo Vila, eds. *Cumbia! Scenes of a Migrant Latin American Music Genre*. Duke University Press, 2013.

Fernández-Planells, Ariadna, Enrique Orduña-Malea, and Carles Feixa. "Gangs and Social Media: A Systematic Literature Review and an Identification of Future Challenges, Risks and Recommendations." *New Media and Society* 23, no. 7 (July 2021): 2099–124.

Fisher, Austin, and Iain Robert Smith. "Second Phase Transnationalism: Reflections on Launching the SCMS Transnational Cinemas Scholarly Interest Group." *Transnational Screens* 10, no. 2 (2019): 114–25.

Fisher, Austin, and Iain Robert Smith. "Transnational Cinemas: A Critical Roundtable." *Frames Cinema Journal*, no. 9 (2016): 1–28.

Fishkin, Shelley Fisher. "Crossroads of Cultures: The Transnational Turn in American Studies; Presidential Address to the American Studies Association, November 12, 2004." *American Quarterly* 57, no. 1 (March 2005): 17–57.

Fitzgerald, David. *A Nation of Emigrants: How Mexico Manages Its Migration*. University of California Press, 2009.

Flores, Juan. "Bring the Salsa: Diaspora Music as Source and Challenge." In *The Diaspora Strikes Back: Caribeño Tales of Learning and Turning*, 151–72. Routledge, 2009.

Flores-Villalobos, Joan. "'Freak Letters': Tracing Gender, Race, and Diaspora in the Panama Canal Archive." *Small Axe: A Caribbean Journal of Criticism* 23, no. 2 (July 2019): 34–56.

Foner, Nancy. *From Ellis Island to JFK: New York's Two Great Waves of Immigration*. Yale University Press; Russell Sage Foundation, 2000.

Foxen, Patricia. *In Search of Providence: Transnational Mayan Identities*. Vanderbilt University Press, 2008.

French, Jan Hoffman. *Legalizing Identities: Becoming Black or Indian in Brazil's Northeast*. University of North Carolina Press, 2009.

Friedman, Elisabeth Jay. "Constructing 'The Same Rights with the Same Names': The Impact of Spanish Norm Diffusion on Marriage Equality in Argentina." *Latin American Politics and Society* 54, no. 4 (Winter 2012): 29–59.

Friedman, Elisabeth Jay. "Gendering the Agenda: The Impact of the Transnational Women's Rights Movement at the UN Conferences of the 1990s." *Women's Studies International Forum* 26, no. 4 (July–August 2003): 313–31.

Friedman, Elisabeth Jay. *Interpreting the Internet: Feminist and Queer Counterpublics in Latin America*. University of California Press, 2017.

Friedman, Elisabeth Jay. "Re(gion)alizing Women's Human Rights in Latin America." *Politics and Gender* 5, no. 3 (September 2009): 349–75.

Friedman, Elisabeth Jay. "Women's Human Rights: The Emergence of a Movement." In *Women's Rights, Human Rights: International Feminist Perspectives*, edited by Julie Peters and Andrea Wolper, 18–35. Routledge, 1996.

Friedman, Elisabeth Jay, Kathryn Hochstetler, and Ann Marie Clark. *Sovereignty, Democracy, and Global Civil Society: State-Society Relations at UN World Conferences*. State University of New York Press, 2005.

Friedman, Max Paul. *Nazis and Good Neighbors: The United States Campaign Against the Germans of Latin America in World War II*. Cambridge University Press, 2003.

Friedman, Max Paul, and Padraic Kenney. *Partisan Histories: The Past in Contemporary Global Politics*. Palgrave Macmillan, 2005.

Fuentes, Marcela A. "#NiUnaMenos (#NotOneWomanLess): Hashtag Performativity, Memory, and Direct Action Against Gender Violence in Argentina." In *Women Mobilizing Memory*, edited by Ayşe Gül Altınay, María José Contreras, Marianne Hirsch, Jean Howard, Banu Karaca, and Alisa Solomon, 172–91. Columbia University Press, 2019.

Fuentes, Marcela A. *Performance Constellations: Networks of Protest and Activism in Latin America*. University of Michigan Press, 2019.

Gago, Verónica. "#WeStrike: Notes Toward a Political Theory of the Feminist Strike." *South Atlantic Quarterly* 117, no. 3 (2018): 660–69.

Gallego Cuiñas, Ana. *Las novelas argentinas del siglo 21: Nuevos modos de producción, circulación y recepción*. Peter Lang, 2020.

Gallien, Claire. "A Decolonial Turn in the Humanities – المنعطف المقوض للاستعمار في الإنسانيات." *Alif: Journal of Comparative Poetics*, no. 40 (2020): 28–58.

García Blizzard, Mónica. *The White Indians of Mexican Cinema: Racial Masquerade Throughout the Golden Age*. State University of New York Press, 2022.

García Canclini, Néstor. "Will There Be Latin American Cinema in the Year 2000? Visual Culture in a Postnational Era." In *Framing Latin American Cinema: Contemporary Critical Perspectives*, edited by Ann Marie Stock, 247–58. University of Minnesota Press, 1997.

García Peña, Lorgia. *The Borders of Dominicanidad: Race, Nation, and Archives of Contradiction*. Duke University Press, 2016.

Garofalo, Reebee. "Whose World, What Beat: The Transnational Music Industry, Identity, and Cultural Imperialism." *World of Music* 35, no. 2 (1993): 16–32.

Gates-Madsen, Nancy J. "Tortured Silence and Silenced Torture in Mario Benedetti's *Pedro y el capitán*, Ariel Dorfman's *La muerte y la doncella* and Eduardo Pavlovsky's *Paso de dos*." *Latin American Theatre Review* 42, no. 1 (Fall 2008): 5–31.

Gatti, Gabriel, ed. *Desapariciones: Usos locales, circulaciones globales*. Siglo del Hombre Editores; Universidad de los Andes, 2017.

Gaudig, Olaf, and Peter Veit. *Der Widerschein des Nazismus: Das Bild des Nationalsozialismus in der deutschsprachigen Presse Argentiniens, Brasiliens und Chiles 1932–1945*. Wissenschaftlicher Verlag, 1997.

Gellner, Ernest. *Nations and Nationalism*. Blackwell, 1983.

Gerson, Louis L. *The Hyphenate and Recent American Politics and Diplomacy*. University of Kansas Press, 1964.

Gilbert, Jess. *Planning Democracy: Agrarian Intellectuals and the Intended New Deal*. Yale University Press, 2015.

Giles, Paul. *Transnationalism in Practice: Essays on American Studies, Literature and Religion*. Edinburgh University Press, 2010.

Gilroy, Paul. *The Black Atlantic: Modernity and Double Consciousness*. Harvard University Press, 1993.

Gleghorn, Charlotte. "Indigenous Filmmaking in Latin America." In *A Companion to Latin American Cinema*, edited by Maria M. Delgado, Stephen M. Hart, and Randal Johnson, 167–86. Wiley Blackwell, 2017.

Glick Schiller, Nina, Linda Basch, and Cristina Blanc-Szanton, eds. *Towards a Transnational Perspective on Migration: Race, Class, Ethnicity, and Nationalism Reconsidered*. New York Academy of Sciences, 1992.

Glick Schiller, Nina, Linda Basch, and Cristina Blanc-Szanton. "Transnationalism: A New Analytic Framework for Understanding Migration." *Annals of the New York Academy of Sciences* 645, no. 1 (July 1992): 1–24.

Gomes, Carla, and Bila Sorj. "Corpo, geração e identidade: A marcha das vadias no Brasil." *Revista Sociedade e Estado* 29, no. 2 (May 2014): 433–47.

González, Roque. "Film, the Audiovisual, and New Technology in Latin America: Public Policy in the Context of Digital Convergence." Translated by Franny Brogan and Randal Johnson. In *A Companion to Latin American Cinema*, edited by Maria M. Delgado, Stephen M. Hart, and Randal Johnson, 71–84. Wiley Blackwell, 2017.

Grandin, Greg, and Gilbert M. Joseph, eds. *A Century of Revolution: Insurgent and*

Counterinsurgent Violence During Latin America's Long Cold War. Duke University Press, 2010.

Green, Nancy L. *The Limits of Transnationalism.* University of Chicago Press, 2019.

Greene, Julie. *The Canal Builders: Making America's Empire at the Panama Canal.* Penguin Press, 2009.

Grewal, Inderpal, and Caren Kaplan, eds. *Scattered Hegemonies: Postmodernity and Transnational Feminist Practices.* University of Minnesota Press, 1994.

Gruzinski, Serge, *Les quatre parties du monde: Histoire d'une mondialisation.* La Martinière, 2004.

Guarnizo, Luis Eduardo, and Michael Peter Smith. "The Locations of Transnationalism." In *Transnationalism from Below: Comparative Urban and Community Research,* edited by Michael Peter Smith and Luis Eduardo Guarnizo, 3–34. Transaction Publishers, 1998.

Guerrero, Gustavo, *Paisajes en movimiento: Literatura y cambio cultural entre dos siglos.* Eterna Cadencia, 2018.

Guglielmo, Jennifer, and Salvatore Salerno, eds. *Are Italians White? How Race Is Made in America.* Routledge, 2003.

Guy, Donna J. *Sex and Danger in Buenos Aires: Prostitution, Family, and Nation in Argentina.* University of Nebraska Press, 1991.

Habermas, Jürgen. *Die postnationale Konstellation: Politische Essays.* Suhrkamp Verlag, 1998.

Hagedorn, John M. *A World of Gangs: Armed Young Men and Gangsta Culture.* University of Minnesota Press, 2008.

Hall, Kia M. Q. "A Transnational Black Feminist Framework: Rooting in Feminist Scholarship, Framing Contemporary Black Activism." *Meridians: Feminism, Race, Transnationalism* 15, no. 1 (2016): 86–105.

Hanlon, Dennis. "From Taking to Making Images of Indigeneity: Reading the Films of the Ukamau Group Ethnographically." *Bolivian Research Review* 9, no. 2 (2013): 1–29.

Hannerz, Ulf. *Transnational Connections: Culture, People, Places.* Routledge, 2010.

Harmer, Tanya. *Allende's Chile and the Inter-American Cold War.* University of North Carolina Press, 2011.

Harvey, David, *The Condition of Postmodernity: An Enquiry into the Origins of Cultural Change.* Blackwell, 1990.

Heider, Karl G. *Ethnografic Film.* Rev. ed. University of Texas Press, 2006.

Herlinghaus, Hermann. *Narcoepics: A Global Aesthetics of Sobriety.* Bloomsbury, 2013.

Herrero-Olaizola, Alejandro. "'Se vende Colombia, un país de delirio': El mercado literario global y la narrativa colombiana reciente." *Symposium: A Quarterly Journal in Modern Literatures* 61, no. 1 (2007): 43–56.

Higbee, Will, and Song Hwee Lim. "Concepts of Transnational Cinema: Towards a Critical Transnationalism in Film Studies." *Transnational Cinemas* 1, no. 1 (January 2010): 7–21.

Higgins, Lynn A., and Brenda R. Silver, eds. *Rape and Representation.* Columbia University Press, 1991.

Hill, Juniper. "'Global Folk Music' Fusions: The Reification of Transnational Relationships and the Ethics of Cross-Cultural Appropriations in Finnish Contemporary Folk Music." *Yearbook for Traditional Music* 39 (2007): 50–83.

Hine, Christine. *Virtual Ethnography*. SAGE Publications, 2000.

Hjort, Mette. "On the Plurality of Cinematic Transnationalism." In *World Cinemas, Transnational Perspectives*, edited by Nataša Ďurovičová and Kathleen Newman, 12–33. Routledge, 2010.

Hosek, Jennifer Ruth. *Sun, Sex, and Socialism: Cuba in the German Imaginary*. University of Toronto Press, 2012.

Hoyos, Héctor. *Beyond Bolaño: The Global Latin American Novel*. Columbia University Press, 2015.

Huntington, Samuel P. *The Clash of Civilizations and the Remaking of World Order*. Simon and Schuster, 1996.

Huntington, Samuel P. *Who Are We? The Challenges to America's National Identity*. Simon and Schuster, 2004.

Hutchinson, Sydney. "Breaking Borders / *Quebrando fronteras*: Dancing in the Borderscape." In *Transnational Encounters: Music and Performance at the U.S.-Mexico Border*, edited by Alejandro L. Madrid, 41–66. Oxford University Press, 2011.

Hutchinson, Sydney. "Entangled Rhythms on a Conflicted Island: Digging Up the Buried Histories of Dominican Folk Music." *Resonancias: Revista de Investigación Musical* 20, no. 39 (July–November 2016): 139–54.

Hutchinson, Sydney. *Focus: Music of the Caribbean*. Routledge, 2019.

Hutchinson, Sydney. *From Quebradita to Duranguense: Dance in Mexican American Youth Culture*. University of Arizona Press, 2007.

Hutchinson, Sydney. "*Merengue Típico* in Santiago and New York: Transnational Regionalism in a Neo-Traditional Dominican Music." *Ethnomusicology* 50, no. 1 (Winter 2006): 37–72.

Hutchinson, Sydney. "Merengue Típico in Transnational Dominican Communities: Gender, Geography, Migration, and Memory in a Traditional Music." PhD diss., New York University, 2008.

Hutchinson, Sydney. "Norteño Corporeality: Body, Gender, Sound, and Economy in Commercialized Norteño Music Videos." *Popular Music and Society* 45, no. 3 (July 2022): 317–40.

Hutchinson, Sydney. "On Social Dancing and Social Movements: Salsa and Resistance." In *Rhythm and Power: Performing Salsa in Latino Communities*, edited by Derrick León Washington, Priscilla Renta, and Sydney Hutchinson, 17–30. Centro Press, 2017.

Hutchinson, Sydney, ed. *Salsa World: A Global Dance in Local Contexts*. Temple University Press, 2013.

Hutchinson, Sydney. *Tigers of a Different Stripe: Performing Gender in Dominican Music*. University of Chicago Press, 2016.

Iriye, Akira, and Pierre-Yves Saunier, eds. *The Palgrave Dictionary of Transnational History*. Palgrave Macmillan, 2009.

Iskander, Natasha N. "Innovating Government: Migration, Development, and the State in

Morocco and Mexico, 1963–2005." PhD diss., Massachusetts Institute of Technology, 2006.

Itzigsohn, José. *Encountering American Faultlines: Race, Class, and the Dominican Experience in Providence.* Russell Sage Foundation, 2009.

Itzigsohn, José, and Silvia Giorguli Saucedo. "Immigrant Incorporation and Sociocultural Transnationalism." *International Migration Review* 36, no. 3 (2002): 766–98.

Jay, Martin, and Sumathi Ramaswamy, eds. *Empires of Vision: A Reader.* Duke University Press, 2014.

Jay, Paul. *Global Matters: The Transnational Turn in Literary Studies.* Cornell University Press, 2010.

Jay, Paul. *Transnational Literature: The Basics.* Routledge, 2021.

Jelin, Elizabeth. *La lucha por el pasado: Cómo construimos la memoria social.* Siglo XXI Editores, 2017.

Jenkins, Henry, Sangita Shresthova, Liana Gamber-Thompson, Neta Kligler-Vilenchik, and Arely M. Zimmerman. *By Any Media Necessary: The New Youth Activism.* New York University Press, 2016.

Jensen, Silvina, and Soledad Lastra, eds. *Exilios: Militancia y represión; Nuevas fuentes y nuevos abordajes de los destierros de la Argentina de los años setenta.* Editorial de la Universidad Nacional de La Plata, 2014.

Joseph, Gilbert M., and Daniela Spenser, eds. *In from the Cold: Latin America's New Encounter with the Cold War.* Duke University Press, 2008.

Juris, Jeffrey Scott, and Geoffrey Henri Pleyers. "Alter-Activism: Emerging Cultures of Participation Among Young Global Justice Activists." *Journal of Youth Studies* 12, no. 1 (2009): 57–75.

Kazanjian, David, and María Josefina Saldaña-Portillo. "Introduction: The Traffic in History." *Social Text* 25, no. 3 (92) (Fall 2007): 1–7.

Kearney, Michael. "Borders and Boundaries of State and Self at the End of Empire." *Journal of Historical Sociology* 4, no. 1 (March 1991): 52–74.

Kearney, Michael. "The Local and the Global: The Anthropology of Globalization and Transnationalism." *Annual Review of Anthropology* 24 (1995): 547–65.

Keck, Margaret E., and Kathryn Sikkink. *Activists Beyond Borders: Advocacy Networks in International Politics.* Cornell University Press, 1998.

Kenrick, Justin, and Jerome Lewis. "Indigenous Peoples' Rights and the Politics of the Term 'Indigenous.'" *Anthropology Today* 20, no. 2 (April 2004): 4–9.

Kirkwood, Julieta. *Ser política en Chile: Los nudos de la sabiduría feminista.* 2nd ed. Editorial Cuarto Propio, 1990.

Knudsen, Jan Sverre. "Music of the Multi-Ethnic Minority: A Postnational Perspective." *Music and Arts in Action* 3, no. 3 (2011): 77–91.

Kyei, Justice Richard Kwabena Owusu, Elizabeth Nana Mbrah Koomson-Yalley, and Peter Dwumah. "Transnational Political Practices and Integration of Second Generation Migrants." *Journal of Ethnic and Migration Studies* 48, no. 5 (2020): 1–16.

Laguerre, Michel S. *Diasporic Citizenship: Haitian Americans in Transnational America.* Palgrave Macmillan, 1998.

Langer, Erick D., and Elena Muñoz, eds. *Contemporary Indigenous Movements in Latin America*. Scholarly Resources, 2003.

Laó-Montes, Agustín. "Afro–Latin American Feminisms at the Cutting Edge of Emerging Political-Epistemic Movements." *Meridians: Feminism, Race, Transnationalism* 14, no. 2 (2016): 1–24.

Larrondo, Marina, and Camila Ponce Lara. "Activismos feministas jóvenes en América Latina: Dimensiones y perspectivas conceptuales." In *Activismos feministas jóvenes: Emergencias, actrices y luchas en América Latina*, edited by Marina Larrondo and Camila Ponce Lara, 21–40. Consejo Latinoamericano de Ciencias Sociales, 2019.

Lastra, María Soledad. *Volver del exilio: Historia comparada de las políticas de recepción en las posdictaduras de la Argentina y Uruguay (1983–1989)*. Universidad Nacional de La Plata; Universidad Nacional de Misiones; Universidad Nacional de General Sarmiento, 2016.

Latham, Robert, and Saskia Sassen. "Digital Formations: Constructing an Object of Study." In *Digital Formations: IT and New Architectures in the Global Realm*, edited by Robert Latham and Saskia Sassen, 1–34. Princeton University Press, 2005.

Leggewie, Claus. "Transnational Citizenship: Cultural Concerns." In *International Encyclopedia of the Social and Behavioral Sciences*, edited by Neil J. Smelser and Paul B. Baltes, 15857–62. Pergamon Press, 2001.

León, Christian. *Reinventando al otro: El documental indigenista en el Ecuador*. Consejo Nacional de Cinematografía del Ecuador, 2010.

Lessa, Francesca. "Operation Condor on Trial: Justice for Transnational Human Rights Crimes in South America." *Journal of Latin American Studies* 51, no. 2 (May 2019): 410–29.

Levitt, Peggy. *God Needs No Passport: Immigrants and the Changing American Religious Landscape*. New Press, 2007.

Levitt, Peggy. *The Transnational Villagers*. University of California Press, 2001.

Levitt, Peggy, and B. Nadya Jaworsky. "Transnational Migration Studies: Past Developments and Future Trends." *Annual Review of Sociology* 33, no. 1 (December 2007): 129–56.

Levitt, Peggy, and Mary C. Waters, eds. *The Changing Face of Home: The Transnational Lives of the Second Generation*. Russell Sage Foundation, 2002.

Levitt, Theodore. "The Globalization of Markets." *Harvard Business Review* 61, no. 3 (May 1983): 92–102.

Lewis, George H. "Ghosts, Ragged but Beautiful: Influences of Mexican Music on American Country-Western & Rock 'n' Roll." *Popular Music and Society* 15, no. 4 (1991): 85–103.

Lie, Nadia. "Lo transnacional en el cine hispánico: Deslindes de un concepto." In *Nuevas perspectivas sobre la transnacionalidad del cine hispánico*, edited by Robin Lefere and Nadia Lie, 17–35. Brill/Rodopi, 2016.

Lienhard, Martín, ed. *Expulsos, desterrados, deslocados: Migrações forzadas na América Latina e na África*. Iberoamericana Vervuert, 2011.

Lim, Song Hwee. "Concepts of Transnational Cinema Revisited." *Transnational Screens* 10, no. 1 (2019): 1–12.

Lindroth, Marjo. "Indigenous-State Relations in the UN: Establishing the Indigenous Forum." *Polar Record* 42, no. 3 (July 2006): 239–48.

Lionnet, Françoise, and Shu-mei Shih, eds. *Minor Transnationalism*. Duke University Press, 2005.

Lopes, Thiago da Costa. *Em busca da comunidade: Ciências sociais, desenvolvimento rural e diplomacia cultural nas relações Brasil-EUA (1930–1950)*. Fundação Oswaldo Cruz, 2020.

Loveman, Brian, and Elizabeth Lira. *Las suaves cenizas del olvido: Vía chilena de reconciliación política (1814–1932)*. LOM Ediciones, 1999.

Loza, Jorgelina Mariana. "Putas feministas en América Latina: La RedTraSex y su vínculo con el feminismo latinoamericano." *Revista Argentina de Sociología* 12, no. 21 (2017): 6–21.

Lübken, Uwe. *Bedrohliche Nähe: Die USA und die nationalsozialistische Herausforderung in Lateinamerika, 1937–1945*. Franz Steiner Verlag, 2004.

MacDougall, David. *Transcultural Cinema*. Edited by Lucien Taylor. Princeton University Press, 1998.

Macón, Cecilia. "Illuminating Affects: Sexual Violence as a Crime Against Humanity; The Argentine Case." *Historein* 14, no. 1 (2013): 22–42.

Madrid, Alejandro L., ed. *Transnational Encounters: Music and Performance at the U.S.-Mexico Border*. Oxford University Press, 2011.

Madrid, Alejandro L. and Robin D. Moore. *Danzón: Circum-Caribbean Dialogues in Music and Dance*. Oxford University Press, 2013.

Maio, Marcos Chor, and Thiago da Costa Lopes. "Entre Chicago e Salvador: Donald Pierson e o estudo das relações raciais." *Estudos Históricos* 30, no. 60 (January–April 2017): 115–40.

Maio, Marcos Chor, and Thiago da Costa Lopes. "'For the Establishment of the Social Disciplines as Sciences': Donald Pierson e as ciências sociais no Rio de Janeiro (1942–1949)." *Sociologia e Antropologia* 5, no. 2 (August 2015): 343–80.

Maio, Marcos Chor, and Thiago da Costa Lopes. "Modernization, Race, and the Rural Past in Brazil: A Transnational Analysis of Donald Pierson's Sociology (1930–1950)." *Latin American Research Review* 57, no. 2 (2022): 298–315.

Mallon, Florencia E., ed. *Decolonizing Native Histories: Collaboration, Knowledge, and Language in the Americas*. Duke University Press, 2012.

Mandolessi, Silvana, and Mariana Eva Perez. "The Disappeared as a Transnational Figure or How to Deal with the *Vain Yesterday*." *European Review* 22, no. 4 (October 2014): 603–12.

Marchand, Marianne H. "Engendering Transnational Movements/Transnationalizing Women's and Feminist Movements in the Americas." *Latin American Policy* 5, no. 2 (December 2014): 180–92.

Marino, Katherine M. *Feminism for the Americas: The Making of an International Human Rights Movement*. University of North Carolina Press, 2019.

Martin, Tenley. *Transnational Flamenco: Exchange and the Individual in British and Spanish Flamenco Culture*. Palgrave Macmillan, 2020.

Matos, Carolina. "New Brazilian Feminisms and Online Networks: Cyberfeminism, Protest and the Female 'Arab Spring.'" *International Sociology* 32, no. 3 (May 2017): 417–34.

Mbembe, Achille. *Necropolitics*. Translated by Steven Corcoran. Duke University Press, 2019.

McClennen, Sophia A. *Globalization and Latin American Cinema: Toward a New Critical Paradigm*. Palgrave Macmillan, 2018.

McFarland, Pancho. *The Chican@ Hip Hop Nation: Politics of a New Millennial Mestizaje*. Michigan State University Press, 2013.

McSherry, J. Patrice. "Tracking the Origins of a State Terror Network: Operation Condor." *Latin American Perspectives* 29, no. 1 (January 2002): 38–60.

Méndez, Mariela. "Operación Araña: Reflections on How a Performative Intervention in Buenos Aires's Subway System Can Help Rethink Feminist Activism." *Revista Estudos Históricos* (Rio de Janeiro) 33, no. 70 (May–August 2020): 280–97.

Merkel, Ian. *Terms of Exchange: Brazilian Intellectuals and the French Social Sciences*. University of Chicago Press, 2022.

Miceli, Sérgio. *História das ciências sociais no Brasil*. 2 vols. Editora Sumaré; Instituto de Estudos Econômicos, Sociais e Políticos, 1989, 1995.

Middents, Jeffrey. "The First Rule of Latin American Cinema Is You Do Not Talk About Latin American Cinema: Notes on Discussing a Sense of Place in Contemporary Cinema." *Transnational Cinemas* 4, no. 2 (2013): 147–64.

Middents, Jeffrey. *Writing National Cinema: Film Journals and Film Culture in Peru*. University Press of New England, 2009.

Mignolo, Walter D. *The Idea of Latin America*. Blackwell, 2005.

Mignolo, Walter D., and Arturo Escobar, eds. *Globalization and the Decolonial Option*. Routledge, 2010.

Miller, Francesca. *Latin American Women and the Search for Social Justice*. University Press of New England, 1991.

Mission, King. *The Official Globalization of the ALKQN / La globalización oficial de la ALKQN*. Translated by King Martyr and King Outlaw. Autoedición, 2008.

Morawska, Ewa. "Immigrants, Transnationalism, and Ethnicization: A Comparison of This Great Wave and the Last." In *E Pluribus Unum? Contemporary and Historical Perspectives on Immigrant Political Incorporation*, edited by Gary Gerstle and John Mollenkopf, 175–212. Russell Sage Foundation, 2001.

Morris, Aldon D. *The Scholar Denied: W. E. B. Du Bois and the Birth of Modern Sociology*. University of California Press, 2015.

Müller, Gesine. "Transnational Challenges for World Literatures: Publishing Caribbean Writers." In *The Transnational in Literary Studies: Potential and Limitations of a Concept*, edited by Kai Wiegandt, 44–55. De Gruyter, 2020.

Müller, Gesine. *Wie wird Weltliteratur gemacht? Globale Zirkulationen lateinamerikanischer Literaturen*. De Gruyter, 2020.

Naficy, Hamid. *An Accented Cinema: Exilic and Diasporic Filmmaking*. Princeton University Press, 2001.

Nakamura, Lisa. *Cybertypes: Race, Ethnicity, and Identity on the Internet*. Routledge, 2002.

Nakamura, Lisa. *Digitizing Race: Visual Cultures of the Internet.* University of Minnesota Press, 2008.

Niezen, Ronald. *The Origins of Indigenism: Human Rights and the Politics of Identity.* University of California Press, 2003.

Noble, Safiya Umoja. *Algorithms of Oppression: How Search Engines Reinforce Racism.* New York University Press, 2018.

Noriega, Chon A., ed. *Visible Nations: Latin American Cinema and Video.* University of Minnesota Press, 2000.

Noriega Bernuy, Julio, and Javier Morales Mena, eds. *Cine andino.* Pakarina Ediciones, 2015.

Nünning, Ansgar. "Transnational Approaches to the Study of Culture." In *English and American Studies: Theory and Practice,* edited by Martin Middeke, Timo Müller, Christina Wald, and Hubert Zapf, 261–70. Verlag J. B. Metzler, 2012.

Nussbaum, Martha C. *Cultivating Humanity: A Classical Defense of Reform in Liberal Education.* Harvard University Press, 1997.

Ó Briain, Lonán. "'Happy to Be Born Hmong': The Implications of a Transnational Musical Network for the Vietnamese-Hmong People." *Journal of Vietnamese Studies* 8, no. 2 (Spring 2013): 115–48.

O'Brien, Cheryl, and Shannon Drysdale Walsh. "Women's Rights and Opposition: Explaining the Stunted Rise and Sudden Reversals of Progressive Violence Against Women Policies in Contentious Contexts." *Journal of Latin American Studies* 52, no. 1 (February 2020): 107–31.

Olcott, Jocelyn. *International Women's Year: The Greatest Consciousness-Raising Event in History.* Oxford University Press, 2017.

Ong, Aihwa. *Flexible Citizenship: The Culture Logics of Transnationality.* Duke University Press, 1999.

Ortega, Julio, *Transatlantic Translations: Dialogues in Latin American Literature.* Translated by Philip Derbyshire. Reaktion Books, 2006.

Palacio, Manuel, and Jörg Türschmann, eds. *Transnational Cinema in Europe.* LIT Verlag, 2013.

Palaversich, Diana. "The Politics of Drug Trafficking in Mexican and Mexico-Related Narconovelas." *Aztlán: A Journal of Chicano Studies* 31, no. 2 (Fall 2006): 85–110.

Parker, Jeffrey Wayne. "Empire's Angst: The Politics of Race, Migration, and Sex Work in Panama, 1903–1945." PhD diss., University of Texas at Austin, 2013.

Pavlovsky, Eduardo A. *Paso de dos.* In *Teatro completo,* edited by Jorge Dubatti, 1:103–20. Atuel, 1997.

Pease, Donald E. "Introduction: Re-Mapping the Transnational Turn." In *Re-Framing the Transnational Turn in American Studies,* edited by Winfried Fluck, Donald E. Pease, and John Carlos Rowe, 1–46. University Press of New England, 2011.

Penny, H. Glenn. "Diversity, Inclusivity, and 'Germanness' in Latin America During the Interwar Period." *Bulletin of the German Historical Institute* 61 (Fall 2017): 85–108.

Penny, H. Glenn. "Latin American Connections: Recent Work on German Interactions with Latin America." *Central European History* 46, no. 2 (June 2013): 362–94.

Penny, H. Glenn. "Material Connections: German Schools, Things, and Soft Power in

Argentina and Chile from the 1880s Through the Interwar Period." *Comparative Studies in Society and History* 59, no. 3 (July 2017): 519–49.

Peres da Silva, Glaucia, and Konstantin Hondros, eds. *Music Practices Across Borders: (E)Valuating Space, Diversity and Exchange.* Transcript Verlag, 2019.

Perriam, Chris, Isabel Santaolalla, and Peter W. Evans. "The Transnational in Iberian and Latin American Cinemas: Editors' Introduction." *Hispanic Research Journal* 8, no. 1 (2007): 3–9.

Pettinà, Vanni, and José Antonio Sánchez Román. "Beyond US Hegemony: The Shaping of the Cold War in Latin America." *Culture and History Digital Journal* 4, no. 1 (2015): 15–32.

Pike, Fredrick B. *FDR's Good Neighbor Policy: Sixty Years of Generally Gentle Chaos.* University of Texas Press, 1995.

Piñuelas, Edward. "Transnationalism in Postcolonial and Subaltern Studies." Oxford Bibliographies, July 26, 2017. https://doi.org/10.1093/OBO/9780190221911-0047.

Piscitelli, Adriana. "Tránsitos: Circulación de brasileñas en el ámbito de la transnacionalización de los mercados sexual y matrimonial." *Horizontes Antropológicos* 15, no. 31 (June 2009): 101–36.

Planas, Melissa Castillo. *A Mexican State of Mind: New York City and the New Borderlands of Culture.* Rutgers University Press, 2020.

Poblete, Juan. "The Transnational Turn." In *New Approaches to Latin American Studies: Culture and Power,* edited by Juan Poblete, 32–49. Routledge, 2018.

Pohl, Burkhard. "Estrategias transnacionales en el mercado del libro (1990–2010)." *Aleph,* no. 25 (2012): 13–34.

Portes, Alejandro. "Globalization from Below: The Rise of Transnational Communities." Working Paper 98:8, 1997. University of Oxford.

Portes, Alejandro, and Patricia Fernández-Kelly, eds. *The State and the Grassroots: Immigrant Transnational Organizations in Four Continents.* Berghahn Books, 2015.

Postero, Nancy. *The Indigenous State: Race, Politics, and Performance in Plurinational Bolivia.* University of California Press, 2017.

Pozo Artigas, José del, ed. *Exiliados, emigrados y retornados: Chilenos en América y Europa, 1973–2004.* RIL Editores, 2006.

Pries, Ludger, and Pablo Yankelevich, eds. *European and Latin American Social Scientists as Refugees, Émigrés and Return-Migrants.* Palgrave Macmillan, 2019.

Putnam, Lara. "Provincializing Harlem: The 'Negro Metropolis' as Northern Frontier of a Connected Caribbean." *Modernism/Modernity* 20, no. 3 (September 2013): 469–84.

Queirolo Palmas, Luca. *¿Cómo se construye un enemigo público? Las "bandas latinas."* Traficantes de Sueños, 2017.

Ragland, Cathy. 2003. "Mexican Deejays and the Transnational Space of Youth Dances in New York and New Jersey." *Ethnomusicology* 47, no. 3 (Autumn 2003): 338–54.

Ramírez, Dixa. *Colonial Phantoms: Belonging and Refusal in the Dominican Americas, from the 19th Century to the Present.* New York University Press, 2018.

Ramos, Alcida Rita. "The Hyperreal Indian." *Critique of Anthropology* 14, no. 2 (1994): 153–71.

Rawle, Steven. *Transnational Cinema: An Introduction*. Palgrave, 2017.

RedTraSex. *La revolución de las trabajadoras sexuales: 20 años de organización de la RedTraSex de Latinoamérica y el Caribe*. 2017. https://biblioteca.redtrasex.org/handle/123456789/146.

Reilly, Niamh. *Women's Human Rights: Seeking Gender Justice in a Globalizing Age*. Polity Press, 2009.

Risse, Thomas, Stephen C. Ropp, and Kathryn Sikkink, eds. *The Power of Human Rights: International Norms and Domestic Change*. Cambridge University Press, 1999.

Risse-Kappen, Thomas, ed. *Bringing Transnational Relations Back In: Non-State Actors, Domestic Structures and International Institutions*. Cambridge University Press, 1995.

Robbins, Timothy R., and José Eduardo González, eds. *New Trends in Contemporary Latin American Narrative: Post-National Literatures and the Canon*. Palgrave Macmillan, 2014.

Robertson, Roland. "Glocalization: Time-Space and Homogeneity-Heterogeneity." In *Global Modernities*, edited by Mike Featherstone, Scott Lash, and Roland Robertson, 25–44. SAGE Publications, 1995.

Rodríguez García, Magaly, Lex Heerma van Voss, and Elise van Nederveen Meerkerk. *Selling Sex in the City: A Global History of Prostitution, 1600s–2000s*. Brill, 2017.

Romo, Anadelia A. *Brazil's Living Museum: Race, Reform, and Tradition in Bahia*. University of North Carolina Press, 2010.

Roniger, Luis. *Destierro y exilio en América Latina: Nuevos estudios y avances teóricos*. Editorial Universitaria de Buenos Aires, 2014.

Roniger, Luis. "Exílio massivo, inclusão e exclusão política no século XX." *Dados: Revista de Ciências Sociais* 53, no. 1 (2010): 91–123.

Roniger, Luis. "Forced Migration and Exile: Analytical and Historical Perspectives." In *The Routledge History of Modern Latin American Migration*, edited by Andreas E. Feldmann, Xóchitl Bada, Jorge Durand, and Stephanie Schütze, 172–85. Routledge, 2023.

Roniger, Luis. *Transnational Perspectives on Latin America: The Entwined Histories of a Multi-State Region*. Oxford University Press, 2022.

Roniger, Luis. *Transnational Politics in Central America*. University Press of Florida, 2011.

Roniger, Luis, James N. Green, and Pablo Yankelevich, eds. *Exile and the Politics of Exclusion in the Americas*. Sussex Academic Press, 2012.

Rosemblatt, Karin Alejandra. *The Science and Politics of Race in Mexico and the United States, 1910–1950*. University of North Carolina Press, 2018.

Roth, Wendy D. *Race Migrations: Latinos and the Cultural Transformation of Race*. Stanford University Press, 2012.

Rouse, Roger. "Mexican Migration and the Social Space of Postmodernism." *Diaspora: A Journal of Transnational Studies* 1, no. 1 (Spring 1991): 8–23.

Russo, Eduardo A., ed. *Hacer cine: Producción audiovisual en América Latina*. Editorial Paidós, 2008.

Safran, William. "The Diaspora and the Homeland: Reciprocities, Transformations, and Role Reversals." In *Transnationalism: Diasporas and the Advent of a New (Dis)order*, edited by Eliezer Ben-Rafael, Yitzhak Sternberg, Judit Bokser Liwerant, and Yosef Gorny, 75–100. Brill, 2009.

Sanjinés, Jorge. "Problemas de la forma y el contenido en el cine revolucionario." In *Hojas de cine: Testimonios y documentos del nuevo cine latinoamericano*, vol. 1, *Centro y Sudamérica*, 117–20. Secretaría de Educación Pública; Universidad Autónoma Metropolitana; Fundación Mexicana de Cineastas, 1988.

Sanjinés, Jorge, and Grupo Ukamau. *Teoría y práctica de un cine junto al pueblo*. Siglo XXI Editores, 1980.

Sassen, Saskia. *Los espectros de la globalización*. Fondo de Cultura Económica, 2003.

Sassen, Saskia. *The Global City: New York, London, Tokyo*. 2nd ed. Princeton University Press, 2001.

Sassen, Saskia. *Losing Control? Sovereignty in an Age of Globalization*. Columbia University Press, 1996.

Saunier, Pierre-Yves. "Transnational." In *The Palgrave Dictionary of Transnational History*, edited by Akira Iriye and Pierre-Yves Saunier, 1047–55. Palgrave Macmillan, 2009.

Saunier, Pierre-Yves. *Transnational History*. Palgrave Macmillan, 2013.

Sayad, Abdelmalek. *The Suffering of the Immigrant*. Translated by David Macey. Polity Press, 2004.

Schelling, Vivian, ed. *Through the Kaleidoscope: The Experience of Modernity in Latin America*. Verso, 2000.

Schiwy, Freya. *Indianizing Film: Decolonization, the Andes, and the Question of Technology*. Rutgers University Press, 2009.

Schiwy, Freya. *The Open Invitation: Activist Video, Mexico, and the Politics of Affect*. University of Pittsburgh Press, 2019.

Scott, James. *The Art of Not Being Governed: An Anarchist History of Upland Southeast Asia*. Yale University Press, 2009.

Segrave, Marie, and Laura Vitis, eds. *Gender, Technology and Violence*. Routledge, 2017.

Seigel, Micol. "Beyond Compare: Comparative Method After the Transnational Turn." *Radical History Review*, no. 91 (Winter 2005): 62–90.

Shaw, Deborah. *The Three Amigos: The Transnational Filmmaking of Guillermo del Toro, Alejandro González Iñárritu, and Alfonso Cuarón*. Manchester University Press, 2013.

Shaw, Karena. *Indigeneity and Political Theory: Sovereignty and the Limits of the Political*. Routledge, 2008.

Sheffer, Gabriel. *Diaspora Politics: At Home Abroad*. Cambridge University Press, 2003.

Shukla, Sandhya, and Heidi Tinsman, eds. *Imagining Our Americas: Toward a Transnational Frame*. Duke University Press, 2007.

Sikkink, Kathryn. "From Pariah State to Global Protagonist: Argentina and the Struggle for International Human Rights." *Latin American Politics and Society* 50, no. 1 (Spring 2008): 1–29.

Silva, Joseli Maria, and Marcio Jose Ornat. "Intersectionality and Transnational Mobility Between Brazil and Spain in *Travesti* Prostitution Networks." *Gender, Place and Culture* 22, no. 8 (2015): 1073–88.

Simonett, Helena. *Banda: Mexican Musical Life Across Borders*. Wesleyan University Press, 2001.

Smith, Michael Peter, and Luis Eduardo Guarnizo, eds. *Transnationalism from Below: Comparative Urban and Community Research*. Transaction Publishers, 1998.

Smith, Robert Courtney. *Mexican New York: Transnational Lives of New Immigrants*. University of California Press, 2006.

Souza, Natália Maria Félix de. "When the Body Speaks (to) the Political: Feminist Activism in Latin America and the Quest for Alternative Democratic Futures." *Contexto Internacional* 41, no. 1 (April 2019): 89–112.

Soysal, Yasemin Nuhoğlu. *Limits of Citizenship: Migrants and Postnational Membership in Europe*. University of Chicago Press, 1994.

Spivak, Gayatri Chakravorty. "Can the Subaltern Speak?" In *Marxism and the Interpretation of Culture*, edited by Cary Nelson and Lawrence Grossberg, 271–316. University of Illinois Press, 1988.

Stam, Robert. *World Literature, Transnational Cinema, and Global Media: Towards a Transartistic Commons*. Routledge, 2019.

Stites Mor, Jessica, ed. *Human Rights and Transnational Solidarity in Cold War Latin America*. University of Wisconsin Press, 2013.

Stites Mor, Jessica. *South-South Solidarity and the Latin American Left*. University of Wisconsin Press, 2022.

Sutton, Barbara. *Bodies in Crisis: Culture, Violence, and Women's Resistance in Neoliberal Argentina*. Rutgers University Press, 2010.

Sutton, Barbara. "Intergenerational Encounters in the Struggle for Abortion Rights in Argentina." *Women's Studies International Forum* 82 (September–October 2020): 1–11.

Sutton, Barbara. *Surviving State Terror: Women's Testimonies of Repression and Resistance in Argentina*. New York University Press, 2018.

Swan, Quito. "Transnationalism." In *Keywords for African American Studies*, edited by Erica R. Edwards, Roderick A. Ferguson, and Jeffrey O. G. Ogbar, 209–13. New York University Press, 2018.

Sznajder, Mario, and Luis Roniger. *The Politics of Exile in Latin America*. Cambridge University Press, 2009.

Tarrow, Sidney. "Transnational Politics: Contention and Institutions in International Politics." *Annual Review of Political Science* 4, no. 1 (June 2001): 1–20.

Taylor, Diana. *Disappearing Acts: Spectacles of Gender and Nationalism in Argentina's "Dirty War."* Duke University Press, 1997.

Taylor, Timothy D. *Music and Capitalism: A History of the Present*. University of Chicago Press, 2015.

Thomas, Greg. *The Sexual Demon of Colonial Power: Pan-African Embodiment and Erotic Schemes of Empire*. Indiana University Press, 2007.

Tierney, Dolores. *New Transnationalisms in Contemporary Latin American Cinemas*. Edinburgh University Press, 2018.

Tilly, Charles. "Trust Networks in Transnational Migration." *Sociological Forum* 22, no. 1 (March 2007): 3–24.

Tilly, Charles, Ernesto Castañeda, and Lesley J. Wood. *Social Movements, 1768–2018*. 4th ed. Routledge, 2020.

Torres-Saillant, Silvio. "The Tribulations of Blackness: Stages in Dominican Racial Identity." *Latin American Perspectives* 25, no. 3 (May 1998): 126–46.

Trigo, Abril. "De lo transcultural a/en lo transnacional." In *Ángel Rama y los estudios latinoamericanos*, edited by Mabel Moraña, 147–51. Instituto Internacional de Literatura Iberoamericana, 1997.

Trinh, T. Minh-ha. *Woman, Native, Other: Writing Postcoloniality and Feminism.* Indiana University Press, 1989.

Tsing, Anna Lowenhaupt. *In the Realm of the Diamond Queen: Marginality in an Out-of-the-Way Place.* Princeton University Press, 1993.

Tufekci, Zeynep. *Twitter and Tear Gas: The Power and Fragility of Networked Protest.* Yale University Press, 2017.

Tuhiwai Smith, Linda. *Decolonizing Methodologies: Research and Indigenous Peoples.* 2nd ed. Zed Books, 2012.

Urban, Greg, and Joel Sherzer, eds. *Nation-States and Indians in Latin America.* University of Texas Press, 1991.

Urry, John, *Mobilities.* Polity Press, 2007.

Valle, Ivonne del, Anna More, and Rachel Sarah O'Toole, eds. *Iberian Empires and the Roots of Globalization.* Vanderbilt University Press, 2019.

Vandebosch, Dagmar. "Introducción." In "Escritores hispanoamericanos en España," edited by Dagmar Vandebosch. Special issue, *Aleph*, no. 25 (2012): 5–12.

Vandebosch, Dagmar. "Transnational Memories in Antonio Muñoz Molina's *Sepharad*." *European Review* 22, no. 4 (October 2014): 613–22.

Vandebosch, Dagmar, and Theo D'haen, eds. *Literary Transnationalism(s).* Brill/Rodopi, 2018.

Van Deusen, Nancy E. *Global Indios: The Indigenous Struggle for Justice in Sixteenth-Century Spain.* Duke University Press, 2015.

Vertovec, Steven. *Transnationalism.* Routledge, 2009.

Vicuña Gonzalez, Vernadette, and Jana K. Lipman. "Tours of Duty and Tours of Leisure." *American Studies* 68, no. 3 (September 2016): 507–21.

Vilanova, Núria. "Descolonización y cine: La propuesta indígena de Jorge Sanjinés hoy." *Bolivian Studies Journal / Revista de Estudios Bolivianos* 19 (2012–2013): 89–104.

Villas Bôas, Glaucia. *A recepção da sociologia alemã no Brasil.* Topbooks, 2006.

Wade, Peter. *Race and Ethnicity in Latin America.* 2nd ed. Pluto Press, 2010.

Waldinger, Roger, and David Fitzgerald. "Transnationalism in Question." *American Journal of Sociology* 109, no. 5 (March 2004): 1177–95.

Wallerstein, Immanuel. *The Modern World-System II: Mercantilism and the Consolidation of the European World-Economy, 1600–1750.* University of California Press, 2011.

Wallis, Roger, and Krister Malm. *Big Sounds from Small Peoples: The Music Industry in Small Countries.* Constable, 1984.

Warren, Kay B., and Jean E. Jackson, eds. *Indigenous Movements, Self-Representation, and the State in Latin America.* University of Texas Press, 2002.

Watts, Michael J. "Antinomies of Community: Some Thoughts on Geography, Resources and Empire." *Transactions of the Institute of British Geographers*, n.s. 29, no. 2 (June 2004): 195–216.

Weeks, Gregory, and John Weeks. "Immigration and Transnationalism: Rethinking the Role of the State in Latin America." *International Migration* 53, no. 5 (October 2015): 122–34.

Weigel, Sigrid. "On the 'Topographical Turn': Concepts of Space in Cultural Studies and *Kulturwissenschaften*; A Cartographic Feud." *European Review* 17, no. 1 (February 2009): 187–201.

Werth, Brenda, and Katherine Zien, eds. *Bodies on the Front Lines: Performance, Gender, and Sexuality in Latin America and the Caribbean.* University of Michigan Press, 2024.

Wilcox, Clifford. *Robert Redfield and the Development of American Anthropology.* Lexington Books, 2004.

Wilson, Pamela, and Michelle Stewart, eds. *Global Indigenous Media: Cultures, Poetics, and Politics.* Duke University Press, 2008.

Wimmer, Andreas, and Nina Glick Schiller. "Methodological Nationalism and Beyond: Nation-State Building, Migration and the Social Sciences." *Global Networks: A Journal of Transnational Affairs* 2, no. 4 (October 2002): 301–34.

Wood, David M. J. "Film and the Archive: Nation, Heritage, Resistance." *Cosmos and History: The Journal of Natural and Social Philosophy* 6, no. 2 (2010): 162–74.

Wood, David M. J. "Indigenismo and the Avant-Garde: Jorge Sanjinés's Early Films and the National Project." *Bulletin of Latin American Research* 25, no. 1 (January 2006): 63–82.

Wood, David M. J. "With Foreign Eyes: English-Language Criticism on Latin American Film." *Journal of Latin American Cultural Studies* 17, no. 2 (August 2008): 245–59.

Wortham, Erica Cusi. *Indigenous Media in Mexico: Culture, Community, and the State.* Duke University Press, 2013.

Wright, Micah. "'Protection Against the Lust of Men': Progressivism, Prostitution and Rape in the Dominican Republic under US Occupation, 1916–24." *Gender and History* 28, no. 3 (November 2016): 623–40.

Yankelevich, Pablo. *Los otros: Raza, normas y corrupción en la gestión de la extranjería en México, 1900–1950.* El Colegio de México; Iberoamericana Vervuert, 2019.

Ybarra, Patricia A. *Latinx Theater in the Times of Neoliberalism.* Northwestern University Press, 2018.

Zamorano Villarreal, Gabriela. *Indigenous Media and Political Imaginaries in Contemporary Bolivia.* University of Nebraska Press, 2017.

Zuberi, Nabeel. *Sounds English: Transnational Popular Music.* University of Illinois Press, 2001.

Zuboff, Shoshana. *The Age of Surveillance Capitalism: The Fight for a Human Future at the New Frontier of Power.* PublicAffairs, 2019.

Contributors

Amalia L. Cabezas is Emerita Professor of Media and Cultural Studies and Gender and Sexuality Studies at the University of California, Riverside. Her publications include *Economies of Desire: Sex and Tourism in Cuba and the Dominican Republic* (Temple University Press, 2009) and two coedited books: *Una ventana a Cuba y los estudios cubanos* (Ediciones Callejón, 2010) and *The Wages of Empire: Neoliberal Politics, Repression, and Women's Poverty* (Routledge, 2007).

Andrew Canessa is a professor of anthropology at the University of Essex. He has worked for many years with Aymara speakers in highland Bolivia and has published widely on issues of indigeneity, race, gender, and sexuality. His most recent book (with Manuela Lavinas Picq) is *Savages and Citizens: How Indigeneity Shapes the State* (University of Arizona Press, 2024).

Ernesto Castañeda is a professor and director of the Immigration Lab and the Center for Latin American and Latino Studies at American University in Washington, DC. Among his books are *Immigration Realities: Challenging Common Misperceptions* (Columbia University Press, 2024), *Reunited: Family Separation and Central American Youth Migration* (Russell Sage Foundation, 2024), *Building Walls: Excluding Latin People in the United States* (Lexington Books, 2019), *Social Movements 1768–2018* (Routledge, 2020), and *A Place to Call Home: Immigrant Exclusion and Urban Belonging in New York, Paris, and Barcelona* (Stanford University Press, 2018).

Reindert Dhondt is an associate professor of Hispanic literature at the University of Antwerp. His research areas include memory studies, violence studies, and decolonial theory. He is currently working on the representation of museums and artifacts in Latin American literature and questions of symbolic restitution. He is the author of *Carlos Fuentes y el pensamiento barroco* (Iberoamericana Vervuert, 2015). Recent edited books include *Transatlantic Practices of Fascism(s) and Populism(s) from the Margins: The Cultural Politics of "Us" Versus "Them"* (Routledge, 2025), and *Afectos y violencias en la cultura latinoamericana* (Iberoamericana Vervuert, 2022).

Carles Feixa is a professor of social anthropology at Pompeu Fabra University in Barcelona. He is author or coauthor of more than fifty books, including *De jóvenes, bandas y tribus* (Barcelona, 1998, 5th ed. 2012); *Jovens na América Latina* (São Paulo, 2004); *Global Youth?* (London, 2006); *Youth, Space and Time* (Leiden, 2016); *Oltre le bande* (Rome, 2020); *El Rey: Diario de un Latin King* (Barcelona, 2020); and *Mierdas Punk* (Mexico City, 2022). He has been principal investigator of the European Research Council's Transgang Project.

Elisabeth Jay Friedman is a professor of politics at the University of San Francisco. Her published works include *Unfinished Transitions: Women and the Gendered Development of Democracy in Venezuela, 1936–1996* (Pennsylvania State University Press, 2000), *Interpreting the Internet: Feminist and Queer Counterpublics in Latin America* (University of California Press, 2017), and *Seeking Rights from the Left: Gender, Sexuality, and the Latin American Pink Tide* (Duke University Press, 2019). Her current research focuses on the impact of new generations and transnational ideas on feminist communities and strategies.

Max Paul Friedman is a professor of history and international relations at American University and the author of *Nazis and Good Neighbors: The United States Campaign Against the Germans of Latin America in World War II* (Cambridge University Press, 2003) and *Rethinking Anti-Americanism: The History of an Exceptional Concept in American Foreign Relations* (Cambridge University Press, 2012). He coedited *Partisan Histories: The Past in Contemporary Global Politics* (Palgrave Macmillan, 2005) and *The Cambridge History of America and the World*, vol. 4, *1945 to the Present* (Cambridge University Press, 2022).

Sydney Hutchinson is a research associate in popular music studies at the Humboldt University of Berlin and formerly associate professor of ethnomusicology at Syracuse University. She has published numerous books and articles on gender, politics, migration, and place in Caribbean and Latin American music and dance, most recently the textbook *Focus: Music of the Caribbean* (Routledge, 2019). Currently she directs the project Second World Music: Latin America, East Germany, and the Sonic Circuitry of Socialism (secondworldmusic.wordpress.com).

Eduardo Ledesma is an associate professor of Spanish at the University of Illinois Urbana-Champaign. He is the author of *Radical Poetry: Aesthetics, Politics, Technology, and the Ibero-American Avant-Gardes, 1900–2015* (State University of New York Press, 2016). His second monograph, *Expanding Cinemas: Experimental Filmmaking Across the Luso-Hispanic Atlantic Since 1960*, was published by SUNY Press in 2024. He is currently completing a third monograph, *Blind Cinema*, about films by visually impaired filmmakers.

Thiago da Costa Lopes is a sociologist, historian, and postdoctoral researcher at the Oswaldo Cruz Foundation's Department of History in Rio de Janeiro focusing on the history of the social sciences and technical cooperation in the Americas in the twentieth century. Lopes has been a Fulbright Visiting Scholar at New York University's Department of History and the Latin American and Iberian Institute at the University of New Mexico. He is the author of *Em busca da comunidade: Ciências sociais, desenvolvimento rural e diplomacia cultural nas relações Brasil-EUA (1930–1950)* (Fundação Oswaldo Cruz, 2020).

Marcos Chor Maio is a researcher at the Oswaldo Cruz Foundation in Rio de Janeiro and a professor in the foundation's Programa de Pós-Graduação em História das Ciências e da Saúde. Maio has been a visiting scholar at New York University's Department of History. He is currently investigating the interfaces between sociology, anthropology, and social psychology in studies on race and racism in Brazil and the United States in the post–World War II period. He is coeditor of *Raça como questão: História, ciência e identidades no Brasil* (2010). Maio's recent articles include "Gilberto Freyre and the UNESCO Research Project on Race Relations in Brazil" (2019) and, as coauthor, "Race, Science, and Social Thought in 20th-Century Brazil" (2021) and "Modernization, Race, and the Rural Past in Brazil: A Transnational Analysis of Donald Pierson's Sociology (1930–1950)" (2022).

Jeffrey Romero Middents is an associate professor at American University. His book *Writing National Cinema: Film Journals and Film Culture in Peru* (University Press of New England, 2009) traces how Peruvian cinema was shaped by local film criticism. Professor Middents has published essays on documentary aesthetics in the films of Chilean Patricio Guzmán, on Peruvian director Luis Llosa's films, on the theoretical perspective of Kathryn Bigelow's *Strange Days*, and more. He is currently working on a monograph on transnational auteurism and the work of Alfonso Cuarón.

Stefan Rinke is a professor of history at the Institute for Latin American Studies and the Friedrich-Meinecke-Institut at the Freie Universität Berlin. He was awarded the Premio Alzate by the Mexican Academy of Sciences and an honorary doctorate by the Universidad Nacional de San Martín in Argentina, as well as the Einstein Research Fellowship. He has been speaker of the German-Mexican graduate school "Between Spaces" since 2019. Rinke has published numerous monographs, collected volumes, and articles. His latest book, *Conquistadors and Aztecs: A History of the Fall of Tenochtitlan*, was published by Oxford University Press in 2023.

Luis Roniger is Reynolds Professor Emeritus of Latin American Studies at Wake Forest University and a professor emeritus of sociology and Latin American studies at the Hebrew University of Jerusalem. His works include *Transnational Politics in Central America* (University Press of Florida, 2012), *The Politics of Exile in Latin America* (Oxford, 2009, with Mario Sznajder), and *Transnational Perspectives on Latin America: The Entwined Histories of a Multi-State Region* (Oxford, 2021). He is currently completing a book on the politics of human rights in Latin America.

Sandhya Shukla is an associate professor of English and American studies at the University of Virginia. Her most recent work is *Cross-Cultural Harlem: Reimagining Race and Place* (Columbia University Press, 2024). She is also the author of *India Abroad: Diasporic Cultures of Postwar America and England* (Princeton University Press, 2003), and coeditor of *Imagining Our Americas: Toward a Transnational Frame* (Duke University Press, 2007). Her work has appeared in publications such as *American Quarterly, symplokē,* and the *Annual Review of Anthropology.*

Núria Vilanova is an associate professor of Latin American studies at American University and associate dean of undergraduate studies in the College of Arts and Sciences. She is the author of *Border Texts: Writing Fiction from Northern Mexico* (San Diego State University Press, 2007) and *Social Change and Literature in Peru (1970–1990)* (Edwin Mellen Press, 1998). Vilanova has published articles on literature and cinema; the Andes and Mexico are her main regional areas of expertise. She is currently working on a book about the representation of Indigenous peoples in Latin American cinema.

Brenda Werth is an associate professor of Latin American studies and Spanish at American University. She is author of *Theatre, Performance, and Memory Politics in Argentina* (Palgrave Macmillan, 2010); coeditor with Katherine Zien of *Bodies on the Front Lines: Performance, Gender, and Sexuality in Latin America and the Caribbean* (University of Michigan Press, 2024); and cotranslator and coeditor (with April Sweeney) of the anthology *Fauna and Other Plays by Romina Paula* (Seagull Press, 2023).

Index

Page numbers in italic text indicate figures.

Abad Faciolince, Héctor, 75
Abuelas de Plaza de Mayo, 57
Afro-Iberians, 67
Afro-Latin Americans, 105–19, 147–49, 167, 184, 186, 251–60
Aguirrezábal, Javier, 302
Aldana Reyes, Xavier, 300, 301
Alemán, Gabriela, 284
alfaguarización, 73
Algeria, 20
Alianza Popular Revolucionaria Americana (APRA) movement, 50
Allen, Chadwick, 250
Allende, Isabel, 74
Allende, Salvador, 55
Amnesty International, 157
Anderson, Benedict, 47, 228
Anzaldúa, Gloria, 81n15
Appadurai, Arjun, 30, 31, 68, 229, 230, 249
Arab Spring, 29, 302, 304
Argentina, 9–10; exile diaspora from, 56; Indigeneity in, 87; junta in, 167; Operation Condor, 167–69; performative protest movements in, 164; political exile in, 53; sex worker network in, 9, 155–58
Arocena, Rodrigo, 58
Ashcroft, Bill, 70
asylum: early agreements on, 49–50; exile

transnationalism and, 24–27; Inter-American treaties on, 50; legal mechanisms of, 41
Austerlitz, Paul, 248
Averill, Gage, 248
Aymara communities, 87, 92, 95, 280, 283

Bakhtin, Mikhail, 136–37
Bal, Mieke, 63–64
Baldus, Herbert, 105
Barcia Zequeira, María del Carmen, 153
Barrera Enderle, Víctor, 73
Barrientos Iyambae, Bonifacio, 95
Barth, Fredrik, 88
Basch, Linda, 229, 245
Bellott, Rodrigo, 278–79
Bergfelder, Tim, 289
Besserer, Federico, 17
Betances, Ramón Emeterio, 52
Biaggi, Pedro, 133–34
binary/dichotomic perspectives, 2, 5, 644, 71, 229, 270, 292
Bodnar, John, 19
Bolaño, Roberto, 71, 76
Bolivarianism, 48, 52
Bolivia: exodus of refugees from, 50; Indigeneity in, 8, 86, 88, 90, 95–96, 100n33, 280, 283; Indigenous migrants from, 87–88;

Bolivia (continued)
Inter-American treaties on asylum and, 50; *March for Territory and Dignity*, 95; Morales regime, 86, 88, 90, 92, 94. *See also* Indigeneity
boomerang effect, 98
border controls/policies: ghost transnationalisms and, 11; Inter-American treaties on asylum and, 50; Schengen area and, 1
border transnationalism, 6, 24, 25, 26
Boschetti, Anna, 73
Bourdieu, Pierre, 30, 31, 73
Bourne, Randolph, 125
Bourriaud, Nicolas, 82n35
Boyd, Stephanie, 270
Brazil: economic development in, 119; Good Neighbor policy, 104, 105, 107, 108, 109, 110, 117, 119; Indigenous identities in, 96, 100n31; inter-American dialogues and, 108–9, 119; modernization and, 108–9, 113–17, 119; Pierson's work on, 104–6, 109–13, 117–18; race and economic development in, 8–9; rural sociology, 106–8; sex worker movement in, 156; Smith's work on, 106–8, 109, 113–17, 118; social sciences developments in, 103–4; US presence in social sciences of, 108, 119; Vargas government, 108
Brexit, 1, 22
Brosens, Peter, 270
Bustamante, Emilio, 284

Cabellos, Ernesto, 270
Cabezas, Amalia, 9, 145–58
Canessa, Andrew, 8, 85–98
Carelli, Vincent, 281
Caribbean, 9, 152. *See also specific countries*
Cartagena Declaration on Refugees of 1984, 51
Castañeda, Ernesto, 6, 7, 15–32

cell phone cinema: *09 La película* (2014 film) (Aguirrezábal), 298–304, 309; accessibility of, 12; *App* (2013 film) (Boermans), 307; cell phone horror genre, 304–9; defined, 294–96; found-footage horror genre, 298–304; future of, 309; as global, transnational, and collective phenomenon, 296–98; *iMedium* (2018 short) (García López), 303, 304–8, 309; *Night Fishing* (2011 cell film) (Park), 297–98; *SMS Sugar Man* (2006 cell film) (Kaganof), 295; in transnational film studies, 289–93
Central America: displacement of refugees in, 51; sex work in, 146–48; unification of, 52. *See also specific countries*
Cerano, Dante, 281–82
Cervantes, Miguel, 72
Chávez Castillo, Susana, 172–73
Chicano Transnation, 70
Childers, William, 72
Chile, 10; exile diaspora from, 54–56; feminist movements and, 10; Mapuches, 55, 86; military rule in, 54, 55–56; Nazi groups in, 233–34; Operation Condor, 10, 53, 55, 164, 167–69, 171, 175; performative protest movements in, 9–10, 163–64; political exile in, 53
China, 23, 92, 93, 147
chronotope concept, 205–6
cinema: contemporary Bolivian films, 278–79; exhibition strategies, 285; Indigeneity and, 274–75; Indigenous activism and, 279–82; Indigenous plots, 278; Indigenous self-representation, 283; international film festivals, 276–78; Llosa's work, 270, 276; non-Indigenous filmmakers, 282–83; transnational approach to Indigenous filmmaking, 283–85; as transnational project, 272–74; transnational turn and, 12, 270, 272;

visual imagery rooted in, 10. *See also* cell phone cinema

Clastres, Pierre, 88

Cold War, 43, 44, 52–53, 54, 168

Collazo, Rocío, 173

Colombia: *corridos prohibidos*, 77; La Violencia, 78; narcofiction in, 73–75; paramilitary death squads in, 5; striking workers in, 5

colonialism: colonial corporations, 64; Puerto Rico and, 126; types of, 21. *See also* settler colonialism

colonial transnationalism, 6, 23, 24, 25, 26

colonization, 20, 94

Colorado Party, 56

computer networks, 12, 193. *See also* Internet

Confederation of Indigenous Peoples of Bolivia (Confederación de Pueblos Indígenas de Bolivia) (CIDOB), 95

Cortázar, Julio, 83n48

cosmopolitanism: of Latin American migrant writers, 71; transnationalism as, 2; in United States, 125–26

Costa Rica, 46–47, 49, 157

counterpublics: defined, 10, 181–82; growth of, 10; Internet and, 182, 185–94. *See also* Latin American feminist movements

COVID-19 pandemic, 1, 51, 163, 191, 261

Cowan, Benjamin, 169

Crack movement, 71, 74, 82n36

critiques of transnationalism, 4–5, 64

Cuarón, Alfonso, 278, 296

Cuba: communism and, 54; independence of, 52; political refugees from, 50, 51–52, 54; sex workers' mobilization in, 153–54, 155; US military interventions in, 146

Cuban Americans, 54

cultural appropriation, 6–7, 248, 258

cultural globalization, 71, 249

cultural imperialism, 5, 64

cultural purity myths, 5, 8, 26, 64, 70

D'Argenio, Maria Chiara, 277, 278

Davis, Shelton, 87

decolonialization, 12, 21, 227

de Faria, Juliana, 192

deglobalization, 22

del Toro, Guillermo, 292, 296

democracies, 295; ascendency of, 69; collapse of, 53; debates over history in, 60n10; in Latin America, 233

denaturalization, 7

deterritorialization: cyber communities and, 73; of nation-state, 229; of Spanish-language culture, 68

Dhondt, Reindert, 4–5, 8, 63–80

diasporic communities: centrality of homeland attachment, 228; development of, 41; images of, 54; political engagement with homeland, 228; predictions of threat from, 228

diasporic networks: establishment of, 8; interconnectivity and, 40; transnational power effects of, 12

diasporism: elements characterizing, 42–43; in Harlem, 9; Latin American diasporas, 53–57; Latino diaspora, 70; Morisco diaspora, 65; in Puerto Rico, 9; Sephardic diaspora, 65; transnationalism as, 2; variables in Latin American diasporas, 56

Díaz, Junot, 71

dictatorships: in Argentina, 56; in Chile, 54–56; in Dominican Republic, 189, 254; drawing on symbols, slogans, and practices of, 10; in Guatemala, 233; in Nicaragua, 233; in Paraguay, 56; in Uruguay, 57. *See also* Operation Condor

digital technology: feminist movements and, 10, 181–82; governance and, 183; Indigeneity and, 12; spatialization and, 7. *See also* Internet displacement: forced, 41–43; internal, 51

Dominican Republic: Dominican Americans, 71; exodus of refugees from, 50; ghost transnationalisms detectable in, 252–56; merengue in, 254; music history in, 11; Trujillo dictatorship, 254; US military interventions in, 146

Dorfman, Ariel, 10, 164, 165–67, 169–70

Dutch East India Company, 64

economic development and race in Brazil, 8–9, 109–13

economic migrants, 28, 54

Ecuador, 10, 156, 201–12, 284

Ehrlich, Ricardo, 58

El Boomeran(g) (blog), 72

elite politics, 51

elite transnationalism 6, 24, 25, 26, 27

El Hachmi, Najat, 67

El Salvador, 49, 87

Emmie, V. J., 285

Erlmann, Veit, 248

Erro, Enrique, 57

Escobar, Pablo, 74

Estrada, Luis, 78

ethnic affinity groups, 7

ethnoscape, 30

Evans, Peter, 296

exile: as colonial practice, 39; exile activism, 53; identity boundaries and, 7; impacts of, 40, 41; studies of, 41

exiles: diaspora communities and, 41; experience of living as, 44–46; role of, 7

exile transnationalism, 6, 24, 25, 26, 27

extradition agreements, 49–50

Fabricano, Marcial, 95

factionalism, 43

Falicov, Tamara, 272, 277

Feitlowitz, Marguerite, 166

Feixa, Carles, 10–11, 201–23

feminist movements: development of, 7; Internet and, 188–94; in Latin America, 185–88; regional governance and, 190–91; transnational perspective on, 184–85. *See also* Latin American feminist movements

Fernandes, Leela, 246

Fernández, Emilio, 283

Fernández, Gato, 173

Ferreira Aldunate, Wilson, 57

film. See cinema

Fischermann, Berndt, 95

Fishkin, Shelley Fisher, 81n15

Foxen, Patricia, 87

Franco, Jorge, 73

Franco administration, 67

Freyre, Gilberto, 109, 111–13, 117–18, 122n25, 122n27

Friedman, Elisabeth Jay, 10, 181–94

Friedman, Max Paul, 6, 11, 227–240

Fuentes, Carlos, 83n48

Fuguet, Alberto, 82n36

Fukuyama, Francis, 69

Gallego Cuiñas, Ana, 73

Galpin, Charles, 115, 116

gangs. See youth gangs

García Espinosa, Julio, 273

García López, Alfonso, 304–5, 306

García Márquez, Gabriel, 82n36, 83n48

Garifunas, 52

Garofalo, Reebee, 248

Gastarbeiter, 43

gender: gender-based organizing, 183–84; ghost transnationalisms intersecting with identities of, 11, 251; international advocacy movements and impact of, 7; merengue and identities of, 11, 251; performative protest movements, 9–10, 163–76

gender violence: definitions of, 176n6; feminicide, 179–80n49; patriarchy and, 167–71; performative protest movements against, 9–10, 163–64, 171–72, 174–76; state violence link to, 10; violence against women (VAW) treaty, 189–90

Germans in Latin America: clubs and associations of, 231, 232; diaspora nationalism, 232; German migrants internment in U.S., 11, 234–38; migrant diaspora of, 6, 227, 230–31; Nazi ideology and, 231–34, 238–39; repatriation of, 237–38; state treatment of, 11; US interventions and, 233

Getino, Octavio, 273

ghettoization, 19–20

ghost transnationalisms, 245–61; building imagined communities through, 6; defined, 11, 246; Dominican Republic/Haiti example of, 252–56, 260; national mythmaking and, 11; US American example of, 256–60, 260–61

Giles, Paul, 13n10

Glick-Schiller, Nina, 17, 30, 229, 245

global: definitions of, 182; global attention, 67; global/local binary, 5, 8; interweaving of, 7

globalization: acceleration of, 40; advocates of, 71; critiques of, 94; globalizing elites, 1–2; homogenization through, 249; narcofiction and, 76; nationalism and, 4, 69; term usage, 3

Global North: digital nomads from, 27–28; flow of ideas with Global South, 108–9; literature and, 73

Global South: access to digital cameras in, 296; digital nomads working in, 27–28; flow of ideas with Global North, 108–9; marginalization of states and peoples of, 6

glocal: category of, 8; cinema, 296; glocalization, 69; Indigenous identities as,

85; interweaving of, 7

Gómez, Sergio, 82n36

González Iñárritu, Alejandro, 296

Good Neighbor policy, 104, 105, 107, 108, 109, 110, 117, 119

governance: digital technology and, 183; feminist protest and, 190–91; in Haiti, 265n43; Indigeneity as tool of, 86, 92; transnational governance structures, 1. *See also* dictatorships; democracies

Great Britain, 23

Great Depression, 142n33

guagua aérea (air bus) metaphor, 70–71

Guarga, Rafael, 58

Guarnizo, Luis Eduardo, 64

Guatemala, 5, 49, 87, 233

Guayasamín, Gustavo, 281

Guerrero, Gustavo, 73

Gutiérrez Alea, Tomás, 273

Gutiérrez Ruiz, Héctor, 57

Guzmán, Jacobo Árbenz, 5

Haiti: Dominican music and, 11; exodus of refugees from, 50, 54; ghost transnationalisms detectable in, 252–56; governance in, 265n43; US military interventions in, 146

Halfon, Eduardo, 71, 72

Handlin, Oscar, 19

Harlem, 9; border-crossing practices and, 126; Italian Harlem, 127–29, 130, 131, 132, 140n5; Puerto Ricans in, 127, 128–30, 131–33, 136; transethnic solidarity in, 6

Hathaway, Michael, 92

Haya de la Torre, Victor Raúl, 50

hegemonic influence: in Brazil, 108; of Castilian beyond Iberian Peninsula, 68; cinema and, 271, 280; contradictions of, 260; critiques of, 76; in Mexico, 77; resistance to, 7, 184, 223

Herlinghaus, Hermann, 79

Herrero-Olaizola, Alejandro, 79

Higbee, Will, 270, 283

Hispanic literary studies: Latin American Boom, 74, 78, 82n36, 83n48; transnational approaches to Hispanic literature, 68–73, 79; transnationalizing of, 65–68; transnational turn and, 8, 63, 79–80; traveling concept and, 63–64

Hispanophone cultures: influence of global, 67–68; reterritorialization and, 71; transcultural dimensions of, 8, 65

Hjort, Mette, 69

Hobbes, Thomas, 88, 89

Honduras, 49, 50

Hostos y Bonilla, Eugenio María de, 52

Hoyos, Héctor, 76

Hugo, Victor, 48

human rights: gender violence and, 170, 189; movements, 4, 9, 54, 168, 184; organizations, 7, 58. See also United Nations

Human Rights Watch (HRW), 157

Huntington, Samuel, 228

Hutchinson, Sydney, 6, 11, 245–61

hybridization, 66, 249

Iberian studies, 67–68

Icelandic protests, 29

identities: boundaries of, 41, 85; German diasporic, 230–32; Indigenous, 85, 87, 94, 96–97, 100n31, 100n33; multicultural identity, 67; national identity discourses, 72; occupational, 153, 155, 158; reformulation of, 146, 150, 151; self-identification, 227; stigmatized, 87–88, 151, 158. See also Indigeneity

illicit transnationalisms, 6, 11

immigrant integration pathways, 21. See also migration

imperialism, 126

independence, 21; exile and, 39, 58n2; movements for, 126

Indigeneity: central paradox of, 85–89, 93, 96; contemporary indigeneity, 95–96, 98; definitions of, 93, 99n21, 100n27, 100n33; global network of people and ideas shaping, 8; in international law and practice, 90–94, 97–98; Latin American cinema and, 269–85; migration and, 87; Morales regime, 86, 88, 90, 92, 94; nation-state and, 88–89; self-representations of, 12, 87–88; as tool for governance, 86, 92; transnationalism as, 2, 4, 8, 86, 98; transnational turn in cinema and video, 12, 280, 283; Zapatistas, 94

Indigenous mobilization, 88, 94, 95–96, 98

inequality: growth in, 2; highlighting of, 249; structural issues increasing, 22. See also marginalization

Institute of Social Anthropology (ISA), 105–6

Inter-American Commission on Human Rights (IACHR), 50, 157

interconnectivity, 40. See also diaspora networks

International Labour Organization (ILO), 91, 97

Internet: activism and, 191–94; counterpublics and, 10; emergence of, 69; feminist movements and, 181–82; feminist organizing and, 188–94; musicians seeking inspiration on, 83n49

Jackson, Kimberly, 304

Jaramillo, Alonso Salazar, 78

Jay, Paul, 71

Jimeno, Victorino Reineri, 153

Jitrik, Noé, 57

Kaganof, Aryan, 295

Kearney, Michael, 228–29, 230
Keck, Margaret, 98
Kelley, Mary Lee, 149–51

La Marea Verde (the Green Tide), 164, 171–72
language: Aymara language, 87, 92, 273, 283; Castilian language, 67; inclusive, 94; Indigenous identity and, 100n31; Kichwa language, 285; linguistic imperialism, 68; Marcantonio on importance of, 134–38, 142n34, 142n36; Mayan language, 87; Mixtec language, 87, 228–29; power effects of, 9; Quechua language, 274, 276, 277, 280, 283, 285; translation, 66; traveling concepts and, 63; unification through, 228
Latino Atlantic, 10
Latino literature, 70–71. *See also* Hispanic literary studies; narcofiction
Latour, Bruno, 28
Ledesma, Eduardo, 12, 289–309
Lemus, Rafael, 74–75
Lessa, Francesca, 168
Letelier, Orlando, 55
Levitt, Peggy, 30
Lichtensztejn, Samuel, 58
Lim, Song Hwee, 270, 283–84
Líneas y Estudios Transatlánticos de Literatura (LETRAL), 66
literary studies. *See* Hispanic studies
Llosa, Claudia, 270, 276, 278
local: local complexity, 6; local culture, 8, 78–79, 85, 248, 275, 285; local economy, 23; local/global binary, 5, 8; local politics, 7; local specificity, 6, 8, 12, 85, 96, 296. See also glocal
Lombardi, Francisco, 274–75, 282
Lopes, Thiago da Costa, 8, 103–19
Loza, Jorgelina, 155–56
Luiselli, Valeria, 71, 72
Luna, Félix, 43

Macías, Teresa, 166
Madres de Plaza de Mayo (NGO), 56, 172
Maier, Charles S., 228
Maio, Marcos Chor, 8, 103–19
Malm, Krister, 247
Malverde, Jesús, 75
Mapuches, 55, 86
Marcantonio, Vito, 9, 125–40
marginalization, 6, 85, 86, 89, 90, 281
Marín, Carlos J., 304
Martí, Farabundo, 52
Martí, José, 51–52, 66
Martínez Cobo, José, 91
Marxism, achievements of, 4
Matto de Turner, Clorinda, 287n23
Maxakali people, 100n31
McClennen, Sophia, 167, 275
McOndo movement, 71, 74, 82n36
media: alternative, 185–87; blogs, 72; digitization of, 72–73, 308; narcofiction, 78–79; portrayal of women, 169, 173; social media, 192–94, 304; visual imagery rooted in, 10
memory studies, 72
Mendoza, Élmer, 73, 75
Mengel, Maurice, 247
Mercado, Tununa, 45
merengue: Austerlitz on, 248; in Dominican Republic, 254; ghost transnationalisms detectable in, 11; pambiche rhythm and, 253; regionalism and, 250, 251
Mess, Conrad, 304
mestizaje, 66
methodological nationalism, 28
Mexico, 10, 11; American country music and, 11; feminist movements and, 10; Institutional Revolutionary Party (Partido Revolucionario Institucional) (PRI), 77; Mixtecs, 87, 228–29; narcofiction in, 73–75, 82n36; sex workers' mobilization in, 154–55; Zapatistas, 94, 96

Meyer, Gerald, 141n15

Michelini, Zelmar, 57

Middents, Jeffrey Romero, 12, 269–85

migrants: agency of, 6–7; attachments to homeland, 227–28; increase in international migrants, 1–2; institutional racism and, 10; migrant communities, 64

migrant transnationalism, 6, 23, 24–27. *See also* border transnationalism; colonial transnationalism; elite transnationalism; exile transnationalism; reactive transnationalism; relational transnationalism

migration: after World War II, 227; Latin American-US migration, 87; lived experiences of, 87–88; migration studies, 17–19; reverse migration, 71; social fields of transnationalism and, 30–32; term usage, 17; transnationalism and, 7; transnationalism as, 2; US investment in Central America and, 147

Minh-ha, Trinh T., 282

Mixtecs, 87, 228–29

Monteforte, Guillermo, 281

Montoya, Pablo, 72

Morales, Evo, 86, 88, 90, 92, 94

Muenal, Alberto, 281

Müller, Gesine, 73

multilateral transnationalism: ALKQN's homelands, 202–5; chronotope concept, 205–6; defined, 11; hyperchronotope connection, 216–19; King Kannabis, 209–13, 224n17; King Manaba, 206–9, 224n17; King Mission, 213–16; synthesis of, 6; youth gangs and, 10, 201–2, 219–23. *See also* transnationalism-from-above concept; transnationalism-from-below concept

music/dance: dualism of, 246–47; ghost transnationalisms detectable in, 6,

11, 246, 260–61; transnationalism in ethnomusicological literature, 247–50; transnational regionalisms, 250–52, 260. *See also* merengue

Nagib, Lúcia, 292

narcofiction, 73–79

nationalism, 1, 4, 6, 29

nation-states: centrality of, 4, 6, 40, 69; citizenship rights and identity in, 39; critiques of, 94; diasporic communities and, 228–29; geographic boundaries of, 4, 86, 89; in Iberian studies, 67; Indigeneity and, 85, 86, 88–89, 94; process of building in Latin America, 39; reactions to transnationalisms, 12; resistance to, 11; rhetorical overcoming of power of, 5; role of exiles in, 7; transmigrants, 70; transnationalism and, 11, 69; Westphalian, 39, 89, 94, 97

Nazi state: in narcofiction, 74; transnational solidarities and, 6, 11. *See also* Germans in Latin America

neocolonialism, 5, 64

neoliberalism: austerity programs, 191, 220; hyperconsumerism, 77; narratives of globalization, 4; neoliberal carceralism, 6, 201; transnationalism and, 1, 22; Washington Consensus' neoliberal policies, 5, 64; zero tolerance policies, 10

Neuman, Andrés, 71

New Deal, 106, 109, 110, 114

Nicaragua, 49, 50, 52, 146, 154, 233

NiUnaMenos, 10, 164, 170, 172–75, 191, 193

Nolan, Christopher, 294

nongovernmental organizations (NGOs): human rights organizations, 7, 58, 158; Indigeneity and, 88, 92–93, 95, 96; international movement by, 16, 183; in LAC region, 157; NGO boom, 157; political exiles and, 51,

56; support of, 205; transnationalism and, 64
nonmigrant transnational studies, 28
non-refoulement principle, 51
North American Free Trade Agreement
(NAFTA), 69, 279
North-South transfer model, 9, 66

Occupy Wall Street, 29
Oliveira Vianna, Francisco José de, 109, 111,
113–16, 118, 122n25, 122n27, 122n34
1.5 generation, 18, 28
Operation Condor, 10, 53, 55, 164, 167–69,
171, 175
Organization of American States (OAS),
51, 157
origins of transnationalism: defining transnationalism, 15–17; migration and
transnational social fields, 30–32;
migration studies and, 17–19; nonmigrant transnational studies, 28;
political science field, 64; types of
transnationalism, 19–28
Ortega, Julio, 66

Padilla, Ignacio, 82n36
Panama Canal Zone, 9, 147–52, 158, 159n10
Pan-Americanism, 67, 72
Pan-Hispanism, 66, 72
Paraguay, 50, 53, 56, 57, 161n35, 168, 176n4
Paravisini-Gebert, Lizabeth, 155
Park, Robert, 104, 107, 109, 110, 111–13, 118
Park Chan-wook, 297–98
Parker, Jeffrey, 149, 154
Pataxó people, 100n31
patriarchy, 167–71
Pavlovsky, Eduardo, 10, 164, 165–66,
169–70
Penchaszadeh, Víctor, 57
Pereira Castro, Francisco, 47
Pérez-Reverte, Arturo, 78
Perriam, Chris, 296
Peru: Chinese laborers in, 52; cinema in,

270, 274, 275, 276, 278, 281–284,
285; Indigenous peoples in, 86;
NiUnaMenos protest in, 191; Operation Condor and, 176n4; Peruvian
army, 279; political exiles in, 50;
RedTraSex in, 161n35
Pick, Zuzana, 272
Pierson, Donald, 8–9, 104–13, 117–19,
122n27
Pink Tide, 170, 190–91
Pinochet, Augusto, 55–56, 167
pocket cinema. *See* cell phone cinema
Polit Dueñas, Gabriela, 76
political exile, 39–58; elements characterizing, 42–43; role of, 39–40;
significance of, 40; transnational
functions of, 44; transnational turn
and, 41. *See also* exile; exiles; exile
transnationalism
postcoloniality: achievements of, 4; diasporic communities and, 229–30;
transnationalism as, 2
postnational utopianism: challenges to, 5;
critical reactions to, 6, 69; digital
technology and, 191–92
progressive politics, 6, 182
Puerto Rico, 9; boundaries and, 126; circular mobility, 70–71; independence
of, 52, 126, 130, 132, 133–34; Marcantonio in, 141n24, 142n34; Marcantonio's solidarity with, 126, 133–35; US
military interventions in, 146
Putnam, Lara, 140n3

Quechua migrants, 87
queer activism, 7

Rabêlo, José Maria, 48
race: economic development in Brazil and,
8–9, 109–19; fear of migrants and,
22; ghost transnationalisms intersecting with identities of, 11, 250–51;
in Harlem, 127; Indigenous identity

race (*continued*)
and, 92; international advocacy
movements and impact of, 7; racial
difference, 6; sex work and, 149–51.
See also Afro-Latin Americans;
Harlem
Ragland, Cathy, 248
Ramos, Alcida, 100n31
reactive transnationalism: arguments,
25; assumptions, 25; defined, 24;
experiencing of, 28; implications
regarding remittances, 26; implied
effects, 26; as type of migrant transnationalism, 6
RedTraSex, 9, 155–58
refugees, 17, 23, 42, 46, 49, 50–51. *See also*
diasporism; exiles
Reineri Jimeno, Victorino, 153
relational transnationalism: arguments, 25;
assumptions, 25; defined, 22, 24;
experiencing of, 28; implications
regarding remittances, 26; implied
effects, 26; as type of migrant transnationalism, 6, 23
relocations, 41–42
remittances: cultural, 70; defined, 18; gang
economies and, 222; to Guatemala,
87; implications of, 26; Latin American states encouragement of, 228;
as migration goal, 31; as resource
extraction, 23; transnationalism
and, 30
renationalization, 1
repression campaigns, 10
resistance: expatriate communities and,
11; to imperialism, 52, 139, 154, 233;
pocket cinema and, 12; resilience
and, 223; as response to carceral and
neoliberal policies, 202, 222
reterritorialization, 1
reverse migration, 71
Reynaga, Elena, 157
Riester, Jürgen, 95

Roa Bastos, Augusto, 57
Robertson, Roland, 69
Rocha, Glauber, 273
Rodríguez, Marta, 281, 282, 283
Rofrano, Peter, 128
Roniger, Luis, 7, 39–62
Roosevelt administration, 105, 106, 114, 233
Rosa, Rodrigo Rey, 71
Rosas, Juan Manuel de, 43
Rubio, Vicente, 304

Salazar, Gabriel, 57
Salazar, Juan Francisco, 280
Salazar Jaramillo, Alonso, 78
Saldívar, José David, 81n15
Sandino, Augusto César, 52, 154
Sanjinés, Iván, 281
Sanjinés, Jorge, 273–74, 280, 282, 283
Santaella, Angelita, 135–36
Santaolalla, Isabel, 296
São Paulo, 87, 105–06
Sapignoli, Maria, 92–93
Sapiro, Gisèle, 73
Sarmiento, Domingo, 231
Saugestad, Sidsel, 93
Sayad, Abdelmalek, 18–19
Schengen area, 1
Schiwy, Freya, 280
Scott, James, 88–89
Segato, Rita, 163, 166, 174
settler colonialism, 21, 23, 93
sex work(ers): identity, 9; mobilization
of, 152–55; sex tourism, 9; trans-
national sex worker organizing,
155–58; understandings of, 145–46,
158; US military occupation and,
146–52
Shaw, Deborah, 296
Shaw, Karena, 89
Shukla, Sandhya, 6, 9, 125–40
sicaresca, 75, 76
Sikkink, Kathryn, 98
siluetazos, 9–10, 164, 172–75

Silva, Jorge, 281
Silva Catela, Ludmila da, 173
Simonett, Helena, 248
Sitnisky, Carolina, 284
Skármeta, Antonio, 74
Smith, Michael Peter, 64
Smith, T. Lynn, 8–9, 104, 106–9, 113–19, 122n27, 122nn34–35
Soderbergh, Steven, 294
Soja, Edward, 68
Solanas, Fernando, 273
solidarity: in Brazilian society, 115–18; committees of, 54; new forms of, 6; in Harlem, 129, 135; street youth groups and, 11; transnational networks of, 41
Somoza, Anastasio, 233
Southern Cone, 10, 52–53, 167–71, 175, 297
South-North transmissions, 5, 108, 256
South-South transmissions, 66
spatialization, 8
state-building, 8, 86
state power, 6–7
Steiner, Niklaus, 51
Stroessner, Alfredo, 56, 168
Surveillance, 12, 181
syncretism, 249
Szanton Blanc, Cristina, 229, 245
Sztainbok, Vannina, 166

technological utopianism, 12, 290, 309
territorial displacements: in colonial times, 43; exile as, 40; legal mechanisms of, 41; transnational impact of, 41; waves of dislocations, 7
theater in Chile and Argentina, 9–10, 163–64
Thomas, Piri, 128–29, 136, 142n33
Thomas, William Isaac, 19
Tierney, Dolores, 271
Tilley, Virginia, 87
Tilly, Charles, 29
Tönnies, Ferdinand, 115

Torres Caicedo, José María, 47–48
Torrico, Juan Carlos, 275
transatlantic studies, 65–66
transcodification, 66
transimperial processes, 4, 65
transnational advocacy networks: development of, 7; exiles' contact with, 44, 53, 54; multiplier factor of, 41. See also ethnic affinity groups; feminist movements; human rights; queer activism
transnational corporations, 5, 64
transnational cosmopolitanism, 2, 6, 9, 71, 125–26
transnationalism (term): combating elusiveness of term, 5–6; contexts and specification of, 15–16; critiques of term, 4–5, 6, 64; diversity in plural usage of, 5, 222, 246; frequency of usage, 1, 13n1, 29, 80n6; range of usage, 2–3, 6, 12, 245. See also origins of transnationalism
transnationalism-from-above concept, 6, 10, 64, 77, 201, 220–21, 222
transnationalism-from-below concept, 6, 8, 10–11, 16, 64, 77, 201–2, 220, 221–22
transnational networks: political exiles and, 40, 41; structural gender violence and, 10; transference of ideas, practices, and forms of, 41, 57–58
transnational organizations. See United Nations
transnational turn: Cold War studies in Latin America and, 168; contribution to migration scholarship, 16–17, 18; developments in social sciences in Brazil and, 104; Hispanophone cultures and, 8, 63–80, 81n15; Indigeneity and, 12, 269–85; Latino/Latina scholarship and borderlands scholarship and, 81n15; nation construction and, 3; pocket cinema and, 289–309; political exile in Latin

transnational turn (*continued*)
America and, 7, 39–58; in scholarly
research, 2
traveling concepts, 3, 63–64
Treaty of Peace and Friendship of 1907, 49
Trujillo, Rafael, 189, 254
Trump, Donald, 22, 107, 228
Tsing, Anna, 89
Turino, Thomas, 258

Ubico, Jorge, 233
United Fruit Company, 5
United Nations, 1; on asylum, 50; General
Assembly, 183; Human Rights
Conference, 189; Indigeneity and,
97–98; on minority discrimination,
91; on refugees, 50, 51; UNAIDS,
157;
United States: American country music,
11; border enforcement, 51; cosmopolitanism in, 125–26; drug wars,
78; gang leaders in, 10; German
migrants internment in, 11, 234–38;
Indigenous peoples of, 86; Inter-
American treaties on asylum and,
50; military presence in Nicaragua,
52; performative protest movements
in, 163, 164; US-Mexico border, 70
Uruguay, 53, 57, 58, 156, 172, 176n4, 275, 302

Valencia, Sayak, 77
Vallejo, Fernando, 76

Vandebosch, Dagmar, 82n35
Vargas Llosa, Mario, 83n48
Venezuela, 48, 50, 153, 254, 258, 281
Vertovec, Steven, 65
Vicuña Gonzalez, Vernadette, 152
Vilanova, Núria, 12, 269–85
Víquez, Pío, 47
Volpi, Jorge, 73–74, 82n36

Wallerstein, Immanuel, 140n3
Wallis, Roger, 247
Washington, Booker T., 111, 112
Washington Consensus, 5, 64
Weinberg, Liliana, 73
Werth, Brenda, 10, 163–76
Willems, Emílio, 105
Wilson, Gavin, 294
Wong, Cindy Hing-Yuk, 276
Woodworth, Jessica, 270
World Bank, 16, 91, 97
World Health Organization, 1, 156, 157

Ybarra, Patricia, 167
Yglesias, Rafael, 46–47
youth gangs, 6, 10, 201–2, 219–23. *See also*
multilateral transnationalism
YouTube, 10, 210, 280, 293, 297, 299, 303

Zarabia, Victor, 285
zero tolerance policies, 10, 201
Znaniecki, Florian, 19

www.ingramcontent.com/pod-product-compliance
Lightning Source LLC
Chambersburg PA
CBHW022259280326
41932CB00010B/920